LONDON 1900

LONDON
1900
The Imperial Metropolis

❖ ❖ ❖ ❖ ❖

JONATHAN SCHNEER

NB

YALE NOTA BENE

YALE UNIVERSITY PRESS   NEW HAVEN & LONDON

Published with assistance from the Mary Cady Tew
Memorial Fund.

First published as a Yale Nota Bene book in 2001.
Copyright © 1999 by Yale University.
All rights reserved.

For information about this and other Yale University Press publications,
please contact:

U.S. office   sales.press@yale.edu
Europe office   sales@yaleup.co.uk

Printed in the United States of America

The Library of Congress has catalogued the hardcover edition as follows:
Schneer, Jonathan.
London 1900 : the imperial metropolis / Jonathan Schneer.
p.   cm.
ISBN 0-300-07625-8 (alk. paper)
1. London (England)—History—1800–1950.   2. Imperialism—
Public opinion—England—London—History.   3. Nineteen hundred,
A.D.
I. Title.
da683.s35   1999
942.1082—dc21   99-20050

ISBN 0-300-08903-1 (pbk.)

A catalogue record for this book is available from the British Library.

10 9 8 7 6 5 4 3 2

to Margaret, Ben, and Seth

CONTENTS

ABBREVIATIONS

APS	Aborigine's Protection Society
BCINC	British Committee of the Indian National Congress
CES	Christian Evidence Society
CIV	City Imperial Volunteers
ILP	Independent Labour Party
INC	Indian National Congress
INLGB	Irish National League of Great Britain
IRB	Irish Republican Brotherhood
LCC	London County Council
RGS	Royal Geographical Society
RIBA	Royal Institute of British Architects
SDF	Social Democratic Federation
SRBM	Society for the Recognition of the Brotherhood of Man
UIL	United Irish League

Introduction

LONDON IN 1900

THIS book is written as the millennium approaches. The British government intends to mark the turn of the great wheel with an exhibition. It has caused to be erected in Greenwich, London, an enormous Millennium Dome vast enough to contain an array of displays intended to demonstrate that two thousand years after the beginning of the Christian era, and despite the many difficulties of the past half-century, Britons still have much to look forward to.

This great exhibition, however, cannot help but evoke Britain's glorious imperial past; undoubtedly it is meant to. Its very scope is reminiscent of the world's first Great Exhibition of 1851 and of the Festival of Britain launched by a triumphant Labour government to mark the Great Exhibition's centenary. Moreover, the dome will be located at the prime meridian, the datum established by British astronomers and used by cartographers ever since for gauging time and navigating geographical space, the point of origin, also, alongside the Thames River and next to London, from which Britain's extraordinary expansion outward was measured.

Today London remains a great and cosmopolitan center, bursting with people and energy. It is still the seat of government, still a departure point for travelers across the world. It is not preeminent, however, nor is it ever likely to be again, as it could claim to be a hundred years ago when the British Empire and its capital city had reached their zenith. No matter the mixture of nostalgia and national pride which the Millennium Dome elicits, London is no longer the imperial metropolis.

Just a century ago, however, almost within living memory, it was. Great Britain controlled territories on every continent except Antarctica, owned islands in every ocean, sent representatives to the four corners of the globe, governed (directly or indirectly) the destinies of four hundred million people. It owned the greatest empire the planet had yet seen.

London was the empire's capital, and the imperial metropolis of the world. It was unique. Paris may have been more beautiful, but it was less imposing than London, and it served as metropole to a smaller empire than the British. Vienna and Rome had once been capitals of great empires, but no longer; their grandeur, like the imperial reach of the Hapsburg family and of the Vatican, was faded and diminished. New York was enormous, but not a capital city; Washington's role as the capital of an informal American empire had yet to crystallize. Berlin was a rough and sprawling city whose time as an imperial center had not yet come. When it did come, during the early years of the Second World War, it was mercifully short-lived. On the other side of the globe, Shanghai and Peking were great cities, but at the turn of the twentieth century the Celestial Kingdom remained inward looking. If anything, its rulers hoped to shut the rest of the world out. The British, however, had the opposite intention; they embraced, they intended to instruct, perhaps even to rule, the world. And the British megalopolis, London, was their Rome.

London at the turn of the twentieth century was sui generis. First of all it was physically enormous. "One may go east or north or south or west from Charing Cross," wrote an American visitor in 1895, "and almost despair of ever reaching the rim." London's "outer ring" stretched from six to fifteen miles in every direction from the center, containing the new suburbs made possible by the development of commuter trains. From the top of the 202-foot-tall Doric column called the Monument, erected as a memorial to the great fire of 1666 and located near the heart of London's financial district, the tourist who had paid the threepence admission fee, surmounted its inner spiral staircase of 346 steps, and emerged gasping into sunlight might gaze in all directions without seeing an end to the vast metropolis spread beneath him.[1]

It was an imposing panorama to behold. At the foot of the Monument and ringing it were the warehouses, offices, and banks of the City or Square Mile, as London's financial district was sometimes called, and immediately to the south, the docks and wharves lining the Thames, and then, stretching as far as the eye could see on the other side of the river, the vast, undistinguished conglomeration that was south London. To the east were "miles of mean streets . . . smokey, dirty, unbeautiful." This was the East End of London in its classic phase, a city unto itself containing nearly nine hundred thousand souls, mainly poor, the population anatomized by Charles Booth and his team of researchers in the first great work of sociology, *The Life and Labour of the People in London*, the haunt a decade earlier of history's immortal fiend Jack the Ripper. To the west, in the immediate foreground, was the massive dome of St. Paul's Cathedral and beyond that the spires of Westminster, while above

1. View from the Monument. "London Bridge and Panorama of South Bank from Monument," watercolor by J. Crowther.

Courtesy of the Museum of London.

and past the Houses of Parliament London's West End contained the "familiar succession of terraces, parks, and gardens, upon which are concentrated the most lavish display of wealth and ostentation at present manifest in the world." To the north were the grimy streets of working-class Holborn, Clerkenwell, Kings Cross, Finsbury, and Islington, above them the greener, leafier reaches of Hampstead, Highgate, Golders Green, Muswell Hill, and other suburbs stretching, so it seemed, to infinity.[2]

Among the streets and squares, alleyways and crescents of London, place-names bore reminders of earlier, more pastoral times: Butterwick Road in Hammersmith, Violet Hill in St. John's Wood, Cherrytree Road in East Finchley. Stand even today on the busy, filthy pavement of Battersea Rise at the end of Lavender Hill in Wandsworth and you can see, albeit cluttered now with shops and houses, the little knoll not far from the Thames where once an ancient village must have stood. In London's grassy parks, in its tree-lined squares, it was easier still in 1900 to forget for a moment that one was surrounded by the greatest city of the world.

Exit the park gates, however, and the bustle, noise, and grime of modern urban life smote the senses. Already London traffic jams were notorious, newfangled horseless carriages and traditional horse-drawn vehicles often merging in near gridlock conditions. Swarms of men and boys darted between them, dustpan and broom in hand, sweeping paths for wealthy, fastidious pedestrians wishing to cross. Pneumatic rubber tires, recently introduced, had begun to reduce the rumble of London's innumerable wagons, trams, trolleys, and omnibuses, but there remained the clatter of horses' hooves on roads still paved for the most part with granite settes, which magnified all street noise. Meanwhile underground electric trains rumbled ominously. "The roar of it comes up to you from all sides," wrote another observer of London at the turn of the century; and with regard to the city scene more generally, "It is one continual strenuous movement. . . . Hour after hour and every day, is the mighty, throbbing life renewed."[3]

In 1900 London was no longer an industrial center, although gasworks, railways, and, above all, the great dock companies employed many thousands in massive factories and yards. The single largest industry in London was the clothing industry, accounting for almost a third of the city's nearly eight hundred thousand manufacturing workers, but it was carried on largely in workshops employing fewer than half a dozen and by "sweaters," who subcontracted jobs to men, women, and children who often worked alone at home. For laborers who escaped the sweater, relatively small-scale manufacturing was the rule. In East London there were breweries and flour mills and numerous small factories producing for the food trade: jam, margarine, candy, sugar, mineral water, and soft drinks. Further west the workers of Clerkenwell turned out higher-quality products, for example, scientific glassware and telephone and (later) radio equipment. Suburban industry also flourished, lured from the center by cheaper rents and the development of modern transport.[4]

Specific trades suggested aspects of Britain's imperial role. The sweated seamstress might sew buttons on the uniforms of soldiers sent to suppress brushfire rebellions throughout the empire. Workers in Eno's Fruit Salts factories perhaps took pride in manufacturing "The antiseptics of Empire," as a typical advertisement put it. The employees of Bovril, a company which produced beef extract thought to contain health-promoting qualities and which was given therefore to soldiers wounded in South Africa, might preen themselves on "upholding the British flag and contributing to the success of British valour." Even the makers of Monkey Brand soap might congratulate themselves on having produced a commodity which, according to advertisements, would "scour the country" as Gen. John French had promised to scour South Africa until it had been cleansed of Boer rebels.[5]

Dockland contained a large labor force whose earnings depended more

directly, although not entirely, upon the maintenance of empire. Built originally round an elbow in the Thames, which snaked through London on its
way to the sea, and stretching, by the turn of the twentieth century, for miles
in either direction, the port of London was the busiest on earth. Into it daily
glided massive steamers, as well as the two- and three-masted sailing vessels
which continued, even in 1900, to ply the world's oceans. Invariably they were
loaded with the fruits of Britain's imperial sway: food, drink, spices, herbs,
teas and coffees, animal hides, furs, feathers, ivory, gold, silver and other metals, precious stones, timber, cotton, curios, jute, hemp, objets d'art, in fact
nearly everything the planet produced. Every sunrise tens of thousands of
men could be seen already hard at work unloading the riches of empire from
the holds of the great ships, then sorting, carrying, trucking it along the
quays and wharves which lined the river, and finally cataloging, stacking, and
packing it in the vast warehouses behind.[6]

Every morning, too, and not more than half a mile from the forest of masts
rising above the turbid waters of the Thames, thousands of businessmen
wearing white collars, wristbands, top hats, and polished boots emerged in
waves from the Bank Street tube station (just completed that year) and fanned
out for their offices. They were lawyers, bankers, insurance agents, stockbrokers, importers and exporters of everything under the sun. They were
buying, selling, and trading goods of all descriptions: bonds, futures, stocks
in Chinese railways, Latin American sugarcane fields, African gold mines,
Borneo rubber plantations, Ceylonese tea farms. For London contained not
only the world's busiest port, but its richest, most cosmopolitan financial
center.[7]

London acted like a magnet not only on the produce of empire and the
funds which facilitated its functioning, but on the peoples of the empire and
the world beyond. Of the more than 6 million who lived in greater London in
1901, tens of thousands had been born in Czechoslovakia, Italy, and Germany.
They clustered mainly in central districts, Soho, Holborn, Kings Cross, and,
a bit to the north, in Finsbury. Many tens of thousands more who had been
born in London were descended, often at the remove of only a single generation, from Czechs, Italians, Germans, and other nationalities. Still, because
they were relatively few in number and relatively assimilable, they never became targets of systematic or organized discrimination. For the Irish it was
different. At the turn of the twentieth century, 60,000 Catholic men and
women who had been born in Ireland made their homes in London; the entire metropolitan Irish Catholic population was estimated at 435,000, and
anti-Irish sentiment, although possibly diminishing, was still widespread.
Anti-Semitism was also rampant in London in 1900, precisely because the

city was being inundated by a wave of Jewish immigrants. In 1881, 46,100 Jews had lived in London; nineteen years later the figure had risen to approximately 135,000, mainly Russian Poles escaping from pogroms. It was estimated in 1899 that 120,000 alien Jews lived in the East End, 42,000 in the borough of Stepney alone, and anti-alien agitation was on the rise. The imperial metropolis was perhaps the most cosmopolitan city in Europe, but not always happily so.[8]

The empire, formal and informal, likewise contributed to the capital's cosmopolitan character. From Asia came Indians, Malaysians, Chinese, and Japanese. Like the Irish and the Jews they tended to live and work in the rookeries and slums, the ghetto which took up a good portion of East London. Twenty thousand "Malay and Lascar" dockers and sailors passed through this part of the city annually, many making it their home base. Along the Limehouse Causeway and adjoining streets there was a small Chinatown. Scattered throughout the poorer sections of the imperial metropolis there was also a sprinkling of African and West Indian immigrants. Few in number, they proved significant historically. In 1900 they organized the world's first Pan-African Conference. The opening sentence of its address "To the Nations of the World," composed by the great African-American delegate to the conference, W. E. B. Du Bois, rings down the ages: "The problem of the twentieth century is the problem of the color line."[9]

In London's crowded streets one might hear all the accents of the empire: the twanging inflections of Australians, New Zealanders, Canadians, and the "goldbugs" of South Africa, the rounded intonations of the Irish, the unfamiliar enunciations of Asians and Africans. At Victoria or Charing Cross station one might witness the arrival of an East Indian prince or maharajah or rajah. "He will be accompanied, perhaps, by over 100 servants, and 50 or 60 tons of luggage," wrote an English observer with more than a hint of jealousy.[10] At the Inns of Court one might see an Indian or Trinidadian student of English law; at a London teaching hospital there might be an East Asian or a West Indian student of British medicine; at the South Kensington Museum one might rub elbows with a Parsee student of Western technology or British business practices.

While London accepted a steady stream of visitors and immigrants it simultaneously sent its own sons and daughters to the four corners of the globe: explorers and researchers sponsored by the Royal Geographical Society; soldiers sent to defend imperial interests in China, South Africa, West Africa, Borneo, India, and elsewhere; missionaries of various denominations; merchants and traders looking for profits; engineers to oversee the construction of roads, railways, bridges, and tunnels; emigrants in search of a new and more prosperous life. Not only London's docks but equally her grand railway stations were scenes of continuous movement, their imperial function as obvious to travelers as the mundane use to which commuters and day-trippers put them. As if to underline this connection, each section of the enormous Waterloo railway station was named for one of Britain's successful imperialist campaigns.[11]

In 1900, London was, in a famous phrase, "the heart of the empire."[12] It was also the brain. The guiding impulse behind the agents sent to oversee four hundred million people originated in Whitehall, a district in central London immediately south and west of Trafalgar Square. Here were the offices of ultimate authority, the rooms, halls, and debating chambers in which were taken the decisions governing the nation and empire alike. The prime minister lived and worked, of course, at 10 Downing Street, a surprisingly modest, not to say dowdy, residence for so exalted and powerful a personage. To one side of Number 10 was the Colonial Office, a grander edifice; to the other the Foreign Office, which extended round the corner to the square tower facing the magnificent prospect of St. James Park. Nearby were the India Office, which extended all the way to Charles Street, the Local Government Board offices, the Home Office, the Privy Council offices, the Board of Trade, and the Treasury, all housed in the imposing if unadorned structures which characterize the area. Along Whitehall, the broad avenue which gave the district its name, lay the Houses of Parliament and Westminster Abbey, grand Gothic compositions; in the other direction lay the Admiralty and War Offices. Taken as a whole the district simply radiated national and imperial power.

British colonists sensed it. Their governments set their London offices as close to the center of power in Whitehall as possible. Walking up Victoria Street toward Westminster Abbey, one passed the Cape of Good Hope Government Agency, the offices of the colony of Natal, of the Canadian Dominion, of Western Australia, Victoria, New Zealand, New South Wales, Tasmania, and Queensland. At the other end of Whitehall, on Trafalgar Square, the government of South Africa eventually established its English headquarters.[13]

Meanwhile the imperial metropolis itself must be governed. Since 1889 this had been the task of the London County Council, a majority of whose members in 1900 were Radicals and socialists. Their project was enormous, not least because London had been badly governed for centuries. Now under the leadership of Lib-Labs (Liberals of the laboring class) who had risen through the ranks, of middle-class Fabians like Sidney Webb, and of a diverse group of Progressives including the aristocratic Liberal leader Lord Rosebery and the Positivist philosopher and Radical Frederic Harrison, city government was taking steps to level slums, to erect decent, affordable public housing, to guarantee trade union rates for city employees, to control vital services such as gas and water. Moreover, there was a dimension to London politics that was absent elsewhere. According to Harrison, the members of the council were "trustees of the Metropolis of the Empire" and must govern accordingly. What precisely this meant, however, was a matter of contention, as will become evident in a chapter below.[14]

Because London was the seat of a great empire, imperial markers were everywhere. Imperial themes and messages saturated daily life: they were present in many productions staged in London's theaters, music halls, and "nigger minstrel" shows; they pervaded popular exhibitions and displays, especially the famous Earl's Court Exhibition Grounds, where the impresario Imre Kiralfy imported wild animals and colonized peoples and presented them in dramatic spectacles based upon Britain's imperialist triumphs in Africa and Asia. They provided the subtext at public exhibitions of artifacts and in museums.

On a more mundane level, imperialist sentiments appeared on the wrappers and advertisements of cigarette packets, soaps, teas, medicines, drinks, and a thousand other items. They were celebrated in textbooks read by London's schoolchildren and on the maps the children studied. They could be discerned in London's very architecture, in its public spaces, its buildings, shops, factories, and offices. They suffused political discourse, including even the discourse of London's anti-imperialists of Asian and African descent.

In short, London in 1900 was a "world city," as Asa Briggs expressed it in a memorable phrase—but it was also something more.[15] Today New York is a world city in the sense that Briggs used the term, a fount of artistic and intellectual creativity and endeavor, an economic powerhouse, a center of communications, an entrepôt without parallel, the heart of world finance. A hundred years ago London was all those things and something beyond, namely, the capital of a formally constituted and governed empire upon which the sun never set, an *imperial* city. Power radiated from it along lines established by an imperial parliament, formal tribute flowed into it from a hundred client states. This imparted a certain atmosphere to the city's built environment; a certain ambiance to its culture; a certain tone to its politics. It stamped London's residents with an indelible if ambiguous identity which distinguished them from residents of other great cities; it produced specific repercussions, some of historic moment, which it will be the purpose of this book to explore and to analyze.

Traditionally scholars have paid little heed to such matters, being more interested in imperialism's impact upon the world than in its impact upon

Britain. Of course the economist John Hobson was concerned with the growth of British jingoism, and Lenin, borrowing from Hobson and Engels, argued that imperialist profits paid the bribe which induced British labor aristocrats, including London's artisans, to ignore their own class interest. More common, however, were the concerns of mainstream investigators of British imperialism, such as Sir John Seeley and Fisher during the pre-1914 period, and their successors, for example, C. J. Lowe or Ronald Robinson and John Gallagher. These scholars focused upon the economic, national-political, and geopolitical roots of British expansion. Such preoccupations continue to recur. The most original and magisterial recent treatment of British imperialism, Peter Cain's and Anthony Hopkins's two-volume study, is not concerned with the impact of British imperialism upon popular culture and political attitudes at home, but rather with the imperializing class itself, which it dissects with great originality and thoroughness, and with the world role Britain enjoyed as a result of the preoccupations of these "gentlemanly capitalists."[16]

Social and cultural historians, however, have long been aware of the impact of empire upon late-Victorian and Edwardian England. Indeed, for the past decade Manchester University Press has published a notable series devoted to it. "Studies in Imperialism," which numbers more than a dozen volumes edited and contributed to by John MacKenzie, demonstrates conclusively that from the 1880s until the Second World War British citizens were subjected to a continual barrage of imperialist propaganda, overt and covert, which helped to produce a general acceptance, even celebration, of empire. Feminist scholars, building on MacKenzie's work—for example, Nupur Chauduri, Margaret Strobel, Antoinette Burton, and Mrinalini Sinha—have likewise sought to explain the impact of imperialist ideology in Britain on the British people and to illumine especially its influence upon British feminist ideology and British understandings of gender.[17]

It is one thing, however, simply to note an imperialist sentiment on a tin of tea or box of Monkey Brand soap, or to underline the cultural imperialism implicit in the public exhibition of African artifacts or even African people at Earl's Court, as, for example, MacKenzie and some of his essayists do; it is quite another to dig more deeply and to fruitfully interrogate advertisements or spectacles as texts. In works of great subtlety and sophistication Anne McClintock and Annie Coombes have done so. Like MacKenzie and the Manchester authors, they emphasize the ubiquity of the imperial theme in late-Victorian and Edwardian England, but then they probe the linkages it posited among race, class, and gender. Coombes analyzes how public knowledge of Africa was transmitted and formed, focusing on the museums and public exhibitions of the period, to illuminate the relation between a putative scientific knowledge and popular imagination. McClintock charts among other subjects the evolution of so-called scientific racism into "commodity racism" in Britain, by which British world power, white supremacy, and male authority were marketed on a hitherto unimaginable scale.[18]

The role of those who were descended from the imperialized peoples but who lived in Britain has also exercised the minds of British historians. Ron Ramdin, Peter Fryer, and Rozina Visram, among others, have followed the example of previous historians who sought to rescue the despised classes of earlier times "from the enormous condescension of posterity," chronicling the lives and struggles of men and women previously unheralded. Laura Tabili has taken this project a step further, tracing the attempts of black seamen during the first half of the twentieth century to forge a British identity in the teeth of a pervasive racism which denied them full rights of citizenship.[19]

Yet another angle of approach is offered by literary scholars. Graham Dawson, Joseph Bristow, Satya Mohanty, and Robert MacDonald, among others, have decoded "the language of imperialism" expressed in works of popular fiction, paying particular attention to the manner in which it was gendered. Like that of the Manchester authors, the feminist historians, and the practitioners of "history from the bottom up," their work is largely informed by Antonio Gramsci's concept of cultural hegemony, by Edward Said's argument about the shaping of Western identity in contradistinction to a supposed Oriental identity, and by the psychological insights of Sigmund Freud, Jacques Lacan, Melanie Klein, and, above all, Michel Foucault, who argued the links between sex and all kinds of power, including imperial power.[20]

And yet for all this good work, historians of London itself have paid little more than lip service to the imperial theme. Studies of the government of the metropolis barely touch upon it. It does not appear in David Feldman's and Gareth Stedman Jones's collection of jointly edited essays. Michael Port's examination of the architecture of imperial London is narrowly focused upon offices of state within a relatively confined area. In his survey of London history Roy Porter treats it, quite properly, as one factor among many; I now believe that he does not afford it due emphasis. In short, despite the fact that historians are increasingly aware of the importance not merely of imperialism in British history, but of the impact of imperialism upon life in Britain, no scholar has attempted to work out how it influenced the history of the greatest imperial metropolis of modern times.[21]

The subject of this book will be the intersection of urban life and imperialism at a particular moment, when both the city and the empire of which it was the capital were at their zenith. It will build upon previous work, but I hope to add a new dimension to studies of the metropolis by showing not merely how the imperial message pervaded everyday life and what were the consequences, but also how some Londoners refused merely to accept the message and sought rather to refine and turn it to their own purposes. In short, the book seeks to explain an interactive process which defined what it meant at the turn of the twentieth century for London to be the world's imperial metropolis.

The general argument of the book is that imperialism was central to the city's character in 1900, apparent in its workplaces, its venues of entertainment, its physical geography, its very skyline; apparent, too, in the attitudes of Londoners themselves. Identity, however, does not reveal itself in an instant, cannot be fixed or defined in a single sentence. What it meant for London to be an imperial metropolis, even at a specific moment in history—that is to say in the year 1900—is something that takes a good deal of unraveling.

Moreover, identity is never fixed or unitary. One object of this book is to explore the meaning of an identity which was fluid, subtle, and the object of contestation. To some Londoners the meaning of their city was plain as a pikestaff. Many investors in stocks and bonds, many bankers and financiers, many men and women with commercial interests in Asia, Africa, the Americas, and the Antipodes believed that imperialism spelled opportunity and that the City of London, the world's greatest financial district, existed to augment their fortunes. To them the imperial metropolis was little more than a unique machine for making money. The better one understood how the machine operated, the more money one made.

Others interpreted the identity of the imperial metropolis in slightly less self-interested fashion. To a number of leading political and military men and to some important architects, London's meaning was disclosed in the city's physical appearance, in the layout of streets and avenues, and in the buildings and public monuments which lined them. London's built environment, such figures maintained, should be appropriately imposing. It should convey a sense of Britain's world role, of its preeminence, so that Londoners would, as if through a process of osmosis, come to understand what their attitudes toward empire and the imperialized peoples should be. To those who embraced this view, the imperial metropolis was not so much a machine for making money as it was, at least potentially, a machine for making imperialist-minded citizens.

Still others drew different conclusions. An imperial people merited respect in the workplace as well as abroad. There were Londoners who were prepared to go on strike to demand this. Because they labored in factories, workshops, and sweaters' dens to make the capital city of a great empire function, because, in other words, their skills and strengths were (indirectly perhaps) as vital to the prosperity and health of the British Empire as were those of imperial explorers, soldiers, and settlers, many London workers believed that they deserved decent treatment and higher wages from their employers.

Finally there were Londoners, mainly women and immigrants from the colonies, who purposively sought to explore, to expand, and in a few rare cases to explode entirely the boundaries of an imperial metropolis which failed to accord them sufficient opportunity for self-fulfillment. For them imperial London was not yet, but could still become, the capital city of a more enlightened and progressive world. It was a microcosm of what the British Empire itself should and could be.

This book argues, then, that the imperial metropolis both shaped and was shaped by Londoners in 1900. Metropolitan residents from all walks of life and holding diverse, even conflicting, understandings of imperialism configured a city that bore their own modest imprimatur as well as the mark of Britain's great empire builders. Certainly Londoners were not merely passive receptors of imperialist propaganda, as a number of historians have depicted them. The imperial metropolis was the product of a complex interaction, of reciprocal, occasionally antagonistic forces and processes, of a multiplicity of rhetorics which this volume will trace and analyze.

Moreover, the diverse meanings with which London residents and the formal architects of British imperialism alike invested the imperial metropolis had direct and indirect consequences themselves. These were played out on the world historical stage, in the ebb and flow of British imperial rule, in British party politics, in Britain's labor and feminist movements, in the history of London itself. This book will attempt to identify some of these consequences, too, and to trace and analyze them, in order to weigh their historical impact.

Early chapters will unveil and interrogate the imperial messages implicit in London's architecture, popular entertainments, and selected workplaces (the City of London and dockland, which I call the nexus of imperialism) as well as reactions to them. Later chapters will explore the divided imperial metropolis, first investigating gender boundaries in the empire's capital city, then providing a taxonomy of anti-imperial London and examining the alternative worldview that some of its inhabitants struggled to articulate. A concluding chapter will focus on the Khaki Election of 1900 in London, during which themes adduced earlier were addressed by leading figures and voted upon by a mass electorate.

PART I

Imperial London

2. Cleopatra's Needle and Sphinxes.
Courtesy of the Guildhall Library.

CHAPTER 2

THE FACE OF IMPERIAL LONDON

I N 1900 the capital city of the greatest empire in the world contained many imperial symbols, statues, shrines, and monuments. At the junction of Knightsbridge and Brompton Road there was the memorial to Field Marshall Hugh Rose, first Baron Strathnairn, conqueror of Syria and India, posed on bronze horse, wearing his Indian helmet with cascading feathers. Towering over the Thames Embankment was Cleopatra's Needle, an obelisk 68 feet high and weighing 180 tons, with two large sphinxes at its foot. There was the facade of the Colonial Office itself in Whitehall, decorated with representative human and animal figures of the five continents over which the British flag flew. London was dotted with such reminders of Britain's imperial rule.[1]

Perhaps most striking among the city's many imperial symbols and monuments was Trafalgar Square, located at the very center of the imperial metropolis. At its front stood the massive column commemorating the great naval hero Lord Horatio Nelson. It was 176 feet high, surmounted by a 17-foot statue of the great man, and set upon a square pedestal 36 feet tall. Each side of the pedestal pictured one of Nelson's famous victories. Four great black lions, symbols of English might, ringed the memorial. In 1900 four additional statues stood in the square commemorating George IV and three imperialist generals, Sir Charles Napier, who fought the Peninsular campaign with Wellington and later helped to crush the Luddites, Sir Henry Havelock, who put down the Indian Mutiny, and Charles George "Chinese" Gordon, the martyr of Khartoum.[2]

Art may exist for art's sake, but public art exists outside and beyond itself. It is meant to affect the public. Benjamin Wyatt consciously, if rather loosely, modeled the Waterloo Place memorial to the former commander-in-chief of the British army, the duke of York, upon the Emperor Trajan's Column in Rome, which had been erected to commemorate the moment when

the Roman Empire reached its vastest extent. William Railton chose a column in the temple of Mars the Avenger in the Forum of Augustus, also in imperial Rome, as his model for Nelson's Column.[3] By the turn of the twentieth
century, with Britain engaged in a full-blown imperial war in South Africa, in
a cooperative international "police action" designed to punish the Boxer
rebels in China, and in brushfire wars against native insurrections in West
Africa and Borneo, British architectural sculptors reflected popular passions
in their art. Perhaps not surprisingly, they displayed what one scholar has
termed "an unattractive Kiplingesque obsession with patriotism, health and
'masculinity.'" No public square, no park, was complete without its bronze
depiction of "lusty 'outward bound' youths."[4]

The work of British architects likewise reflected popular passions. For
decades they had been consciously searching for a style that could be termed
national. But the adherents of the Arts and Crafts movement, those who favored simple, natural English designs, had been overshadowed toward the
end of the century by architects who preferred a grandiose and boastful, even
imperial, style. In 1901, with the Boer War raging, John Belcher and Mervyn
Macartney published what might be termed this movement's manifesto.
"The work of the Later Renaissance [in England] may justly claim to embody and represent many of our national characteristics," the two architects
began in their jointly edited and massively influential *Later Renaissance Architecture in England*. The style was "practical and convenient . . . sturdy, masculine," "graceful" and "sober," precisely fitted to "modern requirements." It
was, in short, and to quote a leading architectural historian, "a suitable basis
for . . . the expression of Britain's importance as the centre of a great empire."[5]

By then not merely the Arts and Crafts movement, but Victorian Gothic
architecture as a whole had given way to a revived classicism modeled on the
works of Christopher Wren and John Vanbrugh. Throughout London, indeed throughout Britain and the empire, buildings constructed during the
quarter century or so before 1914 reflected this political ideal, which was also
an architectural style variously termed baroque classicism or English, Edwardian, or classical baroque. Significantly it became the style of choice for
new government buildings in Whitehall, for example, the new War Office,
designed by William Young in 1899, and the new Colonial Office, designed
in the same year by John Brydon (and subsequently occupied by the Department of Local Government and the Treasury). Large businesses "soon took
it up as a style that was sound and grand and associated with British prosperity," including the North Eastern Railway Company at 4 Cowley Street,
Booth's gin distillers in Cowcross Street, Dewar House in the Haymarket,

Lloyd's Shipping Register offices in Fenchurch Street, and a host of other insurance agencies, among them the Royal London Insurance Company, the Alliance Assurance Company, and the Pearl Assurance Company. Waring and Gillow's department store on Oxford Street was built in "as specifically English a Classical style as any jingoistic patriot would ask for." Hotels, theaters, restaurants, and even a few pubs followed suit.[6]

The public art and architecture of London together reflected and reinforced an impression, an atmosphere, celebrating British heroism on the battlefield, British sovereignty over foreign lands, British wealth and power, in short, British imperialism. The impression was not hegemonic, for London's public art and architecture broadcast mixed messages, and in any event London residents did not all absorb the implicit lessons of the classical baroque style unthinkingly. Nevertheless it was an integral and influential presence in London life. At the same time it remained in toto largely an uncoordinated jumble of disparate monuments, department stores, hotels, public and private offices. Enormous and impressive London undoubtedly was; but the face it presented to the world did not express London's peerless status as the world's greatest imperial metropolis. There were relatively few broad, sweeping avenues and boulevards, as in Paris and Berlin, where architects had consciously celebrated the Third Empire and establishment of the second German Reich, a dearth of structures to compare with the grand buildings facing the Ringstrasse of Vienna, which had been erected to reflect "the greatness of empire," few constellations of linked squares as in St. Petersburg.[7] Men and women who thought about such matters, including a number of important London architects as well as politicians and officials, hoped to see the construction of more such boulevards and buildings, and according to some larger plan.

In 1900, a grand scheme to widen the Strand and to create a broad avenue running north from it up to Holborn provided just such an opportunity, revealing the intersection between politics and architecture. On one level the project was an uncomplicated and much-needed civic improvement. On another level, however, it was an ambitious attempt to give the metropolis an example of the imperial face many thought it needed and deserved.

The authority which oversaw this project was the London County Council (LCC), established in 1888 to give the vast and still-growing metropolis something like coordinated government. The LCC, which replaced a moribund and corrupt Metropolitan Board of Works and whose members were directly elected, soon divided between Liberal, Radical, and socialist Progressives on the one hand and Conservative Moderates on the other. From the outset, however, a few members from both factions shared certain aspirations. They "hankered," as the architectural historian Andrew Saint puts it, "for London's transformation into the imperial capital that Britain merited."[8]

This was not, however, a simple matter. Some wished for the construction of buildings in the style of Edwardian Baroque in order to reflect the glory of Britain and her empire. Others favored various projects of civic improvement and reform which they held to be essential in a truly imperial metropolis. On the grounds that the working class of an imperial metropolis deserved no less, these councilors advocated, for example, the widening of congested streets, the demolition of slums, the construction of public housing. But Progressives and Moderates, whether advocates of urban renewal or

3. Horse buses on the Strand, ca. 1900.
Courtesy of the Museum of London.

4. (*left*) Wych Street (demolished to make way for the Aldwych and Kingsway).
Courtesy of the Guildhall Library.

5. (*right*) Holywell Street (demolished to make way for the Aldwych and Kingsway).
Courtesy of the Guildhall Library.

of a more imperial face for their city, could agree that the metropolis needed a major north–south artery, since most of its wider streets ran east–west. Here was an opportunity for them to work together.

Various schemes for cutting an avenue from the Strand to Holborn had been floated over the decades. In 1892, with Frederic Harrison as chairman of the LCC's improvements committee, a realistic plan began to emerge. Eventually it boiled down to this: the Strand itself must be widened and its buildings refronted. Then a great crescent should be constructed at the street's eastern end (the Aldwych), and running northward from it a broad avenue past Holborn connecting with Southampton Row and thus Russell Square and the Euston and Kings Cross railway stations. This great new boulevard would also improve access to Waterloo Bridge to the south. Depending on one's perspective, the section between the Strand and Holborn was either "a large amount of slum property only fit to be demolished," as one commentator put it, or "an intensely interesting, if somewhat squalid, sector of the Old

London," according to another. In any event, it was an area which neither the architects nor the city planners of the LCC wished to preserve.[9]

Divided though the LCC may have been as to ultimate objectives, it swung ponderously into action. In 1898 its improvements committee, now chaired by the Liberal politician Shaw Lefevre, began purchasing property along the route of the proposed road. In March 1899, the LCC appointed a new chief architect, the former Admiralty surveyor William E. Riley, under whose direction widening of the Strand commenced. He initiated discussions with professional colleagues in the Royal Institute of British Architects (RIBA). At his urging, the LCC announced a competition among eight leading architects for suggestions on treatment of the Strand-Aldwych facades.

The process was not uncontentious, however, because the divergent motives of the project's sponsors mirrored divergent notions among London's populace. No single definition of the imperial metropolis satisfied everybody. Ratepayers, less concerned with the face of London than with their pocketbooks, objected to the additional taxes they would have to pay to fund the project. Radicals, who believed in a more egalitarian imperial metropolis, opposed "the addition of a very large sum to the capital value of the 'property' of the London land monopolists." Socialists like the LCC councilor John Burns approached the issue of egalitarianism from another angle: "I don't want London to confine itself to a few swell boulevards. We want common sanitation to be uniform, to be relatively better in the poor street, which is the children's playground, and in the side street, which is the charwoman's promenade."[10]

Similar objections were to dog the project until it had been completed, testimony to the enduring ambiguity of imperial London's identity. On the other hand, no consequential faction on the LCC was prepared to oppose a project which appealed to both reform-minded and imperial-minded councilors. More immediately troubling if ultimately less significant, therefore, was the LCC's inability to find eight leading architects willing to submit blueprints for the meager £150 fee that had been offered. The LCC increased the sum by £100. This gesture hardly appeased the president of RIBA, William Emerson: "For the London County Council, the most important municipal body in the world, to ... expect to obtain the best professional talent by increasing the paltry fee ... to £250 for designing over a mile of frontage [is] ... derogatory to the dignity of the profession." Another problem was that the LCC would not promise to hire the architect whose plans they eventually chose. But the council ploughed ahead anyway, the faction concerned with London's face increasingly dominant or at least vocal about its aims. As Howell Williams, one of this group, pointed out to the LCC improvements committee, they were "dealing with buildings to be erected on perhaps one of the most important sites in Europe." What was constructed should reflect this fact. The committee was convinced. "The great thoroughfare . . . should," it maintained when it moved the motion in favor of the project, "possess beauty and civic dignity, as some of the grand thoroughfares in certain continental cities."[11]

Architects took the point, too, and expanded upon it. What London required, and what the Aldwych-Holborn project could provide, Emerson argued in the peroration to his presidential address to the RIBA in November 1899, was "an architecture that may enhance the glory of this great empire." Six months later, at an architectural congress, he elaborated upon this theme. British architecture would never enhance the glory of the British Empire if it were left to the vagaries of private enterprise. On the other hand, no county council had sufficient powers to control and guide it. Therefore, "there should be a responsible head [preferably a government minister] . . . chosen . . . for his known cultivated tastes, large Imperial ideas, and love of art, combined with practical common sense. . . . For the Metropolis, in which the whole empire was interested, such a controlling body should [most certainly] be a Government Ministry of Fine Arts." If his prescription was followed, Emerson argued, then "the architecture of the greatest empire the world has ever seen . . . [will] not in the future suffer by comparison with that of other civilised countries."[12]

Emerson's call for an architecture to reflect Britain's imperial grandeur did not fall upon deaf ears. Norman Shaw, perhaps the greatest and most influential British architect of the age, took it up. He had been asked to participate in the competition, had declined because he was retired, but then agreed to act as an unpaid consultant and advisor. In an article on the project which appeared in the *Architectural Review*, he appealed to architects to display British patriotic sentiment and to follow Emerson's injunction by including in their plans for the new road a specific structure. London as it now was cut a sorry figure among the great cities of the world, Shaw admitted: "Fancy having to show a cultivated foreigner Charing Cross Road or Shaftesbury Avenue! [where architectural and street improvements had recently taken place]. How should we feel? And what would his politeness induce him to say to these architectural achievements?" The new project, however, offered "an opportunity for a very striking arrangement." It should include a "great national monument . . . not . . . a thing 10ft. or 15ft. wide, and possibly 20ft. high—but a really grand architectural composition—perhaps 50 ft. wide and 70 ft. or 80 ft. high. . . . Nothing less would be worthy of what ought to be a superb site, in the centre of a city that claims to be one of the most important in the world."[13]

Mervyn Macartney, one of the architects chosen to submit drawings in the competition, agreed with Shaw and Emerson. Now he asserted that because London was "the greatest and wealthiest city in the world," the project must reflect its exalted status. "Where the new street joins the great crescent [which eventually became the Aldwych], a circus should certainly be formed, with a site provided in the centre for a great national memorial (sure to be wanted some day), and on no account to be turned to any baser uses."[14]

The discussion spilled from the pages of the professional journals into the popular press. The *Daily Express* made no comment upon the aims of British architecture but was sure the Aldwych-Holborn project provided an opportunity for imperialist and patriotic display. What was needed was not a single national monument as envisioned by Shaw and Macartney, but something grander, an entire "Hall of Heroes—Lest we forget."[15]

One architect thought that London actually compared well with other great European cities. Vienna, Berlin, and Paris consisted mainly of "narrow irregular streets, in an infinitely worse sanitary condition than those of London," sniffed T. Walter Emden, president of the Society of Architects. But the majority of his colleagues disagreed. "The Boulevard de Sebastopol, the Grand Avenue des Champs-Elysées, the Boulevard Haussmann in Paris; the Boulevard Anspach and others in Brussels . . . the magnificent streets and avenues of Vienna" were the models which W. Woodward of the RIBA thought British architects should follow.[16] John Belcher agreed in the *Architectural Review* for April 1900. So, in the same issue of the journal, did three other prominent architects, T. G. Jackson, W. R. Lethaby, and Ernest Newton. London would never assume its rightful place as the premier imperial metropolis so long as it lacked the sweeping, broad avenues of the continental cities, Paris in particular. The proposed boulevard must be straight as a string and very broad. "I think that 100 ft, building to building, is sufficient for fine effect," Woodward opined. Shaw placed his weighty imprimatur upon this width in his article as well.

What to name the new street likewise exercised the minds of those concerned. Beachcroft, of the LCC, reminded the improvements committee that "as next year was the millenary of King Alfred, the Committee might consider the desirability of associating the name of Alfred with the new street." Others canvassed alternative names. "For our own part," wrote the editors of the *Builder*, "we keep to the suggestion we have already made, that the street be called 'Gordon Avenue,' in commemoration of the noblest Englishman of our time."[17] In the end, however, the LCC dubbed the new avenue Kingsway. An acceptable compromise, it seemed at once patriotic, all-embracing, and dignified.

When finally the eight architects submitted their designs they all reflected the current fascination with Edwardian Baroque and the current political climate. "We see almost every variety of Classic or so-called Renaissance composition," remarked the *Building News* of November 2, 1900, which reprinted all of the designs over the course of several weeks. Shaw, who assessed the entries for the LCC, "enthused upon the English Renaissance" and chose the designs of Henry T. Hare (architect of the Oxford Town Hall), William Flockhart, and Mervyn Macartney, in that order, as the best.[18]

The door stood open to the grandly conceived imperial metropolis of their fond imagining, or so it must have seemed to the LCC's empire-minded visionaries contemplating Hare's plans. And the crescent they caused to be built, and the road they caused to be cut, *were* grandly imperial to look at. "Even now, almost a century later," an urban historian muses, "the strains of *Pomp and Circumstance* still linger. . . . This connection with Edwardian imperialism gives Kingsway character. . . . We are reminded of past glories and long extinguished aspirations."[19] Still the visionaries cannot have been altogether satisfied with the results of their project. The stubborn objections of Radicals and socialists who envisioned an altogether different imperial metropolis were never entirely silenced or overcome; the doubts of Moderates who objected to higher taxes and municipal spending were never completely assuaged; moreover the lack of a single directing figure with appropriate powers proved crippling to the imperialists' larger aims, as Emerson had predicted.

Consider this last difficulty first. From the beginning a congeries of property owners, builders, and architects sought to bring their interests to bear upon the project. "Commercial considerations must give way to some extent," exhorted the editors of the *Builder* on March 10, 1900. "This new road is the biggest affair of our time . . . the undertaking behoves us to enter on it as statesmen not as hucksters," echoed the architect Halsey Ricardo. But in London in 1900, the hucksters could not be excluded. As the buildings went down along the Strand, the advertising posters went up on giant hoardings, much to the dismay of the *Architectural Review*, which found them (and also "the abominable lamp columns which are being erected in the centre of the new roadway") inexcusable. The squalid scene with its puffs for soaps, teas, whiskeys, hotels, and restaurants certainly did not present the face of London which LCC visionaries wished the world to see.[20]

Meanwhile, several of the firms owning property along the Strand had developed their own plans for rebuilding, even as the eight chosen architects were drawing up theirs. The managers of the Gaiety Theatre and Restaurant, for example, employed the architect Ernest Runtz, one of the eight competi-

6. Kingsway completed.
Courtesy of London Metropolitan Archives.

tors but not one of the three finalists. Now he was told by the LCC that he must coordinate his designs with those of the winner, Henry Hare. The two men soon fell out. The *Morning Post* newspaper, Carr's Restaurant, and Short's Limited were other businesses whose facades along the Strand required further attention from the LCC, even though, or rather precisely because, each employed its own private architect.

Then there was the question of how best to utilize the great central area facing the Strand where the Aldwych would be. Some on the LCC wished to build a new London County Hall there. Others favored the great memorial structures broached by Shaw and Macartney. Still others wished to leave it to private enterprise. Council members dithered over this issue. In the end

Australia House and India House and Africa House did locate at the Aldwych, proof positive that the LCC had finally created the atmosphere they sought—but it took more than two decades for these architectural representations of the British Empire to arrive. A similar state of affairs existed along the new avenue, Kingsway. It took five years to complete, and then, the grand aspirations of its designers notwithstanding, businessmen proved reluctant to rent sites along it. Many stood vacant until after World War I. In 1908, according to John Burns, Kingsway was merely "a rendez-vous for Covent Garden waggons, and a pest on account of gangs of betting men who seem to prosper there."[21]

Indeed, so disappointed with the outcome of the project were a number of influential architects, politicians—including at least two past members of the LCC—and a host of other notables, that in 1903 they formed a Further Strand Improvement Committee to press their cause. Their argument was familiar by now: "As pointed out in the 'Report of the Royal Commission on London Traffic,' Paris, New York, Washington, Berlin, Brussels, Vienna, have streets finer than any that London can show. We ask—is London . . . to refuse this opportunity of showing itself in reality an imperial city, a worthy Capital of a world-wide Empire?" London did so refuse. The further improvements which the committee sought would have cost more than £239,400, and this neither the city's ratepayers, nor the Moderates who opposed municipal spending, nor even those Progressives who objected to increasing the value of Strand property owners at municipal expense would approve.[22]

In the end, what was written of Shaw in the *Dictionary of National Biography* might have been written with his role in the Aldwych-Holborn project in mind: "To his advice we owe some attempts to give our capital city a dignity worthy of its imperial position. But . . . [his] projects for straightening out the haphazard muddle of London were mostly blocked."[23] For if the British Empire was the most powerful the world had ever known, it yet lacked an emperor whose every vision of London could become an architect's command. Great Britain was a constitutional empire and a capitalist one.

A few years later, the national government showed that it possessed the political muscle and financial resources to accomplish what the LCC could not. Parliamentary approval had accompanied the Strand-Holborn project, but Parliament had not been the prime mover behind the scheme. Upon the death of Queen Victoria, however, Parliament commissioned a memorial to her in front of Buckingham Palace, and then a new layout of the Mall, which runs along the upper rim of St. James Park all the way to Trafalgar Square, and finally the Admiralty Arch which links them. The architect chosen to complete this project was Aston Webb. Inevitably the style he employed was Edwardian Baroque. Thus Webb and the imperial government finally provided London with at least a portion of the imperial face the city was thought to deserve. Had it not been for the death of a revered monarch and the respectful silence of those who otherwise undoubtedly would have opposed such a project for its expense, or for its inegalitarian implications, however, London might lack this grandest and most imperial of avenues. The price for giving the face of London a thoroughly imperial cast would have been to place limits upon constitutionalism and free enterprise. That was a price few Londoners were willing to pay.

Possibly the London passerby rejected or was oblivious to the nationalist and imperialist preoccupations of public sculpture and architecture and to the messages they were meant to convey. Possibly he missed the classical allusions present at, say, Trafalgar Square, the reminders of British heroism, the justification of Britain's imperial role implicit in the various memorial statues there. Or possibly not. The P. & O., Royal Mail, Cunard, and White Star Line steamship companies all occupied offices on Cockspur Street, within a stone's throw of the square. No doubt there were standard business reasons for choosing this location. But also may there not have been the hope that customers inspired by the square's patriotic themes would be eager to visit scenes made famous by imperialist adventurers? A few steps up the Strand from Trafalgar Square, Henry Gaze and Sons, travel agents, offered, in early January 1900, a sixteen-day trip from Cairo to Khartoum to travelers wishing "to see the scenes of the Sirdar's exploits." The Sirdar was the British military commander in Egypt, the man who had avenged General Gordon.[24]

Architecture affords the backdrop to what takes place in a city. It does not determine events, but, because it contributes to a mood or atmosphere, it can influence them. A young Londoner, moved and inspired by the statue of General Gordon in Trafalgar Square, decides finally, perhaps after months of rumination, to emigrate to South Africa. Twenty paces from him he sees South Africa House, which will furnish him with information about the colony; a dozen steps beyond are the offices of the steamship line which will take him there. His life is changed; perhaps, in a small way, history is changed.

The effect can transcend individuals. During the Boer War the return of soldiers from South Africa was carefully stage-managed, not so much by military as by political and municipal authorities. The idea was to display the heroes in such a way as to create, or to sustain, a mood of imperialist determination among a public which might begin to grow weary of war. But then the heroes must be presented in a proper setting—which means that the arrangers of such scenes believed architecture can be made to serve a political purpose, that it can, in fact, help to shape history.

A specific instance of such attempted manipulation occurred in October 1900 when the City Imperial Volunteers (CIV) returned to London from a tour of duty in South Africa, where they had seen combat. The CIV was the brainchild of the aldermen of the City of London and more particularly of the lord mayor, Sir Alfred J. Newton, Bart. Raised, equipped, and manned mainly by the great firms and companies of the city, the CIV had departed England the previous January amidst unprecedented hoopla. Their return, however, proved to be an even greater occasion.

The soldiers sailed from Cape Town for home on October 7 aboard the steamship *Aurania*. In London the responsible authorities began planning a grand reception for them. Its purpose was to honor the returning military men and the City firms which had funded them and also, more important, to encourage martial and patriotic spirit in the imperial metropolis. A march through the capital and ceremonies at St. Paul's Cathedral and the Guildhall would be followed by a great banquet.

The authorities thought through every detail of the event. The men would march in a certain order designed for purposes of spectacle and display: at their head, astride their chargers, the CIV commander, Col. Henry William Mackinnon, and the commander of the Home District, Gen. Sir Henry Trotter; behind them, mounted only slightly less splendidly, the CIV's cavalry division, led by a sergeant bearing a flag captured in the Orange Free State; next the field battery including Maxim guns; then the CIV cyclists; and then, numbering thirteen hundred, the infantry battalions. Behind these, in horse-drawn brakes, a spectacle clearly designed to whip at patriotic sensibilities: those of the CIV who could not march because they had been wounded.

Moreover, the authorities arranged not only for police, but also for the London Scottish, the Queen's Westminster, and the Surrey Volunteer brigades, themselves arrayed in splendid uniforms, to line the route of march in order to hold back the anticipated crowds. They would lend further picturesque, indeed patriotic, color to the scene. Finally, they scheduled various military bands to perform "Soldiers of the Queen" and other patriotic airs at way stations along the route, so that not only sight but sound itself would feed the imperialist enthusiasm of onlookers.

Equal attention was devoted to the course that the returning soldiers would follow. First of all, they would not begin their march from Waterloo station, the point of destination for all other London-bound trains from

Southampton, including a smaller detachment of sailors from H.M.S. *Powerful* who had been feted earlier in the year although with less hullabaloo, because the route from that terminus to St. Paul's Cathedral, over the Waterloo Bridge and eastward along the Strand and Fleet Street, is relatively short and prosaic. Rather their train would come up from Southampton to Paddington railway station, the terminus for Queen Victoria's special train whenever she traveled to London from Windsor, and the railway station most associated in the public mind with royalty and grand occasions. Then, from Paddington, the soldiers would follow almost precisely the route the queen had taken during the celebrations accompanying her Diamond Jubilee in 1897. These "arrangements . . . were discussed yesterday morning at a special meeting, over which the Lord Mayor presided at the Mansion House," reported the *Daily Mail.* Unavailingly might an officer of the returning corps warn "there is not a man among us who would not rather forego the reception" altogether! But the politicians had much more on their minds than the finer feelings of returning soldiers.[25]

The *Aurania* docked in Southampton on the evening of Saturday, October 27. On Monday morning the CIV disembarked amidst cheering throngs and filed into four great trains which carried them up to London by the circuitous route that brought them to Paddington. The caravan whirled through towns and villages decorated with patriotic flags and banners, past waving, applauding crowds. It steamed into Paddington at two minutes past noon. This was the starting point of the march through London which the men dreaded. And now the careful calculations of the event's organizers began to pay off.

When the men of the CIV filed from Paddington station into Praed Street and then down the Edgware Road, they did not take a direct route toward St Paul's by turning into Oxford Street, which, after all, is lined mainly with shops and is not conducive to the mood the authorities sought to create on this occasion, and which borders at its eastern end on Soho, an insalubrious, even raunchy district. They were also thus able to avoid marching down any portion of Charing Cross Road, whose eastern edge touched the notorious slum district of Seven Dials. Rather, at the end of the Edgware Road they continued south, through the lofty Marble Arch, following Queen Victoria's route of three years before. But whereas the queen had turned down Constitution-hill to Buckingham Palace, in which she spent the night before continuing her progress to St. Paul's on the second day of her Diamond Jubilee celebration, the CIV marched across Hyde Park Corner and then southward toward Apsley House, an imposing mansion which had been the generous gift of a grateful nation to the duke of Wellington, the hero of a previous war. This is as noble a stretch as may be found in London, with Hyde Park on one side and the elegant Park Lane on the other, well designed to impress the onlooker with a sense of the wealth England possesses and, through Apsley House, of the nation's power, historic mission, and past military glories.

From Apsley House the backdrop to the march grew even more grand. The CIV trooped east along Piccadilly with Green Park to their right. Buckingham Palace lies immediately to the south, and here they took up the queen's route of 1897 again, for she, upon leaving Buckingham Palace after the twenty-four-hour hiatus, had turned from Constitution-hill into Piccadilly and then into St. James Street, Pall Mall, the Strand, Fleet Street, and finally Ludgate Hill on the way to St. Paul's. So did the CIV, although stopping briefly at Marlborough House, the Prince of Wales's London residence, where the heir to the throne greeted them, and then departing from the queen's route to make another detour down Whitehall to the War Office, where the secretary for war, Lord Lansdowne, the commander in chief of the army, Lord Wolseley, the adjutant-general, Sir Evelyn Wood, and Queen Victoria's third son, Prince Arthur William Patrick Albert, the duke of Connaught, greeted them. From Whitehall the column marched into Trafalgar Square, perhaps the single most vivid architectural and sculptural talisman of British power, heroism, and imperialism within the metropolis.

This itinerary had been designed to present an appropriately grand and imperial backdrop for the sunburned heroes returning from the veldt and for the members of the royal household and high military men who came to bless them. It fostered an impressive ambiance linking royalty, imperialism, the CIV, and the cheering throng in a shared, glorious endeavor. Moreover, the itinerary was eminently practical. There would have been no room for great crowds along Oxford Street or Charing Cross Road, but as the CIV paraded from Marble Arch to Hyde Park Corner, "the public stretched back among the trees a hundred deep at a time." Indeed Hyde Park, Green Park, and St. James Park could accommodate any number of people. In Trafalgar Square, a more limited space, the crush was so fierce that "accidents were frequent, and the hysterical shrieks of women mingled with the deep-throated huzzas of the crowd." Along the Strand and Fleet Street the mass grew so dense that the CIV could barely make their way. "The multitudes who poured into the streets exceeded in number the crowds that came out to celebrate her Majesty's Jubilee [of 1897]," one witness recorded in disbelief.

From Trafalgar Square the line of march followed the Strand east into Fleet Street, up Ludgate Hill, and into St. Paul's. This was a less imposing section of the metropolis. Indeed, the Strand was a mess as a result of the LCC's decision to widen and improve it; Fleet Street, rather a narrow artery, was lined with the seedy pubs and cafes frequented by journalists and printers

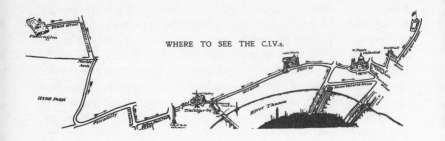

7. London route of the returning CIV. This was one of many such maps
printed in the daily press.
By permission of the British Library.

who worked nearby.[26] No longer surrounded by architectural reminders of
British imperialism and military success, the crowds grew unruly. Did the
lack of an imposing backdrop free spectators from certain feelings of con-
straint? At any rate, as one journalist recorded, at this stage of the march "the
ambulance men were needed every few minutes. . . . At Ludgate-circus a se-

8. CIV marching through Hyde Park.
By permission of the British Library.

rious accident occurred, and on all of the street refuges gasping patients were lying."

Why did the organizers of the occasion not choose to receive the returning soldiers at Westminster Abbey instead of St. Paul's, thus obviating the march up the Strand and Fleet Street and the scrum which followed? The answer must be not merely that St. Paul's could accommodate a larger crowd—although surely this was a consideration which had influenced the queen three years before—but also that they wished to honor the City Imperial Volunteers with a service in the City, which had created and paid for them, and to fete them at the Guildhall, also located in the heart of the City; they wanted to use architecture to underline the connection which the CIV embodied, linking the City of London with imperialism and loyalty.

But now the volunteers were approaching St. Paul's, where the lord mayor, his wife, the sheriffs of London in brilliant red coats, the Cathedral Choir in white, and "a gaudy throng of liveried servants" stood waiting. Above them towered the massive dome of St. Paul's, the very archetype of the classical baroque style. Spectacle was paramount once again. Decorum reasserted itself. The cathedral's "portals flung backward. . . . Out of the dusk rushed a crash of cheering, and through the cheering a clamour of bagpipes and brass. And now the white train of clergy and choir . . . the Lord Mayor and his scarlet throng, and—them [the CIV]. . . . The organ burst out and the brasses of the Royal Military School of Music made the blood tingle, and every throat took up the processional hymn, and everything together wrung tears from many eyes." The bishop of Stepney welcomed the returning warriors with a speech of Thanksgiving: "My brothers . . . Welcome Home!" Sir George Martin stood out on the chancel steps, waved his baton, and "the National Anthem rolled from a thousand strong throats up into the glorious spangled roof." It is hard to imagine a scene better calculated to play upon patriotic emotions or a building better suited for the occasion.

Yet there was another such scene, at the Guildhall, to which the CIV processed immediately following the service at St. Paul's. Exiting the cathedral, the soldiers forced their way through surging crowds, up Cheapside and King Street, which were lined by the Tower Hamlets, the Second London, and the London Rifle brigades. This was the very heart of the City of London, the birthplace, as it were, of the CIV. The great offices and display rooms of imperial merchant princes, their banks and insurance houses, loomed above the crowds, which were well behaved again. The soldiers entered the grand premises of the Guildhall. Portions of this building dated back to the thirteenth century, but much of it had been reconstructed after the great fire of 1666 by the greatest of all practitioners of English Renaissance architecture,

Christopher Wren himself. The soldiers filed through the gallery, dominated by fourteen-foot statues of Gog and Magog, into the great hall, where, "under the shadow of the memorials erected by the City of London to Nelson and Wellington," the lord mayor, General Trotter, and Colonel Mackinnon delivered patriotic speeches. Then, "as the familiar strains of the National Anthem rose from the assembly, the lips of many a khaki-clad warrior quivered with the emotion he endeavoured to conceal."[27]

If there is such a thing as architectural determinism, that is not what this chapter is arguing for. On the other hand, architecture can be made to serve more than one purpose. At the turn of the twentieth century some of London's municipal authorities and, it would appear, most of the country's leading architects thought that architecture meant more than the style of a building. They believed that London was the capital city of the world's greatest empire, but that its architecture did not reflect this fact. London would show the world a more imperial face if the Strand was widened, if a great monument was placed at the Aldwych, if the new road to Holborn was a hundred feet wide, named after General Gordon, and so on. For these men architecture and national identity were linked. Architecture could help to forge a national and an imperial identity.

Some LCC councilors and their allies had a rather different notion of what a truly imperial capital should be. For socialists like John Burns it meant a city which fostered the health and living standards of its inhabitants so that they might play their part in imperial affairs. He supported the Strand–Holborn improvements only when convinced that London's poor would benefit from the new north–south connection between Waterloo and King's Cross and Euston railway stations. Harold Cox, Radical secretary of the Cobden Club, M.P. for Preston, and a future London County councilor, articulated another reason for Radicals and socialists to support such projects. As he put it to a meeting demanding further Strand improvements, the workers of London had "a double interest in the beauty and the spaciousness of our public thoroughfares. Because their homes are so narrow the street is their playground, their drawing room." Councilor Frederic Harrison wished to preserve and enhance not merely London's street views, but the "historic associations" linked to certain sections of the city. The famous Radical was thinking of preserving not merely vistas which opened on London's great buildings like Parliament and St. Paul's Cathedral, or of, say, the view from Hyde Park corner or Marble Arch, but rather the penumbra of radical ideas which encircled humble homes, taverns, and coffeehouses where the Puritan revolutionaries and early trade unionists used to meet, and Kennington Common, where the Chartists assembled in 1848, perhaps even Farringdon Hall, where, that year, the Labour Party's founding conference had taken place. Harrison viewed the members of the LCC as "trustees of the Metropolis of the Empire," but his notion of what the Metropolis of the Empire should be like was not the same as, say, the notion of an architect like Aston Webb.[28]

No wonder, then, that the project was not entirely successful. The broadened Strand, the Aldwych, and the Kingsway promised more in blueprint than they delivered in reality. And here looms yet another competing vision of the imperial metropolis. For the very commercial successes which helped to strengthen the sinews of British imperialism had also produced a mindset among London businessmen and ratepayers which was inimical to the rehabilitation of their city along grand and imperial lines. "We submit," wrote the members of the Further Strand Improvement Committee, "that the matter should be considered from the point of view not only of what is for the moment financially desirable, but also of what is befitting the dignity of the Capital of our Empire."[29] Their plea fell upon deaf ears. Imperial identity and national identity were at odds in this instance, and national identity was more profound. After all, the opposition to high rates stretched back past the cheeseparing of the Liberals in the mid–nineteenth century all the way to the seventeenth century, when John Hampden refused to pay "ship money" to King Charles.

But it was not only a matter of money. It was a matter of power too. The LCC simply could not ride roughshod over the wishes of London ratepayers, even had it wanted to. It lacked the authority to push the Strand–Holborn improvement scheme to its logical conclusion. In Cape Town, Bombay, and, above all, in New Delhi, where architects and city planners suffered fewer constraints, an imperial architecture might take concrete form.[30] Not so in the capital city of the empire, where architects and the civic authorities who commissioned them had to take the wishes and needs of private interests into account. The imperial metropolis was democratic to a degree. Although Britain could take an empire, it could not give its capital city a facelift.

And so London authorities attempted to make do with such imperial face as the capital already possessed. The lord mayor and his colleagues did so in their arrangements for celebrating the return of the CIV from South Africa. They took care to choose an itinerary and a destination which had received the royal imprimatur three years before, linking soldiers, royalty, the City, and spectators in a patriotic, empire-minded, and Christian whole. The march did not begin at Waterloo Station and end at Hyde Park, as it might have done, or in Trafalgar Square, which was a traditional destination for political marches and rallies, or in Westminster Abbey, but rather in the City's own great place of worship where the queen had celebrated her sixty years' reign. Architecture provided the splendidly appropriate backdrop for the route and the endpoint the organizers chose. Few Londoners can have suspected that British imperialists had conscripted the very streets they walked, the very buildings they passed or entered, in an attempt to capture their hearts and minds.

Were the imperialists successful? Can spectacle permanently imprint human behavior? Did ratepayers who objected to further Strand improvements, did socialists and Radicals who questioned the need for a more imperial-looking London, cheer the returning CIV? Even when British authorities attempted to utilize such imperial face as London did possess, competing visions of the imperial metropolis arise to confuse us. Perhaps for a moment, on Monday, October 29, 1900, one meaning of imperial London was unambiguously apparent and triumphant. But the discussion sparked by the LCC's plans for the Strand and Kingsway is a reminder that the imperial metropolis was always in process of construction, that Londoners sought to shape it in different, even conflicting, ways, that they built it as much as it built them.

❖ ❖ ❖

CHAPTER 3

THE NEXUS OF EMPIRE

O N August 20, 1900, the British steamer *India*, bound home from Java with eighty-five hundred tons of sugar, went down in heavy seas about twenty-eight miles from Cape Guardafui off the east coast of Africa. The cargo was lost, but the crew and passengers managed to escape in four lifeboats. The boats became separated in the confusion of the moment. The next day passing steamers picked up two of them, but the other pair had drifted away and could not be found. On August 22 the lost survivors fell in with a Somali dhow whose captain offered to conduct them to shore to find fresh water. There, in the words of an English journalist, "one of the native crew [of the *India*] who understood something of the [Somali] language . . . gathered that the strangers intended making prisoners of the shipwrecked mariners and holding them for ransom or selling them into slavery."[1] The refugees plotted an escape. That evening they threw an armed Somali guard overboard, cut the towline linking them to the dhow, raised their sail, and stood away. The Somalis gave chase. They "could be seen preparing their blowdarts and stones."

The escapees, thirty-nine strong, abandoned the smaller of their two lifeboats. Thus unencumbered they outdistanced their pursuers but were left with practically nothing to eat or drink. On four tablespoons of water every twenty-four hours and, after the first day, no food at all, they sailed for a week. Although they saw several steamers they were unable to attract their attention. "Day after day in the fierce sunshine the Europeans, although longing for water to moisten their cracked lips, manfully kept their courage," a journalist wrote later. By contrast "the native [crew] handed knives to one another and would have induced each other to put an end to their sufferings but for the influence of the officers."

On the eighth day, they sighted Barali, "a friendly village on the Arabian coast." From there it proved possible to contact European authorities, and

9. Shipping wild animals at the nexus of empire.
Credit: Hulton Getty.

soon they were aboard the P. & O. steamer *Egypt*, headed for England. Henceforth it would be smooth sailing. The *Egypt* put into London on October 6. Amid a crowd of well-wishers and curious onlookers, the rescued officers, crewmen, and passengers descended to the quay of the Royal Albert Dock, safe at last in the imperial metropolis.

Three months before the steamship *India* had foundered in the Arabian Sea, the Royal Albert Dock had been the site of a celebration reported in tones less emotional than those used to describe the shipwreck and its aftermath, but no less revealing of certain British attitudes. "On Thursday," wrote a journalist for the *Stratford Express* of May 12, 1900, the "colonial men" of ocean-going vessels berthed in the Royal Albert Dock performed "'Hobson, Jobson' . . . a curious Mohamedan ceremony."[2] The "darkies commenced the festival at an early hour." Many were naked to the waist, dressed only in English trousers, others wore flowing robes and turbans or paper caps of diverse colors. Several had on scarlet tunics. Some "strutted about in old forage caps and busbies." The blackest of them had powdered themselves freely with flour "to make them look handsome," while "those of a lighter colour had applied themselves to the grease pot to adorn their faces in many colours." One or two sported long beards and hair made from sheep's wool. "The appearance of all was remarkably grotesque," the reporter opined.

Shortly after their noonday meal these men formed into marching order and, bearing bamboo poles on which flags of all colors and sizes were fastened, assembled at the end of number nine shed on the north side of the dock. Here they had earlier erected two model temples rising in tiers, decked with multicolored paper and tinsel. Someone began to sing "in doleful fashion," to the accompaniment of "tomtoms." Several others, "one of very fine physique," began "a weird dance . . . surrounded by crowds of men who bowed and bowed and bowed." The procession moved in fits and starts about the dock. At intervals the men passed round cups of water "and some sort of prayer or statement was made." Finally the party reached the dockhead, where it dismantled one of the temples and performed another "curious ceremony," which ended with the men plunging the temple into the water. Then, the reporter concluded, "the darkies departed to their several ships apparently exhausted with their afternoon's celebration."

In 1900 the Port of London was the greatest in the world. It vastly overshadowed all other British ports.[3] Within London it played a critical role as a giant physical space, as the employer of an enormous labor force, and as a critical factor in the city's and the country's economy. Less well understood was the port's role as a crossroads of people and things entering and exiting not merely Britain, but what might almost be termed the *idea* of British dominion. At London's docks the world performed daily a symbolic obeisance to the British Empire, when East End "dock rats" unloaded from ships' holds and then trucked along quays and stacked in warehouses behind them the tokens of African, Asian, Latin American, Middle Eastern, and Antipodean submission, the riches extorted from imperialized peoples. From London's docks men and women boarded ships on their way overseas to defend and to extend British imperial sway. To the docks they returned, sometimes bloodied from battle, especially during 1900 while the Boer War was raging. To the docks returned also the rescued mariners of the S.S. *India*, safe at last from the dangerous peoples residing outside the pale of British imperial civilization. And within them, to the bemusement of local workers and journalists, "colonial" seamen might safely perform strange ceremonies, for the docks were where the empire both ended and began, they were its safe edge.

The London docks were, in short, a crossroads of people, things, and attitudes, a nexus of empire. And they were a nexus of imperialisms. Perhaps

10. Lascar seamen at the docks.
Courtesy of Museum in Docklands, PLA Collection.

the soldiers and emigrants, the explorers and entrepreneurs who set sail from London in 1900 held fairly simple and conventional views of the British Empire: it reflected their country's glory and power and was a source of wealth. The men who labored at the docks shared such views, as will become clear; but they scarcely shared in the wealth. London's dockers, therefore, sought to redefine British imperialism so that it would benefit them too. The imperial metropolis they inhabited, at least in their minds, was different from the one which the generals, architects, and politicians sought to fashion.

The docks, located in the eastern portion of London, lined the northern bank of the Thames River from Tower Hill to the Beckton gasworks, a distance of ten miles not taking into account the great bend in the river around

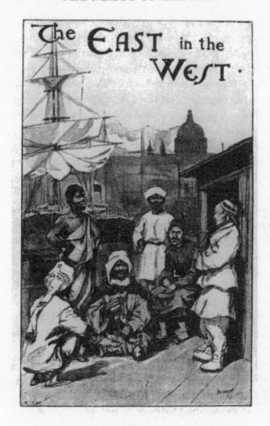

11. Artist's impression of Lascars at the docks.
Photograph courtesy of Pitts Theology Library, Emory University.

Millwall, the Isle of Dogs, and Cubitt Town. At Beckton the series of docks ended and the flat fields of Essex began, but twenty-six miles further downstream was another large dock at Tilbury.

There were four great dock companies in London at the turn of the twentieth century. A single firm owned the Victoria, Albert, St. Katherine's, and London Docks; another owned the East, West, Southwest India, and Tilbury Docks (and the two companies were to merge into a single vast operation later in the year). Then there were the Millwall Docks and, on the south bank of the river, the Surrey Commercial Docks.

These were enormous establishments, employing approximately thirty thousand men. Their warehouses were vast structures, five and six stories tall, some taking up more than an acre of land. The docks contained, too, sheds and outbuildings of various sizes and descriptions, offices, and rough cafes serving cheap food and drink. Altogether dockland occupied 26 square miles of space, 416 acres of land and more than 1,100 acres of water.[4]

Dockland also contained a vast array of wharves and warehouses. A dock is a system of basins, pools, and channels in which ships are moored, as well as jetties to which they may tie up, with warehouses on the land behind. Wharves consist only of quays to which lesser ships may be tied, with warehouses behind them. In 1900, there were more than 320 wharves lining both sides of the Thames, employing collectively 41 percent of the port's labor force. They were engaged in a competition for business with the dock companies that was proving ruinous to both parties. The wharves were not large enough to accept modern steamships or indeed any vessels engaged in foreign trade, but they could accept smaller ones, including lighters, to which the cargoes of oceangoing vessels had been transferred. In 1899, London's wharves accepted from all sources more than 7½ million tons of cargo, the docks a little less. So perhaps, by the turn of the twentieth century, the wharves were winning the competition.[5]

But the harbor as a whole was losing a larger war to Liverpool, Bristol, Hull, and other ports which were modernizing and enlarging their facilities. As a result the number of vessels entering the Port of London and the tonnage of goods received had declined steadily since the 1880s. "London is losing its share of the import trade," the LCC warned in 1900. The port's share of the export trade had "materially declined" as well. In one area only were the London docks expanding business: "There is an increase in the shipping from British possessions." So they really were the imperial docks after all.[6]

It was an impressive sight when a big ship came into the docks: the tugs backing and filling in the river to hold it steady before the dock gates, the enormous hydraulic capstans which opened the gates as if by magic, thus raising or lowering the level of water, then the ship itself sliding silently within the dock toward her berth. But there was something awful about the process too. Joseph Conrad thought that when a vessel tied up, "it ceased to live."[7]

Sailors deserted a ship once it was moored, but then dockers swarmed aboard to unload it. Although London's port workers were generally considered the quintessential unskilled laborers of England, men who needed only strong backs to perform their allotted tasks, in fact, many possessed varying degrees of expertise. Stevedores mainly loaded ships, which demanded great skill, since vessels could be damaged or even capsized by shifting cargoes when they were at sea. Lightermen, who transferred cargo from boats moored in the river to dock quay or wharf via small barges, or lighters, had to know the principles of navigation and the peculiarities of the river, its tides, shoreline, undercurrents, bridges, obstacles, and so on. Stevedores and lightermen were considered the labor aristocrats of the port. So were the skilled men who operated winches and cranes and other dock machinery. Some dockers specialized in handling cargoes which demanded particular skills or strengths that might take years to develop.

The vast majority of dockers, however, were casual laborers who never knew whether they would be hired on a given day and who were glad for the opportunity to help unload whatever cargo a ship brought in. Such men, memorialized by contemporary observers like the famous sociologist Charles Booth and by numerous historians,[8] clamored for hire outside the dockgates every morning, often bribed foremen for a day's work with a fraction of their scanty earnings, and then were forced to run while unloading ships and to labor for twenty-four hours or more at a stretch.

Even when the port was busy and work plentiful, the casual docker's standard of life was low. His diet was meager, his housing cramped and crowded. In bad times dockers starved, sometimes to death. Some slept "rough," under bridges, a deadly peril in wintertime. Dockers who spoke to the House of Lords' Commission on Sweated Industries in 1888 and to the Commission on Labour in 1892 and to researchers employed by Booth testified time and again to the rigors and miseries of East End life. Such accounts form a staple of most historical treatments.[9]

Less well known, perhaps, are the dangers dockers faced when they were fortunate enough to find work. Nearly every week during 1900 a London docker was crushed by a heavy cargo or broke his neck falling into a ship's hold or from a winch or crane he had climbed to repair. Nonfatal accidents and injuries, many of them severe, were even more common. "There is scarcely a man working on the docks, who has been there for one or two years, who has not a mark about him somewhere or other," a stevedore testified in 1892. Some cargoes were dangerous to handle. Sulphur and pitch could blind a docker for days at a time, "stinking hides," wet paper, and guano might make him ill. Phosphorus rock, copper ore, and iron were likewise "very dangerous cargo to work." Those who escaped accidental injury suffered a physical toll from their labor. One docker remembered a gang at the Cutler Street warehouse, "called the 'happy eight,' lusty fellows picked out. Within a few years there was hardly one out of that gang of eight who was not suffering with hernia, most of them with double hernia."[10]

The situation was so bad that the Conservative home secretary, Sir Matthew White Ridley, commissioned an investigation into the causes of accidents at the docks. The report, published early in October 1900, listed 115 deaths in British docks during the previous year and 4,591 nonfatal accidents, but these may have been underestimates. A leader of the dockers' union claimed that more dockers died at the East End's Poplar Hospital alone than had been recorded by the commission for the entire country.[11] The investigators recommended increased supervision, better fencing and lighting, and the provision of proper and efficient life-saving appliances. The home secretary, while reserving comment upon these prescriptions, promised to circulate copies of the report to inspectors of factories and coroners. No further action was taken.

The dock owners were not likely to make the changes which were necessary. "I utterly deny that dock work is dangerous," one of them wrote at about this time. "If we ever received any suggestions from our men how, in any way, we could lessen the liability to accident, do you suppose . . . that we are such brutes as for the sake of saving a few pounds of expenditure [we would] neglect to do all we can?" This was, in fact, precisely what many dockers believed. Because the dock companies fell within the provision of the Factory Acts, they were obliged to pay compensation to the families of men who met death by their negligence and to men who suffered nonfatal accidents for which the companies were responsible. But the men and their families rarely received anything. The companies retained lawyers to argue, usually successfully, that contributory negligence on the part of the docker meant that no compensation need be paid. Moreover, laborers feared retribution from the company if they dared ask for compensation. As one explained, "The men, in nine cases out of ten, do not care about going for it, for fear of losing their employment." Meanwhile, the wharves were excluded from the terms of the Factory Acts, so that wharfingers paid no compensation, regardless of who was at fault for accidents occurring on their premises.[12]

Because neither the government nor the employers would take the steps necessary to improve conditions on the docks, the question was what the dockers could do to help themselves. Over the years they developed two main strategies for coping with their poverty and perils, one emphasizing individual initiative, the other collective solidarity. In examining these strategies one begins to discern both the impact of imperialism upon the men who labored at the heart of the heart of the empire, and their own attempts to develop an imperial identity from which to benefit.

❖ ❖ ❖

One of the great ironies of life in dockland in 1900 was that every day its workforce unloaded, sorted, stored, and catalogued goods with which otherwise they would never have come into contact because they were so poor. They handled furs from Canada, ivory from Africa and India, shells from Australia and New Zealand, spices and drugs, bird skins and ostrich feathers from the furthest outposts of the imperial dominion. Precious stones and metals, fruits, nuts, oils, wines and spirits poured into London every day. Men who could never afford to purchase any but the commonest tea worked in vast storerooms handling chests, half-chests, and boxes of pungent, expensive blends from India, China, and Ceylon, "the atmosphere heavy with the peculiar odour from their wrappers." They labored in warehouses filled with "upright bags of fragrant cinnamon and packages of nutmegs, mace and cloves." They stacked "whole elephant tusks . . . the solid teeth of numerous hippopotami . . . gracefully curved tusks of the walrus." They unloaded ships whose holds contained case upon case of Jamaican rum.[13]

12. The yield of empire: cinnamon quills from Ceylon.
Courtesy of Museum in Docklands, PLA Collection.

"There is so much wealth in the country," mused Michael Hart, a dock-worker, "and [our] share of that wealth is so little." This perception was hardly limited to dockers, but the men who labored along the Thames saw more clearly than most that every day the world paid tribute to Britannia. As citizens of the greatest imperial power the world had ever seen they must have asked themselves why they too were not entitled to some of the tribute. Thus the impact, in part, of imperialism upon the lives of dockers: its bene-fits, in the form of the imperial loot to a portion of which they simply helped themselves; and its drawbacks, in the jail sentences many of them received— for the Thames police court, where dockers who had been apprehended for pilfering were tried, was the busiest in the United Kingdom. Not all its cases concerned thefts from the docks, but East End newspapers record an aston-ishing number of trials for robberies committed in dockland.[14]

Men could steal from the docks in two ways. They smuggled goods out as they left work by hiding them in their clothing. Or they sneaked into the docks at night, seized what they wanted, and snuck out again. On its north-ern boundary, a wooden fence twelve feet high ran the length of dockland pre-cisely to discourage such surreptitious behavior. John Mann, superintendent of the Metropolitan Police, Thames Division, thought, however, that it was "absolutely useless in respect of safeguarding property." The fence was of "a flimsy construction," which made it "a very easy matter to break [through] ... thereby enabling persons and property to be irregularly passed out." In fact, "from a casual observation it can be seen that dozens of the planks form-ing the fence have been destroyed."[15]

The men who snuck into the docks at night were often professional thieves. Theirs were not spontaneous exploits but carefully planned incur-sions. On the night of March 11, for instance, thieves broke into the B Jetty warehouse of the London Docks and stole a bale of bearskins. "They left said warehouse at the extreme end door ... [the] waterside end," wrote Inspec-tor William French, the policeman in charge of the subsequent investigation. They "had evidently a boat or barge to facilitate their escape."[16] Here the rob-bers had to know how to shift their stolen goods to a fence, which argues for their experience and sophistication. They were never caught.

Less fortunate were Samuel Brown, William Dennis, and Thomas Walli-neer, who on the night of April 20 met on the south bank of the Thames, ap-propriated a rowboat, crossed the river, and boarded the lighter *Mallard*, ly-ing at her moorings at Hermitage Stairs. They had been part of a gang unloading the barge that day. In fact, earlier Dennis had attempted, with half a sovereign, to bribe the *Mallard*'s night watchman, John Brear. But Brear, who pocketed the money, went to the police anyway. They were waiting to capture the three men when they boarded the barge.[17]

Almost equally unlucky were the men who planned and partly carried out a big haul from the Royal Albert Dock late on the night of October 6. They managed to pass about eighteen hundredweight of gun metal bearings and other portions of machinery through the fence so deprecated by Superintendent Mann and onto a horse-drawn cart. They were proceeding along Auberon Street when one of the cart's wheels collapsed at a point which happened to be immediately opposite the home of police sergeant Morris of the North Woolwich subdivision. "The lateness of the hour ... the direction in which the vehicle was travelling, and the peculiar contents aroused the officer's suspicions," wrote the crime reporter for the *Stratford Express.* "The services of another officer were requisitioned whilst the driver was seeking help—which, however, never arrived for the sight of two constables scared them away."

The commonest sort of robbery at the docks, however, was unprofessional, even unplanned. It was carried out by men who succumbed to temptation. As one prisoner explained to the judge, his "wife and children were at home starving, and seeing the tobacco lying on the floor of the warehouse, loose, [I] went in and picked some up." Similarly, if less desperately, William Stovely, a stevedore working the steamship *Navarino*, "found the pineapple on the floor and thought there was no harm in taking it."[18]

More commonly dockworkers helped themselves to drink. Thomas McDonough, for example, stole a bottle of Hennessey brandy from the steamship *Ifafa*, which was about to leave for South Africa. "I kicked against it on the quay side when coming from work," he told the dock police, but an examination of the ship's cargo revealed that two cases of brandy had been forced open and seven bottles taken. McDonough was sentenced to five weeks' hard labor.[19]

McDonough's is a typical story in almost every particular. First, it was an alcoholic beverage that he had stolen, for which a ready market would exist if he himself did not consume it. Next, under questioning, he offered a lame excuse for how it had come into his possession. Then it was discovered that other bottles were missing and unaccounted for. McDonough undoubtedly had confederates who had not been caught. Finally, the sentence meted out was remarkably severe.

In one way only was McDonough's case atypical. As often as men were apprehended trying to smuggle unopened bottles from the docks, they were found actually drinking while they were supposed to be at work. For exam-

13. Dock search (1).

14. Dock search (2).

By permission of the British Library.

Courtesy of Museum in Docklands, PLA Collection.

ple, Henry Willis, a stevedore, was caught with two bottles of brandy in either trouser leg. Aboard the ship he had been working "several empty bottles were lying about." (Willis's sentence was one month at hard labor.) On another occasion, Thomas Catmore, Thomas Waters, Edwin Chapman, and Arthur Robinson, working the steamship *Robert*, stole or consumed (the record is unclear on this point) an entire case of gin. At any rate, they were all discovered "the worse for drink" and committed for trial. So too was Arthur Talbot, a laborer in a wine vault, discovered to be "the worse for drink." Having consumed half a pint of brandy, he attempted to take the remaining half-pint home with him. For this the judge imposed a sentence of twenty shillings' fine or twenty days' hard labor.[20]

William Kelly also got drunk on the job. He was seen "bending over a cask" and when searched was found to be hiding in his clothes a tube "supposed for the purpose of obtaining wine."[21] The practice of employing a tube to extract liquor from casks was common enough to merit a name, "sucking the monkey." An entire gang of stevedores was found sucking the monkey on July 28, according to the *Stratford Express*. The men loading the number one hold of the *Winkfield*, bound for South Africa, were all drunk that day, one of them so drunk that he had to be hoisted from the hold to the deck in a basket. The foreman of the gang, Richard Cornelius Foster, was sentenced to two months' hard labor. "That's not justice," he cried when the judge read his sentence.

Justice was rarely what the men received. McDonough, the laborer charged with stealing a bottle of Hennessey's brandy, received "an exemplary punishment, as this kind of robbery was very prevalent." Patrick Casey, a stevedore caught with two bottles of gin while leaving the East India Dock, was told by the judge at his trial that "he took a serious view of these peculations as they interfered with the trade of the port" and received two months at hard labor. Arthur Benford, caught with a bag of green tea, "asked to be dealt with leniently because it was the first time he had been in trouble" but was sentenced to either pay forty-five shillings—a penalty far beyond the means of a dock laborer—or serve twenty-one days at hard labor. Henry Young, a laborer at the Victoria Docks for fifteen years and never before in trouble, was caught with nine ounces of Egyptian tobacco; he was sentenced to pay a fine of twenty shillings or to serve two weeks in jail.[22]

Judges imposed harsh sentences to deter further thefts, but thievery continued unabated. As recorded in East End newspapers, dock laborers helped themselves, during 1900, to an astonishing number of bottles of liquor: rum, gin, brandy, ale, and port wine being the beverages of choice. They also took tea trays, candlesticks, tobacco, packets of wool, bottles of chlorodyne and of Dr. Powell's balsam of aniseed, bales of cowhair, tins of cooked tongue and of condensed milk, a shawl, boxes of Jordan almonds, bags of oats, wheels of cheese, pineapples and other fruits, a typewriter, silk ribbons, stockings, hats, forty-three pounds of lead pipe, and cases of grapes, zinc, and India rubber. And these were only the cases mentioned by part of the press.

For every man caught stealing, many escaped detection. Ten years after 1900, with the docks no longer privately owned but under the presumably more effective policing of the Port of London Authority, stealing continued unabated. By then the dock police force consisted of 1 superintendent, 10 inspectors, 26 sergeants, 384 constables, and 13 officers employed as barge searchers. Yet, as one of the force informed the undersecretary of state, "the Criminal Investigation Staff at present employed by the Dock Authority would, according to my information, have to be increased quite three-fold to be effective in putting a stop to the pilfering for which these docks have become notorious."[23]

Historians have estimated that larceny in Britain declined by about half between 1850 and 1900.[24] But no decline took place in dockland. The fruits of empire (Jamaican rum, pineapples, teas, bearskins, tobacco, and so on) were simply too tempting and too easily appropriated for dockworkers to leave them alone. So they engaged in petty thievery to a greater extent than other British workers. Indeed, given the miserable rates of pay they received, many a London docker's standard of living must have depended to a degree upon such petty larceny. Thus, because the docks were the nexus of empire and because they could not be adequately policed, many of the men who worked in them developed a particular approach toward private property and authority.

Their views were unmeasurable but real. "You are working for a rich firm," two men said to William Baker, a carman engaged in transporting a load of tea from the Cutler Street warehouse. "Can we have the lot?" "It was my only chance of making a bit," said a docker who served five weeks in jail at hard labor for stealing three bags of oats. A lighterman, Harry Gosling, recalled that when he was a boy, "my father [also a lighterman] often used to say to me as we passed the casks" of sugar on the West India Dock, "'Go on, boy, help yourself,' and I took a handful of the delicious stuff."[25]

No doubt many British workers shared such attitudes. Every trade had perks to which workers believed themselves entitled. But dockers daily confronted at their workplace the might and scope and riches of the British Empire and measured that against their own puny efforts to accumulate wealth. The contrast must have been galling, more galling even than the contrasts between rich and poor at factory, mine, and mill. And then, stealing a few bottles of rum hardly seemed to shift the balance. So some objected when authority punished them. "That's not justice," Foster had cried as the judge sentenced him.

Moreover, is there not in dockers' efforts to share in the imperial loot a modest, never precisely articulated attempt to redefine the imperial metropolis in their own interest? If London truly was the capital city of a great empire, perhaps they told themselves, then was it not right that they, the men who made its economy function, should reap the benefits too? Stealing is stealing, but sometimes it is not merely stealing, as, for example, when it is a part of class conflict. In this instance, pilfering at the docks may hint, if only obliquely, at an act of imperial self-definition.

In 1900 the imperial dimension impinged more directly as well, as became apparent during the dock strike of that year. Because it took place at a worksite where imperialism was an inherent component of daily life, and at a time during the Boer War when patriotic feelings were especially intense, the dispute provides further insights into the cultural role of the imperial docks and an angle of approach for investigators of popular imperialism and working-class patriotism.[26] Moreover, the strike offers further evidence of Londoners' attempts to redefine the imperial metropolis in their own interest.

The Dock, Wharf, Riverside and General Labourers' Union of Great Britain and Ireland was relatively young. It had been formed, against great odds, in 1889, when a few dockers laid down their tools and, unexpectedly, gained national, indeed international, support. They demanded a raise of a penny an hour, which seemed exorbitant only to the dock owners, but they were striking for something more than money. If the despised dock rat could organize a union, then organization was beyond the power of no worker. If he could win his strike, then a higher standard of life was within the grasp of every Briton. Many historians see a common thread linking the dock strike of 1889 with the rise of the socialist movement in Britain and the foundation of the Labour Party in 1900.[27]

In 1889 a remarkable triumvirate constituted the first rank of the dockers' leadership. John Burns, a charismatic and flamboyant figure, became first the leading socialist on the LCC, then a Lib-Lab member of Parliament and eventually a cabinet minister under Herbert Henry Asquith. Tom Mann, equally capable if less politically ambitious, remained a primary figure—"a volcanic force" someone once called him—in the industrial wing of the labor movement until his death in poverty in 1940. Ben Tillett, the third great leader of the strike, stayed with the dockers for his entire career but, unlike either Mann or Burns, came to straddle both the industrial and political wings of the labor movement, eventually entering Parliament as a Labour M.P. In 1900 Mann and Burns were already pursuing other interests, but Tillett was still general secretary of the union.[28]

The strike of that year began on Tuesday, June 5, when Scrutton's Ltd., the newly appointed labor contractor for the Victoria and Albert Dock Company, refused to hire dockers outside the dock gates, as had been the practice of the former contractor, and hired them inside the gates instead. Dockers on the D and I jetties immediately walked off their jobs because if the employer, who controlled access to the dock, could hire men inside, then the union would lose its influence over who applied for work. Inspector French of the London dock police force instructed his men "to take strong measures" to clear the strikers from the company's premises. Yet all would have been well had Scrutton's rehired them the next day. Instead Scrutton's locked them out. Thereupon the locked-out men forced their way into the dock, "went to the ships and 'called out' the men, threatening that if they did not cease work they would be maltreated. Most of the men stopped work," but some scuffling broke out, whereupon the police intervened again.[29]

On Thursday morning when the Victoria Dock opened for business it contained more than sixty metropolitan bobbies to reinforce the dock police. They "were stationed along the quay and jetties and prevented unauthorised persons [read, strikers] from approaching the ships, while a number of officers were kept in reserve at Customs House ready for any emergency." Their presence did not have a calming effect. Union laborers hitherto separate from the dispute now began coming out. Scrutton's riposted with a call for free laborers, that is, nonunion men, as replacement workers. More ominously the dock company itself intervened, contacting an employers' organization, the Shipping Federation, to supply the needed strikebreakers.

With this intervention all possibility of compromise had been ruled out. The Shipping Federation existed to defeat strikes. It had been founded during the new unionist era immediately following the dock strike of 1889, when British ports were experiencing a veritable labor war, as the newspapers called it, and the employers felt themselves to be on the defensive. "In August 1890 a conference of shipowners was held," Cuthbert Laws, himself connected with the shipping trade on the employers' side, recalled, "at which it was resolved to combine for protection against the tyranny of the 'New' Unionism, and the result was Nemesis, in the shape of 'The Shipping Federation.'"[30]

Commanding enormous resources, this organization could provide free labor to any strikebound ship at any port in the kingdom. It owned two seaworthy vessels, the *Paris* and the *Ella*, aboard which it could send strikebreakers wherever they were needed, an oceangoing tug, the *Talisman*, and motor launches at Liverpool and the Tyne for local emergencies. In addition, for use in London, it kept a three-masted vessel painted black, which could accommodate up to five hundred men if necessary. This was the infamous *Lady Jocelyn*.

In 1900, a father and son team ran the Shipping Federation. George Laws, a native of Tynemouth, had played the crucial role in founding it. He possessed great drive, talent for organization, and what might be called a stingy attitude toward employees. When Laws was the shipowners' representative on a Board of Trade special committee on safety at sea, "he revealed his fearless advocacy and determination" by opposing adoption of a life belt because it was too expensive.[31] That had been some years earlier, however. By 1900 the leading force in the federation was George's son, Cuthbert.

"His was a powerful personality," wrote the historian of the Shipping Federation. "He never shirked—sometimes, indeed, he seemed to seek—a fight." A turn-of-the-century photograph reveals a short, burly, handsome man with piercing eyes, a mustache, and rather long curly hair. "He was an orator in the grand and classic style," who often "drew many of his analogies and many of his phrases from the bible."[32] This must genuinely have irked Ben Tillett, a great exponent of the "religion of socialism."

Such, then, were the main opponents of the dockers who objected in June 1900 to the policies of Scrutton's Ltd. From the outset it was clear: either the struggle would be short and sharp, in which case surely the strikers would lose; or it would spread from the Victoria to other docks and become protracted, in which case its outcome would be less easy to predict.

The union understood. It attempted to widen the dispute, sending pickets on Monday morning to the gates of the Millwall, West India, and London Docks, in addition to the Victoria and Albert Docks. Meanwhile Tillett was firing off telegrams to Middlesbrough, Hull, Swansea, and Bristol, ostensibly to acquaint dockers in those ports with the state of affairs in the capital, but really to encourage them to strike, too, so that the Shipping Federation could not concentrate on London. He released a defiant manifesto: "The greatest organization of capital ever known in the country [that is, the Shipping Federation] have made a set on all the workers connected with the loading and discharging of shipping and allied industries. . . . [But] we are fighting and shall continue to fight the battle of labour. This dispute will affect 50,000 homes." And he announced with obvious satisfaction that his old friend Tom Mann "was coming into the fight."[33]

Meanwhile the "blacklegs," or strikebreakers, hired by the Shipping Federation had begun to arrive: two hundred from Birmingham, lured with promises of twelve months' regular employment at thirty shillings per week, and similar numbers following similar inducements from Ipswich and North Shields. This was more than the *Lady Jocelyn* could accommodate. The federation opened additional depot ships and sheds capable of housing several thousand men. It was said to be bringing in strikebreakers from as far away as Holland, although the labor correspondent for the *Times* denied this. There were, he averred, plenty of English free laborers—and they were being "well looked after." "Breakfast,—Irish stew, bread, butter and coffee, with half a pint of ale at 10:30," he enthused. "Dinner,—Soup, beef, potatoes, and bread with half a pint of ale, another half pint being supplied at 3 pm. Tea,—cold meat, bread and butter and tea. Supper,—Bread and cheese and half a pint of ale." On Sundays the Shipping Federation entertained the blacklegs: on one occasion eight hundred of them boarded the *Clacton Belle* for a five-hour trip down the river complete "with free beer and tobacco, and a band to accompany them"; on another, a thousand of them aboard another *Belle* steamer went on a jaunt around the Nore.[34]

The response of striking dockers to blackleg labor might have been predicted. On the morning of June 25, James Morgan grabbed the arm of John Shea, a crane operator at the docks. "If you go to work you will get your head bashed in," he warned. Michael Connolly, a sixty-two-year-old dock laborer, broke the arm of George Helby, a clerk at the Royal Albert Dock, because he had no union ticket. When Israel Read, a quay foreman employed by the London and India Dock Company, went with his son to the Peacock Tavern after a day's work, John Eagle and Samuel Carter, both on strike, wanted to know why he had money to spend during a labor dispute. According to the newspaper report, "Witness turned to his son . . . and said, 'Drink up and let us get out'. Carter said, 'we haven't done with you yet' and struck him in the eye several times. Eagle also struck witness in the jaw."[35]

Public houses seem to have been the common location for this kind of fracas. A few days after Eagle and Carter punched Read, Thomas Cooksley was having a drink in a pub in Hallsville Street when James Dooley came in and called him a blackleg. "Witness went outside and the prisoner followed him, knocked him down and took all his money out of his pocket." On another occasion Frederick Pearce and three friends accosted Thomas Martin and Charles Mann at the Liverpool Arms in Canning Town. "Witness replied 'I don't know you.' Prisoner then said, 'You are working for Scrutton's,' but witness answered 'I shall work where I like.'" This was a braver rejoinder than a wise one. Pearce "turned round and hit Mann on the jaw knocking him down. As Mann was leaving the house prisoner struck him several times. Mann was bleeding from the face."[36]

At a time when workers could be sentenced to jail for sampling a single pineapple, strikers convicted of interfering with free laborers received little mercy. Eagle and Carter, the men who had assaulted Israel Read, were each sentenced to a month in jail. Connolly received six weeks at hard labor for breaking Helby's arm, although he insisted it had been a fair fight. Pearce had to wait in jail for seven weeks before his case even came up in court and then to endure a homily from the judge: "England is a free country in which a man need not belong to a trade union unless it pleases him to do so. . . . It ought to be recognized that a man is at liberty to work for whom he likes."

Not all the violence came from the side of the men on strike. Cooped up in the depot ships or sheds within the docks, hooted and spat upon during the working day when, at least, the police were there to protect them, and targets of physical abuse if they dared to show themselves in the pubs and cafes of the East End after working hours, some free laborers were eager to confront their tormentors. Late on the evening of June 25 John Sinister, a docker on strike, was standing with friends outside the Tidal Basin Tavern. He saw a party of free laborers emerge from the dock gates about a dozen yards from the pub: "Someone said it was now *their* time." Another cried, "Now *we've* got a chance to let go." A belaying pin crashed through the window at the side of the door to the pub. "Then witness saw a man throw one deliberately through the big pane." That man, according to two eyewitnesses, was Thomas Bromley, a twenty-seven-year-old dock laborer temporarily residing aboard the *Lady Jocelyn*. He received not so much as a warning from the judge when his case came to court.

Despite the strikers' attempts to intimidate the strikebreakers, their union faced heavy odds. They were about to become heavier. Tillett hoped that lightermen and stevedores would join his strike. Harder for employers to replace with blacklegs than casual laborers, these labor aristocrats could add a crucial measure of support, as they had done during the great strike of 1889. On June 19, Tillett appealed to the executive council of the Stevedores' Union for aid. They withheld it. Possibly there was bad blood between the two waterfront societies, but one of the stevedores' leaders simply explained that "the members of [his] Society could not leave their employment, having recently agreed with their employers upon a new set of working rules."[37] Then the stevedores' executive council voted to send officers to the docks every morning, to make sure their men continued working.

Worse still, Tillett's union was short of cash. As the dispute wore on, strikers and their families became hungry, at a time when work was plentiful if taken on the employers' terms. The union could afford only a one-time donation of four shillings per man. It dispatched an appeal to trade unionists throughout the country asking for "money to meet the wants of 20,000 persons . . . in need of food." It sent men into the streets with collection boxes. They were, wrote one journalist, "a bit persistent and indulged in forcible language toward those who declined to contribute," but still they hardly collected enough. Unless something unexpected happened, the strike began to look like petering out. "It ain't me, it's the old hen and chicks I care for, and I'm going back," one striker said, reflecting a mood becoming all too common from the union's point of view.[38]

The strength of the Shipping Federation, the plentiful supply of free laborers, the refusal of the stevedores and other labor aristocrats on the Thames to support the strike, the lack of funds, all made victory for the union unlikely. An additional factor influenced the outcome of the strike, namely, an atmosphere of patriotism and national pride created by the docks' role as an imperial nexus and exacerbated by the Boer War.

The backdrop to the strike was the continual embarkation of troopships from London to South Africa. Horses, enlisted men, and officers filed through the docks nearly every day, sometimes thousands of them. "Yesterday," reported the *Stratford Express* of January 13 in a typical paragraph, "the *Matiana*, a British-India liner, received 200 men, five officers and a number of horses. . . . Today three special trains . . . will bring 620 men and twenty officers. . . . The *British Prince* left the Royal Albert Dock on Saturday for Southampton and Capetown conveying the 6th Division Ammunition and Mounted Infantry. . . . The *St. Andrew* and the *Pindari* . . . are being got ready for the reception of horses and men." Daily the dockers loaded ships with weapons, ammunition, and other paraphernalia of war. They witnessed the tearful farewells of soldiers and their families. These spectacles seemed almost designed to play upon the patriotism of onlookers. A typical embarkation took place on the morning of April 7, beginning with the arrival from Doncaster of the machine-gun section. This was followed by the Sussex unit from Shorncliffe: "The men all looked extremely smart and each wore on his soft felt hat a raven worked in red, the bird forming the emblem of his company." By noon visitors were ashore, gangways removed, and ropes cast off: "The quay was completely packed and loud cheers were raised as the ship swung into the centre of the dock. A rush was immediately made for the dockhead . . . handkerchiefs and miniature flags were freely waved. The scene was extremely picturesque."[39]

But it showed only one side of the equation. The London docks were also the destination of hospital ships laden with sick and wounded soldiers from the war zone. The disembarkations of these unfortunates also whipped up patriotic sentiments. Perhaps they were meant to. When, for example, on January 6 the *Garth Castle* berthed at the East India Dock, much was made of the thirty-six ill and wounded soldiers aboard. "Before leaving the ship each man was given a glass of port and a sandwich by Sir Donald Currie's direction," reported the *East London Advertiser*. "Each of the invalided men received a pipe, two ounces of tobacco, package of cigarettes, a thick woolen shirt, woolen drawers, a pair of socks, a muffler and a tam o'shanter." Then they were provided with a hot meal while a band, the "Absent-minded Beggar's Relief Corps," played patriotic airs. More solemn occasions received more sober attention. When the body of the marquis of Winchester, killed at the battle of Magersfontein, reached the port of London, "the coffin was carried from the ship to a hearse, which was in waiting, by a detachment of artillery."[40]

Such spectacles carried messages which could only undermine the union's effort. Were not men who refused to load troopships destined for South Africa blacklegging the soldiers defending the empire? Journalists were quick to point out that troopships were being delayed by the strike. The government let it be known that if coal porters did not load the transports bound for South Africa, *it* would find laborers who would. This was enough for some strikers. "Making a virtue out of their position they have decided to work, rather than demonstrate against" the government, one newspaperman smugly observed.[41]

Not surprisingly, even though the leadership of the dockers' union opposed the Boer War (as did most prominent labor leaders), patriotic demonstrations within the docks were common. One of the most famous manifestations of British nationalist sentiment in the country's history took place on May 18 and 19, when news came that the British garrison in the besieged town of Mafeking had been relieved. In London's East End, where the dockers lived, celebrations were intense. They extended into dockland. Tugboats, which "kept up an unceasing round of hooting and tooting," and barges were decked out in the national colors. The big ships moored in the river "flew streamers of flags from topmast to deck." The wharves and warehouses fronting the river hung out banners and bunting. When the captain of a French steamer did not dress his ship, "shore gangs [of dock laborers] informed him that unless he hoisted some token of rejoicing they would cease work." The captain put up flags.[42]

On June 9, with the dock strike in progress, news arrived that Pretoria had surrendered to British troops. Again the flags went up, and first of all at the Victoria and Albert Docks, where the strike had originated. There the Peninsular and Orient Shipping Company took "the lead at 8 am. when, simultaneously and as if by magic, every vessel of the fleet at present in the dock hoisted flags from stem to stern and from foremast to mizzenmast." All other vessels followed suit during the morning.[43]

On June 20, with the strike at its height, came yet another patriotic demonstration, this one on behalf of a fund for Britain's war widows and orphans, sponsored by the *Daily Telegraph* newspaper. The enormous procession took most of the day to wind through the streets of East London. There were men on horseback dressed as cowboys and distributing flags, marching soldiers, horses sporting the national colors hauling replicas of great cannons and artillery pieces. There were allegorical cars depicting "Britannia Rules the Waves," "Our Empire's Defenders," "Mafeking Fort," and the like. Men dressed up as General Buller, the Prince of Wales, Kitchener, Baden Powell, and other patriotic heroes: "Even the president of the Transvaal was not absent, but he somehow always occupied a suspended position." Twenty bands took part in the procession, which stretched three miles in length.

The hoopla accompanying the national effort could not but overshadow a labor dispute. After all, the dockers, too, had marched round the East End demonstrating against their employers. But how tiny and pathetic their

marches must have appeared, and how thin the sound of their single strag-
gling brass band, in comparison with the patriotic demonstrations. Then
union men had solicited funds for the families of dockers on strike. They were
in direct and unequal competition for public support with the *Telegraph*'s fund
for the widows and orphans of British soldiers, just how unequal Frank Har-
mon, dock laborer, discovered on August 10 in Thames Police Court. "You
had no business to go collecting in this way and annoying people," Justice
Gillespie warned the accused, whose crime had been to beg patrons of the
Northumberland Arms public house for funds to help the starving family of
a striking comrade. "You may go now, but you must see to it that it does not
occur again."[44]

Many East End residents took Justice Gillespie's view of dockers' solici-
tations. They would not fill the union collection boxes. But after the *Telegraph*'s procession seventeen hundred collecting boxes were turned in, and
"the committee were . . . engaged the whole of the day in the task of counting
the contents of the boxes and this work, it is anticipated, will occupy them
from ten days to a fortnight." When the socialist newspaper, *Justice*, opened
a fund to support the strike, three readers sent in one shilling each. By contrast, East End residents flooded the *Telegraph* offices with money and offers
of money. Businesses, clubs, societies, political organizations, trade unions,
individuals sent in contributions. In the end residents of Bow contributed
£1,052; residents of Forest Gate and Stratford £834; residents of Stepney
and Bethnal Green £1,200.[45]

Other comparisons reveal equally stark contrasts. When a member of the
union tried to solicit the patrons of the Northumberland Arms, its owner summoned the police; when the *Telegraph* publicized its procession, the owner of
the Cock and Lion promised to provide a waterman's boat, the owner of the
Anchor and Hope promised a large model of a full-rigged ship, the owner of
the Railway Tavern pledged an Irish jaunting car with passengers in Irish
costume.[46] When Tillett appealed for funds from other trade unions they
turned a deaf ear; when the *Telegraph* made its fund known, the East End
Trades Council, local branches of the Railway Servants' Union, the Gas
Workers' Union, the Carmen's Union, the Spitalfields Costermongers'
Union, the Lightermen's Society, the Jewish Bakers' Association, even a society of local shoeblacks, all promised support.

East End residents favored patriotic demonstrations over the strike. So
did the dockers, who were East Enders too. Given the natural sympathy
among Londoners for British troops, their own countrymen, in danger in
South Africa and given the general patriotic hubbub permeating English life
at the moment, it would have been surprising only if they had done otherwise.

But an additional factor may have influenced the dockers. Laboring at the heart of the heart of the empire, where patriotic scenes connected to the war occurred frequently, London's dockers may have been *more* primed than their neighbors to support the empire, and *less* likely at that particular moment to support a strike.

The evidence is indirect and relative on this point. Fifty thousand dockers labored along the Thames, but no more than a few hundred marched on the union picket lines. By contrast, tens of thousands of East Londoners joined the *Daily Telegraph*'s procession. We can never know how many were dockers, but certainly the districts in which they lived welcomed the parade. "The street decorations were perhaps richer and more plentiful in the poorer districts than in the main road," observed one journalist.[47] Tens of thousands also celebrated the relief of Mafeking, Kimberley, and Pretoria. Here dockers played a prominent part, running up thousands of flags, streamers, and bunting on tugboats, lighters, barges, warehouses, wharves, and other structures fronting the river.

What seems then to have been a predisposition among dockers toward a patriotic and prowar stance could not but adversely affect their strike. Laborers who learned at their workplace to regard with awe the reach and power of British rule and the wealth which stemmed from it were now demanding their fair share of imperial largess. "Firms like Scruttons thought they could dictate to the workmen and treat them like slaves," charged a dockers' organizer, Tom Watts, but the strike would "show them that they were human beings as well . . . and had as much right to the luxuries of life."[48]

This was a contradiction. All human beings had a right to those luxuries. The labor movement is built upon that assertion. But dockers were asserting their rights as citizens of an imperial country, as residents of an imperial metropolis, as *imperial workers*, while the employers, even the public at large, were accustomed to thinking of them as London's beasts of burden, metaphorical hewers of wood and drawers of water. "No other class of labor is forced to wait, huddled in groups, at the mercy of and bidding of the employers," Tillett complained.[49] But the nexus of imperialism did not teach that decent treatment was a right, or that rights had anything to do with the way one was treated. Out went the soldiers; in came the fruits of imperialism. The strong survived, the weak went to the wall or submitted to their conquerors, sent them tokens of their submission, accepted their rule, judgment, and charity. Fair play was not part of the calculation at the heart of the heart of the empire, yet it was in part upon the claim to fair play that the dockers based their demands.

Ben Tillett embodied the contradiction. He spent his life demanding bet-

15. Ben Tillett addressing striking dockers.

ter treatment for London's dockers, but what he thought most disgraceful about their situation was not merely that they were treated badly, but that they were forced during times of stress "to eat from the refuse heap thrown out by the coolies and Hindoos." From whose refuse heaps should white men have eaten? But then Tillett was a British chauvinist of long standing. Early in his career he opposed Jewish immigration into the East End, and later he opposed the employment of foreigners on British ships. "I have no objection to the alien as such," he averred in 1896, "but he is always a cheap and obsequious worker, and alternates between slavish humility and too often treachery in the use of the knife." He thought that African-American men in the southern United States were wont to commit sexual outrages against white women. In 1910 he waged an explicitly anti-Semitic parliamentary campaign against the German Jewish industrialist Alfred Mond. And during World War I he once told an audience that the only good German was a dead one. If Tillett believed in the solidarity of labor, then he believed too in a hierarchy of races with the British "race" on top.[50]

No doubt diverse factors shaped Tillett's, and the dockers', outlook: for example, popular discourse influenced by mid-Victorian science and anthropology, plain common sense, as Errol Lawrence has described the roots of British racism, the general atmosphere and tone in parts of the East End, sections of which were already notorious bastions of racism. It seems likely, however, that the docks, because they were an imperial nexus, and especially during the Boer War, which could not but inflame patriotic and chauvinistic sentiments, influenced this outlook too. The docks highlighted the magnitude, puissance, and riches of the empire, the gallantry of its defenders, and, implicitly, the right of Britain to its far-flung possessions. So Tillett preached, at once, internationalism and nationalism, selflessness and selfishness, a confusing hodgepodge which undermined the solidarity and strength of purpose upon which his union's chance for victory in a labor dispute rested.[51]

The dockers' strike of summer 1900 did not quite catch on, although for a moment it had threatened to. It died with a whimper. The men straggled back to work in dribs and drabs. By mid-July it was over.

The dock owners had beaten their employees. For the union the defeat was catastrophic. Membership fell sharply. By 1906 the single metropolitan branch had an income of only £89, compared with £1,308 in 1900. Tillett waxed bitter: "Those very members who were directly the cause of the dispute ratted in a most disgraceful manner." On the other hand, the dock company spokesman, Sydney Holland, reported with pride to shareholders that "the percentage of wages, when compared with gross receipts, is less this year than it has ever been." He also took pleasure in announcing that "the amount of compensation for accidents to the men has not increased at all," taking this as evidence not of his company's parsimony, but rather of the safe work environment it provided for employees.[52]

Meanwhile the docks resumed their wonted appearance. "The P & O steamer *Peninsular*, which left the Royal Albert Dock on Thursday last week carried £67,500 for Bombay," reported the *Stratford Express*. "The *Sobraon*... arrived on Saturday with £92,728. The *China*, due in London on Sunday, brings £213,949 in gold coin from Australia." And one week later, "The *Oceana* left the Royal Albert Dock on Friday with £310,608 including £197,500 in bar silver for Bombay, £73,000 in that metal for Hong Kong and £32,608 in silver coin for Shanghai." And the next, "The P & O steamer *Caledonia* left the Royal Albert Dock on Friday with £252,000 in bar silver for Bombay. A sum of £92,000 in gold has been shipped at Bombay per the P & O liner *Oriental* for London."[53]

This was a traffic London's dock rats could touch but never possess. Petty pilfering, however, which had nearly ceased during the strike to judge from the press, now resumed at an accelerated pace. So did the toll of dead and injured dockers. "The exploitation of labour goes on," Tillett lamented. "It

saves in labour costs by wasting life, driving to an early grave . . . some of our
most robust men." For some the daily struggle, or the union's powerlessness,
were too much to bear. On July 28, Edward Conroy, a laborer at the London
Dock, received less pay than he thought was due him. "He seized a large
shovel with which he smashed 70 windows as well as the frames." Ten days
later Frank Edwards, also a dock laborer, appeared at the Thames police
court, his crime—attempting to commit suicide by stabbing himself in the
chest with a penknife: "Prisoner's wife said her husband had been thrown out
of work through the dock strike and that had upset him. They had five children. Prisoner now said that he was very sorry." He was discharged with a
caution.[54]

Scholars have long recognized the contribution of dockland to the economy of the conurbation in which it was located, to the history of London,
including specifically the East End of London, and to labor history generally.
Historians of labor and of popular imperialism have explored the factors
which helped to shape the ideas of the men who worked at the docks: the roots
of British attitudes toward race, imperial expansion, and patriotism, and their
role in the formation of such institutions as the press, schools, and literary
and scientific establishments. Some have examined working-class attitudes
toward the Boer War, others the inward-looking, solidaristic, and patriotic
aspects of working-class life at the turn of the century. The literature is large
and growing; still I hope to have suggested an additional dimension in the
history of popular imperialism and dockland and its labor force.[55]

The London docks linked the tiny mother country with the rest of the
world and with Britain's vast empire. They were a nexus and facilitator of in-
coming and outgoing people and products, raw materials and finished goods,
attitudes and values. As a result, the docks both helped to shape attitudes and
life chances among the men who worked in them and reflected the dockers'
attempts to redefine the imperial metropolis in a way that would benefit
themselves.

Diverse factors influenced the outlook of dockers, but perhaps none
played a more formative role than their workplace. The formative process was
protracted; I have focused upon the year 1900 because the Boer War, then at
its height, brought to a head and made more visible the long-term trends in
which I am interested. The evidence suggests that the nature of the dockers'
workplace helped to shape their attitudes toward private property and authority and helped inculcate imperial sentiments among them, making them
quick to celebrate their country's triumphs in an imperialist war; that it

helped to weaken their tenuous solidarity, making victory in labor disputes less likely; that it undermined, to a degree, the logic of trade union leaders, who championed mutually exclusive principles of international brotherhood on the one hand and racism on the other. The Boer War compounded these effects.

Moreover the dockers' workplace appears to have shaped indirectly their responses to the rigors, dangers, and miseries of their lives. Dockers did not often protest collectively by striking, and when they did they were likely to be ineffective. They protested individually, however, by stealing from their employers. Here, it would appear, they were successful more often than not.

At the same time, dockers interpreted the imperial metropolis in a different sense from their employers. They sought inclusion; they wanted a share of the luxuries the imperial metropolis made available to London's more fortunate residents. Working at the nexus of imperialism, they knew—who better?—that London was the capital city of a great empire. In seeking their share of life's luxuries they sought to remake their city so that it would accept them too.

CHAPTER 4

THE CITY

OCKLAND and the City were contiguous districts in the imperial metropolis, linked by more than geography. Many City firms were commercial rather than financial and therefore inextricably tied to the foreign trade streaming into the port which was only a stone's throw away. In this sense the two quarters were interdependent. Yet the obvious contrast between them, one a grim reminder of the poverty to which a portion of England's workforce had been reduced, the other a testimony to the country's wealth and power, overrode such links. Ultimately the City was far more significant than dockland to London's, Britain's, indeed, the world's economy. The docks played a prominent and peculiar role in the imperial metropolis, but the City was sine qua non.

From St. Katherine's Dock it was a short walk west to Tower Hill, which formed part of the City's eastern edge. There the mean streets gave way to thoroughfares lined with three- and four-storied brick warehouses and offices, some quite magnificent, and representing nearly every conceivable trade or profession. In many of these buildings lay the goods London's despised but proximate dock rats had trucked along the quays and wharfs only a short time before. The City's southern boundary was the river; to the west it stretched as far as the Holborn Viaduct and the Temple; to the north there was no obvious borderline, it petered out somewhere between the street known today as London Wall and the Regent's Canal.

At the turn of the twentieth century the City occupied an irregular square mile. In fact the City was often called the Square Mile. It contained 638 acres, 48½ miles of streets, lanes, alleyways, and courtyards, representing as intricate a maze as any East End warren, and chockablock with buildings of every shape, size, purpose, and age. At the center was the lord mayor's residence, the Mansion House, its Portland stone exterior, Corinthian portico, and dignified entrance stairway epitomizing the Palladian style which had dominated English architecture during the first half of the eighteenth century. Close by, on Threadneedle Street, was the Bank of England, a vast, gloomy series of edifices, five great domed, single-storied halls designed by Sir John Soane in the style of the Temple of the Sybil at Tivoli. The bank occupied about three acres of ground. Immediately to its east was the Royal Exchange, containing the famous insurance house Lloyds of London. With its imposing classical portico and richly ornamented internal cloister, this structure was "a good example of the grandeur in civic and public buildings . . . characteristic of the Victorian age." To the west, an even more massive dome, St. Paul's Cathedral, and to the east the 202-foot Roman Doric column of the Monument dominated the City's skyline.[1]

Warehouses were ubiquitous in the City of 1900. Some were rather grand, for example, 23–25 Eastcheap, which contained the showroom for the spice merchants John, Hunt and Crombie. Built of brick and stone, this building, which still stands, features second-story windows with semicircular arches above them in red, yellow, and black brick and cornices with terracotta animal heads and geometric designs. More typical was the warehouse at 30–32 Watling Street, which also still survives, and which, eschewing ornate design, was made from plain yellow brick.[2]

Markets, or exchanges, took place within these City warehouses at the turn of the twentieth century, for instance, wool sales, which were held on Coleman Street in a hall "not unlike a small theatre." During the sales, wrote one observer, "the atmosphere is pervaded with the peculiar odour of fleeces, while the samples dragged promiscuously from the bales much resemble London snow-flakes." At 1 Lime Street, the Hudson Bay Company offered periodically "a wealth of furs and bearskins . . . which range in value from muskrats of a few pence each, to rare silver-fox and rich sea-otter, worth, if perfect, £300 or £400 apiece." Paper markets, where the purchaser bought futures, that is, goods en route or still at a colonial port, were also becoming common by 1900. Thus the City's famous commodity markets, including the London Metal Exchange, comprising seven markets in nonferrous metals, the Baltic Exchange, a market in grains, the Coffee Trade Association, and so on. Over the years the markets themselves became public companies owned by shareholders.[3]

By 1900 the City was not only a commercial center, then, but a financial center as well. A market in stocks and shares had developed rapidly during the past half-century. It was located at the London Stock Exchange, whose chief building, immediately east of the Bank of England, was called the House, or "Gorgonzola Hall . . . in reference to the veined marble with which it was copiously decorated." The House consisted of "a vast, oblong hall, irregular in shape, culminat[ing] in a rotunda not unlike that of St. Paul's Cathedral, with a gilt dome and vaulted glass roof upheld by red granite columns." Here the atmosphere was extraordinarily hectic, bidding (to the tune of more than £10 million daily) carried on noisily and often overflowing from the building into Broad Street and Throgmorton Street, "the latter thoroughfare sometimes being completely blocked by the crowd, when a boom or a slump is on."[4]

There had been 864 members of the Stock Exchange in 1850; in 1900 there were 4,227—so large and speedy was the increase that interested parties began discussing ways to limit admission. Members were either brokers, who bought and sold shares for investors, or jobbers, who held blocs of shares in more than one company and who, in selling shares to brokers, "acted as a most useful and efficient buffer between the market and investors." By 1900 shares were being sold at the London Stock Exchange in practically any company, domestic or foreign, with a paid up capital of £100,000 or more. These included relatively small concerns, operating in such fields as industry, commerce, finance, mining and services, larger joint-stock enterprises, such as railways, and, at the top, huge consolidated issues of governments, such as the British National Debt.[5]

The warehouses, markets, and Stock Exchange were among the institutions imparting to the City its particular flavor and role in 1900. England's great banks likewise were crucial. First among these was the national Bank of England. To one observer the bank represented "the real cornerstone of London's business-life, nay of the whole credit system of the Universe." It made England's paper money, administered the British public debt, fixed the bank rate, by which the credit system of the City (and universe) were governed, and maintained its gold reserves. Within its "dimly-lit, heavy-vaulted, white-washed cellar" lay silver ingots and bars of gold worth up to £40 million.[6]

The City contained many more banks. A main theme of financial history during this period is the steady stream of provincial banks which amalgamated and established headquarters in the City, and their rivalry with the Bank of England. The head offices of the London and Westminster, the Union Bank of London, Lloyd's Bank, the London and County Banking Company, the London Joint Stock Bank, the London, City and Midlands Bank, among others, were all located near it, generally in Lombard Street or the lanes branching off from it. These glorified "high-street banks" made enormous profits, paying dividends of no less than 9 percent in 1900, and some considerably more.[7]

The big banks of London, including the most prestigious merchant banks like Barings, Rothschilds, Gibbs, and Hambros, provided much of the credit for world trade. They acted as guarantors for bills and as intermediaries (issue houses) in raising long-term foreign loans. Some of the most important merchant bankers sat upon the court of directors of the Bank of England, helped to determine its policy and through it Britain's financial policy as well. There were also international or imperial banks, with headquarters in the City, which acted as crucial intermediaries for trade and investment between the periphery and the metropole.

Then there were the great insurance companies with City headquarters. The preeminent firm was Lloyds of London, which had grown from a simple coffeehouse, convenient for meetings of seventeenth-century businessmen, to the world center of risk insurance. During the 1890s, Cuthbert Heath, the great figure in Lloyds' modern history, expanded the firm's interests from marine insurance to fire insurance and burglary insurance. Eventually, at his urging, Lloyds would write policies insuring just about anything. In 1900 the company was working from lavish quarters in the Royal Exchange building. Its rooms, according to the *Illustrated London News*, were "enriched after the best Roman models, simple, massive, spacious and brilliantly lighted." Even the lavatories were "on a scale approaching to luxury . . . [with] the elegant soap dishes, the spotless napkins, the china basins, the ivory tipped cocks for the supply of hot and cold water."[8]

Lloyds was the greatest of the City insurance houses, but at the turn of the century there were nearly fifty more which specialized in fire insurance, eighty-seven specializing in life insurance, seventeen, besides Lloyds, selling marine insurance. Many of these were also reaping enormous profits. During the first year of the twentieth century it was estimated that shipping insurance alone earned £90 million.[9]

The City's atmosphere was hectic and crowded. Every weekday morning since the opening of the Liverpool Street Station in 1874, commuter trains had disgorged tens of thousands of men, most sporting beards and dressed in dark suits and winged collars. Then, in 1900, the Bank tube station opened directly in front of the Royal Exchange, feeding thousands more into the Square Mile. "The passengers from the last-arrived electric train crowd to the steps leading to the open air," one observer noticed. "At the foot of the staircase their ranks open. The very young men spring forward. . . . They are not only going to business! They seem to be rushing there."[10]

Few women or children were to be seen in the district at any time, but between nine o'clock in the morning and five o'clock in the afternoon "all is crowded by businessmen, clerks and shopmen hurrying along, in winter generally wearing a silk hat, but in summer often bareheaded," wrote the Ger-

man explorer Carl Peters, who, at the turn of the century, had "looked at England and her inhabitants as I have looked at the countries of the Massais and
the Makalanga." Peters keenly noted the hustle and bustle of City life. "In
front of the Mansion House 248,015 people are passing every day," he reported almost disbelievingly, and "the number of those who pass through
Cheapside, the most frequented street . . . amounts to 91,190."[11]

At lunchtime City restaurants were "truly chock-full of customers which
is not exactly comfortable," the explorer continued. The most lavish establishment, the Throgmorton, boasted "brilliantly illuminated halls . . . wide
staircases glowing with gold mosaic, colour friezes and panels enriched with
metals, while onyx and marbles blend with richly carved oak and handpainted
tapestries." More common were restaurants like Pimm's, where customers
sat on three-legged stools before a long bar, consuming steaks for nine pence
and potatoes for a penny. "The rush . . . is so great that behind our chair there
is already another customer who waits for us to make room for him when we
have finished," Peters complained. "To get a whole table for oneself alone in
a City restaurant is a very exceptional occurrence."[12]

16. Royal Exchange—busy scene in City of London.
Photograph courtesy of Woodruff Library, Special Collections, Emory University.

A City man, H. Osborne O'Hagan, confirms the German's impression of breathless haste and hurly-burly. O'Hagan, who made a fortune in the City, spent no moment of the day in idleness. "I would rise at eight o'clock," he recalled in his memoirs, and

> during the time I was dressing, breakfasting and driving to the City I would be thinking out my programme for the day ... jotting down fresh ideas. Arriving at my office ... I would at once have in one of my secretaries and a shorthand writer ... open and attend to my correspondence, dictating replies as far as possible as I opened each letter. That work completed, I [would take] up the 'phone on my desk and my attendant [would] put me in touch with persons who had asked to speak to me on my arrival, and with persons I had noted down to be spoken to. By the time these matters had been completed there would be several people waiting to see me, some by appointment, others on urgent business without appointments.

And so it would continue throughout the day. O'Hagan claimed that, in his boardrooms, he shuffled between as many as three directors' meetings simultaneously, while "time after time I had to leave these meetings to carry on negotiations for new businesses which were offered me."[13]

The great purpose of this hectic pace was to make money, lots of it. O'Hagan was eminently successful, but many were not. "Can you or any of your readers tell me what is to become of Shansi shareholders?" one unlucky but not atypical investor plaintively queried the *Financial Times* of April 18, 1900. "I am only a small one but my subscription is far beyond my means." This unfortunate person, who signed his letter "Silly Ass," had ordered on credit more shares in the Shansi Company than he could afford. Now he could neither pay for nor sell them: "I have an ugly liability of 15s a share on the whole of my shares, and my brokers tell me I must pay another 3½d a share and a commission to them if I want to get rid of my further liability, which I simply can't do."

Between H. Osborne O'Hagan and Silly Ass stretched a long line of more or less successful investors, brokers and jobbers, clerks, businessmen, and financiers. Increased wealth was their common goal; the City was their common ground. Yet the Square Mile was much more than merely the place where men interacted in a common quest for riches.

In the beginning the City and London had been one and the same. Over the centuries, as London's role as a great port clarified, manufacturers and merchants established headquarters at the center, along the banks of the Thames. Markets developed where there were merchants. Banks located near the markets. The center was becoming the City. By the mid–eighteenth century, with England now in the first rank of world powers, finance overshadowed manufacturing there, although of course City firms continued to focus on commerce as well. Already, however, the area had become a magnet for international money, attracting funds from wherever there was a surplus seeking investment outlets. Meanwhile, although the number of businesses and business-related enterprises in the City had multiplied, the number of people who lived there had declined.

This process accelerated during the nineteenth century, especially with the growth of suburbs and the development of cheap commuter trains. By the turn of the twentieth century, the City's daytime population was 359,940, its nighttime population a mere 26,923. Land near the Bank of England was said to cost £1 million per acre. No wonder hardly anyone lived there anymore. But by then the City was scarcely a residential area. It had become rather, as one historian puts it, "a series of markets and services that facilitated the ever more complex flows between producers and consumers, lenders and borrowers, experts and the ignorant." The focus of world trade, a vast clearinghouse for goods, finance, and expertise, the almost universal provider of both development and other finance for enterprises the world over, the City was now a locus of power and wealth that overshadowed even the great manufacturing districts of northern England.[14]

The City's role depended, to a degree, upon the British policy of free trade; also upon the gold standard, which supported the vast network of bills of exchange, denominated in sterling, which provided the bulk of long- and short-term credit for world trade. Scholars have debated the influence of the City upon Britain's economy, and especially the City's part in Britain's gradual economic decline during the late nineteenth and twentieth centuries. They have examined the City's influence upon national politics and its role in funding and shaping the empire. They have written histories of the Stock Exchange, of various banks, insurance firms, and other companies. They have painted its portrait in pointillist fashion. Perhaps the most influential recent contribution appeared in 1993 in two volumes by Peter Cain and Anthony Hopkins, who argued that at the turn of the twentieth century the City was playing a critical part not merely in defining British affairs, but in shaping and conducting British policies throughout the world. It was dominated by "gentlemanly capitalists," a term and concept which has aroused much scholarly interest.[15]

According to Cain and Hopkins, gentlemanly capitalists composed a complex social and political elite stemming neither from the industrial bourgeoisie nor the aristocracy, although often they had marriage ties with the latter and maintained strong connections to the land. They did not constitute a majority in the City, but as lawyers, bankers, and financiers they largely controlled its key institutions, for example, the big banks and insurance companies. Imbued with certain aristocratic values and ideals—duty, honor, Christianity, love of sport and adventure, to list a few—they composed the very class which over the centuries had come to dominate Britain's government. Naturally, then, City and government cooperated, informally for the most part, to promote what gentlemanly capitalists considered to be the country's world and imperial interests, for patriotic reasons no doubt, but also for profit, by financing various mines, railways, and government bonds throughout the formal and informal empire.

Indeed, Cain and Hopkins maintain, profits, patriotism, and imperialism were inextricably linked in City minds. To cite an example: in 1900, as the Boxer Rebellion raged in China, the court of directors of the Bank of England met at the heart of the Square Mile. The court anticipated restoration of "peace and quietude" to the Celestial Empire. Then, as one court member put it, "the Bank would be appointed the vehicle for the transfusion of Western civilisation into that ancient community, and they would enjoy the honour of being bankers to two-thirds of the human race. Dividends were a very interesting and satisfactory point with them; but these national connections and services greatly added to the value of their proprietary stock."[16]

17. Brokers in the London Stock Exchange.
Courtesy of the Guildhall Library.

Yet if, through the efforts of Cain and Hopkins, the role of the City and particularly its links with the empire have been clarified, much remains to ponder. Imperialism touched the City, helped to define it, in ways historians have yet to consider. Moreover, City attitudes about the empire played a crucial role in defining the imperial metropolis.

In 1900 the London Stock Exchange experienced an unprecedented boom in West African mining shares, so that for a short time the "jungle department," as it was uncharmingly termed, became the center of City attention. To focus upon a company that ran a West African gold mine in 1900, therefore, is to turn a magnifying glass upon turn-of-the-century links between City and empire in a heightened state. The Ashanti Goldfields Corporation was one such company.

In 1890 two native African merchants, Joseph Edward Biney and Joseph Ettrusion Ellis, purchased land concessions containing a goldmine located some forty-five miles south of Kumasi, the capital city of the Ashanti nation. As it happened they now owned one of the richest goldfields in the world. Although for five years they headed a small syndicate to work the mine, in fact they needed additional expertise and capital. Fortuitously Biney happened to be the West African agent of the London merchants Smith and Cade. He sent his employers specimens of gold-bearing quartz that were assayed at more than eight ounces of gold per ton, a very high ratio. Edwin Arthur Cade, a partner in the firm, set sail for Africa immediately.

The antecedents and early life of this man were not what might have been expected of a typical City gentleman—or rather they demonstrate that not all those who made successful careers in the City were themselves gentlemanly capitalists. The son of a successful Ipswich watchmaker who had branched out into the new field of photography, Cade attended neither an elite public school nor Oxbridge, but rather Framlingham in Ipswich, which he left at age fifteen. Apprenticed in 1879 to his brother, who had succeeded to the father's business, Cade proved restless, moving to London in 1882. He worked for Martin's Dry Photo Plates at 24 Soho Square. Although brought up as an Anglican, he attended the Methodist Chapel in Studley Road, Clapham. There he met and married the daughter of John Smith, an established West African merchant with offices in the City. Upon the marriage his father-in-law brought him into the firm as a senior partner.[17]

Whatever Cade's background and previous career, his letters and conduct from 1895 until his premature death in 1903 reveal a man who thoroughly understood the rules which governed the City of London. Upon his arrival

18. Edwin Arthur Cade.
Courtesy of the Guildhall Library.

in West Africa in 1895, he purchased from Biney and Ellis a land concession of one hundred square miles, including the gold mine. He named his new company the Cote d'Or and fobbed off its previous owners with 796 shares each, while reserving for himself and his father-in-law 5,500 shares. This was, perhaps, accepted (if sharp) business practice the world over. But already Cade was thinking in grander terms: "The Cote d'Or Company, I may remark, was a small company formed among friends . . . merely for the purpose of preliminary enquiry as to what was offered and to test its probable value. Our intention immediately upon the Secretary of State allowing it, is to transfer all our interests to a larger working company. . . . This Company will be composed of private friends and connections of the original shareholders of the Cote d'Or Company."[18] Thus Cade planned to exploit the opportunity presented him and to garner additional City backing, while hoping and expecting that his own interests and those of the British government would coincide.

They did. Over the course of centuries Europeans had come and gone in coastal West Africa. By 1895, although France retained a presence to the north and inland, Great Britain, having defeated the Ashanti people in campaigns of 1823, 1863–64, and 1873–74, was the dominant power in the region. After the general election of July 1895, the British secretary of state for the colonies was none other than Joseph Chamberlain, whose attitude toward the further development of West Africa by British finance and expertise was activist and positive. "Mr. Chamberlain is ready and anxious to encourage by every means in his power the development of the resources of the Gold Coast," E. Minfield of the Colonial Office wrote reassuringly to Cade in February 1896. The colonial secretary had already dispatched Col. Francis Scott and a detachment of troops to Kumasi. Scott not only occupied the city but took prisoner the Ashanti king, Prempe, and exiled him first to Sierra Leone, then to the Seychelle Islands. Thus was the way made clear for Cade (and other British businessmen) interested in West Africa. In March 1897 Chamberlain gave Cade's company permission to commence mining operations in earnest. In December of the same year the Cote d'Or Company liquidated in favor of a new firm, the Ashanti Goldfields Corporation.[19]

All this, however, was merely the necessary prelude to Cade's main work. His next step was to assemble for the fledgling company a five-man board of directors, including himself, with interlocking City interests. Frederick Gordon, whom he appointed chairman of the board, was also a director of Maple and Cook, the great furniture firm, and of the Ashanti Company Ltd., which had extensive rubber interests near the mine. Viscount Duncannon, another board member, was already vice chairman of Bovril. Cade made sure as well to invite representatives and former members of the Colonial Office to board meetings. Not himself descended from England's elite governing class, Cade had made sure to obtain the support of gentlemanly capitalists for his enterprise.

Such figures could invest large sums of money in Ashanti Goldfields Corporation and attract additional funds if necessary. When, for example, the company needed to pay for construction of a stamp mill, shareholders, including board members, subscribed more than £21,500 within a matter of days. But already the mine was turning a tremendous profit. From March 1898 to the end of June 1899, 3,108 tons of quartz yielded 2,544 ounces of gold. In the next twelve months 4,673 tons rendered no fewer than 7,812 ounces.[20]

Possibly Cade found it easy to attract and work with the City elite because he shared some of the qualities said to have animated its members, for instance, the spirit of adventure ostensibly typical of public school boys who went on to careers in the City. Cade enjoyed the challenge presented by travel to, from, and within Africa, making the arduous journey to the Gold Coast and inland to the mine no fewer than three times in eight years. He possessed other gentlemanly values as well, for example, a love of formal gardens. He sent to John Daw, the managing director of the mine in Ashanti, "rose-trees, Japanese Maples and like beautiful and sweet-scented shrubs, . . . bulbs of Gladiolus, Begonias and Gloxinas, also about two dozen roses of the most approved kind in Bush form . . . and a dozen or two of gorgeous climbing plants like Bougainvillea, and a few geraniums and fuchsias." Implicit in such a list was the imperialist assumption that the African landscape could be domesticated, made to resemble England. "If as an amateur gardener I may give you one piece of advice it is this," Cade ended one letter to Daw, "do not plant the [bulbs] too close."[21]

But these were secondary attributes of gentlemanly capitalism as analyzed by Cain and Hopkins. Much more important was Cade's ability, demonstrated first in his construction of the corporation's board of directors, to attract gentlemanly support and to work closely with the government. Cade continued to play this game with great skill. For instance, in 1900 it was necessary to hire laborers to carry gold from the mine at Obuasi some eighty miles through the jungle to the railway terminus at Tarquah, where it would be loaded onto a train for the remaining portion of the journey to the city of Cape Coast. Cade wanted the railway extended from Tarquah to Kumasi, the Ashanti capital, or, if that were too distant, at least as far as his own Ashanti Goldfields. But how to persuade the government to fund such a project?

19. John Daw.
Courtesy of the Guildhall Library.

Cade recognized that other businessmen with interests in West Africa would benefit from extension of the railroad. They must be organized into a group which could exert pressure on the government to build it. "I think you will be pleased to know," he wrote to Daw on January 12, "that I have been the means of bringing the Chairman and the leading Directors of the Warsau Company into direct touch with our people, and I am giving a dinner shortly which will be attended by all the more important people of all the sundry and every principle Mining Company on the coast." The dinner took place some two weeks later, as Cade wrote to Daw, "at the Hotel Metropole, [with] twenty gentlemen, amongst whom were Sir John Bramston, Sir Blundell Maple, our directors, Messrs Steinkopff, Walford, Annan, Prince, etc., present as my guests. The object being to back, strengthen and I hope settle the possibility of getting money for the [railroad]. I am very sanguine that the object has been accomplished." Sir John Bramston had been assistant undersecretary of state for the colonies during 1896–97, precisely when Cade was receiving permission from the colonial secretary to expand his company; presumably he and Cade were already well acquainted. Sir John Blundell Maple, best known for owning and betting vast sums on racehorses, was the Conservative member of Parliament for Dulwich and chairman of Maple and Cook, the furniture concern of which Frederick Gordon, chairman of Ashanti Goldfields Corporation, was a director. No doubt Messrs. Steinkopff, Walford, Annan, and Prince were City men with interests in the Gold Coast as well. Again, if Cade himself was not a gentlemanly capitalist he certainly knew where to find them and how to work with them. But then, as Cain and Hopkins have argued, this is how the imperial City got along.

Perhaps, however, Cade was knocking at an open door? Chamberlain had long believed that the government should provide the infrastructure of empire, especially in potentially profitable areas. And he was "more confident than ever that these Colonies will turn out to be a most valuable possession. . . . [F]rom all the information I have obtained . . . the gold industry . . . is going to be, I believe, a most solid, valuable and profitable industry in the Gold Coast Colony." When Cade offered various financial guarantees so that the government need not fear losing money on the railway, Chamberlain decided to go ahead with it. On February 23 Cade wrote triumphantly to Daw that the "agreement to the terms stated for the Railway is to all intents and purposes a fact accomplished." To hasten matters, however, his board of directors further agreed to grant an honorarium of one thousand pounds to the project's chief engineer "if the Railway is so far completed to enable us to get heavy machinery to our mines by 31st May 1903." Interestingly, "Mr. Frederic Shelford, who was in attendance, reported that the Colonial Office had no objection to the course suggested."[22]

Cade intended to make a great deal of money in West Africa, but he was inspired by loftier ideals as well. "I want if I can," he informed Daw, "to hasten forward that time when a great impulse shall make Ashanti the centre of the world's observation." His company must become a model employer of African labor. "I am pressing upon all new offices that great consideration for natives of which you speak," he assured his general manager. Here, indeed, Daw appears to have been the leader. He planned to employ as miners the very men who had engaged earlier in rebellion against British colonizers. Cade responded with enthusiasm. The scheme, if successful, would represent "a most magnificent service to your country as also to that part of the Queen's dominion [Ashantiland] which already owes so much to your endeavour." Ashanti warriors would beat their swords not into plowshares, exactly, but at least into mining picks and shovels.[23]

By 1902 the Ashanti Goldfields Corporation was earning profits in West Africa, attempting to divert the West African people from rebellious to peaceful activities, and doing its best "to promote the welfare of the native," as Daw put it to a meeting of shareholders back in the City of London. Here, seemingly, were married the gentlemanly capitalist goals of service (to West Africans and to a certain idealized version of Victorian imperialism) and honorable pecuniary gain. Cade's and Daw's imperialism, ostensibly selfless, essentially selfish, was typical of the conventional blinkered views commonly held not merely in the City but throughout the imperial metropolis. It was virtually identical, for example, to that of a more significant Chamberlainite, the colonial editor of the London *Times* (see chapter 5).

Deeply embedded in this worldview were condescending, authoritarian notions. Cade's factotum, Daw, thought of Ashanti as "a new land outside the pale of civilisation." He lectured an audience of shareholders that it was "a simple but dreadful fact that the Government, until lately, took no means whatever to improve the conditions under which the natives lived in West Africa; and so long as they are allowed to construct their villages without supervision, and are not compelled to make arrangements for drainage, or to give attention to sanitary matters, to say nothing of the filtration of the water which they drink, so long will malaria abundantly flourish." Failing government intervention, which Daw confidently predicted Chamberlain would eventually provide, private enterprise must play its part. Compulsion was not something at which Daw or Cade would balk. "Our medical officers make daily visits," Daw boasted to the shareholders, "and we reserve their right to enter every hut, and to generally see that the regulations governing the sanitation of the village are rigorously and minutely carried out." Neither would the company permit the sale of liquor on its property, or any but the most inconsequential form of Ashanti self-government. "We have created a native council of men . . . in whom we can feel confidence. They try all cases of a petty character."[24]

In sum Cade, Daw, and the approving shareholders of the Ashanti Gold-fields Corporation saw in it a means of accumulating wealth, of serving their country, of expanding the British Empire, and of uplifting African stan-dards—whether the African wished to be uplifted or not. The principal founder and driving force behind the enterprise, Cade, was an adept at the rules of the game which ruled the City during its imperialist heyday. He brought together City and government representatives and pointed out to both how their interests coincided. As a result Cade prospered, his company prospered, the City prospered, and the empire grew—if with uncertain re-sults for indigenous peoples. Moreover it only seemed natural to conflate the single corporation, Ashanti Goldfields, with the City of London, the City of London with the imperial metropolis more generally, and the imperial me-tropolis with the imperial project as a whole. As Daw lectured his stock-holders, the "essential . . . impulse, the enterprise, the grasp and daring" which had resulted in so profitable an undertaking, stemmed from "the five

20. The kind of men who helped to make the fortunes of Edwin Arthur Cade and
John Daw: two Ashanti Goldfields Corporation Ltd. employees.
Courtesy of the Guildhall Library.

21. Where the gold came from: Offin Camp, Ashanti Goldfields Corporation Ltd.
Courtesy of the Guildhall Library.

gentlemen [who are] the directors of the Ashanti Goldfields Corporation,"
and they, of course, were located "at home, in London, here."[25]

By their activities and attitudes Cade and his business associates helped
to define an imperial metropolis whose double role was to facilitate the extraction of wealth from British colonies and to dispense British values, practices, and justice to colonized peoples. But how did imperialism affect the City
of London more generally and how did the City, taken more broadly, tend to
view the empire? In short, what was the City's contribution to defining the
imperial metropolis?

Put simply, most of the men who worked in the City viewed the empire as
a potential El Dorado, profits from which were occasionally impeded by
terrain and climate, by rebellious natives or settlers, and by liberal do-gooders who took a different view than they did of imperial responsibilities, and
who sometimes inconveniently either caught the ear of or even became members of British governments. It did not occur to the City that El Dorado might

be left to work out its own destiny, only that the City and the British government should overcome such obstacles to profitability as it might pose them. Inevitably then the City favored a "forward" imperial policy; it contained few "Little Englanders."

Difficult terrain presented no insuperable problem to City men interested in profitable returns on imperial investments. The land in El Dorado could almost always be made to yield to modern methods, for example, the construction of railways. The impact upon natural habitats and environment was devastating, but environmental consciousness was not high in the imperial metropolis or anywhere else in those days. As John Daw reported to his shareholders, "The area over which they ruled was 100 square miles. . . . The whole property was covered with primeval forest through which some large rivers ran." But Daw had no doubt that "in two years, after the railway reached their property, they would stand at the top of the tree so far as . . . dividends were concerned."[26]

Climate could represent a more intractable obstacle to profit making than rough terrain. In 1900, the tobacco plantations at New Darvel Bay in Borneo paid a smaller return on investments than had been expected. This was because, as Sigmund Sinauer reported to his stockholders, in Borneo "a very hot sun follow[s] soon after heavy rains. . . . A number of the drops remaining on the leaves are acted upon by the fierce tropical sun just as in the case of a burning-glass such as you perhaps remember having used in your boyhood." The result of hot sunshine focused through droplets of water was a spotted tobacco leaf which yielded a less than satisfactory smoke. Investors in the New Darvel Bay (Borneo) Tobacco Plantations consoled themselves, however, with the hope that by constructing railways, importing Chinese laborers, and increasing trade with Japan, they could make up for the area's peculiar weather patterns and earn profits nevertheless.[27]

Then the indigenous peoples themselves might unintentionally cause problems for shareholders. In Lagos, for instance, the local population was accustomed to collecting sap from rubber trees. Unfortunately this practice damaged the tree trunk and interfered with the rate of return upon investments in the rubber trade. "It is a great pity," opined the editors of the *Financial News* on February 3, "that Government action could not have been applied towards restraining the wicked waste of the trees by the niggers. . . . Might not the Colonial Office do something?"

Often, too, indigenous peoples posed a threat to City profits quite intentionally. Well might an imperialist boast that "every man, woman and child residing in Borneo were [*sic*] practically as free as those living in England"; unaccountably, the people of Borneo remained ungrateful. Sporadic rebellions marred life for European settlers there. On January 31, 1900, British-led troops finally captured and killed the leader of Borneo's rebels, Mat Selleh, but many of his followers escaped into the "jungle [which] is almost impenetrable thereabouts." They continued their struggle against the interlopers, which had something of a depressing effect upon City bondholders.[28]

In Ashanti, where Cade had established his mining operation, rebellion assumed more serious proportions, with correspondingly grave consequences for City investors. The country was rich in natural resources, especially gold and rubber. As we have seen, the British established formal rule of the area in early 1896 but, as in Borneo, without engaging the affections of the indigenous population. In April 1900 an arrogant British governor, Sir Frederick Mitchell Hodgson, summoned Ashanti leaders to a meeting at which he cavalierly demanded they surrender to him the traditional throne of Ashanti kings, the golden stool. He wished to sit upon it himself! ("The whole thing seems to have been founded on the same old tale of trying to force the native instead of leading him," Cade commented revealingly when he first heard of this rash command.) The Ashanti responded with outrage. Twenty thousand fighting men, some armed with modern weapons, marched on Hodgson's forces in Kumasi. Reuters news service hardly reassured concerned English readers by reporting that Ashanti leaders could raise thirty thousand more. In the heavy fighting that ensued, Ashanti warriors came near to breaking into the city before relieving troops arrived.[29]

The shock wave that had originated in West Africa swept across continents and oceans to rattle walls in the City of London. Cade found his hands full trying to reassure the friends and relations of his employees in West Africa that they were safe. "I have done my best to quiet matters," he wrote to Daw with some satisfaction, not least because in the end neither the mine nor its staff had been harmed.[30] In Gorgonzola Hall, however, the repercussions of the Ashanti rebellion were severe. "The readiness displayed by the Ashantis to revolt is evidently a factor that must be taken into consideration in entering upon mining enterprises in that country," warned the editors of the *Financial Times* on April 27. Investors took this advice to heart. On April 9 the *Daily Mail* reported that "the news of tribal fighting in Ashanti has nipped a promising boom in West African mines in the bud."

Those investors who had resisted the boom might congratulate themselves on their caution; those who had jumped early now faced the consequences. "But for the unfortunate rising in Ashanti the directors would have declared a dividend as promised," John Daw, who had left the goldfields just before fighting commenced, reported to 283 concerned shareholders attending an extraordinary meeting. "However, under the circumstances, he thought they would give the directors credit for a certain amount of prudence in not paying away any money for the moment." Investors who had jumped not merely early but deep, confronted catastrophe. The owners of MacIver and Company, West African merchants, for example, found themselves in bankruptcy court: "They attributed their present difficulties to the effect of the Ashanti war on African produce trade."[31]

As soon as British troops rescued Governor Hodgson in Kumasi, however, the boom recommenced. In fact, an almost hysterical resurgence took place, so that Stock Exchange authorities felt obliged to devote a separate corner of the House exclusively to Ashanti dealings, a corner immediately dubbed the jungle department. By late fall, thirty-three companies were trading there. Moreover, as the *Daily Mail* reported on October 11, "several expeditions have left this country for West Africa within the past few days and various new flotations are in course of progress." Established companies like Cade's Ashanti Goldfields, whose shares had sold originally at one pound each, were now up to twenty-four pounds, and the company was finally paying the postponed dividend—at the rate of 100 percent.[32]

Thus El Dorado might bite the hand which intended to pick its pocket. The greater the obstacle to profit making, or, for that matter, the greater the success in removing the obstacle, the greater the impact upon City views and lives, positive or negative. Inevitably City views of empire and the empire's impact upon City views were intertwined. In 1900 the two most significant obstacles to City profits were located neither in Borneo nor Ashanti, however, but in China and South Africa. And their impact upon City behavior and attitudes was pronounced.

Of the many potentially profitable places in which turn-of-the-century City men were interested, China was among the most promising. Figures for 1899 showed an "astonishing expansion" of Anglo-Chinese trade and British-financed railway construction, and, according to one enthusiast, there was no end in sight. "With its 400 millions of population, its fertile soil and great mineral wealth, [China] offered almost unlimited opportunities for the extension of commerce," gushed Joseph Walton, M.P., who seems to have served almost as the parliamentary mouthpiece for English businessmen with Chinese interests. "China is the neutral market which offers the greatest possibilities for trade expansion, and where our commercial rights should be [most] resolutely upheld," he continued in a book devoted to extolling the benefits of further investment and trade with the Far East. Even the relatively sober *Financial Times* acknowledged, on February 5, 1900, that "a good deal of interest is felt in commercial and financial circles in the City in the course of trade in China."[33]

When the Boxer Rebellion of Chinese nationalists began to take shape in the spring of 1900 the City paid close attention. "The increasingly serious aspect of the trouble in China has cast a shadow over the Stock Exchange today," the *Financial Times* reported worriedly on June 7. Investors were proving reluctant to commit funds to Chinese projects: "Consequently 'House' operators who had laid in stocks in anticipation have become disgusted and thrown things overboard." As matters in China worsened, faces in the House lengthened, and the value of portfolios dipped even further. By June 19 "the Chinese situation" had "become practically the dominating influence on the Stock Exchange."

So sensitive was the market now that prices rose and fell according to the latest rumor of events on the far side of the globe. On June 21, "the Stock Market had a bad opening on the unfavourable situation in China, but within a quarter of an hour a remarkable change took place," reported the *Daily Mail*'s financial expert, the author of a regular column called "Chat on 'Change." "A telegram was said to have been received from Shanghai to the effect that Admiral Seymour had reached Pekin and found the Legations all safe." Immediately stocks rose, and not only those connected with the Far East. As the journalist explained, "A fringe of operators hang around every bad market waiting for the slightest evidence of a turn and ready to buy on it. They are a sort of salvage brigade, and their activity yesterday indicated that the worst was believed to be over."

In fact, however, the worst in China was yet to come. Putative telegrams from Shanghai to the contrary notwithstanding, no one in England really knew where Adm. Sir Michael Culme-Seymour was, let alone whether he had rescued the Europeans seeking refuge from the Boxers in the legation in Peking. In late June the empress of China threw her support behind the Boxer rebels. This meant that it would be necessary for the international contingent of advancing soldiers not merely to rescue the besieged Europeans, but to defeat the Chinese government in what bid fare to become a full-scale war. The Stock Exchange "now takes the view," reported "Chat on 'Change" in the *Daily Mail* of July 3, "that it is impossible to gauge the dangers of the outlook. . . . It is on account of China that the Stock Exchange has stopped its advance. It is afraid of the future and it cannot see its way anywhere."

The effect upon small shareholders was particularly grave. Men who had paid ten shillings per share to the Pekin Syndicate in March were now offering them on the open market for as little as two shillings sixpence. Facing this predicament, Silly Ass penned his despondent letter. Apparently he was merely one of many worried investors anxiously seeking advice from experts. The *Financial Times* now confessed to sharing "with curious correspondents some little surprise that the political crisis in East Asia should have produced so marked an effect." But the editors discerned a silver lining: "The Chinese rising has certainly afforded a promising opportunity for the public to secure a speculative investment at bedrock level."[34]

Bedrock levels pertained in South African stocks too. In early 1900, with the Boer War still going badly for Britain, gold and diamond mine stocks were at a low ebb. The repercussions swirled and eddied throughout greater London, sometimes in unexpected, even piquant, fashion. Lady Elizabeth Bertie and her friend May Emily Manby, for instance, had speculated heavily in "Kaffirs," that is to say, in South African mines. With the British reverse at Magersfontein the value of their investment dropped precipitously. "Who could have foreseen the fearful fall?" Manby queried a reporter from the *Financial News*. "Among the wealthiest people are persons I know who have been almost ruined; and these people had had a better chance of studying the risks than I have had. Their calculations have been in error; so have mine; and now I owe my broker money." In fact, between them May Emily Manby and Lady Elizabeth owed their brokers more than £10,000. They claimed not to have it; their husbands had the funds, apparently, but refused to pay. "All this happened while I was away on the Continent," said one of them. "Women have no judgment and have no business to speculate on the Stock Exchange." Given the anachronistic and sexist property laws of the period it would appear that, in this instance, the brokers themselves were liable for the losses incurred by their clients, a twist that may have gladdened more than a few hearts in the imperial metropolis, if not in the City of London itself.[35]

The impact of the imperial war in South Africa upon the City of London may be discerned in less likely quarters. The war led, for example, to higher prices for comestibles. Here, obviously, the repercussions extended far beyond the Square Mile, and the fashionable drawing rooms of those like Manby, who did business with City stockbrokers and who may well have been entirely unaffected by higher food prices. But there was at least one section of the City workforce which suffered from the rise in costs. In February 1900 an association of waiters who worked in City of London restaurants unavailingly requested that the lord mayor open a fund on their behalf "on the grounds that the war has resulted in the abandonment of many festivities."[36]

And, then, investors might suffer from the increased prices for food and drink after all, albeit indirectly. Only a month after the waiters' unsuccessful petition to the lord mayor, holders of shares in the St. James Restaurant learned to their dismay that "as soon as fighting commenced in Africa our receipts fell in an extraordinary way." Because profits had dropped dividends had dropped too. Likewise shareholders of Eastman's, a firm which imported meat, learned from the managing director, J. J. Thomson, that "the war in South Africa has been against the retail meat trade in this country owing to a considerable number of meat-carrying vessels being chartered by the Government." So their investment had declined in value. From E. T. Hargraves, chairman, shareholders of the Chester Lion Brewery Company received an even sadder report. The beer trade had "been prejudicially affected by the war." Not only were former tipplers now choosing to contribute funds to war charities instead of to pubs, but "the Chancellor of the Exchequer thought that the present time was an appropriate one for increasing the duties on beer and spirits, and in consequence for three months we have had to pay an extra 1s. per barrel on beer, and an extra 6d. per gallon on spirits."[37]

In the first instance, then, the empire touched people connected with the City precisely where one might have guessed it would, in their pocketbooks, albeit occasionally in unexpected, indeed unpredictable ways. The bottom line was this: when imperial affairs went smoothly, then brokers, investors, waiters, and many others prospered; when affairs went rough, then they suffered.

In December 1899, the City decided to subsidize, equip, train, and send to South Africa a volunteer force to fight in the Boer War (the very same unit whose return to London was discussed in chapter 1). The lord mayor, Sir Alfred J. Newton, Bart., was the moving spirit behind this enterprise. On December 21 the Court of Common Council of the City of London agreed, at his urging, to provide £25,000 toward the regiment, henceforth to be known as the City Imperial Volunteers, or CIV, which would number 1,000 men. Something like fifty City companies contributed an additional £34,000, while individual City gentlemen found yet another £55,000 for the project. The entire sum of £114,000 was raised within days. Simultaneously three great shipping families, Wilson, Currie, and Evans, announced that they would transport the volunteers to South Africa free of charge. It took only three weeks for the volunteers, all Londoners, all bachelors, many employed in the City itself, and numbering 1,550 in the end, to be registered, medically certified, trained, and sent off to Africa.[38]

The social composition of the CIV suggests that a surprising number of London's gentlemanly capitalists were prepared to fight and die for empire. Forty-four employees of London's leading banks volunteered, according to one count, fifty-two according to another, including "a very good percentage of Bank of England officers." Twenty-one lawyers from the Inns of Court served. Something like two hundred brokers, jobbers, and clerks at the Stock Exchange served as well.[39] "The Stock Exchange has had some very nasty things said about it," boasted the *Financial Times* of January 15, but "what

other similar body of private individuals in the country has sent anything like
so large a proportion?"

It was not only the elite of the City who volunteered, however, but rather
a broad cross section of its working population. According to the *Daily Mail*
of June 16, the officers of the civ were drawn from 26 professions and trades
and the men from 121: "Included in the rank and file were 41 barristers and
law students, 18 bootmakers, 13 bricklayers, 9 butchers, 591 clerks, 29 com-
positors, 49 drapers, 5 dentists, 67 engineers, 7 farmers, 13 gardeners, 10
grooms and coachmen, 18 grocers, 1 hatter, 38 ironmongers, 4 licensed vict-
uallers, 87 labourers, 11 medical men, 1 milkman, 31 porters, 49 painters and
paper-hangers, 37 printers, 26 plumbers, 14 solicitors, 19 stationers, 4 shop
assistants, 5 schoolmasters, 27 travellers [traveling salesmen?], 23 tailors
and 65 warehousemen." It is only logical that so many clerks volunteered for
service because the City employed more clerks than anything else. On the
other hand, I do not know how 7 farmers wound up serving in the City Imperial Volunteers.

The volunteers received an enormous send-off from the City, participated
in the general South African campaign, suffered casualties, and, as we have
seen, returned to an even more tremendous welcome late in the year. The
Daily Mail closely followed their exploits, puffing them shamelessly. Research suggests another dimension, however, which may be alluded to briefly.
"They seem to have great difficulty in realising that they are no longer volunteers," complained one of their officers, whose orders the men had ignored.
"The want of training in march discipline was another weakness with which
we had to contend," recalled the commandant of the regiment a year later. "At
first some of the men seemed surprised that they were not allowed to drop
out without asking leave." The commandant thought that civ "shooting was
scarcely as satisfactory as I had expected," but the volunteers had excelled at
one maneuver, "the quickness with which all ranks dropped flat on the word
'cover'."[40]

Perhaps the assessment is unfair. During their stint in South Africa 1 officer and 13 civs were killed or died from wounds, and 47 died from disease.
Sixty-five were wounded and 130 were invalided home. "The total loss from
all causes was at a slightly higher ratio than in the regular army, giving the
C.I.V.s honourable pre-eminence," writes one historian.[41]

Thus, again, did empire impinge upon the lives of City men, this time in
the most direct and forceful way imaginable. Yet the example raises more
questions than it answers, for surely the men of the civ volunteered to fight
for more than their pocketbooks. Empire meant more than El Dorado to the
City of London.

❖ ❖ ❖

Common sense suggests, and research confirms almost immediately, that the empire tugged not only at purse strings but at heartstrings too. Men were unlikely to volunteer for service in South Africa and to risk their lives solely for their profit margins. They fought and died for something better, something larger.

They accepted British rationales for the conflict at face value and repeated them to one another. "We have been forced to the arbitrament of war," declared the lord mayor to five hundred CIVS at their swearing-in ceremony, "and we shall not sheathe the sword until our supremacy in South Africa is established—a supremacy which will be universally welcomed as securing in that country equality before the law to all nationalities, and, in consequence, real freedom in its best and only true sense." Some may have fought, in part, because they believed that British rule in South Africa would benefit the Africans themselves. "In time, by God's blessing, we may hope to be enabled to extend the benefits of peace, justice and mercy throughout all the dark places of the earth," said one gentlemanly capitalist. More common was the statement of Lord Gifford to the shareholders of the Bechuanaland Exploration Company: the war would assure "equal rights to all white men." This would be "true liberty as we understand it."[42]

But to many in the City the empire stood for more than political principles; it stood for something mystical, based upon blood ties which united the Anglo-Saxon race. "The British Empire is no mere name, no congeries of independent peoples bound together only by the fact that they choose to colour all their lands pink on the map," boasted the *Financial Times* of June 1, 1900. Rather the empire was an organic whole, a family, as the "magnificent enthusiasm with which the colonies have thrown themselves into the fight [against the Boers] and have clamoured for the forefront in the battlefield" demonstrated. In reality Australia sent only a token number of troops to South Africa, Quebec opposed sending any at all, and ultimately Canada sent only one thousand, who were paid by British authorities while they were on service. Yet the City took these dubious demonstrations of solidarity as proof of Britain's unique "colonising genius." Only Great Britain could have inspired such devotion.[43]

Moreover, the City maintained, imperialism would help resolve class differences at home. As Sir Sidney Shippard, K.C.M.G., president of the Australian timber firm M. C. Davies' Karri and Jarrah Company, director of the British South Africa Company, and member of numerous other City boards of directors with imperial connections, put it, "Englishmen of all classes, men of the imperial race, should stand together shoulder to shoulder throughout the world."[44] Here were sentiments that London's dockers were struggling to express. Ben Tillett would have agreed, so long as Shippard paid his workers a living wage.

Possession of empire meant more prosaic things to the City as well, for instance, that Britons always must be on their guard because jealous competitors coveted their colonial possessions. In the *Financial News* of January 25, "a well known City merchant" warned his countrymen that the Indian frontier was at risk. "The true Russian," he averred, "only looks forward to one war—the war with England," which would be launched from Afghanistan. Another City gentleman, Henry B. Sang, discerned another danger. "Our greatest competitor is Germany," he warned the *City Press* of June 6. The eyes of wary City men turned also toward France, as the *Daily Mail* observed on April 23. In the City "the Ashanti trouble is believed to be the result of local French machinations, while the coming mobilisation of the Army corps for the summer manoeuvres is deemed to constitute a possible danger.... Matters may become acute sometime in June." As for the Dutch, they were particularly odious, as Boer conduct in the Transvaal proved. The ostensible loyalty of the "white colonies" during the Boer War cheered City gentlemen partly because so much of the world seemed unfriendly to British policies and interests.

City gentlemen affected to believe, however, that imperial Britain could outface them all. "I think that before this [Boer] war we could not have realised the immense latent strength, or the boundless resources of the British Empire," mused Shippard. "We are beginning now to understand what might be the aggregate of those forces."[45] With more bluster "Justacia" made the same point in the *Financial News* of February 24: "If the Slav is to be kept in a secondary place it must be done by the Anglo-Saxon race. As to the other nations, they are unworthy of notice, and must now begin to 'eat humble pie.' ... They need England; but, thank God, England does not need them."

The corollary to disdain for other Europeans was a smug self-assessment that bordered on the ridiculous. According to Shippard, "England alone has solved the problems of life hitherto." According to Ernest C. Maccatta, chairman of the Anglo-French Exploration Company, "Wherever Great Britain has set her foot, two blades of grass have grown where one grew before." The most peculiar assertion was left to Stanley Shaw, a graduate of the City of London School for Boys. "Londoners make the smartest and cleanest soldiers" he boasted, quoting as his authority "an old soldier of the Confederate Army who had fought [in defense of slavery] with Stonewall Jackson in the old Stonewall Brigade."[46]

Since the empire was ringed by jealous competitors, the City naturally favored increased military spending. Few old Gladstonians remained within the Square Mile. "The whole world is under arms," observed the *Bankers' Journal* of March 14. "Peace and Retrenchment are nowadays looked upon rather as dreams than realities. . . . It is certain that we must be ready to defend our Empire and hold our Trade, and so we must insure ourselves accordingly." This was a theme to which the journal returned repeatedly. A few favored more dramatic departures. When the prime minister, Lord Salisbury, visited the City's annual Conservative Association dinner, the chairman of the Stock Exchange, J. K. J. Hichens, pressed for the introduction of conscription: "As the people realised more and more the isolation in which England stood, surrounded by nations whose feeling towards her were extremely hostile, they would, he thought, be willing to submit to some form of compulsory service. (Hear, hear.)" Sir Blundell Maple, Bart. M.P., one of the attendees at Edwin Cade's dinner party in the Hotel Metropole, had a more startling and inegalitarian proposal: "Every income-tax payer who has not a certificate of three years' service in a volunteer force should contribute £5 per annum to a fund for the national defence of the country."[47]

A vaguer, less obviously militaristic vision also found favor within the City. This was "imperial federation," the ambitious program linked most closely with the later career of Joseph Chamberlain. But the imperialist wing of the Liberal Party was also gaining strength at this time, which perhaps explains why such free traders as the City still contained joined with tariff reformers in the British Empire League, founded in 1897 "to secure the permanent unity of the Empire," as its journal the *British Empire Review* put it.

In the long run, City men who favored imperial federation recorded few triumphs, but in 1900 their movement was at its height. On April 28 the Empire League held its third annual meeting in the heart of the City, at the Mansion House, under the presidency of the lord mayor. The platform consisted primarily of City luminaries, a veritable Who's Who of gentlemanly capitalists belonging to both main political parties. As reported by the *City Press*, "The Duke of Devonshire [a Liberal Unionist] acknowledged the deep interest the City of London had always taken in the League, and moved the adoption of the annual report." "On the motion of the Governor of the Bank of England, seconded by Sir Charles Rivers Wilson [president of the Grand Trunk Railway of Canada, member of the council of the Suez Canal Company, and former finance minister of Egypt], the statement of receipts and expenditure was adopted." Lord Rothschild, of the famous banking family, Lord Brassey, the former governor of Victoria, Lord Strathcona, governor of the Hudson Bay Company, director of the Canadian Pacific Railway Company, and honorary president of the Bank of Montreal, Sydney Buxton, M.P., the distinguished Liberal politician and former undersecretary of state for the colonies, and Herbert Samuel, another Liberal also connected to a famous banking family and destined to go on to a notable political career much concerned with imperial affairs, were also present.[48]

Wound up with City definitions of empire, then, were notions of romance and blood ties, of danger and isolation, of arrogance and defiance. Yet no definition which ignored the racism implicit in these attitudes would be complete.[49] The City's gentlemanly capitalists were probably no more racist than most other Londoners (or Britons or Europeans or white North Americans for that matter), and *racism* is a slippery term whose definition depends upon time and place. But City investors repeatedly heard the chairmen and managers of their companies disparage the very people who made the profits of imperialism possible. "They are a healthy race, good-tempered and tractable, and fairly intelligent," observed Arthur Nichols, secretary of the Bank of Egypt, of the Egyptian people, adding, "They are like children—will suddenly quarrel fiercely over nothing . . . but suddenly the row is over and they are all laughing and joking again." The people of Swaziland, according to another alleged expert, were "untutored, unrestrained . . . savages . . . whose time was divided between gossip, sun baths, and raiding . . . [and] who looked upon the Europeans as curious amphibious bipeds who came out of the sea."[50]

Above all, the colonized peoples were lazy. "Only sheer necessity, borne on him by starvation or taxation—that close concomitant of civilisation— serves to drive the untutored Kaffir to daily toil," opined the *Financial News*, and the City agreed. "Some inducement or policy of the Government should be enacted that will get the labour we require out of the 10,000,000 of natives of South Africa," asserted C. D. Rudd, a director of Consolidated Gold Fields of South Africa. But in Rhodesia forced labor was already common. In Bechuanaland captives charged, but not convicted, of rebellion were indentured against their will. In South Africa the Glen Grey Act taxed at impossibly high rates natives who could not prove that they were employed.[51] At the turn of the twentieth century, the City of London favored for the peoples of the British Empire in Africa something very like a return to slavery.

There were practically no dissenting voices. A City of London Bible Class Union spokesman complained that British "traders treat the people [of the Congo] very unfairly and tyrannically." Few paid heed, which may have been a blessing for the speaker. When a newspaper reported, falsely, that an investment firm whose partners, "needless to say, are not of English extraction" were refusing to maintain places for its clerks on war service, the City's response was violent. According to the *Westminster Gazette* of January 15,

Herzfelder of Kahn and Herzfelder was "set upon by a mob of members who had been awaiting his appearance all day. He was hooted, hissed and hustled. . . . He was thrown down and kicked. He finally fainted . . . but on coming round was maltreated again." His partner complained to the general purposes committee of the Stock Exchange but proved unable to furnish it with the names of Herzfelder's assailants, "owing to the suddenness of the cowardly attack, the pressure of the crowd and [Kahn's] consequent bewilderment." The general purposes committee therefore declined to pursue the matter. Likewise those in government: on February 2, in the House of Commons, Mr. M'Neill, M.P., "asked the Home Secretary whether the government intended to take any steps to bring the ringleaders to justice." The home secretary did not.[52]

The obverse side of the coin, however, was very much in evidence. On numerous occasions the City turned out as one to greet returning soldiers or sailors from South Africa, suspending business to wave flags and national em-

22. Reception on the Stock Exchange of the news of Cronje's surrender.
Note caricature of Jewish broker at right.
By permission of the British Library.

blems, to cheer and sing "Rule Britannia" and "God Save the Queen," above all, it would appear, to drink. When the City learned that Lord Dundonald's troops finally had broken the Boer siege of Ladysmith, for example, "by one o'clock the whole of the year's stock of champagne was sold out ⌈at Mabey's restaurant⌉ and other restaurants enjoyed a similar experience." Upon the relief of Mafeking, the stock exchange devoted three full days to celebrations. Its members arranged even for a movie camera to record these activities, so that later generations could witness the intensity of gentlemanly capitalism's patriotic and imperial sentiment.[53]

The men who gained their livelihoods in the City of London in 1900 contributed to the definition of the imperial metropolis in a number of ways: they sought to enrich themselves, their colleagues, their shareholders and thus to cement the City's role as a financial and commercial metropole; they supported and encouraged the government to pursue a forward imperial policy, to the point of themselves forming a battalion to fight the Boer War. They believed that London was the capital city of the empire, that its destiny was to reap the benefits of imperialism while simultaneously exporting the men, ideals, and expertise which ensured the destinies of millions elsewhere. Self-interested and sentimental, the City of London helped construct the most commonly held understanding of the imperial metropolis. No twists or subtle inflections here. According to the City of London, the imperial metropolis ruled.

CHAPTER 5

◈ ◈ ◈

POPULAR CULTURE IN THE
IMPERIAL METROPOLIS

IT was impossible, in turn-of-the-century London, to avoid the imperial subtext. It was present in the city's architecture, which was meant to display an imperial face to the world (although what that face should be was contentious). It was apparent at the port of London, where dockers who could touch but rarely possess the wealth of empire sought to redefine the imperial metropolis in more inclusive terms. It made unambiguous appearance in the Square Mile, where an unmediated notion of British superiority and London's imperial destiny held sway. The imperial theme appeared too in London's popular entertainments and recreations, and the messages they broadcast were, for the most part, as unproblematic as those trumpeted by the City. From their recreations and entertainments Londoners learned that British imperialists were heroes, the colonized peoples were inferior, imperialism benefited all Britons. But Londoners were not passive consumers of popular culture, they *chose* their modes of relaxation. Thus they indirectly helped to determine what those modes would be. Here as elsewhere they helped shape a constitutive element of the imperial metropolis.

Consider first late-Victorian London's innumerable exhibitions and presentations of peoples and artifacts from the imperialized territories. The South Kensington Museum (today the Victoria and Albert Museum) represented a vast imperial archive, listing, categorizing, ordering, and reordering subject peoples and their arts and crafts. During the late-Victorian period museum directors concluded that Indian objects on display were art and not mere decorations, but the manner in which they exhibited them smacked of hierarchy: Eastern art was excluded from the main part of the museum and confined to peripheral Oriental galleries. As more than one historian has argued, the purpose of the museum was consciously didactic, teaching the scope, necessity, and power of British imperialism. Indeed, even the environs of the museum, containing the Albert Memorial, the Royal Albert Hall, and the Imperial Institute, celebrated empire. It was here that organizers chose to locate the famous Colonial and Indian Exhibition of 1886. As in the South Kensington Museum, Londoners might view "the stoutly-earned results of a wide-spread domination . . . the fruits of British pluck, endurance and industry." More than five million people attended.[1]

Other London exhibitions took a similar line. The Stanley and African Exhibition of 1890 contained maps representing the continuous growth of British power in Africa and a portrait gallery of "the most eminent men connected with African enterprise . . . explorers, missionaries, abolitionists, pioneer traders, sportsmen," but not a single native African. The Greater Britain Exhibition of 1899, staged at Earl's Court (of which more below), taught that "from within the boundaries of the Empire can be procured every necessary and luxury of life more cheaply than from any other part of the globe." The chairman of the company promoting this extravaganza sought public endorsement from the Colonial Office: "There is no room for difference of opinion . . . about . . . the political advantages . . . of this proposed exhibition."[2]

By 1900 exhibitions and spectacles consciously designed to combine entertainment and tuition in the benefits of empire had become a staple of London life. Londoners and their country cousins might visit Portobello Gardens, where "Bush savages from the Wilds of South Africa every night exhibit the Habits and Customs of their Native Country, Tracking and Killing the Lion, Leopard, Buffalo, &c., and their Superstitious Bush Dance." They could call at the Royal Agricultural Hall in Islington, which displayed "70 Singalese and Tamils . . . Devil and Udakke Dancers . . . Nautch Girls, Native Wrestlers, Jugglers, Snake Charmers, and Monkey Performers." They might choose Sanger's Hippodrome and Circus, where "Bedouin Arabs . . . sons of the burning sands and exhausted wells" galloped their horses inside a big tent, or the Livingstone Exhibition at St. Martin's Town Hall, Charing Cross, where were displayed "the food, clothing, medicines and other articles necessary for the health of travellers in tropical . . . semi-civilised lands." Or they could visit the twenty-six-acre Earl's Court exhibition grounds, located in the western part of London, which was, as advertisements boasted, within an hour's railroad journey of no fewer than ten million people.[3]

In August 1900 Earl's Court, "with its deep, cool, shady nooks, its beautiful grounds, its sparkling lake," was immensely popular, but not simply because it enabled Londoners to escape the summer heat. The site contained, among other amusements, Boerland, a shooting gallery where patriots might "wipe something off the slate" and "snipe the enemy," a model goldmine in full operation to remind viewers of the profits accruing to London through the empire and why it was necessary to fight in South Africa at all, and a Kaffir Kraal, ("as inodorous as a Kaffir habitat can well be," one reviewer sniffed disdainfully), described blandly in promotional materials as "a real native village inhabited by the savages of the Dark Continent." Here the visitor could witness "savage South Africans" pursuing "their ordinary vocations, one of the most interesting being the manufacture of the lucky Kaffir bangle."[4]

The pièce de résistance at Earl's Court was yet another collection of hapless human imports: "A horde of savages, direct from their kraals, comprising 200 Matabeles, Basutos, Swazis, Hottentots, Malays. . . . Five extraordinary Koranna Women. Twenty females of various savage tribes. . . . Prince Lobengula, the Redoubtable Warrior Chieftain, who was taken Prisoner by the Troopers during the Matabele War." This was the native African component of the cast of a ridiculous drama highlighting British heroism and African bestiality concocted by Imre Kiralfy, chief among the Earl's Court impresarios. His venue was the Empress Theatre, the largest single-span covered building in London after St. Pancras railroad station. It contained six thousand seats. Under Kiralfy's sway it had been transformed into a great schoolroom where Londoners might learn the necessity of their country's domination over foreign, dark-skinned peoples.[5]

Music halls, no less popular than exhibitions in turn-of-the-century London, taught similar lessons. Whatever may have been the political content of the mid-Victorian music hall (some have argued that it emphasized the liberatory aspect of British foreign policy), in 1900 most London music halls broadcast a clarion imperial and militarist call. During January 1900 alone, at the Pavilion Leo Stormont nightly sang the Sons of Empire; at the Alhambra Harrison Brockbank recited "Sir Arthur Sullivan's fine setting of 'The Absent-Minded Beggar,'" an imperialist and patriotic paean to the British soldier by Kipling; at the Empire Mrs. Brown-Potter declaimed "Mr. Henry Hamilton's stirring poem, 'Ordered to the Front'"; and at the South London "Bonnie Kate Harvey . . . [crooned] a semi-patriotic song, 'Hands Off,' in which England and America unite, if needs be, to face the world." At Gatti's, on Westminster Bridge Road, a "new military monologue in three scenes" entitled "The Volunteer" was just opening.[6]

Music hall acts whose titles did not betray patriotic and empire-minded sentiments expressed them anyway. At the Tivoli (still in January), "Tonight's the Night," by Wal Pink, traced the adventures of Tommy Wuggs, who stumbles accidentally into a fancy dress ball. The host of the ball introduces him to Britannia, to the Boer president, Paul Kruger, to British generals and politicians, and to numerous gallant soldiers, sailors, and nurses. In the end Wuggs awards first prize for fancy dress to Britannia and a consolation prize to Kruger, who, upon inquiring what it is, learns that it will be "a darned good hiding" with the compliments of Tommy Atkins.[7]

Music halls also afforded a venue for entertainers who neither sang nor danced, but whose patriotic and imperialist sentiments remained a crucial part of their act. At the Tivoli an artist and war correspondent, Romi Ashton, nightly drew a half dozen sketches pertaining to the Boer War. "Beginning with an exceedingly ill-favoured Boer scout," reported an observer, "he went on to General Buller . . . winning the enthusiastic approval of the audience," and then in succession and to mounting favor, an Australian soldier with a broad-brimmed hat, Jack Tar, a British Grenadier, and "a Highlander charging a Boer under the motto 'One for Majuba.'" Such war artists were a popular feature of London music halls in 1900. So were "biographs," primitive projectors casting war photographs upon a screen, without which, according to a journalist, "no hall is now perfect."[8]

The editor of *Dramatic World* noted that patriotic and imperialist sentiment ran highest at the Alhambra, whose owner, Dundas Slater, "deserves warm commendation for keeping up the national spirits." Here the main spectacle throughout the early months of 1900 was "the fine tableaux ballet" entitled "Soldiers of the Queen." On January 10 this "triumph of martial military display" attracted the officers of the 17th Lancers, among whom "much enthusiasm prevailed," and, on March 16, the Prince and Princess of Wales, who complimented its producer afterward. The colonial secretary, Joseph Chamberlain, visited the Alhambra periodically. "It does me good," he is reported to have said.[9]

The Boer War provided the occasion for imperialist propaganda at so-called legitimate theaters too. In "The Absent-Minded Beggar," by Arthur Shirley (another spin-off from Kipling's poem), which opened at the Princess's Theatre in January 1900, a Boer villain covets the wife of the hero, an English soldier, but is foiled in the last act. An earlier scene depicted "a very realistic and descriptive representation of the fight on the hills round Ladysmith," including "the rattle of the guns and the thunder of the 'Long Toms,'" and volumes of smoke. "To say that the audience received this show of valour enthusiastically is to understate the fact," wrote a reviewer. "They simply screamed with delight, and cheered again and again in a frenzy of patriotism."[10]

Indeed the London playgoer might have been excused for thinking that it was nearly impossible to avoid patriotic and imperialist themes in 1900. Aside from "The Absent-Minded Beggar" at the Princess's Theatre, one could attend "The Price of Peace" at the Drury Lane Theatre, in which a British prime minister murders a foreign spy in order to maintain England's superiority over Russia, "For Auld Lang Syne" at the Lyceum Theatre, in which Boer assassins and British noblemen battle to the death, "Bootle's Baby" at the Garrick Theatre, in which a gallant army officer raises an abandoned infant, and "A Boer Meisje," in which a Boer maiden takes pity upon a wounded British officer.[11]

Arrogant cultural assumptions and racial stereotyping achieved their acme in yet another form of popular entertainment. "Nigger minstrels" played regularly to packed houses and could be hired for private parties. Sometimes the performers were African Americans; more often they were white Britons who painted their faces black. They sang songs with such titles as "Razors flying in de air," "Il Africano Imbecilio," and "The Funny Little Nigger." One verse of "Susannah don't you cry" serves as an indication of the general flavor:

> I jumped on board de Telegraph
> And floated down the river,
> De electric spark it magnified,
> And kill'd five hundred nigger,
> De engine buss, de boss run off,
> I really thought I'd die,
> I shut my eyes to hold my breath,
> Susannah don't you cry.[12]

Scholars have discerned in "nigger minstrelsy" a double edge: black people were presented as stupid, lustful, vengeful, and savage, but also the "nigger minstrel" "could act back . . . laugh at social pretension . . . mock the holders of authority and power."[13] This, however, is preposterous. Where the characters of music hall comedy might mock authority or even subvert it, the "nigger" of nigger minstrelsy was doomed to eternal subordination. What was comic about his act was his attempt to escape or to "ape" his betters. It is perverse and absurd to discover among all London entertainments the sole if muted plea for racial equality and anti-imperialism in nigger minstrelsy.

But then historians have long known that turn-of-the-century popular entertainments extolled imperial themes, including implicit and often explicit messages about the necessity of empire, Britain's world role, white supremacy, and the like, to enormous approving audiences. A less obvious venue for similar themes also existed.

Perhaps nowhere was a Londoner's identity as resident of an *imperial* metropolis more subtly or fully confirmed than at the zoo in Regent's Park. The Zoological Society of London had been established in 1827 as the result of a campaign led by Sir Stamford Raffles, who had died the year before. In 1829 King George IV bestowed the Royal Charter. The society's published

aims were primarily scientific, to advance the study of zoology and to introduce "new and curious subjects of the Animal Kingdom," but, as Harriet Ritvo
has convincingly argued, in capturing and caging wild beasts from the four
corners of the globe Raffles intended from the outset for the zoo to be a "precise and elaborate figuration of England's imperial enterprise." The very notion that one could list and classify, let alone cage, all species of animals was
an inherently imperial project. Thus the zoo came to play a role not unlike
that of the South Kensington Museum.[14]

At first the society restricted membership to an elite fellowship, while allowing nonmembers into its gardens and menagerie in Regent's Park upon
the recommendation of a fellow. A sponsoring fellow was not always available, however, and the grounds were inviting. By the late 1830s local public
houses were conducting a brisk trade in black market invitations to the zoo
at a shilling apiece. In 1846 the zoo bowed to the inevitable and formally
opened its gates to the general public. A few years later a music hall artist, the

23. Plan of zoo at Regent's Park.
Photograph courtesy of Candler Library, Special Collections, Emory University.

Great Vance, sang "Walking in the zoo is the O.K. thing to do." His song was a hit.[15]

By the turn of the twentieth century visiting the zoo had become a common form of popular recreation. More than half a million people attended annually, admission remained a shilling for adults and sixpence for children, except on Mondays, when the price was sixpence for everyone. Annual income and expenditure exceeded £30,000, and the collection of animals had increased to 2,865. By this time the society numbered nearly three thousand fellows and twenty honorary, twenty-five foreign, and two hundred corresponding members. Its president was the duke of Bedford. It owned offices at Hanover Square.[16]

In 1900 the zoo contained animals from all over the world, but many came from parts controlled by Great Britain. Every day the viewing public, including especially schoolchildren, viewed these representatives of the imperialized territories, as a glance at the zoo's Daily Occurrences book reveals. But it was not only schoolchildren who called at the zoo. The Daily Occurrences book records frequent visits made by parties of foreign visitors and of army regiments. It lists too when aristocrats and royalty stopped by.[17]

The zoo's ascent to great popularity coincided with the period of Abraham D. Bartlett's superintendency. From 1851 until 1897, when he died, Bartlett ran the zoo with great knowledge, punctiliousness, and humanity. He established the routines by which it was governed, oversaw the small army of laborers, craftsmen, and keepers who maintained the place and the animals, while himself keeping an eagle eye upon all that transpired there. He was dedicated to the animals. When the back tooth of a hippopotamus became inflamed, Bartlett extracted it with a pair of pliers four feet long; when nervous new arrivals to the menagerie needed calming, he sat up all night with them. To the dismay of his wife but the delight of his son, he took bear and lion cubs home and nursed them.

Unfortunately, during his final years Bartlett's powers waned. His son, Clarence, who had been appointed assistant superintendent and clerk of the works in 1872, gradually assumed control. The son "was a different type, of lower ability and character, a sycophant with his superiors and a bully with his inferiors." He was also a less capable manager. Under his command, especially after his father's death, the gardens began to lose their allure, the physical plant became dilapidated, the animals grew mangy and dispirited. In 1892 a group of fellows sought to halt the process of deterioration. They suggested introducing a brass band on Sundays, cheaper and more tasty refreshments, additional and better advertising. They did not, however, address the condition of the zoo's animals.[18]

Then, early in 1901, four years after Bartlett senior's death, the *Saturday Review* launched a scathing critique of the zoo's treatment of animals. "There is no exception to Buckle's dictum that wherever, amongst bodies of men, the opportunity for abuses exists there will abuses exist also," the journal declared. "In the case of the Zoological Society the opportunity exists. . . . Accordingly there are abuses." Most of the zoo's cages were too small: "These most cruel and miserable boxes contain, of course, no kind of retreat or dark recess for the animals to retire into, so that they are at the mercy of any tormentor who chooses to spit or wave his stick at them, or even to thrust it through the bars." Indeed, charged the author of this exposé, a number of animals had been literally crippled by such close confinement. Naturally Bartlett and his allies defended themselves vigorously. A revealing debate had commenced.[19]

"The dark places of the earth are full of cruelty," charged the *Saturday Review*, suggesting that the zoo at Regent's Park had become one of them. Here was a provoking assertion. Londoners were accustomed to thinking of Africa and Asia as dark places which Englishmen penetrated to shed light. It was only to be expected that their inhabitants treated animals cruelly. "The negro and the arab kill off [animals] ruthlessly for the enjoyment of the moment," one expert averred. Had the zoo fallen nearly to the level of these people? According to the *St. James Gazette* it had. "Why," it inquired, "do *Englishmen* [emphasis added] keep these splendid creatures in six-foot wire dens?" Presumably the journal would have known why "negroes and arabs" did.[20]

"We have got the best lion house and the best reptile house in the world," Philip Lutley Sclater, the zoo's secretary, riposted defiantly, playing his own nationalist and imperialist cards. It was left, however, to a "Zoological gentleman" to play trumps. The zoo's critics were "extreme humanitarians," he charged in a letter to the *Evening News*. Perhaps their regard for the comfort of animals was such that they "would like to see a diet of negro provided for the crocodiles, and the tigers regaled with best Bengal babies?"[21] Here was the no-nonsense attitude by which the zoo, and the British Empire for that matter, had been acquired and were largely governed. Big game hunters, animal collectors, British explorers, and imperial officials conferred great blessings upon the imperialized peoples and upon the people at home, by establishing the British Empire obviously, but also by capturing dangerous wild animals and transporting them to London where they could do no harm and provide entertainment as well. There was a price to be paid: the animals were less comfortable than they had been in their natural habitat, but this was a small cost. If Londoners wished to enjoy the zoo they should quit caterwauling about conditions there.

A year later the "extreme humanitarians" opened up another front in what had become a continuing campaign. They had learned that zookeepers fed live goats to a python in the reptile house. The Humanitarian League shed light upon this "dark place" with letters to the press and a series of articles in its journal, the *Humane Review*. The loyal Sclater defended this practice too. "No one except officials are allowed to see the snakes fed; it takes place at night, after the Gardens are closed." His protestations cut little ice with critics, who objected less to the spectacle than to the practice itself. They demanded the British public rise up against "the shocking barbarity of feeding reptiles with living beings (living beings, too, infinitely higher in the scale of existence than their devourers)." While barbarians might approve such practices, the civilized, "right-minded . . . British public" could not. As "J.R." wrote to the *East London Observer* at the height of the controversy, "heathens" fed live animals to snakes, but the practice was "a disgrace" in "civilised, Christian" England.[22]

Thus the zoo was as much a source of instruction as of entertainment. Londoners learned, simply by visiting, that the extent of the British Empire was great and that it had the power to capture, cage, transport, and display dangerous and exotic wild creatures. From the debate over the treatment of animals Londoners learned that while dark-skinned people treated animals cruelly, English imperialists did not. Or that if they did, they should not, because Englishmen were more civilized than "negroes and arabs." Or that anyway, as the *Court Journal*, a defender of the zoo, put it, "It may be safely assumed that the many eminent men who are associated with the Zoological Society would never countenance unnecessary cruelty."[23] Or that sentimentalists, "extreme humanitarians," could not run a zoo, let alone an empire.

The scientific method as practiced by Britons tempered hardheaded notions about "necessary cruelty." Readers of *A Walk through the Zoological Gardens*, by F. G. Aflalo, learned that British imperialists had domesticated nature itself. "The temperature of the Insect House is . . . worked out with mathematical precision," Aflalo gushed. "The assistant superintendent goes the round of his House every morning, sets his Six's (registering Fahrenheit thermometers), and notes maximum and minimum temperatures." In the house where frogs and toads were kept, "each species requires a case built on a brick foundation, with hot-water pipes below . . . [and] two feet depth of clean mould . . . for the growth of grass or other vegetation."[24]

But the taming of nature required more than Western science. It required the bravery of British sailors, as readers learned from yet another turn-of-the-century guide to the zoo: "To capture a [polar bear] and incarcerate him without injury in a cask, is a feat which few men would accomplish but the intrepid pursuers of the whale, by whom polar bears are often brought home as a supplemental venture on their return from the northern seas to Peterhead."[25]

Of course, once taken, wild animals remained dangerous. A lion caged at the zoo, "the handsomest in the building," had killed a circus attendant. A wildebeest had gored its keeper. In the reptile house, as the *Daily Mail* instructed readers, there were "cobras, vipers and rattlesnakes. The slightest negligence may mean ... death." Yet the head keeper "will make the rattlesnake and cobra perform after their kind, or show the feeding of the chameleon or venomous helderm (the only venomous lizard known to science)." Perhaps the most imposing animal in the world was the elephant. British imperialism had tamed it too. For a trifling fee children at the zoo could mount and ride one. Thus could they not merely view but touch and even claim to dominate the living, breathing animal representatives of faraway territories under British control.[26]

There is more to be said about the elephant in the Regent's Park zoo. "This well-known animal is represented by a fine female brought home by the Prince of Wales from his Indian tour in 1875–76," reported Sclater. Historians have noted how English imperialists attributed feminine characteristics to all Indians, male as well as female. The docile, sweet-tempered Jingo, as she was called appropriately enough, submitted with good nature to the indignities heaped (literally) upon her back. In this she was a far better symbol of Indian subordination to Britain than one of her predecessors had been: Jumbo had grown so unmanageable that finally his keepers sold him to the American showman P. T. Barnum, who later had the brute destroyed.[27]

One animal only were the zoo's visitors taught to treat with respect and admiration, namely, the emblematic lion. During the summer of 1900, with war fever at its height, London newspapers took particular interest in "Kruger's Lioness," which Cecil Rhodes had presented to the Pretoria zoo, but which the Boers now thought impolitic to keep. They made arrangements to transfer the animal to Regent's Park. At first the London press feared that the Boers had cut off the lioness's tail—a typical manifestation of their ignorance and cruelty, it was thought. Journalists fulminated; the public held its breath; the lioness finally arrived at Regent's Park to great fanfare and with tail intact, where she paced "gracefully" in her allotted space, "a magnificent specimen of her class," symbol of the British nation, safe in London from Kruger's evil clutches.[28]

If the riveted gaze of journalists upon Kruger's Lioness seems disproportionate, remember that one expert believed "the lion [to be] as brave as any Briton, and as little given to the ways of guile and cunning as he," while

24. Gentleman and elephant.
Credit: Hulton Getty.

another suggested that lions were as devout as Britons too because at the zoo "the Lion House was as quiet and subdued as a Quakers' meeting" every Sunday morning. To save from the dreaded Boer creatures endowed with such specifically national qualities was important indeed.[29]

Other animals, less noble in their bearing, reminded viewers of less noble human beings. A fellow of the zoo recorded, "One day I heard a little boy ex-

25. Children and elephant.
Credit: Hulton Getty.

claim whilst looking at an Orang Outan [*sic*], 'Oh ma, isn't he like a working-man?'" More usually the comparisons were explicitly racist. A species of
monkey, Humboldt's Lagothrix, was popularly known as the "nigger monkey" because of its "delightfully absurd resemblance to a black man." At least
one Londoner thought that black men and baboons not only looked, but even
sounded, alike. "There are few more pleasant sights than that of two chained
baboons thirsting for one another's blood," he wrote. "The nearest utterance
I have ever heard to it was a bout of cursing between two kanaka pearl divers
in northern Queensland. But there were no chains there, and the matter was
finally arranged with knives." The same Londoner was reminded by dingoes,
wild Australian dogs, of "their disreputable black owners." A dingo was "but
the dwindling, hunted familiar of a dwindling, hunted remnant of the human
family." Meanwhile, zookeepers had noticed the resemblance between an
orangutan in their charge and another enemy of British imperialism, not a

working man, but rather "a personage of grotesque and repulsive appearance." They named it Oom Paul, after the Boer leader. Which Londoner, then, would not have learned from the zoo that as wild animals must be caged and tamed, so must be "niggers," kanaka pearl divers, and anyone else who questioned British ascendancy in the imperialized territories?[30]

The presence of dangerous animals at the Regent's Park zoo enabled imperialists to teach additional lessons, for example, the foolishness of those peoples to whom the British had generously offered guidance and protection. According to the author of *A Walk through the Zoological Gardens*, Hindus believed that a poisonous hooded cobra like the one displayed in the reptile house had once sheltered "the sleeping Indian god from the rays of the sun" and was therefore sacred, even though the species "claimed twenty thousand victims yearly."[31] Of course, his readers must have reasoned, such uneducated people needed British protection. "The sight of [a tiger] is considered by the ignorant and superstitious Hindoos as an omen of approaching calamity," wrote the author of yet another guide to the zoo, with a condescension that bears no scrutiny. After all, if you saw a tiger in the wild would you not regard it as an omen of approaching calamity too?

In *My Book of the Zoo*, an author also interested in tigers explained to small children another good reason for the presence of Britons in the subcontinent: "Tigers prowl by day as well as by night and the amount of destruction which they cause in India is terrible . . . so that to shoot a Tiger not only gives pleasure to the sportsman but also confers a great benefit upon the natives of that country." Londoners did not have to visit the zoo, they had merely to read about it, to be instructed in the necessity of British imperialism.[32]

Beasts at the zoo often had been donated by subject peoples or by British explorers and imperialists. Visitors learned how each animal had been acquired from a label affixed to its cage. For example, on the cage of a young emu, "the gift of the New South Wales Lancers upon their departure for South Africa." Alternatively they could read about new acquisitions in the daily press: three ostriches donated by Lt. G. F. Abadie of the West African Frontier Force; "a fine young male white-tailed gnu," the gift of C. D. Rudd, member of the board of directors of Consolidated Gold Fields of South Africa, fellow of the Royal Geographical Society, the very gentleman advocating forced labor for native Africans (see chapter 4); two Grevy Zebras, the gift of Emperor Menelik of Abyssinia to "the Great Queen Victoria in England"; two panthers, donated by F. W. G. Simpson, whose husband had been posted to the Mohpaani mines, Central Provinces, India. In April 1901, several newspapers noted that the king had donated to the zoo wild boars originally purchased from India for the Windsor Great Park. Such notices must have reinforced the notion in the minds of Londoners that their city was located at the center of a great empire, that foreigners treated Englishmen and women with deference, that England's representatives, including military forces, had the right to go where they wished and to take what they wanted.[33]

Elite fellows of the Royal Society appear to have believed this. They spanned the globe in search of specimens to kill or capture, laid down the law to indigenous people, even renamed species of animals previously unknown to the collectors themselves but familiar to natives, who saw them often. For example, in 1900, one of the society's fellows, C. V. A. Peel, reported to the annual meeting on a recent expedition he had undertaken to Somaliland. Like Sir Harry Johnston, who had discovered a species of giraffe which the society then named in his honor (although the Congolese people already had a name for it), and Mary Kingsley, for whom three species of fish had been named, Peel journeyed to Africa in hopes of identifying new species of insects and arachnids and potting the occasional lion or elephant. However, at one stage of the trip

> the natives [proved] extremely troublesome, and I had a very anxious time. Several of my rifles, clothes for barter, and a pony were looted from me, and my followers were frequently attacked. . . . I went on to Kadea, looting a pony on the way in exchange for the one taken from me. Upwards of five hundred armed men made their appearance at this point, and I thought we were in for a big fight, some of the young men dancing themselves into a perfect frenzy. I was obliged to fire over their heads to keep them from looting my camels. They succeeded, however, in stealing some rifles, and I was obliged to take out my little army twice against villagers.

In Peel's cavalier theft of a horse from one African to make up for the thievery practiced by another miles away, in his disparaging remark about African warriors "dancing themselves into a perfect frenzy," and in his blasé reference to the "little army" he directed into African villages, the connections between the Royal Zoological Society in London and British imperialism could scarcely have been more starkly revealed.[34]

The London zoo was a kind of prism. Attitudes passing through it were filtered, separated out, bent to reflect imperial ideas. Like visitors to the theater, music halls, and Earl's Court, visitors to the zoo in 1900, adults and children alike, were taught the power, scope, and legitimacy of the British Empire.

✧   ✧   ✧

Londoners in 1900, then, were subjected to a continual barrage of patriotic and imperialistic propaganda. Even in the great Sherlock Holmes stories by Arthur Conan Doyle the bombardment continued. Moreover, in the Holmes stories with their cabs, Cockneys, and the great river Thames snaking through so many of them, London itself figures almost as a primary character. In these tales the relation between urban life and empire is often the axis around which the plot revolves.

Conan Doyle published the first Holmes adventure, "A Study in Scarlet," in late 1887, the second, "The Sign of the Four," in 1890, the first series of short stories during 1891–92. He thought he had killed Holmes off at Reichenbach Falls in 1893, but at public urging resumed writing about him again in "The Hound of the Baskervilles" in 1901. Between 1903 and 1927 Conan Doyle completed three additional series of Holmes stories. Almost all of them deal with events said to have taken place before October 1903, so that the London which Conan Doyle depicts is the imperial metropolis at the turn of the twentieth century.

Conan Doyle held conventional views about the British Empire. He was a patriot who volunteered for service during the Boer War and who wrote two books justifying the British cause. He attempted to invent a gauge for measuring the angle of falling bullets, so that Boers could not take cover in forts from British troops laying down a barrage. Little wonder that the stories for which he is justly famous reflect conventional imperial values.[35]

His two chief characters embody them. Watson, who narrates almost all the Holmes stories, reveals in "A Study in Scarlet" that during the second war in Afghanistan he volunteered to serve as assistant surgeon with the Fifth Northumberland Fusiliers. Holmes in "The Adventure of the Noble Bachelor" bemoans the empire's loss of America. "I am one of those who believe that the folly of a monarch and the blundering of a Minister in fargone years will not prevent our children from being some day citizens of the same worldwide country under a flag which shall be a quartering of the Union Jack and the Stars and Stripes."[36]

Conan Doyle depicts the London of Holmes's and Watson's adventures as an imperial metropolis, but not in the manner one might expect. There is little about the grand imperial buildings of Whitehall and Westminster, the colorful uniforms of its soldiers, in short, about the spectacle which empire put before Londoners. Watson sets the stage in the first of the stories, "A Study in Scarlet." Having left the service, the former army doctor "naturally gravitated to London, that great cesspool into which all the loungers and idlers of the Empire are irresistibly drained."[37]

Occasionally Conan Doyle describes London as a jungle, for example, in "The Adventure of the Empty House" and in "The Adventure of the Bruce-Partington Plans." A jungle requires careful exploration and navigation, the prerequisites to the specialist knowledge which leads to domination. Taking the Holmes corpus as a whole, London may be conceived as the disputed territory of two rival empires, a good one associated with England and personified by two English types, the brilliant amateur detective and his dogged amanuensis; and an evil one associated with criminality, often of non-European origin or when Moriarty, of Irish origin, appears.[38]

The disputed territory is depicted less often as jungle than as quotidian. "It was a very long street of two-story brick houses, neat and prim, with whitened stone steps and little groups of aproned women gossiping at the doors," Watson remarks of Cross Street in Croydon in "The Cardboard Box." Conan Doyle cites familiar streets and landmarks to make the reader feel comfortable with a London he knows, for example, in "The Adventure of the Blue Carbuncle": "Our footfalls rang out crisply and loudly as we swung through the doctors' quarter, Wimpole Street, Harley Street, and so through Wigmore Street into Oxford Street. In a quarter of an hour we were in Bloomsbury." It is this familiar London which "the dregs of empire" imperil.[39]

Or Conan Doyle makes London seem dreary and colorless. In "The Sign of the Four" London's weather is gray, foggy, and dispiriting. "A dense drizzly fog lay low upon the great city. Mud-coloured clouds drooped sadly over the muddy streets. Down the Strand the lamps were but misty splotches of diffused light." The city is as dreary as the weather. Holmes, Watson, and Mary Morstan (who will become Watson's wife) travel by hansom cab to visit Thaddeus Sholto: "Long lines of dull brick houses . . . rows of two-storied villas, each with a fronting miniature garden . . . interminable lines of new, staring brick buildings." These are descriptions of characteristic English weather, English towns, English streets. In the Holmes stories Conan Doyle presents the reader with two Londons: one which is a jungle and one whose Englishness has been emphasized.[40]

Against everyday London the exotic influence of empire stands out all the more. Despite the drabness of his neighborhood, Sholto, for example, lives in a magnificent apartment:

> The richest and glossiest of curtains and tapestries draped the walls, looped back here and there to expose some richly-mounted painting or Oriental vase. The carpet was of amber and black, so soft and thick that the foot sank pleasantly into it, as into a bed of moss. Two great tiger-skins thrown athwart it increased the suggestion of Eastern luxury, as did a huge hookah which stood upon a mat in the corner. A lamp in the fashion of a silver dove was hung from an almost invisible golden wire in the centre of the room. As it burned it filled the air with a subtle and aromatic odour.

Compare this with Watson's first impression of prosaic 221B Baker Street, the address he shares with Sherlock Holmes: "A couple of comfortable bed-

rooms and a single large airy sitting-room cheerfully furnished, and illuminated by two broad windows."[41]

This famous address requires further scrutiny. Conan Doyle always describes it as cozy, comfortable, untidy. No fewer than twenty-seven of the
sixty Holmes adventures mention the coal fire in the sitting room. References
to homey bric-a-brac and furniture abound: cigar cases, armchairs, settees,
side tables, gasogenes for soda water, and the like. It is this refuge and the dull,
quintessentially English city in which it is located that Holmes and Watson
strive to protect from the alien effects of empire.

Often one reads of the strange, menacing influences which the empire ex-
erts upon the great city. Occasionally they are human. In "The Man with the
Twisted Lip," Watson finds himself in an East End opium den. As he enters,
"a sallow Malay attendant" offers him a supply of the drug. The place is run
by "a rascally Lascar," "a man of the vilest antecedents." Isa Whitney, an Englishman, has fallen into their clutches. Sometimes, however, the influences are
more insidious and terrifying than even a "rascally Lascar." In "The Adventure of the Speckled Band," Dr. Roylett murders one stepdaughter, and nearly
does in the other by introducing into her bedroom "a swamp adder . . . the
deadliest snake in India." In "The Adventure of the Devil's Foot," Dr. Leon
Sterndale, the great explorer of "the dark continent," poisons his enemies
with a root used "by the medicine-men in certain districts of West Africa."
And in "The Adventure of the Dying Detective," Holmes "has been working
on a case down at Rotherhite, in an alley near the river," that is to say, near
the imperial docks, where, he tells Watson, he contracted "a coolie disease
from Sumatra." It is far beyond the ability of a conventional medical practi-
tioner to cure. "What do you know, pray, of Tapanuli fever?" Holmes asks the
doctor contemptuously. "What do you know of the black Formosa corrup-
tion? . . . There are many problems of disease, many strange pathological possibilities in the East, Watson."[42]

The evil pygmy Tonga in "The Sign of the Four" stands out as the most
horrible of all the human imperial imports. Tonga was "a little black man—
the smallest I have ever seen—with a great misshapen head, and a shock of
tangled dishevelled hair. . . . He was wrapped in some sort of a dark ulster or
blanket which left only his face exposed; but that face was enough to give a
man a sleepless night. Never have I seen features so deeply marked with all
bestiality and cruelty. His small eyes glowed and burned with a sombre light
and his thick lips were writhed back from his teeth, which grinned and chat-
tered at us with half-animal fury." There was only one way to deal with such
a figure. "'Fire if he raises his hand,' said Holmes quietly."[43]

In "The Sign of the Four," the imperial theme is most evident. The story
turns upon the adventures of Jonathan Small, a Worcestershire man who

winds up in India. Against the backdrop of the so-called mutiny of 1857, Small and three confederates murder a merchant attempting to convey the priceless Agra treasure to safety. They have time only to hide the loot before being captured and imprisoned in a penal colony among the Andaman Islands. Eventually Small escapes with the devoted Tonga, whom he had cured of swamp fever. In London they track down and kill Major Sholto, to whom Small had confided the treasure's location and who had stolen it. In one of the great scenes from the Holmes canon, the great detective and Watson race down the river Thames aboard a police launch in pursuit of Small and Tonga in the cutter *Aurora*. Recognizing that capture is imminent, the doomed Small flings the Agra treasure into the murky waters of the Thames. It seems poetic justice that jewels from India should be consigned to a river known as the "gateway to Empire," for surely the empire had brought nothing but disaster to Jonathan Small.

But the empire can also figure as a positive factor in the Holmes stories, and London is as often redeemed as threatened by imperialism. The empire supplies English men and women with wealth. Miss Mary Sutherland, in "A Case of Identity," has an income left to her by Uncle Ned of Auckland: "It is in New Zealand stock, paying 4½ per cent." In "The Hound of the Baskervilles," Sir Charles Baskerville made his pile in South Africa. In "The Boscombe Valley Mystery," Mr. John Turner "made his money in Australia, and returned some years ago to the old country." In "The Adventure of the Solitary Cyclist," the plot hinges on the attempt of two villains to cheat Miss Violet Smith out of the money her brother earned in South Africa and intended to leave to her.[44]

Or the empire becomes an opportune refuge. In "The Adventure of the Copper Beeches," Mr. Fowler and Miss Rucastle escape a wicked family when Fowler accepts "a Government appointment in the Island of Mauritius." In "The Adventure of the Three Students," which takes place at Cambridge University, Gilchrist, who has been caught cheating at an exam, seeks a new life in the Rhodesian police force. And in "The Disappearance of Lady Frances Carfax," the Hon. Philip Green "[finds] it better to go to South Africa."[45]

In the Holmes stories, then, Conan Doyle presents the empire in double-edged fashion. It is at once a source of deadly peril to Londoners and, paradoxically, of wealth and sanctuary. He dealt with the colonized people themselves in the same double-edged fashion. They are hideous (one of Conan Doyle's favorite words when describing Africans especially) in some stories, but stalwart, imposing, even innocent and deserving of protection in others.

That the author of the Sherlock Holmes stories harbored racist sentiments and that Londoners in 1900 were exposed to racist ideas when they read them is unsurprising. The description of the dreadful Tonga in "The Sign of the Four" stands out, but Conan Doyle usually portrays Africans as savage and bestial. In "The Adventure of Wisteria Lodge," for example, one of the murder suspects is "a huge and hideous mulatto with yellowish features of a pronounced negroid type." Confronted by the police, "he chewed Downing's thumb nearly off before they could master him." But mastering savages is something Conan Doyle regards as a Briton's natural task.[46]

On the other hand, Conan Doyle was capable of presenting black people less unsympathetically. In "The Yellow Face," the mystery turns upon the attempt of a white woman to live near her child from a first marriage to an African American and yet to keep the child's existence secret from her current English husband. Of her earlier spouse the woman says, "A nobler man never walked the earth." And when Holmes explains the situation to Mr. Grant Munro and introduces him to his stepdaughter, this second husband "lifted the little child, kissed her and then, still carrying her . . . held his other hand out to his wife."[47]

This story indicates an altogether different attitude toward race relations than might have been expected from the author of "The Sign of the Four." It is worth noting, however, that in "The Yellow Face" the late lamented first husband is described as having been light-skinned, while the daughter, "darker far than ever her father was," in fact, a "coal-black negress," is treated by Conan Doyle with ambivalence. A lighthearted child who laughs thoughtlessly when Holmes penetrates the disguise her mother so painfully created for her, one wonders how Conan Doyle would depict her if she were no longer a "little creature" (itself a demeaning term).

As with Africans, so also Conan Doyle treats Asians in double-edged fashion. In "The Sign of the Four," John Small describes the famous Sepoy Mutiny of 1857: "Two hundred thousand black devils let loose and the country a perfect hell." The mutineers attack the home of a friend. "I could see hundreds of the black fiends, with their red coats still on their backs, dancing and howling round the burning house." There is something primitive, even bestial, about the aroused Asians. They are like Africans as many Britons supposed them to be. "The beating of drums, the rattle of tom-toms, and the yells and howls of the rebels, drunk with opium and with bhang" repel Small. Yet he cooperates with two loyal Indians, "tall fierce-looking chaps" called Mahomet Singh and Abdullah Khan, in stealing the Agra treasure. Later he refuses to betray them. "'Black or blue,' said I, 'they are in with me and we all go together.'" Presumably Conan Doyle wishes us to admire Small for the loyalty he displays to his inferiors.[48]

Like many imperialists of the late nineteenth and early twentieth centuries, Conan Doyle believed there was a hierarchy of races. Anglo-Saxons occupied the top and Africans the bottom, with "Malays" and "Lascars" perhaps a notch above them and educable Indians located at the next rank. Near this level he slotted in Latin Americans too. In "The Adventure of Wisteria Lodge," the villain is a former Central American dictator who "imposed his odious vices upon a cowering people for ten or twelve years." Watson and Holmes obviously believe that the British people would never have so cowered. Other Europeans might have, or at any rate would have resisted in forms that stouthearted Englishmen would reject with scorn. Conan Doyle presents Italians in particular as adept with the knife, an assassin's weapon; for example, in "The Adventure of the Red Circle" and in "The Adventure of the Six Napoleons," where the villain, Beppo, is described in terms Conan Doyle usually reserved for Africans: "a sharp-featured simian man with thick eyebrows and a very peculiar projection of the lower part of the face like the muzzle of a baboon." In fact Beppo seems nearly as bestial as the evil Tonga: "Swift and active as an ape . . . he glared at us from the shadow of his matted hair, and once, when my hand seemed within his reach, he snapped at it like a hungry wolf." So, a rung above the Latin Americans on the hierarchy came the Italians.[49]

Conan Doyle indulged a mild anti-Semitism as well. In "A Study in Scarlet," Watson is unpleasantly surprised to find calling at Baker Street "a greyheaded, seedy visitor, looking like a Jew pedlar." In "The Cardboard Box," Holmes takes delight in having tricked "a Jew broker in Tottenham Court Road" out of five hundred guineas by paying him only fifty-five shillings for a Stradivarius violin. And in "The Adventure of Shoscombe Old Place," Sir Robert Norbeton laments his terrible position. "I am deeply in the hands of the Jews," he complains, meaning that he is deeply in debt. Perhaps the Jews ranked somewhere below the Italians? The only foreigners for whom Conan Doyle showed consistently positive regard were the Americans, and them he supposed to be largely descended from Britons. Of course the very notion of categorizing and ranking races as Conan Doyle does is inherently imperialist.[50]

In the end, Conan Doyle's approach to racial issues is best revealed at 221B Baker Street on the walls of the sitting room shared by his two protagonists. There Watson has hung portraits of his greatest heroes. One is of the American preacher and abolitionist Henry Ward Beecher. Presumably, then, Watson sympathized with the antislavery northern states during the American Civil War. However, the other portrait on the sitting room wall is of the great British imperialist Gen. Charles "Chinese" Gordon, who died at the hands of the Mahdi in Khartoum. Presumably, then, Watson also believed that

Africans and Asians required the directing hand of British imperialists like the general to guide and, when necessary, chastise them. But there was nothing contradictory about this outlook. By 1900 few Britishers believed in slavery. They would rule the colonized peoples by less odious means. Of course, it would be necessary, occasionally, to use force to maintain their beneficent sway.[51]

The Sherlock Holmes stories, like music hall entertainment, West End theater, the spectacles at Earl's Court, the London zoo itself, preached a rather simple message. Brave and wise Englishmen had established a great empire over vast reaches of the world inhabited by uncivilized, dark-skinned, people. This was good for those who had been colonized and for the colonizers. Meanwhile, foggy, prosaic London accepted as was her due the fruits of empire. Often the fruits of empire were dividends "at 4½ per cent." But when they were dart-blowing pygmies like Tonga or puff adders from India, white men such as the brilliant Holmes and the trusty Dr. Watson would deal with them as they dealt with Italians and Jews. The price of empire was eternal vigilance, but it was a price well worth paying.

Imperialism had created a public in London by 1900. It had done so, in part, through museums, exhibitions, music halls, nigger minstrelsy, the Regent's Park zoo, and the Sherlock Holmes stories. The public was enormous. The Regent's Park zoo attracted nearly a million visitors annually.[52] More than five million people visited the Colonial and Indian Exhibition; more than ten million lived within easy reach of Earl's Court, which contained a theater with six thousand seats. Music halls and theaters flourished in 1900, and the Sherlock Holmes stories were immensely popular. When Conan Doyle revived Holmes in "The Hound of the Baskervilles" in 1901, the *Strand Magazine*'s circulation rose by thirty thousand.

The public cut across class lines. If music hall primarily attracted a working-class audience, we have seen that it also charmed royalty, at least one cabinet minister, and military officers. Nigger minstrelsy likewise appealed to all classes. The "Happy Darkies" could be hired to entertain childrens' parties. They advertised in *Queen, the Lady's Newspaper*, which the working class did not read. Amateur nigger minstrels performed at church benefits, presumably for audiences not confined to workers, while the most popular professional groups, the Mohawk Minstrels and the Moore and Burgess Minstrels, performed at St. James Hall, which was located at Piccadilly and Regent Street, hardly a working-class address. The Regent's Park zoo appealed to workers, bourgeoisie, and aristocracy alike. There is no indication that the schoolchildren who visited were primarily of the working class, and in any event the zoo's day books record visits from all classes. Moreover contemporary photographs reveal obvious gentlemen and lady visitors. As for the Holmes stories, we cannot be sure who read them, but the *Strand Magazine*, costing sixpence per issue, was accessible to nearly everyone.[53]

If London's imperialist public was enormous and heterogenous, the message broadcast to it was not complex on the face of it, although the Holmes stories and perhaps a few dramas and melodramas may have qualified it to a degree. Brave Britons had brought civilization to savages, ruled them wisely, disciplined them when necessary, accepted as their due the bounty which imperialism made possible. London was the capital city of a proud and mighty empire upon which the sun never set. It was open to the colonized peoples, but if they failed to behave according to British norms then they would be punished.

There was also an implicit message transmitted in London's popular entertainments, not so readily apparent perhaps, but equally powerful. The comingling of classes at so many of London's recreations helped to dissolve inter-British differences by emphasizing inter-imperial ones. Thus the crowd which gawked at Kruger's Lioness, or which applauded the Mohawk Minstrels at St. James Hall, or which purchased for sixpence the *Strand Magazine* in order to breathlessly follow Holmes down the Thames in pursuit of evil black Tonga learned as Sir Sidney Shippard, the company director had put it, as even the leaders of the Dockers' Union believed, that "men of the imperial race should stand together shoulder to shoulder" against outsiders.[54]

The relationship between audience and performers, authors, and directors of zoos was also reciprocal, however. The men, women, and children who attended exhibits and entertainments, who read Conan Doyle's stories, were not mere sponges passively accepting imperial ideas and spouting them when squeezed. They *elected* to visit Earl's Court and the zoo and the rest and to ignore, say, George Bernard Shaw, who placed only three plays resulting in a total of seventy-eight performances during the entire decade preceding 1900.[55]

And when the London audience sat before music hall artistes or nigger minstrels, what was their relationship to them? Players play to an audience or risk losing it. Music halls and theaters, actors and authors depended upon the men and women who purchased tickets and books. The audience helps to shape the performance and its message, too. With the Sherlock Holmes stories the audience quite literally determined the text. Conan Doyle wished to quit writing about the great detective in 1892, but his readers would not let him. Presumably they wished to read not merely of Holmes's continuing adventures, but of the London which his creator depicted variously as a jungle territory disputed by rival empires and a familiar prosaic town embodying English virtues but menaced by empire and guarded by a brilliant sleuth and his gallant friend. Even when taking their relaxation Londoners helped to make their city the imperial metropolis.

PART II

Alternative Imperial Londons

CHAPTER 6

LIMNING FEMALE GENDER
BOUNDARIES

THIS discussion of female gender boundaries in the imperial metropolis begins in an unexpected place: the hallowed, elegant halls and chambers of an exclusively male organization, the august Royal Geographical Society (RGS), the body which sponsored David Livingstone, Sir Henry Morton Stanley, Sir Francis Younghusband, the polar explorers, and many others. An admiral had founded the RGS in 1830, its first president was a viscount, "its original members included the King, fifty officers of the army, all the leading statesmen of both parties including the Duke of Wellington (then Prime Minister) and men eminent in all branches of science."[1] In 1870 the society took a spacious house called Burlington Gardens at 1 Savile Row for its headquarters. In addition to sumptuous galleries, display rooms, and offices, this large square building contained a library of 31,000 volumes, map-mounting and map-drawing rooms, smoking rooms, an observatory, and an imposing, book-lined council chamber with a great fireplace at one end. It was in this room seated round the long table at its center, in an atmosphere redolent of fine cigars, leather easy chairs, masculine endeavor, and general male clubbiness, that the council of the RGS resolved with little ado on July 4, 1892, to admit women to the society on the same terms as men. In November it elected fifteen ladies as members.

Although the move to admit women seems counterintuitive given the past history and general character of the society, the council anticipated little trouble. Women travelers occasionally addressed the RGS; to the council it seemed absurd that they should be invited to speak and yet be barred from membership. Moreover women were permitted to join any number of other scholarly and popular societies headquartered in London, for instance the Zoological, the Royal Asiatic, and the Royal Historical. They might attend lectures or even deliver them, and they were entitled to make use of their facilities on equal terms with men.[2] Perhaps the factor that weighed most heavily with the council, however, was financial: the RGS was short of funds, and women members would pay subscriptions.

In fact, however, by its action an unsuspecting council had loosed the furies. A clique of reactionary members rallied by various admirals and generals and led by George Curzon, future viceroy of India and Conservative cabinet minister, questioned the legality of the move, maintaining that the decision to admit women en masse on equal terms with men required a change in the society's constitution. "That and that alone is the question at issue between the Council and ourselves," Adm. Sir Leopold McClintock argued disingenuously for the resisting members. Really the admiral and those for whom he spoke believed that women should be excluded because they were incapable of serious thought or scholarship, while moreover as fellows they would be entitled to become officers of the society, which then would inevitably degenerate under petticoat rule. "I should be very sorry to see this ancient Society governed by ladies," lamented Adm. J. Halliday Cave. "I think that if we were to admit ladies into this society it would seriously detract from the scientific value of the society, impairing our prestige and reputation in the eyes of foreign scientific bodies and thereby do[ing] irreparable damage to our interest and well being," cautioned Gen. William Francis Prideaux.

The advocates of women's admission fought back. "He certainly is behind the period who proposes the exclusion of ladies from any legitimate rights," argued Robert Needham Cust, a former president of the society. "I really could not see in what way the Society could deteriorate by the open admission of women into Membership," echoed Prof. W. H. Flower. Meanwhile the council's lawyers assured it, incorrectly as it turned out, that the decision to admit women was permissible according to the society's constitution. Thus the battle raged at specially summoned meetings and in the letters columns of the *Times*. In the end Curzon and his confederates successfully reversed the new policy on narrow legal grounds, although failing to force out the handful of women who had benefited from it. Women would not be admitted as equal members to the RGS until 1912, when, ironically, Curzon himself reversed positions to become their champion.[3]

Historians who have examined this episode have viewed it as a particularly blatant example of the pervasive sexism which afflicted not merely the RGS, but late-Victorian London as a whole. No doubt; and yet it is also true that the champions of female membership nearly succeeded in their plan and that, although they were defeated in 1893, even then they probably represented the majority of members. Three thousand five hundred and forty-six individuals belonged to the RGS in 1890. A postal ballot of the membership taken in June 1893 revealed 1,165 in favor of women being admitted "as Ordinary Fellows of the Society," 100 suggesting they be admitted "under diverse restrictions," and only 465 "direct negatives." The greatest explorer of the day, Henry Morton Stanley himself, probably spoke for many in the RGS when he supported the council: "Ladies should be admitted" he argued and went on to list some of the "distinguished women travellers" worthy of that honor. The episode, then, is as notable for revealing opposition to misogyny as for revealing the existence of misogyny.[4]

What was true of the RGS was true of the imperial metropolis more generally. No doubt imperial ideals served to buttress sexism throughout London as well as at Burlington Gardens, 1 Savile Row, that meeting place of masculine adventurers, scientists, missionaries, and geographers, all men, all dedicated to expanding, protecting, and understanding the empire. On the other hand, as Messrs. Cust and Stanley and Professor Flower had argued, the bonds of gender were not fixed or immutable in London at the close of the Victorian era. Rather, like most things, they were subject to interpretation and contestation. And as with the RGS, so with the imperial metropolis: it was not simply a fixed construct but rather a flexible and porous entity whose female gender boundaries were permeable to a degree and ever under question.

Indeed if the imperial dimension hindered women's activities it also provided space for them, presenting openings which they could scarcely have seized upon anywhere except the imperial metropolis.[5] I trace here the attempts of four extraordinary London women to explore and, where necessary, to re-limn the borderlines of feminine gender roles in their city. The four were hardly representative figures: two were aristocrats, two from the upper middle class; each was more intelligent, talented, and determined, better connected, and wealthier than the vast majority of women (or men). Neither were the four alike in their aspirations and accomplishments. Their achievements were not of a piece: the aristocrats took advantage of their elite status in negotiating the gendered margins of the imperial metropolis; the two middle-class women, who sought always to assuage popular understandings of gender roles, nevertheless subverted them to become influential imperialists in their own right. Each woman's story is intrinsically interesting and suggestive. Each yields general insights into the opportunities and obstacles all women in London faced because of their sex. Taken together the four demonstrate yet again that Londoners, women as well as men, helped shape the imperial metropolis as much as they were shaped by it.[6]

In 1900 British women could vote in some but not all local elections if they satisfied existing property requirements, but they were not permitted to serve on local elective bodies such as the London County Council; neither could they vote for or stand as parliamentary candidates. In fact it was generally held that such influence as women might bring to bear upon national politics must take place behind the scenes, where perhaps they could influence men who possessed the franchise or who were themselves involved in parliamentary politics.

What was held to be true of woman's role in national affairs applied equally to imperial politics. Women might serve as nurses, missionaries, servants, and wives to male emigrants, or upon the boards which recruited such people, but only rarely as the explorers, pioneers, soldiers of fortune, engineers, farmers, merchants, and entrepreneurs who were carving out the British Empire in faraway places, and never as the shapers of imperial policy. Yet there were women in London sufficiently privileged and ambitious to bend the rules, to enlarge the very limited space accorded members of their sex in matters political and imperial. Precisely at that point where imperialism and traditional female roles intersected most obviously in London, in the drawing rooms and dining rooms of the elite class which ran the empire, a handful of women staked their claim to a role in imperial affairs too.

At the turn of the twentieth century those who still believed in separate spheres for men and women held that women were custodians of a domestic space to which men might retreat when in need of nurturing and sustenance and from which they would emerge refreshed, to struggle and conquer in the wider world. In late-Victorian London a few advantaged women who nominally accepted this notion discovered how to satisfy orthodox expectations while fashioning for themselves a larger, more interesting, demanding, and potentially liberating role. At luncheons, dinners, and receptions which they organized, these women might meet, converse with, impress, even influence the men who ran Great Britain and the empire. They could not have accomplished the same thing elsewhere because in no other part of the country were there gathered so many politicians, cabinet ministers, and diplomats. As one political hostess, on holiday in the wilds of Sussex, put it in a letter to her friend, the great essayist and man of letters Edmund Gosse, "How dreadful it is that the country is so full of ladies."[7] She preferred London, where she might be in touch with the men who took decisions affecting the lives of hundreds of millions.

At the turn of the twentieth century perhaps a dozen great political hostesses were entertaining more or less regularly in what we may call the stately homes of London. "Lansdowne House was a favorite resort of the politicians and their followings," recalled Frances, Countess of Warwick, no mean hostess herself in her day. "It had a wonderful setting and Lady Lansdowne possessed a flair for entertainment. The Duchess of Buccleuch, at Montagu

House, received only the most exclusive circle in London." "Clever Lady St. Helier, then Mrs. Jeune, . . . could always secure a plentiful supply of Ministers, ex-Ministers, or Ministers yet to be," remembered Ralph Nevill, himself a socially rather than politically distinguished guest. "I want your astute opinion on a matter," Lord Charles Beresford, a prominent Conservative politician, wrote to Mary Jeune. And although we do not know what the matter was or what her opinion turned out to be, his request suggests the influence such women might come to wield among the great and mighty.[8]

Among political hostesses, Lady Dorothy Nevill, the daughter of Lord Orford, a descendent of Sir Robert Walpole, and the mother of Ralph Nevill, was among the best known. She was a "very small and neat" woman, recalled Gosse, who wrote a memoir of her in 1913, shortly after her death. Even in old age she had been "very pretty with her chiselled nose, the fair oval of her features, the slightly ironic, slightly meditative smile, the fascinating colour of the steady eyes, beautifully set in the head, with the eyebrows rather lifted as in a perpetual amusement of curiosity." Gosse made her laugh once, "because I told her she was like an acidulated drop, half sweet and half sour. 'Oh! Any stupid woman can be sweet,' she said, 'it's another name for imbecile.'"[9]

Lady Dorothy Nevill was far from being an imbecile. She lived and entertained less grandly than some other London political hostesses, but the range of her contacts and the extent of her political knowledge were unsurpassed. Moreover her ambitions were realistic, if limited. She aspired less to an influential voice in political and imperial affairs than to inside knowledge of them. Striving to attain this goal over the years, she managed to establish her regular Sunday luncheon as the liveliest political salon meeting on a weekly basis in the imperial metropolis.

Lady Nevill put her luncheons together with care. Her son once described her system of issuing invitations as "discriminatingly indiscriminate." Mainly she invited politicians, but she leavened her gatherings with a sprinkling of authors, artists, journalists, even actors and actresses. She seemed to know everybody, from Benjamin Disraeli and Robert Arthur Talbot, the third marquess of Salisbury, to Richard Cobden, John Bright, and William Gladstone. She regularly entertained Randolph Churchill (whom she called Randy Pandy) and his Fourth Party, which included Sir Henry Drummond-Wolff, Sir John Gorst, and occasionally Arthur Balfour. Indeed it was at one of her luncheons that Churchill and his friends conceived the Primrose League, which became the women's adjunct of the Conservative Party. Liberals and Radicals were frequent visitors as well. Joseph Chamberlain was an habitué in both his Radical and Conservative political incarnations. The Positivist philosopher Frederic Harrison was a customary guest; so was John

26. Lady Dorothy Nevill.
Credit: Hulton Getty.

Burns. And so Lady Nevill realized her ambition. Her house at 45 Charles Street, Berkeley Square, became "a sort of whispering gallery; all her friends were *dans le mouvement*," judged Lady St. Helier (formerly Mary Jeune), perhaps a trifle jealously. "Cabinet Ministers in moments of *epanchement* confided their secrets to Lady Dorothy . . . her information on every subject was most comprehensive and accurate."[10]

There was something impish or, at any rate, unpretentious about Lady Nevill. On one occasion she served fricassee of guinea pig to her unknowing guests. Reactionary in her political opinions ("I already see Keir Hardie ordering Citoyenne Nevill for execution," she worried), she was remarkably tolerant of those who disagreed with her, coaxing Radicals like Burns and Chamberlain in his early phase to her dinner table with cajoling letters. "Have I the thinnest ghost of a chance that I may see you at any time?" she importuned Chamberlain. "I am going to ask if I could ever have the pleasure of a visit from you to shew you many things that I am sure would interest you," she wrote almost beseechingly to Burns. And although her friends disapproved of her contacts with these wild men of British politics, perhaps there was method in her madness. After all, she lived to see both Radicals made tame. "The shield of your influence is really marvelous," she wrote to the man who once had set "the upper ten thousand" agog by asking what ransom they proposed to pay in order to keep their private fortunes. And to the former "man with the red flag," the erstwhile socialist new unionist Burns, now a Liberal cabinet minister under Asquith, "You are such a good member of this government that we really feel you don't want to hurt us as the other terrors do."[11]

Although ambitious for herself, Lady Nevill was no suffragette. How could she sympathize with a movement whose aim was "Votes for Women" when she did not believe in democracy? "It is inconceivable," she once wrote, "that a really enlightened society will take an admiring view of the system by which a number of individuals, the large majority profoundly ignorant and a great number quite indifferent, are . . . accorded the right of electing other individuals, generally not much better equipped for ruling than themselves." On the other hand she was something of a feminist: "Woman was formed as the help-meet for man; she was not [meant] to be the slave to a tyrant but the companion of an equal."[12]

Nevill's manner and mode of interaction with men never made them uneasy, but rather conformed to stereotype. She gossiped with her guests about social as well as political affairs. "I hear the awful news that Mr. Chamberlain is going to enter into a dual existence with a Miss Potter—what a bore," she confided, inaccurately as it turned out, to the editor of the *Fortnightly Review,* Thomas Hay Sweet Escott. And some years later, to Chamberlain himself, "What do you say to Lady Tweedale's marriage—35 and 46—and 2 husbands before. The Jeunes, I hear, very angry." So shrewd a judge of character is unlikely to have chosen this tone without calculation. Occasionally she played the helpless or ignorant female, which she certainly was not. "If you have a moment to dispose of," she wrote to Chamberlain, "waste it on a poor woman who is really improving under your tuition." She flattered the great men who sat at her table: "You are a savior as well as a wonder," she wrote to Chamberlain again. Above all, she encouraged their confidences. "You know how discrete I am," is a line that recurs more than once in her correspondence with political men.[13]

Yet she was far more than the passive, admiring female that most Victorians expected women to be and that perhaps unperceptive observers imagined her to be as well. When she chose to act on their behalf, Nevill could prove useful to her many guests. For example, when Escott wanted an interview with the Liberal cabinet minister Henry Fawcett, she arranged for one by inviting John Gorst of the Fourth Party to luncheon. She suggested that Gorst bring Fawcett, with whom he was friendly. Her guest agreed to do so. "Mr. Gorst is, I believe, going to bring Mr. Fawcett to luncheon tomorrow," Nevill then wrote triumphantly to Escott. "Will you come?" And she was more than a mere go-between. As the hostess of London's best-known and most popular political salon she acquired a profound knowledge of her country's politics and thus could serve as something of an advisor to her friends. "Mr. G. Russell has not made up his mind whether he will contest Lord Baring's seat," she informed Chamberlain at one point. "I hear if he did he would have a good chance."[14]

If there were Victorians who still believed that a woman's sphere was the home and that women were charged with overseeing the gustatory and social realms in particular, then Dorothy Nevill did not challenge them. She triumphed over them nevertheless. Not herself an actor on the political or imperial stage, she knew the actors, proved helpful to them, possibly even influenced them. She leveraged her seeming acquiescence to public expectations of women into a role that was more active, interesting, and important than women customarily filled. She leveraged, too, her privileged position. After all, it was not she who cooked the food or set the table for her illustrious guests. The path she followed to the edge of the gendered imperial metropolis, an edge she took care not to cross, was one which the vast majority of women could not take.

Other, grander political hostesses cherished grander ambitions. Recalling these now-forgotten figures as she approached the end of her own extraordinary career, "Daisy," Countess of Warwick, gave pride of place to "the most Conservative woman I have known," the "born dictator" Theresa Susan Helen Chetwynd Talbot, who became the sixth Lady Londonderry when, nine years after her marriage in 1875, her husband Charles Stewart, Viscount Castlereagh, succeeded to the title. At the turn of the twentieth century, Lady Londonderry had not, perhaps, reached the height of her powers and influence. That would come in 1906, when, again according to the Countess of Warwick, she single-handedly "broke up the Liberal-Conservative association . . . [because] Asquith and Lloyd George began to show that reform would not wait any longer upon the convenience of the governing classes," and again in 1911, when "her influence was behind the revolt of the peers, which led to a threat that the House of Lords should be flooded with new creations." We may take Daisy Warwick's claims for the marchioness with the proverbial grain of salt, but even in 1900 Lady Londonderry was a force with whom the political world had to reckon.[15]

"I began liking politics when I was only ten years old," the marchioness wrote toward the end of her life, and she never ceased her passionate involvement with them. Her father, the nineteenth earl of Shrewsbury, had been a Conservative M.P. who introduced her to Disraeli and Gladstone. Her husband the marquis, earl of Londonderry after 1884, was also an active Conservative who served in Salisbury's and Balfour's governments and who took a leading role as a "Die-hard" opponent of Home Rule and reform of the House of Lords. It is a moot point, however, as the countess of Warwick points out, whether he or she was the real leader.[16]

In any event, Lady Londonderry aspired to more direct influence over political and imperial affairs than Dorothy Nevill. There is a reliable report that in 1903, when her husband was lord president of the council in Arthur Balfour's Conservative government, the marchioness presided over one of his meetings, quizzing the permanent secretary and his staff "while Lord Londonderry sat in 'isolated dignity' at the head of the table."[17] Three years into the twentieth century such practices could not continue. They seemed to subvert a natural order. But she understood very well how else, and above all where else, a woman with her advantages, abilities, and ambitions might significantly influence matters of state.

Lady Londonderry was a short woman. In the words of one historian, "Her head seemed to be a little too large; but her features were beautifully moulded, and she would have seemed even fairer to look upon had it not been for her haughty expression." "Clearheaded, witty and large-hearted, with unrivalled experience of men and things, social and political," according to one who knew her well, she was also "one of the most striking and dominating feminine personalities of our time." E. F. Benson, the novelist, thought "she liked violence and strong colour." Lady Londonderry, he recalled, "'went for' life hammer and tongs. She collared it and scragged it and rooked it like a highwaywoman in a tiara, trampling on her enemies, as if they had been a bed of nettles." She was, in short, a remarkable figure who saw, perhaps more clearly than Dorothy Nevill did, how a woman in her position might turn conventional notions of female space and place inside out.[18]

Obviously the domestic sphere she occupied was hardly typical, but the course she charted ensured that, in any event, she had no need to leave it while transcending conventional feminine roles far more completely than Lady Dorothy Nevill ever did. The scene of her many triumphs was her home, Lon-

27. Lady Londonderry.
Credit: Hulton Getty.

donderry House, in Park Lane, a huge private palace with vast, high-ceilinged state rooms leading one into another from a wide, pillared gallery above the most magnificent square staircase in London. Its walls were hung with damask, while from the ceilings were suspended crystal chandeliers. The palace "provided a perfect setting for the fashionably dressed crowds glittering with satins, jewels, stars, orders and decorations which so often filled" it. Perhaps Lady Londonderry already understood that architecture can influence history.[19]

At any rate she used her home for her own purposes, reveling in but also expanding the nature of the traditional womanly role of hostess. On the one hand she "frankly and unmitigatedly enjoyed standing at the head of her stairs when some big party was in progress, hugging the fact that this was her house, and that she was a marchioness from top to toe and was playing the part to perfection."[20] On the other, as the familiar, soon the confidante, of statesmen, diplomats, politicians, cabinet ministers, even royalty, she placed herself at the center of events without ever having to venture from Park Lane. Like Dorothy Nevill, she navigated the very edge of gendered London from her home, but she probed it more thoroughly and, as a result, triumphed more completely. She embraced with open arms her role as the queen of receptions, luncheons, and dinners in order to transgress gender roles in the broader sense, in order, that is, to participate on near-equal terms with men in the wider world of national and imperial politics.

Under the marchioness's direction Londonderry House became a meeting ground not merely for her own country's but for the world's leaders. She did not seek to replicate the informal atmosphere of Lady Dorothy Nevill's luncheons, which politicians found "a pleasant relaxation," and where, "knowing how discreet their hostess was they could freely discuss political moves and counter-moves."[21] Lady Dorothy Nevill had carved a peculiar niche for herself in the male domain of politics, but Lady Londonderry aimed higher. She wished not merely to meet and to know the political elite, nor even occasionally to prove useful to them, but rather, through them, to influence events herself.

Her receptions, always conceived on the grandest scale, became famous. Men whose names did not yet appear on her guest lists angled for invitations. "I hope to be in England six weeks at least, perhaps longer and shall be in or quite near London all this time," Alfred Milner, who in fact became a frequent guest, wrote to her importuningly upon his return to Britain from South Africa. No one was too grand or too important to dine with her, while to decline an invitation was to risk the political wilderness. Lady Londonderry would accept only one excuse, an invitation from the single woman in Britain higher in the pecking order than herself. These were forthcoming more often than she may have liked. "I have just been telegraphed for to Balmoral," apologized Britain's foremost military man, Gen. Redvers Buller, explaining why he could not attend at Londonderry House the next day. "I have just been commanded to Windsor," repeated Chamberlain when he could not accept a similar invitation. "I have just got a telegram ordering me to Windsor tomorrow," explained Balfour. "There is an end of dinner with you. Isn't it a bore?"[22]

More often than not, however, invitees accepted Lady Londonderry's summons with alacrity. The marchioness hosted Indian princes, the Khedive of Egypt, the Aga Khan, the colossus of South Africa, Cecil Rhodes, who was a frequent guest while he was in London, and, on a more or less regular basis, practically every important British political figure of the era, including Prime Ministers Salisbury, Balfour, Archibald Philip Primrose, earl of Rosebery, and Gladstone, Britain's first commander-in-chief during the Boer War, General Buller, and most of the era's important cabinet ministers, especially if they were Conservative. Nor were even these the most august of her guests. "The King desires me to say that, should you be at home at 5:30 this afternoon, he would much like to call on you then," his secretary, Lord Knollys, penned in precise copperplate early in 1901.[23]

Lady Londonderry's entertainments were designed to impress. "Champagne, quail, *fois gras*," the countess of Warwick remembered nostalgically. "The meal was sumptuous," recalled John Morley of a luncheon at London-

derry House in 1891, "the music not too loud; each table with a little moun-
tain of roses, all pink here and deep rose there and so forth. Coffee and cigarettes in the fine gallery." Of course, the handsome marchioness was impressive in her own right. Sir A. D. Wolff, British ambassador to Spain, thought
her London's "most intelligent, beautiful and winning hostess." Gladstone's
elderly former chancellor of the exchequer, Sir William Harcourt, paid court
as if smitten: "Your society has not only a physical but an intellectual charm
about it. 'With thee conversing I forget all time.'" And in another letter: "It
is more agreeable to differ from you than to agree with other people." Conservatives were equally enchanted. "I should so much like to have a long talk
to you again. It is useless to attempt to write," complained Milner, now returned to South Africa. "I have been longing to see you to talk over all the ex-
citing events of the last six weeks," George Wyndham, a rising Conservative
politician, wrote to her early in 1896, shortly after Frederick Jameson had
launched his ill-starred raid in South Africa.[24]

Clearly, however, there was more to it than her champagne and charm.
Had Lady Londonderry been merely a good-looking and well-spoken woman
who provided a grand setting for lavish dining, then she would have been in-
distinguishable from a number of other socially prominent hostesses. Governments, however, did not turn to them for assistance; they turned to Lady
Londonderry. The luncheon in 1891 described by John Morley had been
given in honor of the German emperor upon his first visit to England since
ascending to the throne. This was an event that must have been arranged at
the behest of government. More than a decade later British governments
were still requesting Lady Londonderry to entertain visiting notables. "I en-
close the [guest] list [of Spanish dignitaries], cut down as much as I can,"
wrote Sir Douglas Dawson from Ambassador's Court, St. James Palace. "The
names, after the four ladies, are in what I think is order of importance. There
are reasons for all on the list being shown all the civility possible."[25]

Tact and judgment were necessary when entertaining foreign guests.
They were called for when entertaining British politicians as well. Like Lady
Dorothy Nevill, Lady Londonderry possessed these virtues in abundance,
else she would never have gained the confidence of so many important political figures. Harcourt engaged in a kind of political gossip with her which
suggests great trust. "G. Balfour will be a bad appointment at Board of
Trade," he noted cattily in one of his letters to her. "He is hopelessly unfit to
deal with men and quite incapable of handling such business as strikes &c."
And in another letter he ticked off the members of a reshuffled Conservative
cabinet: "Lansdowne . . . that he can [speak?] French does not prove that he
can act English. . . . Harbury . . . no good. . . . Ritchie hardly of calibre for the

first Lord." The Conservative politician Matthew Ridley equally counted on her discretion. "You were so kind in talking to me about political arrangements," he wrote immediately after the Conservative victory in the general election of 1900, "that perhaps you may care to have from myself (of course in confidence till the Queen's pleasure is known) that I have accepted the Home Secretaryship."[26]

Such letters cannot replicate what was said at the receptions and dinners over which Lady Londonderry presided, but they are suggestive. Political gossip and confidences were obviously a staple; that her guests discussed "political arrangements" with her suggests something more. The marchioness was more forthright in her attempts at active intervention than Lady Dorothy Nevill. "I am glad you have written to Devonshire" supporting physical education at school for girls as well as boys, Lord Lansdowne affirmed after one of her dinners. And she was more likely to see her designs translated into action. "I have spoken to the Prince of Wales about what you said to me today respecting the Paris Exhibition and the Irish Industries, and he thinks the idea is a very good one," Lord Knollys reported in a typical note. And a week later: "The Prince of Wales . . . has no doubt it can be carried out." Thus without leaving the domestic sphere or offending men who still believed that woman's place was in the home, Lady Londonderry managed, as one historian puts it, to "influence, introduce, exert patronage and dazzle." Another scholar writes, "Junior Cabinet Ministers deferred to [her], flattered [her], went in fear of incurring [her] displeasure. . . . One suspects that [even] Cabinet lists were drawn up . . . at Londonderry House."[27]

Only one politician failed to accord her the respect she demanded and deserved. The Liberal leader Lord Rosebery, with whom Lady Londonderry exchanged letters for nearly two decades, treated her, at least in his correspondence, as a foolish woman not fit for serious discussion of important matters. He was charming, witty, and, probably unknowingly, condescending. One letter, written from 10 Downing Street, while he was prime minister, establishes his tone. At a dinner the previous evening Lady Londonderry had chided him for accepting her invitation with a typewritten note. Rosebery defended his use of the machine and, next day, returned to the subject in another brief (typewritten) letter: "This great question . . . like that of the House of Lords, cannot now rest here. It requires a solution. Men cannot solve it: it belongs to the large, growing and delicate class of what are called 'Women's Questions.' . . . I would respectfully ask you to impanel a jury of matrons—highborn and fastidious, but alive to the spirit of the age—to decide this knotty point."[28] No other of Lady Londonderry's correspondents adopted this tone with her. Perhaps none dared to.

Her correspondence with General Buller is among the most revealing in the vast collection of her papers contained at the Northern Ireland Public Record Office in Belfast. Lady Londonderry was, according to Buller's wife, "his greatest woman friend."[29] Perhaps this partly explains why she became among the best informed of all British citizens about the progress of the Boer war, the morale of British soldiers and officers, Britain's military strategy, and relations between the army and the government. But there was more to their relationship than simple friendship. Buller tried out his ideas on Lady Londonderry, looking to the marchioness for wise counsel and, more, for help. In this way Lady Londonderry may have come to exercise some influence over imperial affairs.

On June 23, 1899, while British representatives were still negotiating in Bloemfontein with the Boer president, Paul Kruger, and while most Britons were waiting in suspense to learn their government's intentions, Buller shared with her the news that he had been given "command of the expedition to South Africa . . . (this is supposed to be a secret)." Two weeks later he confided to her that Lord Lansdowne of the Foreign Office had instructed him to prepare for embarkation in six weeks' time.[30] He did not depart on schedule, but as the date approached he maintained a steady correspondence with her, confiding Britain's military strategy in the process. "The real military questions turn about the action of the Orange Free State," he wrote in a letter of September 24. "If they join the Boers we shall go up through Bloemfontein. That will mean that the expedition will start from the Cape Colony and not from Natal." Ten days later he was discussing with her the military timetable: "The Reserves are to be called out on [October] the 7th, and the first troops will embark on the 20th. I go out on the 14th." Needless to say this kind of information was hardly available to the general public.

Once arrived in South Africa, Buller continued to be astonishingly indiscreet with his favorite correspondent: "I am going to make my main advance not through Natal but through the Orange Free State, from Cape Colony. This is *secret*, so please tear this letter up and keep it dark; we are trying to make the press and everyone believe that we go through Natal." And when the Boers confounded his plans he made new ones which he again confided to Lady Londonderry: "I hope myself to leave . . . for Natal to try conclusions with the Boers there. Lord Methuen should start on Monday towards Kimberly. . . . After these two operations are on I might be able to commence an advance on Bloemfontein without delay." Moreover, Lady Londonderry was more than the passive recipient of such confidences. When Buller changed his military strategy she asked him why he had done so, and the general felt constrained to make explanations: "You ask in your letter of the 24th . . . why

I went to Ladysmith and abandoned my original plan of going through the Free State. . . . The main point is this. On 2nd November Kimberley and Ladysmith were invested and 4000 Boers had invaded the Cape Colony. My troops sufficient for the attack on Magersfontein could not arrive till 15 December. . . . Could I let Natal be overrun and Kimberly fall while I was waiting?" Doth the general protest too much? Can Lady Londonderry have been disputing tactics with him?[31]

Probably not, but Buller did believe that she had sufficient influence over policy makers at home to be of use to him. He returned to London, his military reputation tarnished irretrievably as a result of his failed campaign, to discover that he had been demoted to command of the Fifth Army Corps. Worse still, his command would be for two years only, after which he must retire. Generals Broderick and Roberts had authorized a statement to the press to this effect. "That is to say," the former commander-in-chief complained, "they openly ally themselves against me. . . . I wish you would find out for me if you can whether Broderick was a party to doing it. Honestly I thought he was a fairer, better fellow." In other words, General Buller thought that Lady Londonderry's sources of information were superior to his own. Nor was this the only occasion when he turned to the marchioness for assistance. "I have today had the most curious experience of my whole life," he wrote to her, rather mysteriously, shortly after his return to London from South Africa. "I have not digested it yet sufficiently to write it, but I will tell you when we meet, and I think you may be able to help me."[32]

Thus Lady Londonderry. "Rising politicians became her protégés," notes one historian.[33] Those like General Buller who were no longer on the rise continued to seek her help and protection too. The "highway woman in a tiara" had taken advantage of her privileged position not to explode gender boundaries for all women but rather to stretch them for herself. In so doing she demonstrated that London's female gender boundaries were elastic, at least for a select few at the pinnacle of the high society of which she was queen.

Ladies Nevill and Londonderry were figures who subverted and expanded roles open to women without, as it were, blasting the gendered spaces to which custom and tradition might have confined them. There were women in turn-of-the-century London, however, who pushed the boundaries to the limit, although even they conformed in their public manner to orthodox expectations. One such woman was Flora Shaw, a journalist who by 1900 had worked her way to the very apex of her profession, becoming the first colonial editor of the *Times*. "I went to see Miss Flora Shaw [because] I thought she might know something," a frustrated Buller wrote to Lady Londonderry when he felt that Salisbury's colonial secretary had been insufficiently forthcoming with him. And his trip was not in vain: "She told me that she believed Mr. Chamberlain was meditating sending Kruger an Ultimatum on the 15th or before."[34]

In Flora Shaw's career one may trace not merely the boundaries of female space and the caps put to female aspirations within the imperial metropolis, but also the singular path of a forceful and intelligent woman who managed to transcend them more completely than even Lady Londonderry had done. Because she was successful at a highly competitive, male-dominated profession, she was in a position to deal with men of affairs differently from the political hostesses, who sought information and influence without leaving the domestic sphere. Shaw, however, was equally at home in the Colonial Office questioning permanent officials, principal private secretaries, and colonial ministers and at London's great political receptions and dinners, of which she was a regular attender, and where she might have the chance to quiz such figures a second time. For that matter, she was also at home on the African veldt, the Canadian Yukon, the Australian outback, and in chancelleries, consulates, and embassies everywhere. As a world traveler, as the first woman to deliver a lecture to the Royal Colonial Institute, as the author of the *Times*'s regular "Colonies" articles, above all, as an influential editor of the most influential newspaper in the world, Flora Shaw helped not merely to disseminate but also to shape Britain's imperialist ideology and policy.

Like the elite political hostesses, Flora Shaw came from Britain's ruling class. Her grandfather, Sir Frederick Shaw, Bart., a prominent public figure, had been secretary for Ireland in 1846; her father was a general, her mother a French aristocrat said to be descended from Louis XV. The family was not wealthy, however, and Flora Shaw, who received little formal schooling, took it upon herself to fund the education of her younger sisters. This decision suggests in itself a person dissatisfied with traditional expectations for women. To earn money she began writing a historical romance. In 1877 she published her first novel, *Castle Blair*, which was enormously successful, and a number of short stories for girls in *Aunt Judy's Magazine*. Earlier she had befriended and beguiled Ruskin; now a well-known author herself, she gained entrance to literary circles, becoming friends with George Meredith and Robert Louis Stevenson, among others.[35]

From literature to journalism: the step was logical for a young woman increasingly aware of her intelligence and powers and determined to pay her own and her sisters' way. Meredith had introduced her to W. T. Stead, editor of the *Pall Mall Gazette*. When Shaw discovered and interviewed the notorious Sudanese slave trader Zebehr Pasha, whom the British had exiled to Gibraltar, Stead published her sympathetic account of their conversations. This launched her journalistic career. When she crossed over from Gibraltar to Morocco, Stead again published her acute, well-informed observations. She followed up this exploit with a series of articles for the *Contemporary Review*. Established now as the author of penetrating and popular analyses of southern Mediterranean conditions, she traveled to Egypt, where she greatly impressed Sir Evelyn Baring, Lord Cromer, the British agent and consul-general, who "recognized in Flora one too intelligent and clear-sighted to be confused by sentimentality, [and] who might influence the [Radical] *PMG* to a more realistic approach to Egyptian politics."[36]

Cromer's insight was a shrewd one. Like a number of upper-class women during the 1880s Shaw had been drawn to charity work in East London, which accounts in part for her early affinity with the Radical Stead. But as she watched the tall ships entering and leaving dockland, it occurred to her that the solution to Britain's poverty lay not in Britain itself but in the lands overseas, which were, to her mind, rich in resources and opportunities for British emigrants. To this idea she adhered for the rest of her life. Even at the outset of her journalistic career in 1887 she was a convinced imperialist. Of equal note, imperialists like Cromer recognized in her a potentially valuable ally. Somehow, in the governor's mansion in late-Victorian Cairo, where one would have least expected openness to new ideas about women's roles, a young female journalist had broken through.

In November 1889, C. P. Scott sent her to Brussels to report for the *Manchester Guardian* on an international conference on the slave trade and other African questions. There she interviewed the conference president, the Belgian Baron de Lambermond, who told her that two civilizations were contesting for control of Africa: Islam, which was "spreading from the north like a stain of oil" and which represented the civilization of the East, and Christianity representing the civilization of the West. "They will decide their quarrel by force," the baron predicted, but the West would prevail, not least because it insisted upon raising Africans from all forms of degradation, including the slavery which Islam brought in its train. This was particularly rich coming from a subject of King Leopold, despoiler of the Belgian Congo, but Shaw found Lambermond's views to be "at once the most moderate, hopeful and practical that I have yet had exposed to me."[37]

At this conference Shaw attempted, possibly for the first time, to influence British imperial policy not through journalism, but extrajournalistically, as it were. If the West was to win Africa by abolishing degradation there, then obviously, according to many imperialists, it must ban the sale of arms

28. Flora Shaw.
Courtesy of News International Associated Services Ltd.

and liquors to Africans, who, they believed condescendingly, were unlikely to use them wisely. Shaw thought that Britain should take the lead in establishing such prohibitions. She had learned, however, that the British Foreign Office was permitting interested parties to influence its policies. Flora Shaw wrote to W. Allen of the Anti-Slavery Society back in London, suggesting that his organization raise an agitation against the arms and liquor traders: "Have you any means of conveying to the Government a conviction that the public is with it, and will support it?"[38]

Shaw's connections with the Anti-Slavery Society, however, and even with the *Manchester Guardian*, standard-bearer of British liberalism and of British anti-imperialism, or Little-Englandism, were uncharacteristic. She would leave them behind as she had forsaken Stead's *Pall Mall Gazette*. While in Egypt Shaw had made contact with a journalist whose views on imperialism coincided more nearly with her own than Stead's or C. P. Scott's. This was Moberly Bell, who in 1890 became assistant manager of the *Times*.[39] The relationship with Bell developed into both a professional association and a life-long friendship. "If you were a man you would be Colonial Editor of the *Times* tomorrow," Bell told her and, although it took a little longer than that and required Bell to engage in some fancy footwork to persuade his superiors to hire a woman, colonial editor of the *Times* Flora Shaw duly became.

By late 1891 Shaw was writing not merely a regular column on colonial matters for the *Times*, but even leaders for its editorial page. In 1892 Bell sent her to South Africa, where she met and interviewed all the principal figures, not merely Rhodes, whom she had known and admired since his visit to London three years previously, and Rhodes's confederates, but his Boer enemies, including the Transvaal president, Paul Kruger. The *Times* published her "Letters from South Africa" as they arrived in Printing House Square and later made them available as a short book, further cementing her reputation. Shaw's journey, however, had only begun. From Africa she sailed to New Zealand and Australia, where, again, she met and interviewed all the most prominent men, thence to San Francisco and Vancouver, and finally, by rail, across Canada to Montreal, posting reports of men, conditions, and politics along the way. The *Times* printed them all. Returned to London early in 1893, she was asked to deliver the address on Australian affairs to the Royal Colonial Institute, which made her the first woman to speak before it. By now she really had seen much of Britain's empire and was rightly regarded as an expert on colonial matters.

At this stage of her career, as for the rest of her life, Shaw's view of the British Empire was relatively unproblematic. She believed that the further it extended, the better, not merely for Britain but for everybody. It was self-evident to her that, at the close of the nineteenth century, European civilization was more advanced than any other and that among Europeans, as she once wrote to Chamberlain, "we are the first." Why this should be the case, she did not attempt to decipher—"The mystery of the decadence of peoples is among the great operations of Nature for which we have no explanation," she wrote—but she was determined to do all in her power to strengthen and expand Britain's undecadent imperial reach. She believed such work was holy, "raising and enlarging our plane of existence and making of us a finer race than history has seen before."[40]

Her approach to subject populations was inherently imperialist. In a typical article for the *Times*, she classified "the three main divisions" among Nigeria's inhabitants as if they were lepidoptera and she a scientist sent to study them. Of human solidarity there was none. The "pagans" of Nigeria represented "the lowest civilization of the country." The "Foulahs" were "Mohamedan Arab[s], relatively light coloured, of the well-known type," that is, vicious slavers. The "Hausas" were "the most interesting of the races which inhabit the country." They originally had migrated to Africa from Asia, Shaw believed, which perhaps explained why, although "the pure-bred Hausa is perfectly black," he was also "of a far higher type than the ordinary negro, and differs from him especially in the fact that he is naturally active, persistent and industrious."[41]

Shaw ascribed, then, to the so-called scientific racism of her era. Ordinarily she was not so crude as Professor A. H. Keane, F.R.G.S., who attributed the "hopeless inferiority" of Africans "to the premature closing of the sutures of the Negro skull, thus preventing the development of the mental faculties up to the normal level of the higher races." Shaw merely believed, as she put it in one of her "Letters from South Africa," that "the black man" was "behind the white man in civilisation, but subject to precisely the same laws of human development." Of course, she admitted, some lagged farther behind than others. As against the industrious Hausas of northern Nigeria there were the "pagan races [of southern Nigeria, who] . . . may be seen in a condition not far removed from the primitive nudity of the forest apes," and the people of Pondoland, whose "ruling chief Sigcan, roasted his stepmother the other day," and "the majority of the chiefs" of Basutoland, who "have become habitual drunkards." Then "there is a tribe which is reported to have tails, and there is another which would appear to justify the Greek legend of the Amazons." Perhaps the differences between the journalist and the academic were not so great after all.[42]

Shaw believed that the first aim of British imperialism must be to establish the rudiments of European civilization among such peoples and then, over the course of many decades, to bring them up to European standards. Obviously British rule would have to be introduced and maintained by force, but "the administration of India, where this aspect of the question has long been appreciated," and "the work done by England in Egypt" were proof "of our capacity for autocratic rule."[43]

The profits which accrued to Britain as a result of empire were never far from Shaw's mind either. She was particularly interested in West Africa, in part because she idolized Sir George Taubman Goldie, whose Royal Niger Company originally pacified the region and paved the way for formal British rule there, later because from 1897 on she was much interested in the career of a young army officer, Frederick Lugard, whom the government had sent to West Africa and whom she would eventually marry. Over the years she wrote dozens of articles extolling the potential wealth which Britain might tap in that corner of the world. A typical column listed the "rubber, she butter [whatever that is], palm oil, wood, oil, gums and many other articles of modern trade . . . in quantities which represent an almost limitless addition to the circulating wealth of the world."[44] Her "Colonies" articles for the *Times*, however, ranged over the full extent of Britain's dominion, cataloguing the riches it contained, from the lobsters of Newfoundland to the gold and gems of South Africa, all of which, Shaw assured her readers, helped ensure prosperity at home.

A more staunch defender of Conservative policy toward the colonies and of individual British imperialists, it would be hard to conceive. Her articles on the Royal Niger Colony were so laudatory that Goldie's biographer believes Shaw asked him to help her write them. Her articles on Rhodes, "the statesman . . . the visionary," were worshipful. When it came to Rhodes, even in private she could hardly contain herself. "I have met now most of the English public men of my day and the impression conveyed to me by Mr. Rhodes is of an unselfishness of aim greater and more complete than I have ever recognized before," she gushed to Lugard. She favored every development which might strengthen and bind the colonies more closely together, for example, Australian federation, which came in 1900, and a railway from the Cape to Cairo, and the Pacific cable, which linked Canada with Australia. A firm believer in imperial preference, Shaw advocated the abolition of tariffs between Britain and the colonies. She was thus a fervent supporter of Joseph Chamberlain, the great exponent of imperial free trade and imperial federation, with whom beginning in July 1895, when Salisbury appointed him as colonial secretary, she held weekly meetings. Indeed, as events were to demonstrate, Shaw would go to great lengths to support the new colonial secretary's designs.[45]

Just how far that was, however, is a matter shrouded even today in mystery. Recognized, in the mid-1890s, as an authority on colonial matters by the class of people who read the *Times*, Shaw burst upon the consciousness of a wider public during the summer of 1897, as a result of a parliamentary inquiry into the infamous Jameson Raid of the previous year. The raid, we now know, had been intended by Cecil Rhodes and Chamberlain to overthrow the Boer government in the Transvaal. They intended to take advantage of the resentment felt by *Uitlanders*, British residents of the Transvaal who were denied full rights of citizenship, to remove a troublesome and potentially threatening regime north of the Cape Colony and to establish a loyal British outpost there instead. The problem was that, although the Uitlanders were prepared to protest and agitate against Kruger's government, they were not prepared to overthrow it. When Jameson, carrying the British flag, launched his ill-fated raid into the Transvaal, the Uitlanders failed to support him. Consequently Jameson and his men were captured, Rhodes was implicated in their abortive scheme, Chamberlain's name hovered in the background, and in London the Liberal opposition launched an inquiry into the government's role in the affair.

The complex intrigues of this plot have never been fully revealed, but it is clear that Shaw and other *Times* editors played an important role in it. In particular Shaw and Moberly Bell acted as go-betweens for the South African plotters led by Rhodes and Chamberlain. Shaw knew well both archconspirators. Perhaps not surprisingly Rhodes entrusted her with the British South Africa Company's private code for secret cablegrams and registered her as Telemones London to receive them.

Three of Shaw's cablegrams to Rhodes during the weeks before Jameson's Raid have come to light. The first asks, "When will you commence the plans?" The second warns, "Delay dangerous." The third, dated December 17, 1895, reads in part, "Chamberlain sound in case of interference European powers but have special reason to believe wishes you must do it immediately." In addition Shaw received secret telegrams from Rhodes and his agents during the run-up to the raid and was mentioned by name in a number of telegrams sent to Rhodes by his chief assistant, Dr. Rutherford Harris. Also, when the raid proved a fiasco and Chamberlain felt compelled to denounce it from London, Shaw carried to him at the Colonial Office a telegram from Rhodes protesting the denunciation. We know, too, that the *Times*'s special correspondent in South Africa during the critical months, Captain Younghusband, was also acting as an agent for Chamberlain and that at a crucial meeting of Uitlanders who were considering whether to rebel, he read to them a letter from Shaw reporting Chamberlain's view of affairs.[46]

When the parliamentary inquiry convened in July 1897, one of its aims was to discover precisely the role Shaw had played. It failed to do so. Shaw worried that two letters she had written to Rhodes might come to light, but they never have. It did not occur to her to worry about the telegrams which the committee did discover because normally the Eastern Telegraph Company, which she had used, destroyed its extra-European copies after twelve months. During her testimony Shaw played the charmingly helpless female and thereby succeeded in convincing even dubious Liberals that all she had known was that something big was brewing in Johannesburg. She claimed to have had no idea that either Rhodes or Chamberlain were involved in a plot to overthrow the Transvaal government. An observer, Herbert Vivian, reporting for the *Saturday Review*, was convinced. He had formed a low opinion of Shaw's abilities. If a deep conspiracy did exist, he wrote, Shaw had not been party to it. She was "a mere pawn in the game."[47]

But the evidence suggests otherwise. The telegrams she sent to Rhodes have something of a hectoring quality. "What is undeniable," write the historians of the *Times* after reviewing the telegrams, "is that [she] was egging Rhodes on."[48] Astonishingly she and Bell also requested that Rhodes not allow the insurrection to begin on a Saturday because then the Sunday newspapers would report it, while the *Times*, which did not print a Sunday edition, would have to wait until the following day. Shaw wanted a scoop for her newspaper. More seriously, it is apparent that Shaw, Bell, and the other *Times* editors aware of the conspiracy viewed themselves not as mere reporters of news, but rather as shapers of events and molders of opinion. They were determined, Shaw as much as any of them, to push the forward imperial policy closely identified with Chamberlain's Colonial Office.

The most persistent and critical of Shaw's interlocutors, the anti-imperialist Radical M.P. Henry Labouchere, believed that Shaw hid her knowledge cunningly behind a facade of feminine vagueness. "A more difficult lady to induce to say what she did not want to it would be difficult to find," he wrote in the popular magazine *Truth*. "Her manner was most charming. When asked a question, she went off at a tangent, and made a clever speech on things in general. If I mildly suggested to her that, however interesting the speech, I had not got a very clear answer to my question, she smilingly expressed her regret, and did it in such a pleasant way that everyone thought that it was due to my abnormal density of apprehension. Then she made a second speech of the same character." From the other side, Rhodes's confidantes were delighted with her act. "She was in a difficult position," Earl Grey of Howick wrote to the chief wire-puller back in Johannesburg, but Shaw had "kept her head and come through the ordeal well." Throughout she had managed to keep Chamberlain's name out of it. "The great thing," Grey thought, "is [that] England is not implicated. There will be all sorts of surmises, conjectures and suspicions for a week or so, and then indifference and forgetfulness."[49]

In the plotting of the Jameson Raid and the reaction to it in Britain Shaw was taking part in imperial political affairs in a manner far beyond the capacity of Lady Dorothy Nevill or even Lady Londonderry. If she felt constrained to act the helpless female as a witness before the committee, in reality she was anything but. George Wyndham, the Conservative M.P. and confidante of Lady Londonderry and now a member of the committee, told his cousin Wilfrid Scawen Blunt that he had been seeing a lot of "the gang that have been running the Transvaal business . . . with Buckle, the *Times* editor and Miss Flora Shaw, who is really the prime mover in the whole thing, and who takes the lead in all their private meetings, a very clever middle-aged woman."[50] Obviously the leaders of the plot were not the editors of the *Times*, but Rhodes and Chamberlain. On the other hand the ability of the *Times* to help shape public opinion was critical to their scheme, and Shaw was a genuine player on the *Times*, perhaps even a leader among its editors.

Moreover as the controversy surrounding Chamberlain's role in the affair died down, Shaw returned to the original theme. Throughout 1898–99, in article after article she continued to urge the genius of Rhodes, the backwardness of Kruger, the virtues of Milner, who in the aftermath of the raid had been sent out by Chamberlain as South African high commissioner (and who surely understood the colonial secretary's larger aims), the disabilities under which the Transvaal Uitlanders suffered, and the inevitability of conflict there between Briton and Boer. In short she continued, as a journalist, trying not merely to report events but also to shape public opinion so that it would support certain policies.

The committee of inquiry had done nothing to damage her reputation with the Conservative government. If anything her relations with it were closer than before. A Colonial Office official minuted, "It has never been our practice to send out advance copies of papers to any journal (always excepting Miss Shaw)."[51] Meanwhile Moberly Bell was showing drafts of her articles to the Foreign Office before printing them, drafts Shaw had composed with the aims of the Conservative government in mind. "I am, of course, glad that the articles seem to the F.O. likely to be useful in the sense in which I intended," she wrote to Bell early in 1899.[52] If she was not a prime actor in the drama then surely she was among the most significant of the supporting cast. Among the rulers of the *Times*, all men with the exception of herself and all accustomed to exercising authority and to receiving deference, she was an equal, possibly first among equals.

When war finally came, as Rhodes, Chamberlain, and Milner had intended it should all along, she arranged another trip to the Cape. There, incidentally, she formed a distinctly lower opinion of General Buller than Lady Londonderry ever expressed. "He did not seem, either in tactics or strategy, to be able to rise above the child's conception of frontal attacks on the Boers wherever they were to be found," she wrote to Bell; but her loyalty to the cause for which Buller fought never faltered. She argued that Britain was battling not merely to secure its own place in South Africa, but the place of all civilized peoples. Her country's "ascendancy" there would "guarantee to Europe that from the Zambesi to the Indian Ocean every citizen of every nationality shall enjoy the same protection and profit by the same opportunity as if he lived under the shadow of his own flag." By then it had become her habit to argue that British imperialism was good for everybody.[53]

Shaw wrote on complex subjects clearly and with great authority based upon prodigious research. Perhaps because she was an autodidact she never ceased to read and to study. There is a revealing letter in her correspondence with W. T. Stead in which she sketches out a reading list for Cecil Rhodes, who apparently had requested one. Despite protestations of ignorance—"my knowledge of literature is much too partial and superficial; and when it comes to the affairs of today I realize afresh every hour that I am grossly ignorant of even ordinary fundamental facts"—she draws breath and makes suggestions. Among classical authors she recommends that Rhodes begin with Homer, Aeschylus, Euripides, Sophocles, Herodotus, and Tacitus. "Thucydides is better than any novel and Plutarch's lives he can't do without." From a later period she advises reading *Don Quixote* (in Spanish) and *Pilgrim's Progress*, which reminds her that the Bible "is of course indispensable." Among the great French authors whose works she has read and whom she believes Rhodes must read, she cites Pascal, Bossuet, Fenelon, Nicole, Racine, Corneille, Descartes, and "Montaigne's essays—so infinitely preferable to Bacon's." As for German literature "I know so little. . . . In the original I have only read . . . Goethe, Schiller and Lessing, besides a few modern novelists." Of English literature, she writes modestly, "there is no need for me to speak. You know it in all probability far better than I do." Then she turns to "the best works of reference," citing studies of Imperial Germany, the Swiss Federation, the American and Canadian Constitutions. Finally, "It is impossible to omit Burke's best speeches and Burke draws Fox and Pitt." Her postscript reveals how well connected this well-read, if self-taught, woman really was: "You ought to consult Lord Rosebery for political works and Mr. Morley for literature."[54]

To formidable learning was attached a formidable personality. If Shaw had played upon male fantasies of female helplessness during her testimony before the parliamentary committee, she knew how to crush those fantasies when it suited her. At work in the offices of the *Times* it suited her. Her colleague Donald MacKenzie Wallace, the newspaper's foreign editor, might dare to correct her in condescending tones, but only once. "Dear Miss Shaw," he wrote, "I was off duty on Sunday night and did not find time till today to read your article on the Colonies. You speak there of very friendly relations between France and Belgium in Africa. In reality the relations are very strained. . . . I send you this hint for future guidance." Little more than a month later, he was writing to her in nearly sycophantic tones. Moreover he now confined his suggestions to minor rather than substantive points. "My dear Miss Shaw," he begins this time, "Your work is always so good that I feel reluctant to seem querulous, but I think you will not be displeased if I venture to suggest a way in which you could greatly assist us, without very much additional trouble to yourself. . . . What I would venture humbly to suggest to you is that you should revise your M.S. a little more carefully, and that unfamiliar proper names such as rivers and native chiefs . . . should be written very distinctly. . . . When the names are used for the first or second time it would be well to print them in the margin." Possibly Miss Shaw had asked her patron, Moberly Bell, to have a word with Wallace; perhaps she had had a word with him herself. It seems evident, anyway, that someone had spoken to him.[55]

How was it possible in misogynist, turn-of-the-century London for a woman to ascend so high? Flora Shaw, though merely a journalist who shunned the public eye, had outstripped the political hostesses, not simply breaching the empire's governing inner circle, as they had done, but taking part as an equal in its planning sessions and then, through her articles for the *Times*, helping to give those plans substance, to make them a reality. Her success, however qualified, demonstrates the permeability of female gender borders in turn-of-the-century London, at last for an elite few, and the protean nature of the imperial metropolis as a whole. Of course Shaw inherited advantages, for example, social, literary, and political connections and even, according to her biographer, good looks and a manner which encouraged the men she was interviewing to confide in her. She possessed, too, intelligence, determination, knowledge, and character in abundance. These qualities and advantages, a rare combination, were necessary for a woman who wished to relimn London's feminine gender boundaries.

Still Shaw walked a tightrope in the gendered imperial metropolis. She was a player in the political world, "advising Cabinet Ministers and those controlling public affairs," according to one who knew her very well, and through her journalism influencing public opinion, upon which the policy makers depended. She never indulged in false modesty: "To have helped to rouse the British public to a sense of imperial responsibility and an ideal of Imperial greatness, to have had a good share in saving Australia from bankruptcy, to have prevented the Dutch from taking South Africa, to have kept the French within bounds in West Africa, to have directed a flow of capital and immigration to Canada, to have got the Pacific cable joining Canada and Australia, are all matters that I am proud and glad to have had my part in." Yet, with the exception of her appearance before the parliamentary committee, she had remained almost always in the background. Politics, above all imperial politics, were her lifeblood, but she could not become a politician because she was a woman. She became a journalist instead, but: "I never thought of my work exactly as journalism, but rather as active politics without the fame."[56]

The admission is significant. As a journalist she attained the outermost of the rings which girdled women's ambitions in the gendered imperial metropolis, but she never went beyond. Possibly she resented it. "We have, all of us, to be content if we can do a part of what we dream," she wrote to Lugard, and later in the same letter: "Don't break your heart in striving for the impossible."[57] Was she advising her future husband or herself? Or did she acquiesce more or less willingly in the bounding of her career, understanding that she had ascended to the highest "glass ceiling" a professional woman might bump up against in imperial London? After all, Flora Shaw attained financial independence, recognition as a preeminent journalist, the friendship and respect of the empire's most interesting and powerful men, influence over British imperial policy. In fact she attained everything a man could attain, except for fame, and "fame somehow doesn't interest me."

The bonds of gender that held Flora Shaw tightest were the ones she internalized. She broke free of the domestic sphere with relative ease, thus far outdistancing the political hostesses who sought to expand feminine roles (if only for themselves), but she could not free herself from the idea that women did not belong in the spotlight: "I daresay that is only the bent of a woman's mind. We are brought up that way—rather to shun than to court public notice." In that sense journalism permitted her to satisfy rather than to explode gender boundaries. She attained the inner circle but remained behind the scenes. Journalism "lives not in itself, but in its results," she explained to Lugard afterward, and as a self-abnegating woman, "I liked being nothing while the work remained."[58]

At the height of her career, Shaw married Lugard and resigned from the *Times*, although she continued to write for it on occasion. Her biographer believes that ill health played an important part in her decision to retire, also possibly political differences with the newspaper's editor-in-chief, Walter Buckle, who may have been kept in the dark during the lead-up to the Jameson Raid.[59] There may have been more deeply personal considerations as well, which will be considered below. Conceivably too Shaw believed that her career had taken her as high as it could. She would never break through the glass ceiling. Perhaps the struggle to reach it, to prove herself in a man's world, had finally exhausted her.

As Lugard's wife Flora Shaw fulfilled a more conventional, less emotionally fraught role until her death in 1929. Determined to remain at the center of events, she devoted herself to her husband's career, lobbying the politicians and officials whom previously she had interviewed and with whom she had occasionally collaborated. Initially from Nigeria, of which Lugard was the first British governor, then from within the imperial metropolis itself, to which she returned from Nigeria for reasons of health, she bombarded Chamberlain at the Colonial Office with letters extolling Lugard's accomplishments in West Africa. When a Liberal government replaced the Conservatives in late 1905, Lady Lugard, as she now was, burst in upon the new undersecretary for the colonies, Winston Churchill, intent upon maintaining her close connection with the man at the top. "The upshot," she reported back to her husband in Nigeria, "was, I think, really satisfactory."[60]

There is evidence to suggest that the erstwhile journalist approached marriage in the manner she had approached her other relationships with men: either she would lead or, at the least, she would work as an equal with her husband. She looked forward to Lugard's return to London, she told him just before they were married, "when occupation will be found for you at home and we shall work in the thick of it side by side." This sounds like the "partnership" Sidney and Beatrice Webb arranged. Indeed, like Beatrice Webb, whose dinners for politicians became legendary, Lady Lugard, formerly a regular attender of political dinners, now presided over them herself. After all, she assured her husband, "one conversation with the S[ecretary] of S[tate for the Colonies] at your own dinner-table will undo the effect of a dozen of Mr. Antrobus's despatches." In the end, however, marriage took the bite from even Lady Lugard's approach to life. "So you come home" from Nigeria, she wrote welcomingly to her husband in the spring of 1905, "tired from the labours of the field to rest a little in the sheltered spot which you have provided . . . for your wife to live in. And the wife whom you have left there will be very very glad to see you. She has been making ready for you for eighteen months, and hopes to give you now peace and gladness and perhaps fresh strength with which to go out again to the work of life." She had retreated to the domestic sphere after all.[61]

Flora Shaw's attitude toward British imperialism was relatively unnuanced. She was brilliant, thorough, tough, and resourceful; aggressive British imperialism possessed in her a powerful advocate. She offered influential support to practically any attempt to extend its borders. In the person of another formidable woman, however, it faced an astute and determined critic, one whose untimely death in 1900 nursing Boer prisoners in South Africa cut short a career already remarkable for the displeasure and discomfort it had caused the likes of Chamberlain, Rhodes, and Flora Shaw.

A veritable cottage industry of scholarship has grown up around the career of Mary Henrietta Kingsley, whose charm and originality of mind remain nearly palpable a century after her death.[62] She wrote with extraordinary verve and wit; her surviving letters, of which there are hundreds, and likewise her published articles and books, coruscate with wickedly insightful observations on people and events. The explanation for her continuing attractiveness to modern scholars, however, lies in more than just her clever pen. It is also due, in part, to the success with which, like Ladies Nevill and Londonderry and Flora Shaw, she negotiated a deeply sexist society, and perhaps even more to the respect she demonstrated for African people and culture at a time when few shared such sentiments.

Mary Kingsley never advocated Africa for the Africans or even equality of treatment for blacks and whites. She always hoped "to see English trade in West Africa, the greatest raw material market in the world, succeed" and for Great Britain to control the region. Nevertheless, she fought hard to limit the impact of British imperialism upon African culture, which, through her travels and studies, she had come to understand and appreciate better than all but a few fellow scholars. She abhorred the banal simplicities of pseudoscientific racism; moreover, her approach to racial matters never ceased to evolve. At the end of her life she seems to have been moving toward a more truly egalitarian position.[63]

Whereas Flora Shaw identified with power and gloried in its exercise, Kingsley identified viscerally with underdogs. Characteristically she directed the only romantic feelings of which her biographers are aware toward a Jewish official in the Colonial Office, Capt. Matthew Nathan (who scarcely noticed let alone returned them). She could not abide sanctimony, hypocrisy, and complacency, qualities she discerned in abundance among many of Nathan's Colonial Office colleagues, as well as among the missionary and official elements in West Africa with whom she had stayed during her journeys. Drawn to Africa for reasons which orthodox imperialists could not begin to fathom, she instinctively sympathized with and befriended a variety of people, including native Africans, upon whose wisdom the Chamberlain school never thought to draw. Lecturing once in Richmond, she was impressed by the intervention of a member of the audience, "a black man named Maxwell connected with the Gambia." Within two weeks they had become friends, and Kingsley had "found more things about Gambia . . . which may come in handy." This was not an isolated instance. "I have had quantities of Blacks" to visit, she reported to a friend, listing "Blyden, Cole, Robbins, Lewis, Barclay and Stevens," among her guests. One cannot imagine Flora Shaw performing a similar hostly role.[64]

Sadly Kingsley flashed across the firmament of British imperial politics for only a moment. Until the age of thirty-one, she lived in Cambridge with her parents. Her father, George Kingsley, was the younger, n'er-do-well brother of the famous author and Christian socialist Charles Kingsley. Her mother had been a maid in George Kingsley's household whom he had made pregnant and married only days before Mary Kingsley's birth. When, in 1893, both her parents died within months of each other, the daughter finally broke free and sailed to the Canary Islands, jumping-off point for a four-month trip through West Africa. After a second West African journey, she wrote *Travels in West Africa* (1897) and *West-African Studies* (1899). These important ethnographic works, whose main scholarly contribution was to explicate the "fetish" or religious practices of the Fang (or Fan) people of the French Congo region, also contained accounts of her many adventures, usually in places where few if any Europeans had previously set foot and were written in so stylish a manner that they attracted a mass audience.

Kingsley had little respect for Europeanized Africans, as she called them, men and women, usually residing in the coastal towns, who had been successfully pressured by missionaries and other agents of imperialism to adopt Western manners. During her travels inland, however, she had gained a very different impression of the less cosmopolitan "bush" Africans, who had received her with dignity and generosity. She felt a deep affinity with their approach to nature, religion, culture in the broadest sense. Consequently, when in December 1895, shortly after Kingsley's first return from Africa, Meredith Townsend, editor of the *Spectator*, wrote in a typically bigoted article that Africans were "a people abnormally low, evil, cruel," she felt called upon to rebut.[65]

Kingsley's travels had convinced her that Africans were not so much "men and brothers," as the abolitionists maintained, but rather the fruit of a different branch of the evolutionary tree altogether. "I . . . feel certain that a black man is no more an undeveloped white man than a woman is an undeveloped man."[66] Thus while Africans might be inferior to Europeans in some ways, they could be superior in others; in any event they and their customs, traditions, laws, and religious beliefs were worthy of respect. Kingsley defended West African polygamy to Victorian England. She argued that slavery and even cannibalism, when viewed in the West African context, should not be condemned out of hand.

This made her an advocate of anthropological relativism at a time when most Britons believed in the absolute superiority of their own civilization. When imperialists like Chamberlain, Lugard, and Shaw, or the Christian missionaries concerned with Africa, or even ostensible critics of imperialism in the Anti-Slavery or the Aborigine's Protection societies, advocated banning the sale of alcohol to Africans, arguing that like children they must be protected from it, Kingsley declared robustly that "in the whole of West Africa there is not one quarter the amount of drunkenness you can see any Saturday night you choose in the Vauxhall Road." When arrogant colonial officers ig-

29. Mary Kingsley.
Credit: Hulton Getty.

nored or trampled upon West African beliefs or denied the existence of West African law, Kingsley attempted to educate them. "How do people think natives keep . . . order without it?" she queried disgustedly. When Chamberlain betrayed his ignorance of the West African conception of property rights by imposing the infamous "hut tax" in Sierra Leone, sparking violent resistance, Kingsley attempted to explain to an uncomprehending Colonial Office that the Sierra Leoneans believed it impossible to own and pay taxes on property simultaneously. According to their law, the right to tax an object implied ownership of it. Thus they viewed the hut tax as tantamount to British confiscation of their homes.[67]

Kingsley believed in imperialism as a critical component of British trade and prosperity. She approved the methods by which the empire had been established in earlier centuries. The Elizabethan explorers had possessed "an intense love of knowledge of the minor details," she wrote in the *Spectator* of January 13, 1900. In contrast, however, she thought that England's modern-day imperialism was characterized by "emotionalism . . . windy-headed brag and self-satisfied ignorance." Kingsley heaped scorn upon the government's claim to be "taking up the white man's burden," to be "introducing civilization," and to be "giving the pax Britannica to wildly disturbed savage districts." These were all lies. She scoffed at the missionaries who claimed to be "saving thousands of souls . . . winning Africa for God." She wrote to a friend, "No one dare say this is a lie, because these are great words, but it is a lie for all that." Neither could she bear the indifference of her countrymen and women to the cruelties inflicted by British imperialists upon the African people: "England's heart has had a case built round it."[68]

Ineluctably, then, she was drawn into active politics. Journalism beckoned, as it must have any woman in turn-of-the-century London interested in influencing affairs, for it might provide a megaphone to one essentially voiceless in a sexist society but extraordinarily talented with the pen. A rush of articles followed in the major weekly, monthly, and quarterly political journals. Through these Kingsley came to play a role not unlike the role Flora Shaw played as author of the "Colonial" articles for the *Times*, except that she rarely agreed with Shaw's opinions. Indeed, as will become apparent below, Kingsley, who never published in the *Times*, became a sort of anti-Shaw.

Still, Mary Kingsley had to pick her way through the minefield posed by the gendered imperial metropolis. Never afraid to offend when it came to expressing her views on West Africa, she was careful to be inoffensive about other things. She dressed conservatively, always in black, and took care to disassociate herself from the feminist movement. She would not support women who wished to join all-male learned societies like the Royal Geographical. "These androgens I have no use for," she explained to Scott Keltie, secretary of the society after 1893. Unlike Flora Shaw, however, she had no hesitation in mounting the public platform to pursue her political aims. "I am lecturing all this month on an average three times a week, and telling people to trust the traders and the bush Africans," she informed a friend late in 1898. As a result, by the time of her death early in 1900, she had become as significant a player in imperial circles as the *Times*'s colonial editor. Today most would agree that of the two her legacy is the greater.[69]

Kingsley's approach to West African affairs was more complex than Shaw's. Shaw, in 1900, simply wished to see as much of West Africa as possible administered by the Colonial Office through her husband-to-be, Frederick Lugard, in the interests, as she maintained, of Britain, the native inhabitants of the region, and the world. Kingsley, on the other hand, although she admired "bush" Africans, had conceived an even greater respect, indeed a romantic and not altogether rational admiration, for the British traders operating in West Africa. She had witnessed such figures in their element during her own peregrinations. Tough, hard-bitten, self-sufficient men little given to cant or self-promotion, they reminded her of the Elizabethan sea dogs. She believed that they understood West Africa and its people more thoroughly than Colonial Office agents ever would or could. Moreover their prosperity as traders depended upon the prosperity of West Africans in general. They would make the best governors of the area, then, because the well-being of its native inhabitants was in their self-interest.

Already embroiled in public disputations with the pseudoscientific bigots and the antialcohol contingent and well known for her defense of West African customs and people more generally, Kingsley became the leader of a movement to make the British West African traders governors of the region in which they did their business. She conceived a three-step program for the accomplishment of this goal. First the traders, many of whom were connected either with Sir George Taubman Goldie's Royal Niger Company, whose primary stockholders were Glaswegian, or the African Association led by John Holt of Liverpool, must organize themselves. Then they must discover parliamentary allies in Britain who would vote en bloc in their behalf. Finally they must fashion a mechanism to govern West Africa with.

The obstacles to Kingsley's scheme were legion. First of all, as she often wrote to friends, "I am only I." She did not have the weighty influence of the *Times* behind her, nor despite her lineage was she immediately privy to the influential circles to which Flora Shaw belonged. Moreover, she was opposed by the Colonial Office of Joseph Chamberlain, which was determined to assert its own control of British West Africa. Then there were the sexist attitudes of her opponents to overcome. However, "I do hate humbug," she once wrote to a friend; and this instinctive revulsion proved a powerful fuel.[70]

In her war with humbug Kingsley's confidante and ally became John Holt, the most prominent of the Liverpool traders with West African interests. "I know the battle has only just begun," she wrote to him in November 1898, "and we want a Moltke and a Bismarck. . . . I invite you to be Bismarck. I'll do my best as Moltke."[71] She really did conceive of the campaign upon which they embarked as an exercise in nation building. If they should succeed, British West Africa would become, under the guidance of its traders, a self-governing federation of colonies like Canada or Australia.

Kingsley's articles put her in touch with the editors of Britain's foremost political journals and, through them, with the politicians themselves. Within a year she had become a regular at the great political dinners and salons, as familiar to government and Colonial Office officials as Dorothy Nevill, Lady Londonderry, or even Flora Shaw. Moreover she had ascended to the very top. "I am going down among that Salisbury-Balfour set on Saturday til Monday," she informed Holt on one occasion. "I have just had a long talk with Chamberlain over the hut-tax affair," she reported on another.[72]

Kingsley sought influence, moreover, not merely through her journalism and growing number of personal contacts, but also by recruiting to her campaign "big ju-jus," as she called them, by which she meant important sympathizers. She and Holt had identified Goldie as the recruit they wished most to attract; in fact, if only he would join they were prepared to cede leadership of their crusade to him. "He is a splendid weapon both to fight red tape and foreigners with," thought Kingsley, who knew him and his wife well.[73] Goldie's Royal Niger Company, which Flora Shaw had celebrated so shamelessly in the *Times*, was due to be wound up in 1900, and the territory it had pacified and controlled, now to be called Nigeria, was to be incorporated formally into the British Empire. Chamberlain would send out Lugard to be its first governor. This, according to Kingsley and Holt, was merely another example of Colonial Office aggrandizement and undervaluation of the traders' contribution. Would not Goldie, the greatest of West Africa's merchants, agree? Could he not become both the spearhead of a West African parliamentary contingent and leader of the united West African traders? But the great imperialist, an enigmatic figure, refused to be drawn.

It was not only to Goldie whom the two wire-pullers looked. They also fixed, if only for a moment, upon the famous African explorer H. M. Stanley, another of Kingsley's ever-expanding number of contacts. But, they concluded, "Stanley as member for Africa is too nervous and thinskinned." In fact, Kingsley wrote upon second thought, Stanley "is a cocktailed ass." But then there was the very same Lord Cromer whom Flora Shaw once had charmed, "a beautiful big ju-ju I have secured, and I have thrown Northcote [a former chancellor of the exchequer] to him, and I think he will do Northcote good for he will pay more attention to the thing when said by Lord Cromer than when said by me."[74]

These were potential leaders. Kingsley was also looking for parliamentary foot soldiers. "I sent you a message about Maclean, M.P. for Cardiff," she wrote to Holt. "When you are again in town sometime I want you to . . . go and have a quiet talk with him." Moreover, Maclean was friendly with "Lord Randolph Churchill's son who is going into Parliament forthwith. . . . Young Churchill is full of go, no doubt full of foolishness [too], but he will, like his father, make the fur fly." "Meanwhile," Kingsley plotted in yet another letter to Holt, "the government should lose its by elections." There was one forthcoming in Kirkdale. Kingsley and Holt thought either Sir Alfred Lyall of the India Council or Sir Spencer Walpole might stand as Radical alternatives to the government's candidate. In the end, however, neither would accept their nomination.[75]

Meanwhile in her second book, *West-African Studies*, Kingsley had presented her cherished plan to "get the government of my beloved coast out of the hands of the permanent official"—and into the hands of the traders. Here it seems appropriate to ask why she did not want the power to be in the hands of "bush" Africans or at least shared equally between traders and Africans. "I like . . . W[est] A[frica] under a government form that would include the

native," she asserted at one point. "They should be powerful enough to reg-
ulate their own side," she wrote to Holt on another occasion. Still, there is no
doubting to whom Kingsley felt the greatest allegiance: "I have and feel more
dislike and alarm at the position of English traders than at the position of the
African. . . . It is gall and wormwood to me, worse than downtrodden blacks."
Even Mary Kingsley could not conceive of West Africa in 1900 ruled solely,
or even in large part, by Africans. Her plan advocated only what subsequent
generations called indirect rule for native Africans.[76]

In its final form Kingsley's scheme proposed a supremely powerful
British-based grand council composed of representatives nominated by the
Chambers of Commerce of Liverpool, Manchester, London, Bristol, and
Glasgow, the British cities with the most important West African interests.
Its members would appoint a governor-general for West Africa (Goldie being the obvious first choice) who would reside six months there and the rest
of the year in Britain, so that he would not lose touch with either base. In West
Africa there would be two subcouncils, one made up of medical and legal experts appointed by the College of Physicians and the lord chancellor, the
other consisting of African chiefs. The governor-general would act as a liai-
son between the grand council and the subcouncils.

To serve under the governor-general in each West African colony and to
run the coastal towns according to British laws, the grand council would appoint district commissioners. These would be advised by municipal councils
of British and African traders. The grand council would also appoint sub-
commissioners to govern smaller interior districts, largely through local
chiefs, who would be responsible for administering African law within their
own communities. The entire revenue for the expenses of government would
be raised from customs duties to be collected in the ports of Liverpool, Havre,
and Hamburg.[77]

Critics fixed immediately upon the lack of parliamentary oversight in
Kingsley's scheme. But, of course, that was her main point. She believed that
the West African traders were supremely qualified to govern themselves.
Moreover she wanted them to rule untrammeled by red tape and regulations
emanating from London. As for the indirect rule component of her plan, critics fixed upon it too. "All the part of West Africa which is not Europeanised
[i.e., the interior regions] would be left in the hands of its chiefs," worried
the *Saturday Review*.[78]

Kingsley's vision was Janus-faced. On the one hand it looked backward,
as far back perhaps as the late eighteenth-century radicalism of John Wilkes,
opponent of overweening government, and certainly to the radicalism of a
mid-nineteenth-century figure like John Bright, who hated aristocratic pre-

tensions and privileges and wished for nothing more than a democracy of manufacturers and merchants. "After all," Kingsley once wrote to Holt, "you and I are the surviving representatives of the old Liberal party of retrenchment and reform."[79] On the other hand it looked forward to the policies of indirect rule by which some twentieth-century imperialists would seek to soften the impact of their domination. In this sense Kingsley is a transitional figure. She occupies the pivot point on which traditional British radicalism foundered. If behind her stood Wilkes and Bright, then before her and striding into the future one may discern the figure of her disciple E. D. Morel, who, inspired by the antiestablishment tenor of her articles, went on to become A. J. P. Taylor's quintessential "trouble maker." Morel founded the Union of Democratic Control during World War I, becoming afterward an important figure in the Labour Party.

Kingsley's untimely death only a few months after she had presented her plan to the public put an end to her ambitions for British West Africa. The Colonial Office shelved her scheme. The West African traders proved incapable of unifying without her prodding; and, absent her guiding hand, no parliamentary bloc took shape to forward their aims. Her death meant, too, that native West Africans had lost a brilliant, if idiosyncratic, champion and that British imperialism had lost an original, if quirky, critic. Yet the meteoric rise to prominence and influence of this extraordinary figure is also important for illuminating the strategies and processes which women in turn-of-the-century London who wished to play a role in imperial affairs were forced to employ.

Again the importance of those political luncheons, dinners, and salons leaps out at the historian. Time after time Kingsley refers to them in her correspondence with John Holt. "Joe [Chamberlain] is in London for a few days and I may see him Saturday night at the *Spectator* dinner," she wrote to him on the last day of November 1898, at a time when she hoped to educate the colonial secretary on hut-tax policy. Two weeks later she dined with and succeeded in buttonholing the French ambassador, De Manville: "A Frenchman would not listen to an Englishman talking to him about how to manage his colonies, but he don't mind a woman doing so." And where but at a dinner party could a woman like Kingsley have had access to such a figure? Then, shortly after a government investigator, Sir David Chalmers, had released a report critical of the hut tax and vindicating Kingsley's position, "I went down to tea with Mrs. Antrobus," the wife of a permanent undersecretary at the Colonial Office. Kingsley was wondering how Chamberlain and his aides had reacted to the report, and Mrs. Antrobus told her: "She, looking deeply vexed, said his report was ridiculous and he must have been got hold of."[80]

These are only a few samples. Kingsley's correspondence contains many more references to similar occasions. She had grasped what Ladies Nevill and Londonderry understood before her: in turn-of-the-century London, where space was overly determined and profoundly gendered, such events represented a nearly unique opportunity for women to mix with and to educate the men who shaped Britain's imperial policies. Kingsley, who took pains not to transgress other gender boundaries, was simply making use of an uncontroversial channel of access to power.

Unfortunately, however, "in a great crowded dinner party one cannot quietly talk over facts calmly." Kingsley favored smaller affairs. She often dined *en famille* with Goldie, with the Antrobuses, with Stanley and his wife, and in small parties with various politicians and Colonial Office men. "I am suddenly asked to lunch by Toby M.P. . . . to meet 'some Members of Parliament who want a word' with me." Like Flora Shaw, however, Kingsley was determined to influence events more directly than even these gatherings allowed. No wonder, like Shaw, she was drawn to journalism. But the ideals she advanced in her writings were anathema to the colonial editor of the *Times*.[81]

The two women, both of whom scaled the limits of the gendered imperial metropolis, detested each other. Kingsley was famous in the first place for having traveled deep into the African interior where no white woman had journeyed before, and then for writing about it in a distinctive and highly engaging manner. Shaw, whose prose was clear and businesslike but lacked Kingsley's sparkle, may have been jealous. "Books that were amusing were not always accurate," she remarked rather spitefully to another woman traveler, Isabella Bird, within Kingsley's earshot. And then early in 1899 Shaw projected a journey of her own, from Cairo to the Cape, tracing the route along which Rhodes hoped to build a railroad. Did she wish to trump Kingsley's travels in West Africa? If so, it was Lugard who dissuaded her: "Any brainless and energetic person can travel,—whereas you are very urgently required for far more difficult and important work."[82]

It is hardly surprising that Kingsley should tell John Holt that "Miss Flora Shaw . . . is . . . supposed to hate me." For her part, Kingsley despised the "smug, superior *Times* ways" which Shaw personified and dealt with them in her inimitable fashion. "Sarcasm is my natural weapon and is the best weapon to fight these *Times*es-minded people with, it gets them on the raw." To cite only one example, an article for the *Fortnightly Review* of April 1898:

> I beg to state that I have the greatest admiration for *The Times*, and moreover
> I owe it many debts of gratitude, for I always made a point when on my extremely occasional visits to an English Government House on the West
> Coast of Africa—the only sort of place in that country where you can get that

newspaper—of securing copies and storing them, because when well wetted and beaten up into a pulp mixed with gum, and then boiled gently in a pipkin, there is simply nothing equal to *The Times* for stopping cracks or holes in one's canoe, which is, as Mr. Pepys would say, an excellent thing in a newspaper.

This particular example of Kingsley sarcasm had almost certainly been prompted by a bombastic anti-French assertion of British rights to nearly all of West Africa written by Shaw for the *Times* of February 7, 1898. "I detest *The Times* articles on West Africa," Kingsley confided to Holt shortly after the offending piece appeared.[83]

Personal antagonism was thus inseparable from more substantive issues. Shaw and Kingsley articulated and fought hard for alternate conceptions of empire. Inevitably they fought one another. In their battle, although it was never wise to underestimate Mary Kingsley, the better established, highly respectable, and well-respected Shaw enjoyed all the advantages. The contest between them casts further light upon the modus operandi forced upon ambitious women in the gendered imperial metropolis.

"The truth is, Mr. Holt," Kingsley confessed in the spring of 1899, "every bit of solid good work I have done has been through a man."[84] This was to underestimate the impact of her writings and platform appearances but points to a remarkable fact: for all her independence of mind, Kingsley's first political objective was to gain the support of Sir George Taubman Goldie for her alternative plan; while, for all her accomplishments as a journalist, editor, and political intriguer, in the end, Flora Shaw chose safety and influence through marriage to Frederick Lugard. There is, indeed, a sense in which the two women competed for the allegiance of both Goldie and Lugard.

By 1898 Lugard had become temporary point man for the antialcohol contingent, whose vicarious teetotalism he endorsed on the stump and through letters and articles in the press. Kingsley fought them, and him, with all her strength, going so far at one point as to have the contents of the alcohol sold by West African traders chemically analyzed in order to prove that it was not even all that strong. Yet she became fond of Lugard. Perhaps she hoped ultimately to convert and make use of him.

Kingsley's first assessment of Lugard's character was not flattering: "a very fine explorer and soldier I have no doubt—but a man who acts under orders and does not think," she wrote late in 1897 after meeting him at the inevitable dinner party. Nevertheless she was soon on a personal basis with him. Within a year her opinion of him had changed to a degree: "I can't help liking Lugard." The two had attended a dinner the previous evening, at which Kingsley detected a softening in her opponent's approach to the liquor question. What he objected to, Lugard told her, was that the Germans monopolized the trade in question, and after all "we were in Africa for our own ben-efit." Here, incidentally, was a revealing admission from the future husband of the advocate of British imperialism on behalf of all the world, but in any event Kingsley, who wished only to defend British traders from the charge that they were demoralizing Africans by selling them drink, was pleased. "This sort of thing I need not rise up against," she happily informed John Holt. Indeed, it appears to have occurred to her that Lugard might serve in the role as leader of West African traders which originally she had cast for Goldie. "You are wrong in your attitude toward Lugard," she corrected Holt, who ob-viously disagreed with this adaptation of plans, "though he is not a second Goldie."[85]

Kingsley may have changed her mind about Lugard precisely because she found him so suggestible. As she had first written of him, "Order him to go anywhere and he would go. Tell him such a thing is good or bad and, if he rec-ognizes the person who tells him so is a proper pious person, he throws all the weight of his authority in backing up what he thinks is the proper pious thing." Could he not be told, then, that the West African traders were good and the Colonial Office bad?

If this really is what Kingsley had begun to hope, she was entirely off the mark. About her there always hung a whiff of bohemianism and eccentricity which would have alarmed so pious and proper an object of her plans as Lu-gard. Moreover, her rival for Lugard's political allegiance was far more re-spectable and decorous than she. And it is conceivable that Flora Shaw found Lugard's suggestibility attractive too. Their surviving correspondence re-veals that, once they married, Shaw was continually dispensing political ad-vice to her husband and telling him what to do.

The contest for Sir George Taubman Goldie's political allegiance was more complicated. Kingsley wanted Goldie to serve as spearhead of the West African traders' movement. "No one knows him so well as I do," she boasted to Holt. Her letters are filled with accounts of her unavailing attempts to win the great man over. He would not commit. In fact, despite his close connec-tion with the West African trading community he would not support her even on the liquor-traffic question, no doubt because if he had done so it would have signaled his support of her larger plans. Lugard, meanwhile, wanted Goldie's backing for the antiliquor position. A tug-of-war ensued. "I have used all my influence on G[oldie] for months," Kingsley reported to Holt. "It is a fight between Lugard and me. Which of us will win I do not know. At pres-ent I have the best of it."[86]

Kingsley realized that Flora Shaw was adding her weight to the same side of the rope as Lugard, because she was anxious to see Colonial Office control extended to West Africa and therefore happy to see the West African traders discredited. Shaw attempted to keep Goldie sweet by writing articles for the *Times* praising him to the skies. Kingsley could not bear to read these puff pieces: "I keep my head cool by keeping away from it." This, in a manner of speaking, was the same approach adopted by Shaw toward Kingsley's writings, as Kingsley understood. Shaw, she wrote to Holt, "keeps Goldie cool by keeping away from me on Liverpool."[87]

What Kingsley probably did not know or even suspect was that for Shaw the political issue between them was colored by a personal one. The *Times*'s colonial editor had conceived a romantic passion for Goldie, and when his wife died unexpectedly in the spring of 1898, she proposed marriage to him. Goldie, an independent-minded and charismatic figure to whom leadership came naturally, could not have been pointed in any direction, let alone managed by a wife, as Shaw must have realized. Perhaps she envisioned a partnership between two great exponents of British imperialism. Perhaps she was already considering semiretirement and subordinating her own ambitions and talents to a husband's. At any rate Goldie brusquely turned down her proposal. Shortly thereafter a shattered Flora Shaw accepted Lugard as her spouse. Her professional career had ended.

Thus two powerful women, perfectly capable of acting independently on the political stage and in the public eye, found it necessary to wage political campaigns by proxy, through men. Shaw won the contest for the allegiance of Lugard, though it is unclear how seriously Kingsley fought on this front, and there is evidence to suggest that, in any event, the victory tasted of ashes; the battle for Goldie was cut short by Kingsley's death.

Mary Kingsley met her end on June 3, 1900, in the fever-ridden camps for Boer prisoners whom she had volunteered to nurse. For once, if only momentarily, she chose to practice a profession which society approved for women, and it killed her. Had she, too, wished for a temporary refuge from the criticism and snide commentary to which, as a woman attempting to influence affairs, she was continually subjected? Did nursing represent the kind of safety that marriage seems to have done for Flora Shaw? Shaw's career did not end with her literal death, of course, but the wedding with Lugard ended her professional activities as surely as the microbes did for Kingsley. Both women stretched gender boundaries to the limit, but when they submitted to society's gendered expectations of them their real contributions ceased.[88]

❖   ❖   ❖

The methods of coping with society's gendered expectations which Dorothy Nevill, Lady Londonderry, Flora Shaw, and Mary Kingsley fashioned for themselves would not have worked anywhere in Britain except

London. Nevill, as we have seen, loathed even visiting the countryside because it took her so far from the center of things. She could never have become a successful political hostess whose home base was a country house, or
even a town house unless it was located in London. Nor, for that matter, could
have Lady Londonderry, who entertained grandly at her country estate, Wyngard, but reserved her main political efforts for the Park Lane establishment.

As for Flora Shaw, she owned a beloved country cottage to which she re-
paired as often as possible. Yet as a journalist for the *Times* "there was much
that could be done only in London," as her biographer observes. "She went
up to town, therefore, constantly, starting often by a very early train, and
sometimes writing her articles in the waiting-room at Charing Cross."[89] The
meetings with Rhodes and other visiting imperialists were most convenient
in London too, which always was the base of operations for such visitors. And
then there were the regular sessions with Chamberlain at the Colonial Office,
not to speak of the luncheons, dinners, and at homes which she was continually attending.

Kingsley, of course, lectured up and down the country and, presumably,
could have written her articles anywhere; moreover her strongest political
and philosophical ties were with the Liverpool traders led by John Holt. All
the more significant, then, that she established her home base in London.
Only there could she have easy and regular access to the men who governed
and made policy for the empire. Only in London was she likely to meet the
steady stream of visiting dignitaries from Africa and elsewhere who were
passing through. "The best way here is by underground railway from Charing Cross to Kensington High Street Station, and then an omnibus will bring
you in a very few minutes to outside my gate," she wrote to one of them.[90]

Kingsley, Shaw, and Ladies Nevill and Londonderry, of course, were
hardly typical Londoners. Their tactics of self-definition were not available
to the vast majority of London's female residents. The four women were extraordinary not only for their talents, but for their opportunities. Even Mary
Kingsley, the least privileged and least well connected of the quartet, was the
niece of a famous author and the heir to an independent income. Still the
strategies employed by these four remarkable women reveal some of the difficulties that confronted all women in the imperial metropolis at the turn of
the twentieth century as well as some of the possibilities open to them.

In a sense Ladies Nevill and Londonderry were less ambitious than Flora
Shaw and Mary Kingsley. Determined to know, to be of use, perhaps in the
case of Lady Londonderry to sway and to guide the men who governed the
empire, nevertheless they sought influence outside the domestic sphere without making themselves conspicuous by leaving it. This gave little opportu-

nity for condemnation to misogynists who believed, for example, that women did not need the vote because they exercised political influence at home, since that was precisely what Nevill and Londonderry were doing. Thus, consciously or not, both women turned traditionally gendered expectations of female behavior to their own advantage. On the other hand, they were hardly striking a blow for the emancipation of their sex.

Flora Shaw went much further. She entered a profession in which she cannot have been welcome, ascended to its top by dint of brains, drive, and hard work, and gained entrance to the same circles which Ladies Nevill and Londonderry entertained as hostesses. Like Lady Londonderry, Shaw insisted upon taking part in policy discussions as an equal, not merely at the banquet table, which was Lady Londonderry's realm, but also at the conference table in the Colonial Office, Foreign Office, and in Printing House Square, headquarters of the *Times*. Yet only a select few knew of her influence, even after the parliamentary investigation into the Jameson Raid and her role in planning it. Shaw gained no following, had no disciples, served as mentor to no one. Later, perhaps, women with journalistic ambitions might read her single biography and become inspired. While she lived, however, relative obscurity was the price Shaw willingly paid for success.

Of the four women examined here only Mary Kingsley might have motivated her contemporaries to reach beyond traditionally gendered boundaries, because she became a visible champion of the Liverpool traders, often speaking on their behalf in public. Yet Kingsley did not wish to fill any such role. Unorthodox in her approach to imperial issues, she was conformist when it came to the wider part her sex might play in society. She opposed the admission of women to all-male societies, argued that "Votes for Women" could wait at least until the male traders of West Africa had been empowered. Why be surprised or disappointed? Historians should know better than anybody that we are all products of time and place.

The imperialist views expressed by the four women examined in this chapter bore little relation to their sex; not one advocated the maternal imperialism feminist historians have discerned elsewhere, although Shaw hoped that "industrious, cheerful and healthy women, prepared to exert themselves in their natural capacity as home-makers" would emigrate to the colonies. Kingsley, for her part, hoped female nurses would volunteer to "support those noble men, our doctors, who too long unaided have fought Death in British West Africa." She volunteered to fight death in Africa and lost. In any event neither Shaw nor Kingsley appear to have believed in the capacity of other women, with a few exceptions, to travel and study Africa as they had done. Men were empire builders, women their helpmeets, present company excluded. Flora Shaw and Mary Kingsley wore gendered blinkers too.[91]

The four women whose struggles to define a role for themselves in the imperial metropolis form the subject of the present chapter were largely successful. Operating under constraints which confronted every woman of the time and place, Shaw, Kingsley, Londonderry, even Nevill attained special access to or influence over imperial policy. Each explored the outer limits not so much of permissible behavior for women as of gendered expectations for them. Each, in her own way, stretched the bonds of gender without ever seeking to make them snap. The very fact that the bonds were stretchable suggests the unstable nature of the gendered imperial metropolis, never a fixed entity, always in process of becoming, a process which women as well as men helped forward.

CHAPTER 7

LONDON'S RADICAL AND
CELTIC FRINGE

THE imperial drumbeat was steady and all-enveloping in turn-of-the-century London. Greater than mere thrum or background noise, it provided the city's defining tone and rhythm. Nevertheless, because London was an imperial metropolis it was cosmopolitan and because it was cosmopolitan it contained anti-imperialists and critics of empire. These men and women did not attain the influence of their imperialist counterparts, but neither were they a negligible force. Moreover, just as the champions of empire helped to shape the imperial metropolis, so too did they. Organized in a dense web of overlapping organizations, they spoke in a multitude of voices, for there were many anti-imperialisms as well as many imperialisms in London in 1900. The views and goals of those anti-imperialists who were of European extraction and had been born in England, Scotland, or Wales is familiar territory to a point.[1] But one cannot understand London's anti-imperialists of Asian and African descent without first establishing the broader context in which they worked.

Native-born Londoners might belong to a number of anti-imperial organizations and political parties. Leaving to one side for the moment those of Irish descent and beginning from as close to the middle of the political spectrum as possible, one comes first to the old Gladstonians on the Radical wing of the Liberal Party, many of whom belonged to ginger groups like the Liberal Forwards or the League of Liberals against Militarism and Aggression, and the members of London's numerous Working Men's Clubs whose umbrella organization was the Metropolitan Radical Federation. Then there were the main socialist organizations: the Independent Labour Party, the Fabian Society, and the Social Democratic Federation. A constellation of more narrowly defined bodies, not political parties, also attracted London's native-born Radicals who were critics of empire: the Positivist, Ethical, and Quaker societies, the Land and Labour League, the Anti-Slavery Society, the

Aborigine's Protection Society (APS), and the British Committee of the Indian National Congress (BCINC).

Liberal and Radical anti-imperialism was something of a misnomer. "The word Imperialism stood to them as a hissing and an execration and a laughing stock," cried George Russell in February 1900 at the foundation meeting of the Gladstone League, which later changed its name to the League of Liberals against Aggression and Militarism. In fact in 1900 many old Gladstonians and working-class Radicals were galvanized less by anti-imperialism than by the Boer War, which they opposed at least in part because they feared it would *weaken* the empire. "Disguise it how we may," wrote one Radical critic, "this Transvaal War is naught but sheer buccaneering—the Jameson Raid on an Imperial scale. . . . Shall we then call the promoters of the present raid 'Empire Builders'? Shall we not rather call them 'Empire wreckers'"? And there was more than one way to wreck an empire. Another Radical worried that the war had "greatly lessened both the respect and the fear which the natives feel for their rulers, and unless when it is over, those rulers can unite in some common policy towards them, the prospect of a great native uprising can never be very far off."[2]

Of course "pro-Boers" had additional reasons for opposing the war: they believed it had been provoked by South African mine owners, some of whom were Jewish, for greedy purposes and served no British interest; it diverted attention from needed reforms at home, wasted money, and disrupted trade; Dutch South Africans were patriots defending their land and liberties as they understood them from alien invaders; war never solved anything anyway. Pro-Boers organized more than one antiwar body to publicize these arguments, for example, a Stop the War Committee, led by Flora Shaw's original employer, the crusading journalist W. T. Stead, who made his *Review of Reviews* its chief organ; and the South African Conciliation Committee, which included Frederic Harrison, leader of the Positivists and sometime guest of Dorothy Nevill (and, as noted in chapter 1, a member of the LCC), and Leonard Courtney, a nominal Conservative at this stage of his career but really an independent with radical views.

Antiwar sentiments mixed with orthodox imperialism in such groups, although their members were often termed traitors to the empire. Stead, for his part, advocated "the true policy of the Liberal Party . . . Imperialism plus common-sense and the Ten Commandments." Courtney once addressed the APS "in no spirit of opposition to colonies or colonisation, in no attempt to prevent the growth and outspread of the English race, but with a desire to make that movement better than it has been." John Clifford, the famous dissenting minister and prominent supporter of Stead's Stop the War Committee, underlined his devotion to "the greatest Empire the world has ever seen." "One question only is left," he added, "whether its ascent to supremacy is to be made pacifically or with violence." He favored the peaceful ascent, which was why he opposed the Boer War.[3]

For these men the rights of indigenous—or at any rate of native black African—peoples did not figure. "An Imperialism based upon common-sense and the Ten Commandments would ... address itself with vigour to the opportunity of restoring peace to South Africa on the only possible basis," Stead averred, "namely one that is compatible with the self-respect of the majority of the European population."[4] He was hardly concerned with the self-respect of black Africans. They must hope for kind treatment from their British overlords, who presumably would be governed by common sense and the Ten Commandments if men like Stead had their way. As "M" put it in the *Speaker*, another Radical journal, "It behoves all those who are solicitous for the success of our rule in West Africa to ... insist that the native gets fair play." But M did not question that British success in West Africa was desirable or that Britons must deal fairly with West Africans from positions of authority over them.

Racism underlay such assertions and omissions. Almost all of London's Liberal and Radical dissidents ascribed to the pseudoscientific Darwinism noted in a previous chapter, positing a hierarchy among races, with white Anglo-Saxons at the top and native black Africans at the bottom. Orientals and Indians inhabited a middle ground in the racial hierarchy and required more delicate handling.

British critics of empire regarded the Chinese with grudging respect tinged by fear. "Open up China," warned Mary Kingsley, "and you liberate the greatest mass of high-class handicraftsmen in the world—men who can beat you, Germany, and America hollow in the production of manufacturers for the world's markets when liberated from their present state." As another critic put it, China had been "a mighty organised power thousands of years before any European country had a national existence." Stead drew the logical conclusion: "Above all let our aim be to leave the Chinese as much alone as possible to manage their own affairs in their own way." When the Western powers invaded China to defeat the Boxer Rebellion, these Anglo-Saxon anti-imperialists offered less than enthusiastic support.[5]

India, too, had been the center of a mighty civilization when native Britons ran about in forests painting their faces blue. That table had turned: British imperialists governed India. But perhaps it could become a self-governing colony. "Let the Indian people ... keep their eye on Canada," advised the *New Age*, a radical journal with Christian socialist overtones. Others favored more far-reaching measures: "Speedy arrangements should be made for winding up our affairs in India, meeting in a suitable manner all legitimate claims."[6] Many British friends of India supported the British Committee of the Indian National Congress. A few held important positions in this organization.

Even the most radical critics of empire took a paternal, usually condescending, interest in Africa, however. Except for Mary Kingsley, who was a cultural relativist, they believed that whites and blacks belonged to the same human species, but that whites had evolved further. Black Africans "were like children," wrote Thomas Hodgkin of the APS, and therefore required the guiding and beneficent hand of British colonizers and governors: "They must be protected against the superior brain power of the races which had reached maturity." The bishop of London, Mandel Creighton, who also belonged to the APS, told an audience, "The great interest of the future [lies] in raising these black races by a continuous process to a level that, however different from ours, might be almost equal with our own." H. R. Fox Bourne, organizing secretary of the APS, made a similar point: "White men are, or should be, in the position of guardians, or of elder or more fortunate brothers, to the blacks with whom ... they are in contact." It was self-evident to such men that Great Britain had a role to play in Africa.[7]

Ever since 1837 the role of the APS in England, or more specifically in London, where its headquarters were located, had been "to assist in protecting the defenceless, and promoting the advancement of uncivilised tribes." Over the more than half-century since its foundation no aboriginal people touched by British imperialism had escaped its well-meant if often patronizing attention. The APS issued a journal, the *Aborigine's Friend*, and innumerable pamphlets, organized countless meetings and demonstrations, and lobbied officials at the Colonial Office and politicians at Westminster to ensure that British imperialism lived up to its "civilising mission." A number of Radical M.P.s, some of them Quakers, belonged to its "parliamentary committee," which oversaw its activities in Westminster.[8]

The organization also served as a kind of guardian angel to "aborigines" who found themselves in Britain. For example, when Edward Cleary, managing director of the Savage South Africa exhibition, brought his cast to London he invited the APS "to come out and inspect them at your leisure." Fox Bourne did so and then with the aid of the Society for the Propagation of the Gospel provided Cleary's "guests" with "such supervision as was possible," including "a lady teacher acquainted with the Zulu language [to teach] English and other elementary subjects."[9]

In reading about aborigines' friends, who rarely seem to have offered true friendship, the friendship of equals, to native peoples, and critics of empire who really were critics of specific imperial policies only, one is irresistibly re-minded of the tone employed by another group of good Samaritans. Josephine Butler's appeal on behalf of Indian women is notorious: "Their helplessness appeals to the heart, somewhat in the same way in which the helplessness and suffering of a dumb animal does, under the knife of the vivisector." Some of the same people who were active in the APS, the Anti-Slavery Society, even the British Committee of the Indian National Congress contributed also to the *Humane Review* and belonged to its parent organization, the Humanitar-ian League, which sought better treatment for animals in the Regent's Park zoo. Here is Fox Bourne again, writing in an article entitled "The Claims of Uncivilised Races": Africans "need to be treated with justice—such justice as will make allowance for their defects and seek to remove them by kindly and reasonable methods—such justice as will prevent their being made victims of the cruelties and treacheries, the tyrannies and meannesses, which are spu-rious concomitants and corrupt idiosyncrasies of civilization." And here is an unnamed "Zoophilist" demanding kindlier handling of the creatures kept at Regent's Park: "We want a more humane and intelligent appreciation of an-imal life, and that sense of kinship which would make us desirous of seeing our rudimentary brethren under happier and more natural conditions." One suspects that the two crusades, for better treatment of animals in the zoo and of aborigines in their homelands and elsewhere, were related in the minds of at least a few who took part in them.[10]

When most Liberal and Radical critics of the Boer War claimed to be anti-imperialist, really they were anti-jingo. They shrank from the "Brag, . . . emblazoned monuments, invidious national songs, [and] coarse buffoonery" which they identified with Joseph Chamberlain and his followers in the Con-servative Party. Jingoist hooligans routinely disrupted antiwar gatherings and demonstrations, often with violence. They drunkenly paraded London's streets following the announcement of British victories against the Boers, looting and smashing. Inevitably anti-jingoism verged on antidemocracy in some Liberal and Radical minds. "The people are even more eager for the fray than their rulers," lamented A. E. Maddock in the *Westminster Review* of July 1900. "Notwithstanding the ignorance of the masses their political franchise has become so enlarged that its effect is seen in the nature and composition of our Government," complained another elitist pro-Boer. After the wild cel-ebrations of Mafeking Night even some of Britain's staunchest democrats were moved to observe sorrowfully that "the great masses of our people are largely swayed by sentiment."[11]

Frederic Harrison was another old Gladstonian whose romantic longing for the liberalism of an earlier period influenced his current outlook. "Today we have lost much of the higher spirit which inspired our public and private life not more than thirty years ago," he noted sorrowfully in his annual address to the Positivist Society on New Year's Day, 1900. "The reek of the pothouse, the music-hall, the turf, of the share-market, of the thieve's fence, infects our literature, our manners, our amusements, and our ideals of life."[12]

The Positivist critique of British imperialism was more thorough than anything offered by the APS or Anti-Slavery Society. Where the latter might criticize the compound system, pass laws, and hut taxes in South Africa, or the government's failure to ban the sale of liquor to black Africans, and where certain old Gladstonians writing for the *Westminster Review* or *Land and Labour* might argue for nationalizing the land as a solution to every problem, including problems caused by imperialism, the Positivists went much further. "Empire within fifty years has swept away the old barriers of the Constitution against Martial Law on English land," Harrison thundered on one occasion:

> It has introduced taxation of the people's food, by which the whole fabric of Free Trade is undermined. It has re-opened in Ireland the discredited and fatal engine of coercion and arbitrary government. It has driven wild horses through the system of financial policy built up by Peel, by Gladstone, by Stafford Northcote and by Harcourt. It has handed education over to the Church, which has received a new and vast endowment. It has broken up the ancient traditions of Parliament, making both Houses mere engines to carry out a hasty plebiscite. It has brought the English labourer within sight of conscription, whilst it has brought his defensive Trade Unions into peril of total extinction.

This was not an isolated jeremiad. Harrison specialized in the booming remonstrance. In the *Positivist Review* and at the society's weekly meetings, he, S. H. Swinney, Edward Spencer Beesly, and many less well known members of the society maintained a steady flow of criticism of British imperialism and its effects at home and abroad. "We at any rate," Harrison observed with satisfaction toward the end of 1900, "have tried to do our duty."[13]

Almost uniquely among London Radicals, the Positivists explicitly condemned racism. "African, Asiatic, American, the Egyptian priest, the Hindoo Brahmin, the Confucian master ... All are honoured alike [Harrison once said] if only they did useful work in their own age according to their own lights." Yet even among the Positivists a hint of noblesse oblige, or something worse, occasionally appears. For example, in the *Positivist Review* for October 1900, F. S. Marvin observed unobjectionably enough, "It is the same spirit which prompts the white man to drive 'niggers' in the tropics and the capitalist to break up trade unions at home. And the solution must be the same in both cases—combination among the exploited and a stronger sense of human obligation among the governing class." But he ended on rather a different note: "With the weaker and less advanced races, combination, courage, foresight, and tenacity are so much more difficult to attain [than among exploited white workers] that the obligation on the stronger party becomes tenfold greater." And it is striking that not even the great scourge, Harrison, would condemn British imperialism lock, stock, and barrel. "I am a *Meliorist* about our empire," he qualified at a National Liberal Club dinner. "Our business is to make it better, to make it a source of real strength to these islands, of fine progress and moral and material improvement to all who inhabit its soil, whatever their race, whatever their religion, whatever their habits, manners, and ideals of life."[14]

It took an exceptional Radical to develop a systematic critique of British imperial expansion, as opposed to an emotional indictment or one limited to specific charges. The only significant public figure in London from the radical wing of the Liberal Party to do so was J. A. Hobson, the journalist and economist, and not even Hobson believed in racial equality. His writings, like those of almost everybody else in 1900, were replete with references to lower, less civilized, and less advanced races. He was, too, an anti-Semite who believed that Jewish financiers in South Africa had manipulated his country into the Boer War. He opposed Chinese immigration to Britain. Yet for all that, he had fewer illusions about British imperialism than Frederic Harrison. It was, he argued, nothing more than the capitalist escape hatch from a home market glutted with products which underpaid workers could not afford to buy.[15]

Atop this theoretical foundation Hobson easily pierced the hypocrisies and cant offered up for public consumption by the champions of British expansion. He once wrote, "The desire to promote the causes of civilization and Christianity, to improve the economic and spiritual condition of lower races, to crush slavery and to bring all parts of the habitable world into closer material and moral union enter into Imperialism . . . but are not its most powerful directing forces. . . . The real Imperialism . . . is in large measure resolvable into capitalist or profit-seeking influences." Unlike Harrison and other critics of specific imperial policies, Hobson did not believe that a humane imperialism was possible.[16]

Hobson found his primary audience not so much among the old Gladstonians and traditional Radicals (although his social contacts were primarily among them—he was friendly with C. P. Scott, proprietor of the *Manchester Guardian*, whose daughter he married, the historian J. L. Hamond, the journalist and politician, H. W. Massingham, and the philosopher-sociologist-journalist, L. T. Hobhouse), as among the most advanced members of the

Ethical and Positivist societies and socialist parties. He played a leading role[17] in the South Place Ethical Society and eventually abandoned the Liberals for the Labour Party, in which his theories had come to have an impact. In 1900 many London socialists shared Hobson's two-pronged approach— anti-imperialist but racist as well.

In fact racist ideals saturated the London socialist milieu. Admittedly they did not take center stage in the Independent Labour Party (the party's metropolitan presence was minimal anyway) or among the Christian socialists grouped around the weekly journal *New Age*, although the journal diluted its antiracism with romantic calls for principled imperialism, but these were honorable exceptions among London's socialist community. More typical in their approach toward issues of race were the London Fabians, influential in the capital far beyond their numbers. If the Fabians rarely indulged openly in anti-Semitism (although Beatrice Webb held some rather peculiar notions about Jews), they nevertheless certainly regarded Africans and Asians (and Boers, for that matter) with enormous condescension. The Fabians believed that countries of higher civilization should take over backward countries. "The test of a higher civilization is nowhere precisely defined," notes their historian, A. M. McBriar, "but it apparently meant Western European countries and the U.S.A. as against African and Asiatic countries." The whole point of George Bernard Shaw's famous pamphlet *Fabianism and the Empire* was that "a Great Power, consciously or unconsciously, must govern in the interests of civilization as a whole."[18]

In the Social Democratic Federation (SDF), London's largest socialist body, Hobson's double-edged approach was even more clearly evident. Belfort Bax, the party's leading Marxist ideologue, developed a theory of imperialism owing much to Hobson. Bax argued that imperialism was nothing more than the latest stage of capitalist competition for markets, raw materials, and labor. If successful it offered capitalism a new lease on life. Socialists, therefore, should oppose it. He wrote in the SDF organ, *Justice*, "It cannot be too strongly insisted upon that the only hope of the early realization of Socialism lies in some combination of events which shall postpone or abort the further spread of European civilization on a large scale."[19] On this basis the members of the SDF consistently opposed all manifestations of British imperialism. With forthright consistency they condemned their country's activities in West Africa, South Africa, China, and India in equal measure.

Simultaneously, however, SDF leader Henry Hyndman was arguing that "rich Jews" dominated the money markets of the world, the trade in bullion, quicksilver, and copper, the stock exchange, and the press, and that "the negro's brain was not constructed like that of the white man. Its convolutions were different." He made this statement at the party's annual conference in 1900. He was followed by a speaker who said that "some Kaffirs were like wild horses, so inferior were they to the whites" and then by Bax (possibly influenced by the writings of Mary Kingsley), who thought "it would be a mistake to put African natives into colleges and varnish them over with a veneer of western civilization." An ugly strain of racism and anti-Semitism was always present in London's premier socialist body. Scholars who have neglected or minimized this aspect of its history have provided less than a full and realistic picture of the organization.[20]

The fact remains, however, that the SDF also contained antiracists, and that if one is to find among any notable group of Anglo-Saxon Londoners in 1900 the articulation of anti-imperialist sentiments which did not also contain condescending, if kindly meant, references to lower or less civilized races, then it is to the Social Democratic Federation that one must turn. The Jews who belonged to it, and of course many who were not Jewish, opposed the anti-Semites in their ranks. At the conference in 1900 they forced through a resolution regretting that "any impression should have gained ground that *Justice*, by its articles, or the S.D.F. generally, is in any way anti-Semitic" and declaring that the movement opposed "all anti-Semitic parties and national antagonisms without distinction of race or creed."[21]

Nor were Hyndman's utterances about Africans accepted unquestioningly. If his speech at the 1900 conference had been followed by others equally objectionable, it had been preceded by that of Harry Kay, the Dockers' Union delegate, who argued that "under equal conditions the black man was the white's equal" (one wonders what Ben Tillett would have made of that statement). Following the conference, *Justice* carried a letter rebutting Hyndman's pronouncement about convolutions of the brain. "I would like to know on whose authority Mr. Hyndman makes this assertion," queried George Ferdinands, M.D. "I, for one, thought our comrade had too much insight into 'the ways that are mean' than to credit the statements of those who, desiring to salve their conscience for the exploitation of the African, invent all manner of 'root differences' and difficulties."[22]

Moreover, racist and anti-Semite though he undoubtedly was, Hyndman himself believed in an independent India. Over the years he proved himself to be among the staunchest British allies which the Indian nationalist movement possessed. Further, because he was a revolutionary Marxist, Hyndman did not shrink from the possibility that violence would be needed to fulfill his hopes for the subcontinent: "I, as an Englishman whose ancestors and relatives have had their share in the conquest and reconquest of India, declare plainly that I hope to live to see the day when a well-organised rising of the whole population will sweep aside for ever the greed and iniquity of the British rule in Hindostan."[23] Such sentiments placed him beyond the pale not merely among most Anglo-Saxon supporters of Indian nationalism, but among the Indian nationalists themselves, as will be shown in a later chapter.

The SDF, then, contained members who opposed British imperialism for instrumental reasons while believing that lower, barbarous, and savage races occupied the bottom ranks of a racial hierarchy, and members who opposed imperialism on both moral and material grounds while insisting upon the essential equality of the races.[24] And it contained members who appear to have held these apparently mutually exclusive attitudes simultaneously. Nevertheless, so far as I can tell, this contradictory body, or rather a section within it, came closer to articulating an all-out critique of British imperialism than any other organized group dominated by Anglo-Saxons in London.

E nter into Celtic, that is to say, Irish, anti-imperial London and, on one level, little changes. On another level, however, the London-Irish critics of empire were altogether different from their Anglo-Saxon counterparts. They claimed to be descendants of the original victims of British imperialism and to be victims of it still. This gave their anti-empire rhetoric a distinctive slant which deserves separate consideration.

Historians estimate that 60,000 people, or 1.31 percent of London's population, were Irish-born at the turn of the twentieth century and that 435,000 men, women, and children of Irish descent were living in the imperial metropolis at that time. A despised ethnic minority themselves, most of the Irish in London had been directed into casual or unskilled jobs, often along the riverside and frequently at the docks. They clustered in London's poor districts, especially St. Giles, Smithfield, Camberwell, St. George's in the East, and Southwark. By 1900, however, some London Irish were escaping the most egregious forms of discrimination through assimilation into the dominant culture, while a minority had emerged from poverty, entering into the labor aristocracy or the various grades of the middle class.[25]

This was a significant community, larger than any other non-Anglo-Saxon population in London, one whose political influence might be considerable and whose political opinions, accordingly, were much assayed, at least during election campaigns. The London Irish were politically eclectic. Mainly Liberal since Gladstone's conversion to Home Rule, some had moved over to Labour (many were active in the dockers' and gasworkers' unions), while others supported the Conservatives at the behest of the Catholic

Church, which was strongly patriotic and therefore progovernment during the Boer War. The fact of the matter, however, is that contemporaries exaggerated the Irish influence on elections, apparently forgetting that a high proportion of the community was too poor and too peripatetic to qualify for the vote or too politically apathetic to cast one.[26] On the other hand, in select London constituencies the Irish probably did play a crucial role (see chapter 10 below), and, in any event, voting is not the only way to register political opinions or to affect the wider political context.

In 1900 the Irish nationalist movement was at a low ebb. The Irish Republican Brotherhood (IRB), or Fenian movement, which advocated an independent Irish Republic attained by revolution if necessary, maintained a shadowy underground existence on both sides of the Irish Sea, but its morale was low, its presence and impact in London close to nil. The Home Rule movement and Irish Parliamentary Party, which under the leadership of Charles Parnell had come tantalizingly close to victory during the late 1880s, had fractured after Parnell's fall from grace in 1891 and was, for the moment, also a negligible force. Nevertheless a surprising number of nationalist associations survived in the imperial metropolis, some serving as umbrella organizations for affiliated offshoots and branches, so that, despite the general quiescence, more than a few Irish nationalist groups were meeting regularly within the greater metropolitan area.[27] In looking for evidence of organized anti-imperialist sentiment among the London Irish the place to begin, perhaps counterintuitively, is not with the explicitly political organizations and leagues among these groups, whether revolutionary or constitutional (although I shall come to them), but rather with the ostensibly politically neutral cultural societies like the Gaelic League, the Irish Texts Society, even the Gaelic Athletic Association.

By 1900 these had taken firm root in Ireland, where the "Irish Ireland" idea was strong. They had taken root in London too, and fear of assimilation made them inherently anti-imperial in a general sense, perhaps more so than in Ireland because in London they sought to preserve Irish culture from the unalloyed prevailing Anglo-Saxon ethos. "Once our people become wanderers over the face of the world, racial sentiments and ties seldom outlast a generation," warned William O'Brien, formerly a Fenian, now an Irish M.P. and editor of a nationalist newspaper, the *Irish People*. The task of the London Irish, therefore, was to maintain their ethnic identity even though they resided in the imperial metropolis, or as "Mr. P. T. MacG" put it in the *Half-Yearly Magazine of the Gaelic League of London*, "to retard the Anglicising process."[28]

In reading about the London Irish one is reminded of the London Jews, whose coreligionists from eastern Europe also were flooding into the imperial metropolis at this time (and who held a Zionist congress in London in 1900). The Irish did not have to recreate a national homeland to return to, as the Jews did, and the Jews were not themselves a people who had been colonized by the British. Nevertheless the parallels are striking. Like the Jews, the Irish strove, not merely individually but through various organizations, to keep their language alive, to celebrate national holidays (like St. Patrick's Day) and other important moments in their history as a people, to maintain traditional practices and customs, in short, to preserve their culture as an autonomous force within the larger Anglo-Saxon context.

The leader of this culturally assertive movement among the Irish in London was Frank Fahy, originally from Galway, who founded the Southwark Irish Literary Club in 1883. This body, whose premises (although frequently shifted) became an important meeting place for Irish men and women in the metropolis, sponsored dramatic sketches, concerts, lectures, readings, and numerous social events. In 1891 it changed its name to the Irish Literary Society of London. Fahy also organized a Junior Irish Club, edited a *Child's Irish Song Book*, and wrote a *Child's History of Ireland* in rhyme.[29]

In 1896 this indefatigable figure helped to establish and then became president of the London section of the Gaelic League. The league, whose branches swiftly proliferated throughout the metropolis, took an even more active role than the literary society in preserving Irish culture in London, first of all by teaching Gaelic. It achieved some success for, by 1900, "all meetings of the London Gaelic League [were to] be formally opened . . . conducted and formally concluded in the national language," and moreover, according to an enthusiast who probably exaggerated, whereas "ten years ago you might never hear a word of Irish spoken in London . . . now in Irish circles it is everywhere spoken and the Irishman who cannot speak it is wont to feel very much ashamed of the fact." The league lobbied Parliament to enact laws mandating the teaching of Gaelic in all Irish elementary schools and the establishment of an Irish university that would cater to the Catholic majority. In March 1900, much to the league's satisfaction, John Redmond, leader of the Irish Parliamentary Party, promised to support this two-pronged campaign.[30]

Meanwhile, the league was holding fortnightly debates in Irish, at which lecturers "extolled the literary value of our tongue and pointed out that philologists and ethnologists the world over set a high value on it." The lectures were crowded. "Over 120 members attended the weekly central meeting at 3 Bedford Street, Strand, on Monday the 5th inst.," recounted one of the audience in a typical report. The Gaelic League of London held classes in Irish singing and step dancing and social events as well.[31]

An Irish Texts Society, formed under the auspices of the Irish Literary Society of London, appeared in 1898. Dedicated to the preservation and republication of traditional Irish folk literature, myths, and fairy-tales, the group counted 470 members in its London chapter by 1900, and its subscriptions totaled £305 10s. 8d.[32] Through the Gaelic Athletic Association, whose London section was founded in February 1899, the Irish strove also to maintain interest in such Irish sports as hurley and Gaelic football.

Although these groups claimed to be nonpolitical, in fact their members usually "remembered that they were Irishmen first and non-political afterwards." At a typical meeting of the Irish Literary Society early in 1900, for example, the audience heard a lecture by Thomas Lough, M.P., entitled "One Hundred Years of Irish Finance." It read in part, "In 1795 the Imperial and local taxation [in Ireland] was only 9s. per head of the inhabitants; by 1897 it had increased to 55s. or a total of 12¼ millions. While the burden of the country had thus been increased the population fell to half, pauperism doubled, the country towns sank into ruin, methods of agriculture exhibited little improvement, the value of crops and stock declined and land was going out of cultivation." Not the speech one would expect at a literary event, but cultural nationalists were likely to be political nationalists too. In 1898 the London Gaelic League supported the celebrations of the centenary of Wolfe Tone's abortive insurrection.[33]

Still, the essential thrust of the Gaelic League, the Irish Texts Society, and the Gaelic Athletic Association remained cultural. This served not to dilute but rather to strengthen their anti-imperialism. It probably never occurred to Anglo-Saxon critics of British imperialism that the *cultural* hegemony of their country could or should be disputed; most were concerned only with criticizing specific imperial policies. By insisting on the merits and distinctiveness of Irish sports, traditions, customs, literature, and language, indeed upon their right to an existence apart from English sports, traditions, and so on, the Gaelic League and the others were rejecting England's right to impose its culture upon Ireland and upon Irish emigrants in England. This was a profound if perhaps slightly amorphous anti-imperialism which few Anglo-Saxon critics of empire can have shared or sympathized with or even understood.

And yet the anti-imperialism of these cultural groups was more visceral than political. To find articulated and sharply expressed, if not necessarily more sincere or profound, anti-imperialist sentiment among the London Irish one must turn to the conventional political societies, both the revolutionary republican and the Home Rule constitutional: to the Irish National Club for the former; to the Irish National League of Great Britain (INLGB), later renamed the United Irish League (UIL), for the latter.

In Dublin the IRB was moribund at the turn of the twentieth century; in London its supporters confined themselves to celebrating historic anniversaries, like the centenary of Wolfe Tone's insurrection, and to delivering the occasional bloodcurdling speech. The brotherhood's traditions and memory remained green, however, in the mind of Mark Ryan, who, although he did not belong to the INLGB or UIL, seems to have taken a leading role in practically every other London-Irish organization, including the Young Ireland Society, the Irish National Club, the Gaelic League, and the Gaelic Athletic Association. A devoted Fenian of long-standing, a former gunrunner, now in addition to talent spotting and fund-raising for the IRB,[34] Ryan strove to maintain in London both intellectual and physical space for those who still believed in an independent Irish Republic achieved by revolution.

A not altogether straight but nevertheless traceable line runs from London's Young Ireland Society, which Ryan helped to form in the 1880s, through the London branches of two more organizations with which he was involved, Sinn Fein and its precursor, Cumann na nGaedheal, founded in 1899, all the way to the Easter Rebellion of 1916. Along this line another nodal point is the Irish National Club, located until late 1900 on Henrietta Street and then removed to Chancery Lane. Ryan took an interest in its establishment and operation too. On the one hand this body provided a venue for the London-Irish assertion of cultural anti-imperialism. Its social events offered "a rare treat to the young Irishman or Irish woman who has the least spark of love for the old songs, the old tunes or the old dances to which one was accustomed during the days 'when we were young and free.'" On the other hand it also made a point of expressing *political* opposition to British imperialism. During the Boer War, the club "passed resolutions denouncing the action of England in trying to grab more territory, and pointing out that Irishmen assisting their old enemy in the work of enslaving the Boers were acting treacherously to Ireland and to the cause of freedom. [It] subscribed towards the Irish Ambulance corps, and distributed leaflets with the object of preventing Irish soldiers from serving England against the Boers." Thus an imperial war helped to politicize Irish anti-imperialism and to give it point.[35]

How much point remains debatable. "We made no disguise [at the club] of the fact that our principles were the principles of Fenianism, and we got many recruits for our underground movement," Ryan boasted in his autobiography. To a degree the evidence bears him out. In October 1899 a constitutionalist who attended at Henrietta Street reported dubiously, "There was a lot of speech making of a warlike kind—one young fellow wanted no County Councils, no Parliament. Frank Hugh told of the important work

Arthur Lynch (of Galway) was doing ... apparently on the lines of Wolfe Tone." And some months later J. Mulcahy argued before the club that "the National Ideal was always more effectively brought nearer by physical force than by constitutional methods." Revolutionary rhetoric was rare among Anglo-Saxon critics of imperialism in 1900, though perhaps not absent in the SDF. Among the Fenian element in London, however, it was the distinguishing characteristic.[36]

Whether it was meant or taken seriously remains unclear. That the British authorities did not entirely ignore it is suggested not only by Ryan himself, whose memoirs are sprinkled with references to spies sent by Scotland Yard to keep tabs on him and his organizations,[37] but also by the existence among the Home Office papers at the Public Record Office in London of a curious document written on October 14, 1896, by Theophilus Farrall, an Englishman of Irish descent lately returned to London from New York City. Farrall claimed to have penetrated Irish nationalist revolutionary circles in both cities:

> I saw maps of the British Isles and portions of maps of the British Isles in districts with certain railway bridges marked down for destruction and bridges at or near London, I think on every railway entering into London. The *modus operandi*... is to get a man quietly stationed ... and at a given time the bridges are to be blown up....
>
> I overheard them on several occasions discussing "incendiary fires" to take place at the country mansions of noblemen and MPs, etc.... They discussed the way to use a new "Greek" fire they have, and the ease with which the work could be done.... They had the locations marked of perhaps all of the Government powder magazines in the country....
>
> What appeared to me of the greatest importance and the most devilish scheme of all was the quite frequent discussion about the "battleships," and they certainly have commenced for some time now to get one or two "good men"... on the different men of war for the express purpose of damaging the propelling and other machinery.

There is no mention of the Irish National Club or of Ryan in this "Confidential Statement," or of other Irish revolutionaries in London except for "Malloy and[or] Harrity," of whom Farrall learned while in New York City, but "which was the London man and which the Manchester man I did not overhear." Farrall, who was down on his luck, hoped the government would pay him a thousand pounds for this information, but in the end he received only fifty. Yet it is suggestive that so obscure a personage managed to penetrate the highest levels of British officialdom. He found a ready listener in Sir Robert Anderson, assistant commissioner of the Metropolitan Police, who contacted the former Irish secretary, Arthur Balfour, who eventually brought the prime minister himself into the picture. It was Lord Salisbury who stipulated the sum Farrall eventually received.[38]

While some Irish nationalists living at the heart of the empire resisted imperial absorption by upholding Irish culture, then, others claimed that only violent revolution would suffice. It is fair to wonder, though, how much hardheaded planning, as opposed to fantastical dreaming, they had undertaken. Most historians emphasize the dreaming.[39] The vast majority of metropolitan Irish nationalists refrained from revolutionary rhetoric altogether. Militant cultural anti-imperialists they would have been, which already distinguishes them in the anti-imperial metropolis, but by and large they were political moderates focused, at least for the time being, on Gladstonian Home Rule.

At the turn of the century, however, this movement too was far from vibrant. Gladstone was dead, the current Liberal leaders thought Home Rule a vote-loser, and meanwhile the Conservatives were in the middle of a ten-year stint of power. In London the INLGB was weak. According to Lynn Hollen Lees only ten branches remained, while Paul Thompson counts "less than ten." Yet there were signs of revival. In the spring of the year the the INLGB changed its name to United Irish League as part of the movement to reunite Parnellites and anti-Parnellites. By then fourteen branches were reporting activities to the London columns of the Irish press. As a token of good faith the league appointed an old Parnellite, John Brady, to be its north London organizer. The former London organizer John Denvir, who had sided with the anti-Parnell forces, now confined his efforts to south London. On May 26 the *Irish Weekly Independent* refers to the formation of nine new branches, most of them north of the Thames. On June 2, the same newspaper counted something "under thirty branches in the metropolitan district." Unfortunately it is impossible to estimate average branch membership. In November 1900 the Hoxton branch of the UIL had eighty-six members paying dues of sixpence monthly, while the Bermondsey branch reported "over four hundred members." Most branches must have been much smaller. And it is not known how active their members were. Yet it seems safe to believe that the league's fortunes were improving during this year.[40]

In 1900 the national organizer of the INLGB (and then of the UIL) was an Irish M.P., James Francis Xavier O'Brien, resident of Clapham, although he "hate[d] living in the enemy's country and long[ed] to return to Ireland." A veteran Fenian who had taken part in the abortive insurrection of 1867, afterward he had endured a long term of imprisonment under difficult conditions (preferable, however, to his original sentence, which was to be hanged, drawn, and quartered). O'Brien had sided with the anti-Parnellites when the split came. Now responsible for league activities throughout Britain, he spent much time corresponding with Liberal M.P.s and candidates, arranging for Irish speakers to support them in select constituencies, and making sure that Irishmen had registered to vote. He was also a ubiquitous presence at London UIL branch meetings. Furthermore he oversaw the efforts of the two London organizers, John Denvir and John Brady.[41]

From O'Brien's papers and from newspaper reports it is apparent that INLGB (and later UIL) branches were almost as much social as political bodies, which means almost as much culturally as politically anti-imperial. One reads in the Irish press of London UIL-organized concerts, dances, festivities marking St. Patrick's Day and other important anniversaries in Irish history almost as often as of political debates and historical lectures. According to the minute books of the Father Purcell branch of the INLGB, members, who met in Macklin Street, off Drury Lane, spent nearly as much time organizing such gatherings (and raising funds for such worthy causes as Catholic orphanages and hospitals) as they did on nationalist politics.[42] Still the main aim of the UIL in London was to promote not merely a sense of Irish identity among members, but also nationalist political purpose, and to recruit as many members as possible.

This wing of London's Irish nationalist movement consciously eschewed revolutionary language. "Though the remedial legislation was far from perfect," Denvir once admitted to the Peckham branch, "they had secured machinery for the fixing of fair rents. . . . [Then] the County Councils in Ireland were a step in the direction of Home Rule and no doubt a further extension of self-government would come." The Father Purcell branch took pains to distance itself from Fenian methods too, resolving on one occasion "that we view with feelings of horror and detestation the abominable outrage in Dublin resulting in the death of Constable Lynott and unhesitatingly express the conviction that the murderous deed was the work of an enemy of the Irish National cause." At the same meeting it reaffirmed its devotion to the Liberal Party, "render[ing] warmest felicitations to Mr. Gladstone on the completion of his 83rd year."[43]

Yet even in constitutional circles the advocacy of physical force as a legitimate tactic was not inconceivable under certain circumstances. The Boer War brought it to the surface. One branch of the London UIL expressed "sorrow at the surrender of that gallant man, [Boer] General Cronje," and gladness that "he succeeded in getting some of his guns away" which could "be used once again against the British." In the House of Commons, Michael Davitt sympathized with the Boers "because they are absolutely in the right in defending with their lives the independence of their country." Davitt quit his parliamentary seat and traveled to South Africa to aid a pro-Boer contingent of Irish volunteers. Upon leaving Britain he asserted, "No cause of right will ever find support from the House of Commons unless it is backed up by force."[44]

The Boer War also elicited from UIL clubs their most vehement anti-imperialist resolutions. "Nothing is to be gained from the shedding of Irish blood in defense of the British Empire," warned the UIL's East Finsbury branch. "All their sympathies were with the handful of gallant Boers who were carrying on an unequal struggle against the gigantic forces of [English imperialism]," J. F. X. O'Brien averred to the Bermondsey branch. The British colony of Natal, "acquired by force and fraud of the usual character that had built the British Empire," a Mr. Brogan informed the Deptford branch of the UIL, had become "at the present moment the scene of one of the most heroic struggles that history had ever recorded."[45]

Another manifestation of anti-imperialism among the London Irish: they sympathized with Indian nationalists too. It is well known that Frank Hugh O'Donnell and other Irish M.P.s helped establish what later became the British Committee of the Indian National Congress and that Parnell briefly considered allowing an Indian to stand for a safe Irish nationalist seat. Nor was it lost upon Irishmen that Indians in 1900 were suffering from a famine as brutal as the one that had devastated their own country half a century earlier. When Englishmen celebrated a Royal Feast Day on June 23, William O'Brien urged his readers to remember "about one hundred millions of Indians who did not 'charge their glasses' . . . nor did their hearts throb with devotion to the Queen. For they are starving." Irish nationalists identified with Indians to a degree.[46]

It proved possible for London-Irish nationalists to cooperate with anti-imperialist socialists who were also interested in India. Here the relevant figure is the East End SDF activist John Scurr, who became a frequent speaker at UIL gatherings and for some period presided at meetings of the Brian Boru (Tower Hamlets) branch. Scurr belonged to the antiracist wing of the SDF. Eventually he became a Labour M.P., an ally of the great anti-imperialist George Lansbury, and the author of a pamphlet advocating Indian independence. On February 10, 1900, he spoke to the Clapham branch of what was still the INLGB. During the next two months he spoke as well to the Bermondsey branch, his own branch in Tower Hamlets, and the Bow and Bromley branch. His theme was imperialism, and although no detailed report of these speeches survives, given what we know of his later history it seems safe to assume at the very least that he placed his subject in the context elaborated by

Belfort Bax and J. A. Hobson. "He dealt particularly," according to the one brief report we do possess, "with the question in connection with the British Empire, showing that whatever benefit certain classes might derive from the plunder of other nations, under the Imperial system sooner or later Imperialism would ruin the people of England." At the conclusion of this effort he received from the members of Bermondsey UIL a "hearty vote of thanks." He received a "hearty vote of thanks" too after lecturing at Bow and Bromley. Perhaps these expressions were mere formulaic endings to reports of such occasions, but then, "Mr. Scurr is an able speaker," reported one of his auditors; his speech had been "most interesting and eloquent," reported another. Scurr's perspective on imperial affairs cannot be entirely discounted as an influence among London UIL members.[47]

Another intriguing figure among London-Irish anti-imperialists is the saintly former Irish M.P. Alfred Webb. Brought up in Dublin as a Quaker, nevertheless he joined the movement of the Irish Catholic majority. "It is like breathing a purer and higher air to have learned to love and trust my Catholic fellow countrymen," he wrote. But then neither creed, religion, gender, nor race interfered with Webb's regard for anybody. Raised in Ireland's most prominent antislavery family, he knew personally most of the American abolitionists, white and black, from childhood. When he became M.P. for West Waterford, he discovered his best friends not only among Irish nationalist members, but among the early socialists like Burns and Hardie and especially in the Radical wing of the Liberal Party with whose members he was in constant touch. "My most congenial work [in Parliament] was with Henry J. Wilson and men of that class on humanitarian questions," he recorded. This meant speaking up for the Irish, but it meant speaking up, too, for all "oppressed people that could not help themselves—such as slaves, women deprived of the franchise, the Indian people, practically without a voice in the government of their own country—the Chinese with the use of opium almost forced on them." He took seriously the Gladstonian injunction to sympathize with subject peoples struggling to be free.[48]

Webb opposed the Boer War, although by the time it broke out he had given up his parliamentary seat (1896) and returned to Dublin. But his letters to the Irish and British press were read in London by the Irish community, and he retained a beneficent influence. While Webb condemned British practices in South Africa, he did not, as so many other Irish nationalists did, ignore the plight of Africa's native population. "They are neither 'as ferocious as wild beasts,' nor as 'irrational as children,'" he wrote. "In their nature they, like the Hindus, are perhaps more really Christian than we. Whatever they might have done if they had had the power and opportunity they have not, in fact, like us, degraded, decimated or extinguished every race with which they have come in contact and which it was their material interest to degrade, decimate or extinguish." When the African American Ida B. Wells brought her antilynching campaign to Britain, Webb "joined in giving a breakfast to her" at the House of Commons. Later he was to help the West Indian Henry Sylvester Williams to organize the African Association and prepare for the world's first Pan-African Conference.[49]

Webb made his greatest contribution to the anti-imperialist cause in Britain through his connection with the Indian nationalist movement. Frank Hugh O'Donnell notwithstanding, Webb was India's best friend among the Irish Parliamentary Party. He joined the executive of the BCINC, traveled regularly to London from Dublin to attend its meetings after quitting the House of Commons, and contributed frequently to its journal, *India*. Dadabhai Naoroji, India's first M.P. (1892–95) (see chapter 8), recognized Webb's importance. In 1894, much to Webb's surprise, Naoroji invited him to preside at the tenth annual meeting of the Indian National Congress in Bombay. Webb gladly accepted the invitation.

Given the Irish response to the Boer War and to the plight of India under British rule, and the influence of men like Scurr and Webb, the logical conclusion seems to be that Irish nationalism and British imperialism were fated antagonists (as Indian nationalism and British imperialism would prove to be), that even Home Rule could never be more than a stepping-stone toward complete independence. For how could any subject people exist as a nation, which is what even the constitutionalists demanded for their country, without overthrowing their imperial masters?[50] It may be, therefore, that anti-imperialist statements uttered by Irish nationalists opposed to the Boer War or on behalf of the starving Indians or condemning British imperialism more generally, as John Scurr and Alfred Webb had done, were in some way qualitatively more anti-imperial than like statements uttered by Anglo-Saxon anti-imperialists.

Or perhaps not. Irish nationalists were also capable of a grating, macho boastfulness and chauvinism. The British Empire had been built and sustained not by "the stunted Cockneys, the dull Hodges, the stupid yokels from Somerset," nor by "the pasty weaklings of the English towns and the craven clods of the English shires," but rather by "the country which gave the Dublin Fusiliers and the Connaught Rangers," William O'Brien crowed after those regiments helped the British to victory in South Africa. "Responsible spokesmen of England sought to hide and . . . to minimise" the contribution of Irishmen to the empire, another Irish journalist claimed.[51]

Such statements reveal something more complicated than simple pride in

Irish accomplishment. Irish nationalists, like Radical and socialist critics of empire, sometimes objected not to imperialism as a whole but rather to specific imperial policies, while approving generally of Britain's world role. But then the nationalist movement and British imperialism were not necessarily in conflict. The editors of *New Ireland* announced on the front page of their March 10, 1900, edition, "Imperialism in its truest sense demands Home Rule for Ireland;" the *Irish People* demanded "a share in the Empire."[52]

From these sentiments much could follow (as it did with Radical and socialist critics of empire who were critics, really, of specific imperialist policies only), for instance, racism and anti-Semitism. The Hoxton branch of the UIL, for example, condemned the British for fighting the Boers "at the bidding of the Jewish money mongers of the Stock Exchange." On October 13, *New Ireland*, much read in London-Irish circles, rebuked William O'Brien, M.P., editor of the rival, *Irish People*, for marrying "Mddle. Sophie d'Affalovich, the daughter of a wealthy Jew banker in Paris." The *Irish Weekly Independent*, also popular in Irish London frequently vented anti-Dreyfusard sentiments. So much for the hope that two despised immigrant groups in London would make common cause.[53]

During the Boxer Rebellion Irish nationalists cast the Chinese as a people with "little regard for human life," who waged war "after a more infamous fashion than the soldiers of Christian England." They scorned the indigenous inhabitants of Africa as "naked black savages." Wishing to express sympathy "for another gallant little nation which is struggling to preserve her distinct existence while a great Empire is striving to merge it into its body politic," the Irish never considered the rebels of Ashantiland or the followers of Matt Sellah in Borneo, let alone the Boxers in China: they chose instead to "deeply enlist [their] sympathies" on behalf of—the Finns.[54]

Thus Irish nationalists, the very ones who claimed to be anti-imperialists, asserted their whiteness, their distinctness from other victims of British imperialism. They wanted not the abolition of British dominion, but rather that England "treat Ireland as she has treated the Australians and the other self-governed peoples in her dominions." What grated was not that British imperialists had decimated and conquered the Sudanese, for example, but instead that "the Irish are still 'Hottentots'—on a level, after seven hundred years of British rule with the remnant of Dervish tribes who were subdued in Central Africa in 1898."[55]

It was left to T. M. Healy, a leading member of the Parliamentary Party, to demonstrate that racism and anti-imperialism, far from being mutually exclusive, were indissolubly linked in certain Irish minds. Speaking before the House of Commons, Healy condemned the government for sending Irishmen to their deaths in South Africa on behalf of "a number of German Jews." The Boers resisted incorporation into the British Empire, he thundered, because they objected to the "pleasure of having a nigger as a magistrate probably, certainly as a policeman" ruling over them.[56]

Thus Irish anti-imperialists in London were prey to the same tensions, ambivalences, and contradictions as Anglo-Saxon critics of empire. Some advocated cultural, others political anti-imperialism; a few championed physical force, the majority believed in moral suasion; bigots and antibigots peopled the movement too.

Yet it was the atypical Alfred Webb who represented what was best in the Irish nationalist movement. He stood upon a pivot-point in anti-imperial London, the nexus where Anglo-Saxon Radicals, Irish nationalists, Indians, Chinese, and men and women of African descent might converge. It was on this spot, if anywhere, that an all-encompassing, color-blind opposition to British imperialism could take root and grow, and, in fact, that is where it did grow, to a degree. On the other hand, as the next two chapters will also show, the historian who listens will hear diverse anti-imperial voices amidst the overwhelmingly patriotic and imperialist cacophony of London noises, and the particular note sounded by Webb was comparatively weak and most usually disregarded.

✧   ✧   ✧

CHAPTER 8

DADABHAI NAOROJI AND THE
SEARCH FOR RESPECT

T the turn of the twentieth century anti-imperial London contained an active, well-organized, well-connected, and politically sophisticated Indian contingent. Its size can only be estimated, not least because the number of Indians resident in the metropolis was constantly changing. Possibly a thousand Indians lived in London in 1900. They were mainly students of law, medicine, or technical and business practices, or they were professional men and their families, or they were seamen called Lascars, who when in London usually stayed in the East End. At most several hundred could be counted on to attend nationalist meetings and demonstrations. In a city of six million this was an insignificant figure, yet India was the jewel in the crown of the British Empire, occupying a vital space in the imaginations of Londoners. Consequently India's children in the capital city had a role to play disproportionate to their numbers. They were active not so much in local affairs as in helping to shape the emerging ambiguous and much-qualified national discourse of anti-imperialism.[1]

During the late-Victorian period the undisputed leader of this community was Dadabhai Naoroji, a small, elderly gentleman with square jaw, fine features, spectacles, and white beard. Naoroji, born in Bombay in 1825 the only child of a poor Parsi family, arrived in the imperial metropolis in 1855 as partner in the Indian commercial firm Cama and Company. Already he had made his mark in Bombay as professor of mathematics and philosophy at his alma mater, Elphinstone College, and as a nationalist and advocate of female education. Within three years of arriving in London he had established his own cotton company. He also taught Gujarati at University College. Both the business and the university setting were suitable bases from which to recruit promising young Indians to take the Indian civil service exam, which, strangely if logically from the British point of view, was held not in India but in London.

Throughout the mid-Victorian period Naoroji shuttled between England and his native land, playing an active role in both countries. In India he was appointed the *diwan* (prime minister) of the state of Baroda but resigned within the year because he believed the prince of the province to be corrupt; he won election to the Bombay municipal corporation and the town council of the corporation. He served a term on the Bombay Legislative Council. He had come to believe, however, that reform in India depended upon the imperial Parliament in London. In 1885, therefore, he returned to the imperial metropolis, where he remained without significant interruption until 1907. In London he came to act as father figure and counselor to Indian students and immigrants, and as leader of the minority who were active in the Indian nationalist movement. In 1888, when Mohandas Gandhi arrived in Britain to study law, he found that "Indian students had free access to the G.O.M. [Grand Old Man] at all hours of the day . . . no matter to which province or religion they belonged. He was there to advise and guide them in their difficulties. . . . And so Dadabhai became real Dada to me." Thereafter Gandhi often looked to the elderly Parsi for wise counsel.[2]

Naoroji played an important role as a public figure and participant in the various Indian societies active in late-Victorian London, many of which he helped to found. He was Britain's most indefatigable advocate of Indian causes, as a public speaker and as expert advisor to various government-sponsored commissions and committees of enquiry. Well connected with Liberal and Radical politicians, he contested Holborn as a Gladstonian in 1886, losing to the Conservative candidate, Col. F. Duncan, but winning attention and sympathy when Lord Salisbury, the Conservative leader, publicly doubted whether "we have yet got to that point when a British constituency will take a black man to represent them." At the next general election, in 1892, Central Finsbury at any rate gave the reply to Salisbury by electing Naoroji, who had stood again as a Liberal.

Salisbury's Black Man, as Naoroji was often called during this period, became an active constituency M.P., but by then he had helped to fashion the political instrument in which he and other Indians resident in London were most interested. This was the British Committee of the Indian National Congress (BCINC), the organization charged by its parent body with educating British public opinion on Indian matters. From the late 1880s until the outbreak of World War I this was the most notable Indian nationalist organization in England. Yet scholars of British history have scarcely attended to it.

The BCINC's prehistory extended back half a century. In 1839 Englishmen sympathetic to India formed a British India Society. In 1855 like-minded figures established the India Reform Society. These precursors were relatively

CENTRAL FINSBURY
PARLIAMENTARY ELECTION, 1895.

D. NAOROJI.

Address to his Fellow Electors
in Central Finsbury, July, 1895.

30. Dadabhai Naoroji election address.
Courtesy of the London Borough of Islington—Libraries Department.

obscure and uninfluential; each was short-lived. In 1865, however, Naoroji
and W. C. Bonnerjee, who was also to play a prominent role in Indian nationalist politics both in India and in England, founded a more noteworthy
body, the London Indian Society. Its purpose was to discuss "political, social
and literary subjects relating to India with a view to promot[ing] the interests of the people of that country." This society merged a year later with the
East India Association, of which Naoroji was also a cofounder but which had
come to be dominated by retired English officers who wished to supply M.P.s
and the public with information on Indian subjects. The enlarged organization prospered for about a decade, attracting prominent English and Anglo-
Indian sympathizers, including influential Liberal and Radical M.P.s. It sponsored meetings at which papers on Indian subjects were read. It lobbied
Westminster, organizing deputations to the House of Commons. As late as

1883 an offshoot of the committee chaired by one of England's leading Radicals, John Bright, was attempting to rally pro-Indian sentiment in Britain. The association's conservative members, who disliked the radicalism of Bright and of the original Indian founders, managed to take control, however, and succeeded eventually in turning it into little more than a discussion group.[3]

There were by then a number of other London-based political clubs and societies for Indian nationalists to join. Of these the most influential was a second London India Society, founded in 1872 by an Indian student at Cambridge, A. M. Bose, to "foster the spirit of nationalism among the Indian residents in Britain." Naoroji played a leading role in this organization too, assuming its presidency. It may be that Naoroji had become dissatisfied with the East India Association and encouraged Bose to start the new group. In 1898 the India Office considered the London India Society important enough to send spies to its meetings.[4]

Meanwhile Indian nationalists at home, including a number of Anglo-Indians, also had been active. The failed revolution of 1857 (which the English shrewdly termed a mere mutiny) suggested that violent resistance to imperialism would be futile; instead the Western-educated Indian elite followed British methods of constitutional agitation. Inspired by the writings of such English radicals as Percy Bysshe Shelley, Thomas Paine, and John Stuart Mill and then by the activities of reformist bodies like the Anti-Corn-Law League, they were much influenced also, as noted in chapter 7, by Irish nationalists like Frank Hugh O'Donnell, M.P. for Dungarvan and London correspondent of the *Bombay Gazette*, who in 1878 had mooted plans for Irish-Indian nationalist cooperation. O'Donnell believed that the Irish party were the "natural representatives and spokesmen of the unrepresented nationalities of the Empire" and hoped Parnell would offer a safe seat to Naoroji. But it was Irish organization which most piqued Indian interest; and when in 1882 O'Donnell and his associates founded the Irish National League of Great Britain, in India the nationalists set about establishing an equivalent body. The Irish remained helpful. At three meetings held in London during the spring of 1883 to carry out the resolutions of the embryonic organization in India, O'Donnell was conspicuous among several Irish parliamentarians.[5]

In 1885 success crowned the efforts of these Indian patriots and their sympathizers: on the subcontinent they established the Indian National Congress (INC), the organization which, under the leadership of Gandhi and Jawaharlal Nehru, eventually would guide the country to independence. Within months they had also begun to take the steps which would lead to formation of an INC branch in London, the BCINC.

At first, perhaps, this latter step did not seem necessary. INC leaders believed that moderate organized advocacy in India on the British model would suffice. Their aim was to rouse educated Indians to agitate peacefully for better conditions, and even these were carefully limited. Virtually no one in the INC demanded outright independence for India or, despite Irish influence, even home rule, let alone violent revolution, to attain such goals. The congress's most advanced members, including Anglo-Indians like founder-member Allen Octavian Hume, son of the great Radical M.P. Joseph Hume, looked toward Canada and other white-settler colonies for models of government, while the majority of Indian members wished merely for additional seats at the table with the imperialists who governed their country. At the first congress, in 1886, W. C. Bonnerjee (who had helped Naoroji to form the first London Indian Society twenty-one years earlier), declared in his presidential address that Indians wanted "to be governed according to the ideals of governments prevalent in Europe" and that, in agitating for reforms, the INC was merely following in India the example set by Richard Cobden and John Bright in Britain.[6]

A modest agenda was natural for a body whose founders thought they had learned the lessons of 1857. Yet even to the carefully nuanced expression of limited aims which the INC allowed itself, British authorities were unsympathetic. "You cannot awaken and appeal to the spirit of nationality in India," Curzon once wrote, "and at the same time profess loyal acceptance of British rule."[7] No matter how moderate the INC proclaimed itself to be, the imperial government insisted, correctly as it turned out, that its goals were inherently radical, that potentially the INC was a revolutionary organization.

This adamantine opposition proved to be the final impetus for the foundation of the BCINC, for the INC answer was to extend its agitation to Britain itself. INC connections with that country were strong, as has been demonstrated, and England, after all, was where the decisions affecting India ultimately were made. "The least that we could do," Hume thought, "would be to provide ample funds for sending and keeping constantly in England deputations of our ablest speakers to plead their country's cause . . . to flood Great Britain with pamphlets, leaflets, newspapers, and magazine articles, in a word to carry on an agitation there, on the lines and scale of that in virtue of which the Anti-Corn-Law League triumphed."[8]

The INC had been established in 1885. The immediate progenitor of the BCINC was the Indian Political Agency, founded in 1888 by Dadabhai Naoroji and his old friend Bonnerjee, who now was serving on the Calcutta High Court. The Bengali Motilal Ghose, one of the founders of the INC and editor and coproprietor of the Calcutta newspaper *Amrita Bazar Patrika*, guaran-

teed funds up to five hundred pounds per year for the fledgling body.[9] A handful of Anglo-Indians and London-based English sympathizers, most of whom
had spent time in India, also played a crucial role. Among these the most important were William Sprotson Caine, the former Chamberlainite and present Radical M.P. for Barrow-in-Furness, who became the agency's chairman;
and William Digby, a radical journalist, author, and failed parliamentary candidate, who became its secretary. Hume, in India, and his friend in London
the Scottish M.P. Sir William Wedderburn, Bart., were also primary actors
at this early stage, Wedderburn proving to be a more reliable source of funds
over the long haul than Ghose would be.

The Indian Political Agency survived only for seven months, but it laid
the groundwork for future agitation. It installed Digby in an office just off
the Strand at 25 Craven Street, Charing Cross. It enlisted the support of another great English Radical, Charles Bradlaugh, who toured the country lecturing on Indian subjects. But, though directly linked to the INC, the agency
was not its formal instrument. Early in 1889 Wedderburn wrote to Lord
Ripon, yet another well-placed English sympathizer, "I hope that A. O. Hume
will be able to come home and arrange for the organization of the Indian Committee, which is no doubt a necessity."[10] Hume did return. Consultations took
place. In July 1889 the Indian Political Agency dissolved itself and established
the Indian National Congress Agency in its place. Directly responsible to the
INC, it took the name British Committee of the Indian National Congress in
September 1889. So the organization remained until Gandhi wound it up after 1920.

✧   ✧   ✧

The BCINC represented the culmination of a decades-long struggle to
found a viable Indian nationalist organization in Britain. Taking its
place as one among many anti-imperialist bodies agitating the capital city
during the late-Victorian period, it would come to preach a distinctive variety of opposition to empire.

The date of the BCINC's establishment is significant. After all, 1889 was
the year of the great London dock strike, of the successful countrywide organizing drive among unskilled workers which ushered in the tumultuous
movement known as the New Unionism, sparking the revival of British socialism and leading ultimately to the foundation of the Labour Party. In Ireland the influence of Parnell and the INL was at its height. The situation in India provided the primary impetus to the formation of the BCINC, but the British
context was important too. The committee's establishment late in the 1880s
reflected the optimistic radical current sweeping the country then. The

minds of British workers and Irish and Indian nationalists traveled on parallel tracks: combination would enable them to wrest better lives from their masters.

This commonness of purpose is worth recalling not least because, during the interwar era, militant Indian nationalists excoriated the early BCINC for being tame and ineffective, while more recently Indian scholars have wished to rehabilitate its reputation as the very model of a moderate pressure group. No doubt the committee preferred from the outset to work for small, realizable goals rather than for independence or even home rule. No doubt, too, its leadership was middle class and aristocratic. On the other hand, it was only natural for the turbulent scene in Britain to color BCINC attitudes and to influence its strategy. Its first aim was to rouse "the English working classes, to whom political power had so largely passed, to a sense of the duties which England owes to India."[11]

In 1889 the new body selected an executive committee of fifteen. It designated Wedderburn as chairman, a position he would hold until 1918, and Digby as secretary, a post he kept only for three years. Over the long haul Wedderburn was to prove the more important in the history of the BCINC, but until 1892, when Digby left the committee, apparently for financial reasons, he played the larger role.

The two men represented different poles within the BCINC. Wedderburn, a wealthy man, had been a civil servant in India when he came into contact with A. O. Hume, then a High Court Judge in Bombay. When he returned to Britain and became Liberal Member for Banffshire in Scotland, he gravitated to the Gladstonian wing of the Liberal Party. He was not the most forceful of personalities but rather "gentle, a little sad, suggesting melancholy over the sadness and sombreness of the human lot rather than power to relieve it." He was an appropriate figure to preside over a Humanitarian League meeting advocating "repression of the more debased forms of sport such as tame stag-hunting, pigeon-shooting, and rabbit-coursing." Digby, on the other hand, was more radical and more lively, as befitted a journalist with fewer means and larger ideas. His articles and books, including *India for the Indians—and for England,* which John Bright praised in the House of Commons, hammered at British greed and brutality in India. His political connections were not limited to the party of Gladstone, even though he had been secretary of the National Liberal Club during 1882–86; he numbered the SDF leader, Henry Hyndman, among his friends.[12]

As BCINC secretary it fell to Digby to establish the organization on a firm basis. He was energetic and effective. "We had hopes and, as a matter of fact, we won in several matters," Ghose wrote nostalgically to him more than a decade later. Digby had carried on the correspondence, coordinated the propaganda, prepared and circulated agendas for BCINC meetings.[13] He proved a great success at arranging deputations and other meetings at Westminster. And when, in 1890, Hume and Naoroji pushed for establishment of an official organ, to be called *India*, Digby became its editor. The journal appeared at irregular intervals to begin with, then as a monthly in 1892, and, finally, starting in January 1898, as a weekly. By then Digby was no longer associated with it or the organization. But in the year of his departure, he helped arrange for the BCINC to take new and larger offices at 84 and 85 Palace Chambers, Bridge Street, Westminster, opposite the House of Commons, to furnish them suitably, and to hang portraits of congress leaders on the walls. Naoroji donated a library dealing with Indian subjects.

Of course Digby could not have established the BCINC alone. In Westminster Bradlaugh worked closely with him, cultivating radical contacts; outside the House, Bradlaugh continued to travel the country lecturing on Indian subjects. Looking back twelve years later, Caine paid tribute to "the Bradlaugh-Digby combination." It had "made an excellent impression upon Parliament." But Caine himself had hardly played a negligible role. A bluff and hearty if puritanical figure who doubled as a lay preacher and advocate of temperance reform, he was known in the House as "the genial ruffian." In 1890 he traveled as a delegate to the INC at Calcutta and upon returning contributed a series of articles to the *Pall Mall Gazette* which, according to his biographer in the *Dictionary of National Biography,* "ably advocated large measures of self-government."[14]

A year later, when Bradlaugh died, Caine replaced him as the BCINC's main contact at Westminster. With Wedderburn he organized a parliamentary committee of members (including a number of Irishmen) who could be relied upon to support measures favored by the BCINC. Within a year the two men were joined at St. Stephen's by Naoroji, whose successful campaign for Central Finsbury, in 1892, Digby had directed. Wedderburn, Naoroji, and Caine, a capable trio, directed the parliamentary committee of the BCINC for three years. Then, in 1895, both Naoroji and Caine lost their seats in the general election. Caine temporarily returned to temperance campaigning. Hume, who had returned to London in 1894, stepped into the breach. He, Naoroji, and Wedderburn now became the acknowledged leaders of the BCINC. Wedderburn was the main parliamentary contact, head of the BCINC's parliamentary committee. The Scotch laird, who favored breakfast meetings at the House of Commons, was like the missing Digby in at least one sense: he "had a large circle of political friends, and he was able to call together at these gatherings many men."[15]

Mr. Naoroji: "You are an alien people"

31. Dadabhai Naoroji in Parliament.
By permission of the British Library.

Outside Westminster the BCINC also carried on a sustained agitation. During the decade following its formation this was the committee's primary means of attracting public attention and influencing opinion. By the turn of the century it was holding up to 130 public meetings per year, many of them addressed by visiting congress dignitaries. Members of the committee spoke frequently also, Naoroji most frequently of all. Possibly his efforts were matched by those of the author Alison Garland, who served as one of the committee's organizers and as its delegate to the Indian National Congress in March 1900; returning to Britain early in April, she had addressed 44 meetings on Indian subjects by mid-September.[16]

BCINC speakers often addressed radical or socialist organizations, but in fact they were willing to appear before practically any body that would hear them. Nor did they confine their efforts to the spoken word. Naoroji's *Poverty and Un-British Rule in India* (1901), Romesh Dutt's *Economic History of India under Early British Rule* (1902), and Henry Cotton's *New India* (1907) all argued that Britain was responsible for the poverty in India which led to famines and that self-rule within the British Empire such as the Canadians and Australians enjoyed was the only realistic solution. Digby's second major book, *Prosperous British India* (1901), was particularly effective. W. T. Stead read it and was aghast. "I address you as an expert who can throw some light on this subject," he wrote to the Indian economist and historian G. K.

Gokhale, a congress supporter with a reputation for moderate political views, "and I should be delighted if you could give me some solid assurance that in your judgment Mr. Digby is all wrong. If he is right, then—but I recoil with horror from such a conclusion."[17]

Not that Stead's relative openness to BCINC arguments was typical, or that the organization experienced smooth sailing. English reformers tended to hold aloof, except when they could actually support the imperial government as an agent of progress and reform on the subcontinent. For all the BCINC's activities, the Indian cause remained not merely unpopular but, to a degree, unregarded in Britain. When Indian subjects were debated in the House of Commons, M.P.s deserted for the terrace and smoking rooms in droves or failed to show up at all. On one occasion Bonnerjee attended the Indian budget debate. Sir Roger Letheridge was addressing the chamber. The only member present to hear him was the speaker of the house.[18]

Perhaps these meager results help explain a certain lack of harmony within the BCINC. The organization was riven by personality conflicts. "Wedderburn is a good generous fellow, but terribly weak in a crisis," Caine confided to Gokhale. "Hume was once a man of energy, but his day has passed," opined J. P. Goodridge, a member of the executive committee who resigned late in 1898 because "as at present constituted [it] performed no useful purpose and did positive harm to the cause." His "dear friend[s] Dadabhai and Wedderburn," Goodridge judged to be "impracticable men without much tact." Another member of the committee, W. Martin Wood, former editor of the *Times of India,* informed Gokhale, who was about to visit London, "I have, in some directions, had longer and closer opportunities of observation [of public figures in Britain] than has scarcely anyone else with whom you are likely to confer," thereby implicitly denigrating the powers of observation of all his colleagues. Meanwhile Ghose had fallen out with his INC cofounders Bonnerjee and Hume, "men who are serving their own interests by means of the organization,"[19] while Hume and his associates held a low opinion of Digby. "They have libelled you behind your back in a most horrible manner," Ghose helpfully noted in a letter to his English journalist friend.[20]

This kind of sniping continued through the 1890s and beyond. Early in the new century Ghose was scheming to reorganize the congress itself and to establish a new committee in London to replace the entire BCINC, in whose trio of leaders, Naoroji, Wedderburn, and Hume, he reposed no confidence. Ghose hoped that Digby would again become secretary and that Caine, returned to the House of Commons in 1900 after a five-year absence, would play the role in Parliament that Bradlaugh had played previously. A. M. Bose was involved in this design too. But lack of funds proved a stumbling block, and then first Caine died in 1903 and Digby, "from nervous exhaustion," according to his biographer in the *Dictionary of National Biography*, a year later. The plan came to naught.

Lack of funds also plagued the BCINC. During 1894–1901 the congress guaranteed it almost twenty-six thousand pounds but supplied less than sixteen thousand. "Again and again the Committee have pointed out the difficulties and anxiety in which they have been involved owing to the Congress not performing its part of the agreement," Wedderburn complained in 1901 in a letter to Dinshaw Edulji Wacha, joint general secretary of the INC. "And the Congress work in England must long ago have come to an end if the Committee had not by their personal exertions and sacrifices collected (from sources apart from the Congress) large sums to meet the deficiencies." During the late 1890s and early twentieth century Hume, Naoroji—who once paid *India*'s journalists twelve months' salary and rent for the committee's offices out of his own pocket—and, most of all, Wedderburn kept the committee going with subventions. Naoroji estimated in 1901 that Wedderburn had spent "not less than £10,000 or perhaps up to £15,000 in various ways in the furtherance of the cause of our country." Financial worries were recurrent in the BCINC; one finds correspondence on this subject in the private papers of its members even on the eve of World War I.[21]

Despite these difficulties, however, the BCINC never ceased to hammer at its themes. "Self-government is the only remedy for India's woes," Naoroji exhorted. As the Irish argued for their country, so Indians argued that Britain must grant them greater scope for participation in local and national government; and also permit more democratic elections, allow them to compete for all civil service positions, serve as officers in the Indian army and the Indian police force, teach and administer at all schools in India. Such reforms would "make India a blessing to you and England a blessing to us," Naoroji explained. These goals were not chimerical. BCINC speakers often reminded Londoners that Britain had promised by "great and solemn proclamations of 1858, 1877, and 1887, to treat Indians exactly like the British people, as British Citizens."[22]

The BCINC pushed its demands assiduously and shrewdly. It orchestrated the reporting in England of nationalist gatherings in India. "The public here do not read Indian papers," Naoroji once instructed Gokhale, so he should send to *British* newspapers telegrams summarizing Indian newspaper reports instead: "The telegrams attract . . . immediate notice and the impression is at once made." The committee also coached parliamentary sympathizers. "I helped Mr. Caine with notes and you have seen what he said on the Bill [Bombay Land Code] in the House of Commons," boasted Romesh Dutt, an economist who had served in the Indian civil service and who was close to the BCINC, although not a member of its executive committee.[23] And it lobbied the India Office and other offices of state through private memorials. Here Naoroji played the leading part. In June 1895 he commenced a lengthy correspondence with the War Office. He wished to discover whether officer candidates for the Indian army could be excluded simply because they were Indian, when there was no act of Parliament to that effect. Five years later he conducted a similar correspondence with the India Office on whether qualified Indians could be appointed to posts in the Indian Educational Service. These efforts tried his patience, but they must have tried the patience of his correspondents too. Insisting on clear language and understandings, Naoroji would not be fobbed off with half promises. If the India Office was determined to discriminate against Indian applicants for educational posts in India, then Naoroji was determined to get them to admit as much. His letters offer evidence that those like Macaulay who from the 1830s had advocated turning Indians into Englishmen had wrought better than they knew or, perhaps, even wished. Naoroji in particular, but most of the members of the BCINC generally, understood as well as anybody the intricacies of parliamentary governance, of lobbying government ministers in person and by pen, of conducting a popular agitation along constitutional British lines. Now India's nationalists were adopting England's own traditional forms of protest and turning them against Britons.[24]

What strikes the historian a century later is the patience and moderation with which they conducted the campaign. The origins of the BCINC may be found in the new unionist era, but Naoroji and his colleagues were more diplomatic than Ben Tillett or Tom Mann ever tried to be, certainly more diplomatic than most Irish nationalists. Even in his vexing correspondence with high officialdom Naoroji never allowed his temper to run away with him. When the India Office endorsed discrimination on the basis of race Naoroji merely accused it of following an "un-English course." Speaking before rougher audiences, he remained equally tactful. "The British influence [has] brought great good to India," he began reassuringly in a speech to the Mildmay Radical Club at Stoke Newington. "We are grateful for many good things," he reiterated a few weeks later, this time to an audience at Toynbee Hall in the East End, listing an end to infanticide and the burning of widows in India, the introduction of law and order, education, and "your other institutions, free speech and a free press," as among the benefits of English rule in India.[25]

In sharp contrast to the Irish, no Indian nationalist demonstration or rally or written remonstrance in Britain was complete during this period without its protestation of loyalty to the Crown. "Such agitation as there was in India was merely for the purpose of securing their rights," G. P. Pillai insisted characteristically before a dinner of the New Reform Club at St. Ermin's Hotel on July 17, 1900, and he "looked forward to such constitutional changes as would make India one of the strongest limbs of the Empire of which Englishmen were so proud." When Gokhale visited London in 1897 he carried a letter of introduction from E. C. K. Ollivant, a former Indian civil servant and current member of the Council of the Governor of Bombay. The letter attested not only that he, Ollivant, believed Gokhale to be a political moderate, but that Sir George Birdwood, former sheriff of Bombay and an influential senior figure in the Anglo-Indian community, and Florence Nightingale did too.[26]

BCINC declarations of loyalty to the Crown were genuine. In their private correspondence these nationalists professed moderate purposes to each other. "You will, I hope, live to see . . . Indians largely predominating in all branches of the Government and the Anglo-Indians accepting them freely as their best safeguards," Hume confided to Gokhale. "My desire and aim has been not to encourage rebellion but to prevent it and to make the British connection with India a benefit and blessing to both countries," Naoroji wrote to Hyndman.[27]

The BCINC took pains to establish that Indians *deserved* to be treated by the Britons as equals. "Let them remember that the Indians were not a race of savages," Naoroji reminded the Plumstead Radical Club. "Two thousand years ago they were the most highly civilised nation in the world. And what sort of people were the natives of England when at that period they were discovered by Caesar?" "We were the first to emerge from barbarism," Gokhale boasted, "and my nation was not only great, but was the greatest of all on the face of the earth, long before anyone had heard anything of the oldest States of the West." Caine thought that in some respects Indians were better than Britons still. "The Sikhs and Gurkhas had proved themselves superior to the British soldier in the Frontier War." Indians must simply demonstrate to Britons their admirable qualities. Then they would receive their reward, as English workers had done in 1867 after demonstrating that they deserved the vote. During the Boer War, Gandhi, who was living in South Africa, organized Indians, who were not permitted to fight for Britain, as stretcher bearers. "He mobilized support," writes a biographer, "on the grounds that participation in the war effort would add substance to the merchants' claim to be desirable citizens."[28]

The search for respect and respectability had a dark side. Once argue that races and peoples deserved esteem for general characteristics, and it was but a short step to suggesting that other races did not deserve it. The BCINC took that step. *India* accepted anti-Semitic stereotypes. The Boer War was being fought "to make Hebrew millionaires richer."[29] Like many anti-imperialists in Britain at the turn of the century, BCINC leaders accepted the view that there was a hierarchy of races, so long as it was understood that Indians did not occupy the bottom of it. "The Government were willing to massacre savages in South Africa in order to find markets for British goods," Naoroji argued in a speech cited above, "whereas if they would only develop the resources of India with her three hundred millions of population they would find ample outlet for British trade."

The BCINC continually drew attention to the disabilities under which Indians labored in Natal. But it never urged Gandhi to make common cause with black Africans who lived there too and whose disabilities were greater. Rather it drew distinctions between "ignorant and lawless Kaffirs," and "educated and highly civilised Indians in that ultra-loyal colony." S. K. Mullick of the BCINC said, "The British were fighting the Boers because the latter refused them equal rights, whilst the colonists were refusing Indians, whose valuable help in the war had been acknowledged, a similar equality of rights." He made no plea for Africans. "Equal rights for all whites [in South Africa] is a principle that we do not quarrel with, but we are strongly of opinion that it is incomplete for the object in view," began *India* in one editorial. But it did not advocate extending "a charter of freedom and justice" to all nonwhites living in South Africa, as might have been expected from an anti-imperialist organ, only to "British Indians."[30] One of the rights Indians in Natal were entitled to which the BCINC thought proper to emphasize was the use of rickshaws drawn by African runners.

Thus the leaders of the BCINC in the anti-imperial metropolis in 1900 objected not so much to imperialism or even to the imperial worldview as a whole as to specific policies and most pointedly specific attitudes toward Indians which they wished to change.

And yet the historian may perceive, however dimly, the outline of a more radical and a more inclusive anti-imperialism among Indians resident in London at the turn of the twentieth century. In part it was provoked by the terrible Indian famine of those years. Millions were starving on the subcontinent, partly as a result of drought but also, as the BCINC had come to believe, because most Indians were too poor to purchase food when drought made it impossible to grow their own. Moreover, they had been impoverished as a direct result of British rule.

Here the BCINC divided: Naoroji had been arguing for years that Indian poverty was due to "deliberate spoliation, ruthlessly carried out." First of all Britain had forced India to pay for wars in Afghanistan, Persia, China, Abyssinia, and against tribes and factions within its own borders, which benefited the imperial power only. Then, every year for a century British capitalists had purposefully drained £30 million from the subcontinent in a brutal, selfish quest for profit. This was why Indians nearly starved when weather was good and died by the million for lack of food when it was bad. Romesh Dutt, possibly influenced by discussions on the rights of absentee Irish landlords, refined Naoroji's argument: the main form the drain took was less deliberate spoliation carried out by capitalists than it was overtaxation of Indian land values. What needed curbing in India was not British capitalism as such, but rather the British government's tax policy, particularly that part of it which entitled alien landlords to spend in England the taxes their agents had collected on the subcontinent.[31]

On one matter, however, Naoroji, Dutt, and nearly the entire Indian community in Britain were as one. The London Mansion House Fund, collected over the course of the famine and by the end of 1900 totaling half a million pounds sterling of charitable contributions, was inadequate and could make no substantial difference to India's suffering multitudes. The British government must pay whatever was necessary to cope with the present emergency. Then it must take more fundamental steps. Increased self-government and increased representation in the educational, police, military, and civil services were necessary. But the paramount necessity was for Britain to cease drawing off India's wealth.

The BCINC had long since lost hope that a Conservative government would take this drastic step. Some BCINC members continued, however, to pin their faith on Liberals. Gladstone, after all, had sympathized with "subject peoples struggling to be free." But Gladstone was dead by 1900, and the Liberal Party was no longer the organization it had been in 1886, or even 1892, when it had last formed a government. Since then the vanguard of radical workers had left it for the ILP, founded in 1893, or for another of Britain's socialist parties, or for the fledgling Labour Representation Committee (direct ancestor of the Labour Party). The BCINC had looked to Britain's working class as a natural ally originally; what more natural in 1900, the year of the Labour Representation Committee's formation, than to reemphasize that historic link?

Naoroji above all emphasized it. He maintained that ending the drain would benefit Britain's workers. Enriched by the £30 million they took out of the country annually, "the capitalists were ever stronger, and how, then, could the workers struggle with them?" If the drain were ended so that Indians might prosper, however, then India would purchase British goods and

British workers would also prosper. At present Britain exported goods to India to the value of only eighteen pence per year per head: "If you could send goods to the extent of £1 per head per annum India would be a market for your whole commerce. If such were the case you would draw immense wealth from India besides benefiting the [Indian] people."[32]

The BCINC in 1900, then, did not speak with one voice, if ever it had. *India*, which publicized the meetings and speeches of such moderates as Wedderburn and Dutt, publicized also Naoroji's more class-conscious addresses. Emphasizing the capitalist causes and consequences of the exploitation and appealing to British workers rather than to well-heeled sympathizers in Liberal drawing rooms and gardens meant associating with the few anti-imperialists in London who favored genuine independence for India rather than incremental increases in self-rule under British control. This tension had always been present within the BCINC. In 1900 *India* opened its pages to Edward Carpenter, who wrote, "These fatuous Empires . . . this British Lion . . . will fall and be rent asunder. *And the sooner the better*." It opened them to Hyndman, who believed the famine presaged revolution in India and who thundered at the SDF annual convention that he was "glad the downfall was coming. He would gladly see the people of India rise. . . . India belonged to them. They had made India. We had ruined it." In one column *India* might emphasize "how entirely it is in the interest of the Indians to be loyal." In another, however, it recognized India's "true British friends" to be the audience and organizers of a socialist meeting in the Battersea Town Hall addressed by George Lansbury, "a colleague of Mr. H. M. Hyndman." There were plenty more such friends in Britain, *India* averred, if only the BCINC "knows where to look for them."[33]

The Indian nationalist movement had warm supporters among British socialists, especially in Henry Hyndman's SDF. "Mainly owing to his influence there are found sympathetic references to India and its people in almost every issue of the excellent and widely-circulated weekly paper *Justice*," noted one Indian in London.[34] The drain theory fit precisely into SDF notions of how international capitalism operated. But what should follow from this? Did the SDF offer the kind of support which the BCINC should accept? The SDF was Britain's premier Marxist organization. It claimed to be working for a revolution which would finally destroy British capitalism. Revolution was its goal for India too.

The BCINC was caught on the horns of a dilemma. If it accepted the SDF embrace it would fulfill the dire prophesies of its early opponents who had labeled it a revolutionary and seditious organization. If it rejected the SDF it risked alienating "true British friends."

Naoroji and Hyndman had been comrades since the 1870s. The socialist leader often paid tribute to the Indian leader's thirty years of selfless work, but he believed it lacked impact. The prerequisite for BCINC success, he asserted, was a more robust, even confrontational posture. After all "you are a representative of 250,000,000 people, a great position and one which in my judgment calls for even haughty language on your behalf." If the BCINC continued to follow its tame path, he warned, it might "take another century to drive the thick end of the wedge."[35]

Naoroji was clearly torn. At one point he went so far as to attempt to sever the long-standing connection: "I cannot any more work with you and the SDF on Indian matters. My desire and aim has been not to encourage rebellion but to prevent it." In fact his position was more tactical than fundamental, as he made clear in another letter: "John Bull does not understand the bark. He only understands the bite, but we cannot do this."[36]

Naoroji's heart was with his old friend; his head was with the moderates. Neither invective nor violence would move an imperial government which possessed all the big guns. The only tactic was for the BCINC to keep doing what it had been doing all along. "We must persevere and never flag in our agitation," he advised Gokhale. And two years later: "Of course our work of reform is an uphill work. We will have troubles [?] and difficulties, but we must be prepared to surmount them. . . . The Irish have been struggling for 800 years and here they are struggling all the same now. They won't be beaten." This was hardly the most inspiring line to take, and there is evidence that by the turn of the twentieth century it was beginning to pall even among the Indian community resident in London.[37]

BCINC leaders feared that less patient men and women were waiting in the wings. The committee had always claimed to be Britain's best bulwark against a repetition of 1857, but now a sense of urgency appeared. Thus the policy of refusing officers' commissions to deserving Indian soldiers "involved the danger of converting the most loyal and patriotic subjects of the Queen into a discontented group which would always try to subvert the Government and plot against the foundations of the Empire." Further encroachments upon such Indian self-government as still existed were equally dangerous. Dutt recalled that he "personally knew the state of feeling in Bengal from the Days of the Mutiny," and he "could say that during that period there never had existed such alarm" as now: "The impression was gaining ground that it was not possible to obtain new privileges by peaceful and constitutional methods." If the British government further limited freedom of the press in India as it planned to do, warned B. C. Dal, a Brahmo lecturer, then "it must be prepared for an outburst which would shake the British Empire to its foundations." Naoroji put it best. "There is justice in heaven," he reminded Lord George Hamilton at the India Office, "and retribution will come as sure as night follows the day." Not that he was threatening the secretary of state for India. He was merely quoting Hamilton's own master, the present prime minister: "Lord Salisbury has truly said 'Injustice will bring down the mightiest on earth to ruin.'"[38]

At the end of the nineteenth century, however, neither the BCINC's presentiments of catastrophe, nor even Naoroji's urgings to keep soldiering on could silence all doubters. At its meeting in 1898 the London Indian Society unanimously passed the usual resolutions. Representatives of the old guard professed confidence in Britain's good faith, but from the floor an Indian student, R. C. Sen, objected: "As one of the younger generation he looked at this matter from a different point of view. . . . English justice was a myth. English government meant the administration of slow poison to the people. It was a mistake to rely too much on the generosity of the English people. . . . they only yielded when other countries proved by acts their determination to enforce demands." Sen sounded like a Fenian. And the spy sent by the India Office to keep tabs on the meeting noted a "specially demonstrative and sometimes noisy group" at the back of the meeting hall from which "Mr. Sen came forward. This report," he warned, "does not err on the side of exaggerating their language." But, in fact, the entire meeting had Fenian overtones: "A special feature of the oratory was . . . presages of disaster in which all the Indian speakers indulged. . . . Allusions to the heroic conduct of the sepoys did only evoke enthusiasm. Applause was not wanting for remarks of a partisan character as between rulers and ruled, official and non-official."[39]

According to the new generation of militants whose representatives so worried the India Office agent, the drain would cease only when Indians stopped it. But would it be right for Britain to cease draining India of her wealth while continuing its extractive practices in other parts of the empire? Some thought not. Now a few Indians began to take the first steps to extend their links with other imperialized peoples beyond the Irish.

Again Naoroji, a complex, even contradictory man, was the pioneer. Convinced that peaceful agitation alone could end the drain, nevertheless he was closest of all the BCINC leaders to London's revolutionary socialist movement. A believer, as we have seen, in the hierarchy of races, still in 1893 Naoroji joined an extraordinary, probably unique for its time, interracial group, the Society for the Recognition of the Brotherhood of Man (SRBM) (see chapter 9). With Alfred Webb, the Quaker Irish nationalist, Naoroji was elected to this body's governing council and remained a member until it ceased to meet upon the death of the African-Caribbean Samuel Jules Celestine Edwards of Dominica, British West Indies, who was its driving force.

A few years later another West Indian, the Trinidadian Henry Sylvester Williams, founded a successor organization to the SRBM called the African Association. Again Webb and Naoroji supported. Only the rare Irishmen sympathized with anti-imperialist struggles of Africans and West Indians, but Webb befriended Williams. Possibly he suggested that Williams locate the office of his association at 139 Palace Chambers, in the same building as the offices of the BCINC. Africans and Asians in the imperial metropolis had opened formal lines of communication. In 1899 Wedderburn attended a meeting organized by Williams protesting Chamberlain's decision to dissolve the Municipal Council of Port of Spain. In 1900 Williams organized in London the first Pan-African Conference. The project was ambitious and expensive. Naoroji, who was sending begging letters to wealthy supporters in India on behalf of the BCINC and who had poured his own personal fortune into it, nevertheless made a donation.[40]

The possibility, distant as it was, that Britain's subject peoples might make common cause troubled officials. At the London Indian Society meeting in 1898 an India Office spy noticed that "a young African native . . . was among those on the left of the platform." At a meeting of the London Indian Society early in 1901, another India Office informant made note of one speaker, Joseph Royeppen, because he was "an Indian born in South Africa (evidently with some negro blood)."[41] The activities of Royeppen are obscure, but he literally embodied the protoalliance British imperialists were coming to fear.

Thus the BCINC at the turn of the twentieth century shared with London's Irish nationalists and Anglo-Saxon critics of empire the usual ambivalencies regarding program, race, and even British imperialism itself. Still it was an important body within the broader anti-imperial movement, if one that historians have largely neglected. Moreover the speeches by members to radical societies and garden clubs, the lobbying, the activities of the parliamentary committee, the books, pamphlets, and newspaper helped to shape London in 1900, contributed to the ongoing process by which the imperial metropolis defined itself. Imperialists shaped London in 1900, but anti-imperialists, among whom Indian nationalists were an important force and influence, helped shape it too.

CHAPTER 9

ROOTS OF THE PAN-AFRICAN
CONFERENCE

U P to the mid–nineteenth century a vibrant community of
African-Britons lived in London. By the turn of the twentieth
century, however, this was no longer so. Assimilation and an
end to immigration had reduced it to a fraction of its former
size and vitality. In 1900 there remained only a small black population in London, desperately poor, composed largely of West Indian sailors, living in Canning Town in the East End. In addition a few exceptional individuals had
prospered, usually in the liberal professions. The imperial metropolis also attracted the occasional student of law, medicine, or business from Africa or the
West Indies and the equally occasional African American.[1]

This tiny population, smaller, less advantaged, less politically experienced, more despised than the Irish or Indian communities in London, nevertheless played a significant role in the anti-imperial metropolis. In 1900 it
organized the first Pan-African Conference, issuing a proclamation "To the
Nations of the World" whose opening lines, written by the great African-
American delegate, W. E. B. Du Bois, reverberate down the ages: "The problem of the twentieth century is the problem of the colour line."[2]

During this period the Pan-African Conference was the outstanding
achievement of London's black community and among the most momentous
accomplishments of all anti-imperial London. Usually it has been treated as
an early exhibition in Britain of the long struggle against European imperialism and for racial justice and, more specifically, as the first significant manifestation of the Pan-African movement.[3] But the conference also represented
the climax of years of organizing. It takes its place in the anti-imperial agitation of the era, bound up with the the the APS, the BCINC, the London labor and socialist movements, the Irish National League. Its organizers, too, can be understood only in this context. Outside forces impinged upon them, but
London helped make them. The Pan-Africans fashioned their own discourse,

but they stood upon the shoulders of men and women steeped in British radical traditions.

The origins of black anti-imperialist activity in London may be traced back at least as far as the British antislavery movement. Yet during the late-Victorian period, as we have seen, the organizational descendants and remnants of that earlier crusade, especially the APS and the Anti-Slavery Society, were not so much anti-imperialist as they were critical of specific imperial policies. The more immediate origins of modern black anti-imperialism in London, therefore, are to be discovered in the trans-Atlantic links forged between African Americans and British Radicals, generally religious nonconformists, during the decades after the American Civil War and in crusades conducted by religious and temperance and thrift societies during the same period. They may be discovered as well in what Stephen Yeo termed the "religion of socialism" movement.[4]

First the trans-Atlantic links. Consider the village of Street, in Somerset, which contained one of the largest Quaker communities in southern England. It was dominated by the Clark shoe factory, run by William Clark, who had married the daughter of the great Quaker Radical John Bright. In 1878, Catherine Impey, a Quaker from Street who knew the Clarks, visited the United States, staying as "the guest of a coloured family" and forming a lifelong hatred of racial segregation and "race prejudice with all its inhumanities."[5] When the nineteenth century's greatest African American, Frederick Douglass, made his last visit to Britain in 1886–87 he met Impey at Clark's home in Street. Douglass and Impey became friends. The next time Impey visited Washington, D.C., in 1891, she stayed with him.[6] In the meantime she had founded a newspaper, *Anti-Caste*, whose masthead "assume[d] the Brotherhood of the entire Human Family, and claim[ed] for the Dark Races of Mankind their equal right to Protection, Personal Liberty, Equality of Opportunity, and Human Fellowship." The foundation of this newspaper and the first steps leading to the establishment of the BCINC took place at roughly the same time, that special moment when the New Unionism and the revival of socialism began to rock Victorian Britain's certainties. Modern anti-imperialism in Britain dates from that era, grew from the same soil.

Impey's goal in the newspaper she produced from her home in Somerset was "not to direct public attention . . . to the mere effects or violent exhibitions of race-prejudice," though this she certainly did, but rather to discover and explain their cause, which she believed to be rooted in race segregation, or caste, as she called it, perhaps with the untouchables of India in mind.

Impey wrote, "The idea that colour has any place whatever in determining the relationship of members of the human family towards each other must everywhere be wiped out. . . . How slow we are to recognise that the darker members of the human family have absolutely the same claim to equality of opportunity and to fellowship as if they were white." Compare this with the condescending attitudes of the APS. Impey rejected out of hand racist justifications for imperialist endeavors in Africa and Asia.

This was a lonely position to maintain in late-Victorian Britain, and Impey's columns reveal her sense of isolation. She would continue her crusade, she once vowed, "even though for a time we should be called to stand alone, outside every human organisation." Her aim was to "secure personal introduction and organise public meetings for those members or friends of oppressed races who come occasionally to plead their cause in this country." If she failed it was not for want of trying. A thin but steady stream of African Americans visited England during the latter part of Queen Victoria's reign, and the Quaker editor from Street appears to have contacted most of them.[7] The most important was Ida B. Wells, the antilynching campaigner, whom Impey met at the home of Frederick Douglass in 1891. Impey, Wells, and a Scottish woman, Isabella Fyvie Mayo, organized an antilynching campaign in Britain too. Wells toured the country several times during the 1890s, lecturing to church, women's, temperance, and political clubs and societies and breakfasting at the House of Commons, courtesy of Alfred Webb. The plan was to collect signatures to a great petition condemning lynchings which would then be sent to the American president, Grover Cleveland.

During the spring of 1893 Impey and Mayo established the Society for the Recognition of the Brotherhood of Man (SRBM), as an adjunct to the antilynching crusade. They founded branches in the main English and Scottish towns and appointed a governing council, which met in London and on which Dadabhai Naoroji and Alfred Webb both served. An expanding society needs an official organ. Impey prepared to give up publishing *Anti-Caste*, which, perhaps, had become a burden. With the support of the society's governing council the two women approached a charismatic West Indian, Samuel Jules Celestine Edwards, inviting him to edit a new journal, *Fraternity*, and to become general secretary of the society as a whole. In July 1893 this fascinating, little-known figure assumed both posts.[8]

In Edwards's life and struggles one may trace the African-British anti-imperialist movement's second taproot, the one running through temperance and church bodies and informed by Christian socialist ideas. Edwards was born in Burns, near the seaport Prince Rupert on the island of Dominica, British West Indies, on December 28, 1857. His ancestors, he once wrote, had "proudly trod the sands of the African continent; but from their home and friends were dragged into the slave mart and sold to the planters of the West Indies."[9] His father, who died in 1867, was a sailor, his mother had charge of his nine siblings. He attended Roman Catholic schools and then a Wesleyan Chapel School, which apparently was very good, at St. John on the island of Antigua. One of his teachers there was the Rev. Henry Mason Joseph, who later moved to London, joined the SRBM, and played an important role among anti-imperialist African-Caribbeans in the imperial metropolis.

In 1870 Edwards stowed away aboard a French vessel sailing to Guadeloupe. This relatively short journey was the prelude to a series of travels which spanned the globe. Eventually the adventurous teenager sailed to North and South America and Asia, including India. What he saw "stirred within his noble nature the ardent desire to assist in securing both the true elevation of his own and the other races of the earth."[10]

But how to accomplish his goals? For native-born Britons who likewise had been stirred the path was obvious. Ben Tillett, for example, shipped all over the world beginning at about the same age and during roughly the same period as Edwards. Having come to similar conclusions, although not so much about the treatment of races as about the exploitation of labor, he was drawn ineluctably into the trade union movement. Edwards did not have that option. Few reformist societies were likely to welcome a black man on equal terms with whites. Therefore, in Edinburgh, where he first settled after his travels (the city was something of a mecca for Africans and West Indians, a number of whom were enrolled at the Edinburgh University medical school at roughly this time),[11] he worked as a laborer and joined, not the trade union, but rather the Hope Lodge of the order of Good Templars. He himself was not a heavy drinker, but he had seen what drink did to sailors when they were ashore. Edwards's first attempts to elevate his own and other races were speeches promoting abstinence from alcohol.

Perhaps it was easier for an organization whose aim was to salvage drunkards to accept black members on equal terms with whites than for organizations of middle-class do-gooders or organizations composed of class-conscious workers who often feared foreign competition. Maybe that is why Williams, the main organizer of the Pan-African Conference in London in 1900, also got his start in Britain lecturing for the temperance movement. Of course many white men also began in this fashion. Tillett again comes to mind, although he lived to become the scourge of "the temperance bleating martyrs." For some, however, like William Caine of the BCINC, the temperance crusade remained a lifelong adjunct of their radical politics. In affiliating with the Good Templars, Edwards had chosen a traditional launching pad, although it may have been the only one available to him; what marks him out is where it launched him to.

An extraordinary figure, Edwards was ripe for launching. "His was truly a most marvelous personality," wrote a friend. "The bright and merry twinkling of his piercing eye, the motion of the head and limbs, the erectness of stature, every one of them silently t[old] volumes, and len[t] to his words an irresistible charm." His conversation, marveled another, "was so interesting—his knowledge of men and books and places and character so wide and thorough, that an hour passed before you knew where you were." In one lecture Edwards quoted Voltaire, John Stuart Blackie, professor of Greek at Edinburgh, Isaac Newton, Tom Paine, and Herbert Spencer, and referred to Lycurgus, Plato, Seneca, Aristotle, Zeno, Diogenes, and Chrysippus. The young temperance advocate "was a born orator"—but not a demagogue. "The way in which he would take up the threads of an opponent's argument, and unravel, disentangle and expose them," recorded another admirer, "caused him often to be greeted with a wild and frantic cheer of triumph and delight." Testimony from yet another who heard him speak: "Personally I never met his equal as a lecturer; there was about him that something which you can't define; a unique personality on the platform he undoubtedly was.[12]

32. Celestine Edwards.
By permission of the British Library.

From the beginning Edwards was interested in more than drink. His early speeches must have ranged over a variety of subjects because before long he was quoted as saying, "I was requested to lecture upon my country and my people." The anti-imperialist was about to reveal himself.[13]

Again, however, Edwards did not choose conventional political channels. He had been led to see, he once recorded, that "the real work of God in this world was the salvation of sinners, not from drink only, but from their sins."[14] He became an evangelist working for the missionary committee of the Primitive Methodist Church. Like the Good Templars, so perhaps the Methodists offered a more hospitable atmosphere to the youthful African-Caribbean radical than a trade union or socialist society would have done. The dissenting churches, like the Good Templars, often attracted young radicals who later went on to careers as social reformers.

Edwards hoped that the Methodists would send him to Africa. They sent him to London instead. Possibly they paid his tuition at the Theological School of King's College, which he attended at about this time and from which he earned "the diploma of Associate" and the accolades of fellow students and professors.[15] Edwards could not have paid his fees by himself; later when he studied at the London Hospital hoping he could go to Africa as a doctor as well as a minister, poverty forced him to withdraw.

It was as a Christian evangelist that Edwards discovered his true metier. He wrote several religious pamphlets: "Atheism a Failure," "Theosophy Old and New," "This Worldism, a Scathing Exposure of the Fallacies and Fraudulent Pretensions of Secularism to Benefit Mankind." Then he began to introduce some of his social concerns, for example, in a pamphlet entitled "From Slavery to a Bishopric, Being a Sketch of the Life, Struggles and Successes of Bishop Hawkins." His lectures evolved along similar lines. To begin with "very frequently he held spell-bound many an audience, while either speaking of his trips to far-off lands, or in speaking upon some Gospel picture."[16] Then he began to combine subjects. By the late 1880s he was preaching mainly against the hypocrisy and greed of European imperialists who claimed to be motivated by the desire to spread civilization and Christianity.

Edwards relished the give and take which accompanied British public speaking. He was fascinated by the speakers' corner in Victoria Park. "It was to this lively spot one Sunday afternoon some ten years ago, that Mr. Edwards first made his way," a friend recalled in 1894. Listening to a debate between a Christian and an atheist, Edwards "interrupted Mr. Atheist, who very suddenly (without in the least counting the cost, or endeavouring to measure his man) began to be somewhat insolent, having an uncontrollable tendency to indulge in personalities of a somewhat low type. 'Holloa, darkie,' 'Bravo,

Sambo,' and 'What do you want?' were expressions which fell from his lips."
Edwards easily demolished this rash man. "There was that in his face which
told you before you began that you were leading a forlorn hope, and there was
that in his eye which, while it pitied you, told you as plain as two and two make
four, 'May the Lord have mercy upon you, for I am after you.'"[17]

From then on he was a frequent speaker in Victoria Park. He also maintained a hectic schedule of public lecturing for the Primitive Methodists. He
never tailored his message to his audience. When he addressed a meeting of
the Society for Propagating the Gospel among the Heathen in Bishop's
Waltham, for instance, "it was a most pleasant sight to notice how well he was
received by the ladies and gentlemen of the highest society in that part of
Hampshire. Yet in his speech he hit out, in his usual style, against the effects
of the white civilisers who go to Africa for what they can pocket." Wherever
he spoke the halls were packed. "While conferences are discussing how to get
people to church," marveled one of his auditors in Bristol, "Mr. Edwards is
filling a hall with 1,000 people five nights in the week, and a much larger one
three times on the Sunday."[18]

Sometime toward the end of the 1880s Edwards quit the missionary committee of the Primitive Methodists and joined the Christian Evidence Society (CES), whose objects were "To declare and defend Christianity as a Divine
Revelation. To controvert the errors of Atheists, Secularists, and other opponents of Christianity. To counteract the energetic propagandism of infi-
delity, especially among the uneducated. To strengthen the faith of the doubting and perplexed. To instruct the young in the reasons for believing
Christianity to be true. To promote the circulation of Publications, Books and
Tracts in defence of the truth." Edwards became leader of the East London
branch of the CES. During the summer of 1892 he launched a CES newspaper,
Lux. He received no salary for his efforts but earned his bread traveling as an
independent Christian evangelist, exhorting his audiences to live up to Christian ideals, not least by condemning and opposing British imperialism (which
so many Christian missionaries supported).

Under Edwards's editorship *Lux* took a line more forthrightly in defense
of the rights and equality of all peoples than even Catherine Impey's *Anti-
Caste*, which he knew and admired. His Christian Evidence newspaper hardly
limited itself to articles about Christianity. Rather in its pages he met the exponents of so-called scientific racism head on and attempted to rebut them:

> A consistent advocate of Darwinian theory . . . will, and can have no difficulty
> in allowing the obvious truth that, given favourable environment, the Negro
> race is just as likely to give a good account of itself as the European. He must
> grant to all men . . . an equality or commonality of origin, and he is bound to

explain the mental peculiarity of the Negro as of any other race by the influence of external circumstances, over which he may or may not have control, which have acted upon the physical organism favourably or unfavourably, which either hindered or assisted the development of the Negro's mental facilities.

Edwards also condemned the imperialism which the scientific racists practiced: "Dr. Knox said: 'As regards mere physical strength, the dark races are generally much inferior to the Saxon and Celt.' Perhaps that will account for the ferocity with which the latter seized North America . . . South America . . . Hindostan, Australia, New Zealand and Africa." Another extract from the same article reads, "Sir Samuel Baker says: 'In Europe is all truth and sincerity, but the Negro is cunning, and a liar by nature.' Does he ever read, or has he ever witnessed, [British] cunning in seizing the Negro's country, the lies [they] have told . . . the abominable greed of the Europeans of the West Coast, and the injustices inflicted upon the Negroes of South Africa?" Englishmen "boast about the Empire over which the sun never sets," Edwards thundered on another occasion. "How many have been murdered, robbed, and enslaved to acquire dominion?"[19]

Edwards's meetings for the CES were as much political rallies as religious gatherings. His listeners behaved accordingly. On Christmas Eve, 1893, he lectured to three audiences in Liverpool: "The address on the Matabele War was an eye-opener to the majority of the audience, and we were not astonished when a strong resolution condemnatory of the gross injustice was carried nem. con."[20]

Edwards's anti-imperialism was rooted as much in his Christianity, in the teachings of the fathers employed long ago at the Wesleyan Chapel School on Antigua, as in his experiences traveling around the world and his observations since then. The application of reason alone to the problems caused by imperialism would solve nothing, he once argued. Only reason and faith combined would prevail. "When would the horrors of the Middle Passage—and with it the slave trade—have been abolished, if men had done no more than thinking?" he queried an audience. At times he grew impatient with the failure of the church to live up to its universalist prescriptions. "Why don't missionary societies raise the country against the continual injustices perpetrated against the Negroes in West and South Africa?" But, until the very end of his life, it never occurred to him that he might leave the church, as it did occur to a number of radicals who began as lay preachers and eventually became prominent labor and socialist leaders. When he accepted the invitation to edit *Fraternity* and to become general secretary of the society which sponsored it, he nevertheless maintained his connection with the CES, continuing to edit and write for *Lux*. Tolerant of other religions, he never ceased to rail against atheists, freethinkers, theosophists, Positivists, Marxists, all of whom he might have considered to be natural allies in the anti-imperialist crusade.[21]

For Christian socialists, however, Edwards made an exception. He once wrote, "Christianity must cultivate that individualism which partakes of the nature of the highest socialism, and the socialism which promotes the noblest individualism. Christianity must maintain the significance of humanity by the continual re-assertion of God's grandest affirmative: 'Whatever ye would that men should do unto you, do ye even so to them.'"[22]

The editor of *Fraternity* built its circulation at remarkable speed. Launched in July 1893 with an initial subscription list of three thousand, the journal achieved a readership of seven thousand by mid-September. Here again note the historical conjuncture. The times were propitious: in 1893 the New Unionism was still in full flow and the socialist revival climaxed with the formation of the Independent Labour Party. In addition, the Indian National Congress had recently established its British committee. "How exceedingly popular *Fraternity* is getting," Edwards wrote in *Lux* on the second to last day of 1893. "In one week the Editor had calls for it from West Africa, the West Indies—especially his own island—and even Norway wants it." But of course the majority of readers were British.

Edwards strove to combine Christian and socialist ideals. "Did it ever occur to you that men ought to have a share of the good things of this life, as all men have a share of God's sun and rain," he quizzed an audience. "I believe it is not of the economy of God to portion that some of his creatures should be in destitution, whilst others have more than to spare, and food to fatten pigs upon." And he sought to merge the religion of socialism with anti-imperialism. As he wrote in the first issue of the journal, "The human race—whatever be their creed, colour or nationality—are from one common origin, with like feelings, ambitions and desires; this oneness of the race forces upon us the great fact that the woes of one ought to call for the immediate relief of the others."[23]

Edwards was now editor and chief writer for two weekly newspapers, leader of a CES weekly bible class, and a lecturer of renown. According to James Marchant, one of his subeditors on *Lux*, "He was not intoxicated with his great and sudden success." Marchant was present once as Edwards strolled down the Strand. "Within one hundred yards he was stopped by Ben Tillett, a well-known lawyer, and three religious leaders. Everybody seemed to know him and to everybody he was homely, gentle, dignified."[24] He remained a poor man. All his efforts on behalf of the CES and the SRBM were unpaid. He earned his living as a lecturer. The problem was that, given his onerous editorial duties, he had to squeeze the lectures into spare moments, and often he had to travel great distances to deliver them.

The schedule was too hectic. From late 1893 references to his sickly demeanor and ill health began to appear in *Lux*. Early in 1894, while on a lecture tour in Brighton, Edwards collapsed. Within a week he was up and speaking again. "People say, why does not the Editor take absolute rest for about a month?" wrote a colleague. "Unless the Editor can lecture, and the lectures pay, he must starve."[25]

But Edwards had become too weak to continue. He took to his bed, wrote to his newspaper on April 14, "We have been lingering between life and death for months." Through popular subscriptions *Lux* raised a fund of £206 10s. 6d., which enabled him to sail in mid-May for the West Indies, where it was hoped he might recover his health. He embarked from Liverpool aboard the *Bernard Hall*. On the eve of his departure he managed to deliver one last lecture. It conveys a bitterness of tone new to him:

> Talk about old age pensions; 5s. a week when you are sixty. When I see it in the papers I look upon it as a huge joke. It ought to come in God's Universe that righteousness must prevail and wrong must be overthrown. Fancy the man who toils all day, and only has 18s. a week, and has to save out of that. . . .
>
> In London I know lots of people who never earn more than 20s. a week. But I said there was a revolution, and it must come when the labourer will receive not only the equivalent of his labour, but also participate in the profits derived. Oh! What a hell upon earth for some of our countrymen and women! Think of men driving in the streets (I speak particularly of London), women sewing away a dozen shirts for 7½d. . . . Look, the revolution must begin there; you preach till you are black as Sheffield, the carrying of the Gospel in the slum has some consolation, but it is poor consolation to a hungry stomach. . . . [And] the pulpit has frequently played the coward.[26]

Thus, at the very end of his life, Edwards seems to have been working toward a more socialist, less overtly Christian position.

He arrived at Bridgetown, Barbados, on June 1 and died in his brother's home seven weeks later, on July 25.

With Edwards's death in 1894 and the petering out of Catherine Impey's *Anti-Caste* a year later, the anti-imperialism which insisted that Britain had no redemptive mission in Asia and Africa, that it should make restitution for past imperial practices and then mind its own business, practically lapsed in London. The hopeful and optimistic moment, 1888–95, had passed. Now the labor and socialist movements were relatively quiescent,

Gladstonians languished in opposition. After 1895 Conservatives would rule for a decade characterized by labor defeats, jingoism, and colonial wars. In London people of African and African-Caribbean descent viewed these manifestations of aggressive imperialism with dismay. And so one comes, finally, to the third taproot of modern black anti-imperialism in Britain, the small group of London-based men and women who organized in 1897 the African Association and who then, in the teeth of the imperialist gale sweeping Britain in 1900, went on to put together the world's first Pan-African Conference.[27]

Although scholars have outlined the early history of the African Association, its origins have never been fully described. The most effective way to fill out the picture is by tracing the activities and connections of another remarkable West Indian, Henry Sylvester Williams. This man, whose activities have been chronicled to a degree, was born in Arouca, Trinidad, on February 14, 1869, the son of an architect from Barbados. He so impressed his teachers at a local elementary school that they singled him out, training him to become a schoolteacher too. This, however, did not satisfy Williams. He wished to become a lawyer.

In 1893 Williams left Trinidad, possibly under a cloud, and headed for Canada. He studied law for a year at Dalhousie University in Halifax, Nova Scotia, but withdrew, perhaps with the intention of enrolling at Rutgers College in New Jersey. His experience of racism in the United States, however, soured him on North America, while inspiring him to "do something for his people." Having conceived an admiration for Great Britain, which he believed to have promised equality of treatment to all subjects of the Crown, he moved to London in 1896. Still planning to become a lawyer, he enrolled at King's College. On June 5, 1897, he applied to Gray's Inn, one of the Inns of Court, to study law; on December 10 he was admitted.[28]

Meanwhile he had to earn his daily bread. Williams attempted to solve this problem as Celestine Edwards had fifteen years earlier, joining a temperance society and lecturing for it, but this "simply defrayed the cost of living."[29] Again like Edwards he did not confine himself to lecturing solely on the evils of drink. Clearly the temperance movement afforded a platform to people with more on their minds than alcoholism. Williams, for example, had discovered, as he later put it, that "the British public was not cognizant of . . . the oppression and the unrighteous circumstances our people were existing under" in South Africa. This was a subject upon which he was prepared to speak.

Traveling the lecture circuit for the Church of England Temperance Society in 1897, Williams arrived in Birmingham, where he met A. V. (or possibly E. V.) Kinloch, the native South African wife of a Scottish engineer. Kinloch had experienced South-African bigotry firsthand. Williams wrote, "She told me her story.... I said this statement should be made known to the British public." He offered to share his platform with her: "I was indeed pleased to see a woman of our own race ... telling the people in England things that they knew not ... convincing them that there was something to be done by the British public." Williams had made the first connection which would lead to formation of the African Association and thence to organization of the first Pan-African Conference.

Kinloch wished to join the Writers Club, an association of progressive women. The club was chaired by Lady Somerset; its members included the daughter of Richard Cobden, Jane Cobden Unwin, one of the first women elected to the London County Council and who would serve on the executive committee of the Pan-African Association, which emerged from the Pan-African Conference of 1900; also the daughter of Bishop John William Colenso, Henrietta Colenso, who followed in her father's footsteps as a champion of African rights, and whose brother, R. J. Colenso, would become treasurer of the Pan-African Association.[30] Sometime after her speech in Birmingham but still during 1897, Kinloch read a paper to this body "fully explaining the compound system in Kimberley and Rhodesia, and showing under what oppressions the black races of Africa lived."[31] H. Fox Bourne, of the APS, may have been among her audience, for soon afterward he engaged Kinloch to tour Britain for the APS, lecturing on South African conditions.

In the meantime Williams had befriended two figures who would play a role in founding the African Association and guiding its subsequent activities. The first was none other than Celestine Edwards's old mentor from Antigua, the Rev. Henry Mason Joseph, who, as noted earlier, had moved to London with his wife and daughter and served on the council of the SRBM. The second was a fellow law student at the Inns of Court, T. J. Thompson, of Sierra Leone. Joseph, Kinloch, Williams, Thompson, and others discussed European and particularly British imperialism. The need for a formal organization which could bring the African-British community in London into closer contact with and serve as a pressure group on behalf of Victoria's black subjects everywhere was apparent. Perhaps the four also shared the broadly nationalist sentiments of the era and hoped to plant the seeds of a Pan-African movement which might take its place alongside Pan-Slavism, Zionism, and Pan-Germanism. They met with English sympathizers, probably representatives of the APS, who told them, according to Williams, that "coloured people though eager enough to join the whites in any enterprise would never be able to unite and hold together so as to have an organization of their own."[32] This certainly sounds like the APS.

Williams, however, "determined to . . . defy the prediction." On September 14, 1897, he convened the meeting which resulted in the formation of the African Association. Its aims were to "encourage a feeling of unity, and to facilitate friendly intercourse among Africans in general, and to promote and protect the interests of all British subjects claiming African descent, by circulating accurate information on all questions affecting their rights and privileges, and by direct appeal to the Imperial and local Governments." A month later, on October 15, Fox Bourne spoke to a second meeting on the possibilities of cooperation between his society and the new one, which had inserted a rule proscribing non-African members, although making provision for honorary non-African sympathizers. A week later "several representative members of the race who lived in London" ratified the new group's constitution and appointed officers: Joseph as president, Thompson as vice president, Williams as general secretary, and Kinloch as treasurer.[33]

The African Association began holding regular meetings, sixteen during its first year of existence, "at which information [was] exchanged on important questions affecting the welfare of Africans, not only on their own continent, but also in the West Indies and elsewhere." By the end of 1898 the association had attracted forty-seven members, mostly student "representatives from different colonies including the West Indies, Gambia, Sierra Leone, Gold Coast, Lagos, Cameroons, Kimberley South Africa," as well as the United States. At several carefully chosen junctures it intervened publicly, urging politicians to support more generous treatment of Britain's black imperial subjects. Eventually it organized the Pan-African Conference. This brought together an illustrious assemblage of men and women of African descent from around the world and resulted in the famous proclamation "To the Nations of the World." With that, however, the association had shot its bolt. The delegates dispersed. The association itself withered and disappeared.[34]

But there is more to this story. What place did the the African Association hold in the historic anti-imperial metropolis? Its members stood on the shoulders of the men and women of the APS and Anti-Slavery Society, of Celestine Edwards's SRBM, of Dadabhai Naoroji's BCINC. Its aims were broader than those of the charismatic Edwards, its tactics, which, as we shall see, were derived in part from the BCINC, were more sophisticated. Edwards had represented African and African-Caribbean sentiments to Europeans in the CES and SRBM as well as to church-related audiences across Britain; the members of the African Association represented the *organized* expression of the African and African-Caribbean desire to humanize a historical movement, British imperialism, which they could not yet defeat or even conceive as defeatable, and they spoke directly to the movement's governors. Naoroji more than Celestine Edwards was their political paragon.[35]

Williams was certainly conscious of the Indian model. He shared a platform with A. E. Fletcher, the editor of *New Age*, who, addressing a social gathering of the association and its friends a few months after its formation, predicted that "if its work is efficiently carried on [the African Association] will equal in importance that of the Indian National Congress." The association, according to Fletcher, must enlighten British public opinion "upon matters pertaining to the welfare of the coloured races inhabiting this vast empire."[36] This meant, as for the BCINC, a public campaign modeled on the old Anti-Corn-Law League's: lobbying Parliament and government ministers and publishing books, pamphlets, and a newspaper.

It meant, as a first step, establishing formal offices. Initially the association met in private quarters, and Williams, as general secretary, used his Gray's Inn address for all correspondence. Then it took a room at 139 Palace Chambers, Bridge Road, Westminster, next to the office of the BCINC. That this decision could have been taken without reference to the older organization is inconceivable. Later the association moved to 61–62 Chancery Lane. From here Williams, as general secretary, loosed a stream of correspondence upon the world. Not only was he in touch with sympathizers and potential sympathizers throughout London, but he contacted the black editors of newspapers in British Africa, the West Indies, and the United States as well as black public figures, intellectuals, and churchmen the world over.[37]

Meanwhile the association had embarked upon a public agitation. Williams, for example, gave lectures entitled "The Treatment of Native Races" and "England's Responsibility to Native African Races" in Birmingham, Manchester, Liverpool, Edinburgh, Stirling, Dundee, Glasgow, Belfast, Dublin, and throughout London: "A large number of persons was thus reached, whose sympathies . . . must have been touched by the object lesson presented to them of a member of the race pleading on behalf of his people."[38]

The African Association's first direct attempt to influence policy occurred during the spring of 1898 after hurricanes had devastated the Caribbean islands. Again taking a leaf from the South Asians, the tone was studiously moderate. "Sir, We beg now to avail ourselves of your courteous offer to consider any suggestions which we may have to offer concerning the distress in the West Indies," began the association's memorial to Colonial Secretary Joseph Chamberlain. "The law-abiding character of our people, their intense loyalty and docility in the hands of the friendly, their efficiency as labourers, are most favourable to the success of the reconstruction that is inevitable." But we may hear a faint echo of Catherine Impey's voice in the memorial too.

33. A deputation to the colonial secretary.
By permission of the British Library.

H. M. Joseph, a signatory to the memorial, would have remembered *Anti-Caste*. Perhaps he was responsible for reminding Chamberlain that the "weaker classes" in the British West Indies, "are those . . . who . . . have the most to fear, according to the customs and habits of thought which prevail in a caste-ridden country."[39]

Later in the year the association sought to influence the colonial secretary again. It hoped that the constitution about to be drafted for Rhodesia would protect Africans in the same manner as the Canadian constitution protected North America's indigenous inhabitants. "This, in the humble wisdom of the Association, Sir, will help to create confidence in the minds of the natives, and thus it will also operate as a great preventative of disturbance and unrest."[40] The BCINC could not have put it more chastely. Chamberlain, however, sanctioned the rule of Rhodes's Chartered Company. Thus the African

Association began to discover, as the BCINC was discovering, that moderate tactics would not necessarily bring results.

Williams took another leaf from the BCINC, cultivating British politicians. In this he was unlike Celestine Edwards, whose political contacts had tended to be with less "respectable" laborites and socialists. Williams did not ignore that band of the political spectrum, but he looked mainly to Liberals. Early in 1899, for example, he helped to organize a meeting of M.P.s and others interested in Trinidad. He "had for some time been in communication with Mr. Harold Cox, Secretary of the Cobden Club." Perhaps through Cox, Williams reached Leonard Courtney, who agreed to chair the meeting, which was held on March 17, 1899. The gathering attracted twenty-one other M.P.s, including Sir Charles Dilke, a former cabinet minister under Gladstone and a member of the APS, and Sir William Wedderburn of the BCINC. Williams addressed this group, criticizing the colonial secretary for dissolving the municipal council of Port of Spain, while favoring the rich planters who benefited from a sugar monopoly.[41] He later claimed that this was the first time a black man had spoken publicly in the House of Commons.

Williams's political views at this point fell within traditional British Radical categories. Lecturing to the Bridge Ward Liberal Club in Stoke, Ipswich, he suggested that the principle of "No taxation without representation" be applied to African-Caribbeans, demanded abolition of the compound system in South Africa, and concluded by reminding his audience that "it remained the duty of England to use the ballot-box as a means of rendering this question a practical issue in the politics of the day." Again taking a leaf from Naoroji, who had argued that British prosperity depended to a degree upon Indian consumption of British-made goods, Williams pointed out to the South Place Institute Debating Society that there were close to eighty million people of African descent living within the British Empire: "This vast population consists of consumers, and assuming each individual to utilize ½d. per day of British made goods, that would net £125,000 per day, and in a year £45,000,000, a sum in this commercial age not to be despised."[42]

Also like Naoroji, Williams took pains to remind doubting English men and women that his people possessed education and culture. As he told the Woman's Pioneer Club on Grafton Street, Africans possessed a glorious history and were capable of glorious things. "The discovery of the ancient remains of gigantic structures and coinage in the Upper Nile, Mashonaland, and Matabele, now called Rhodesia, tell an African tale which goes back thousands of years," he reminded them. "No race has to regret more sincerely the demolition of the great Alexandrian Library than the African, because treasured therein were the writings of eminent Assyrians, and Arabian historians who bore testimony to the enlightenment of the so-called Negro and Negroid races." In a lecture called "The Ethiopian Eunuch," delivered at the Peckham Theological Forum in London, Williams referred to a biblical character mentioned in the eighth chapter of the Acts of the Apostles, an Ethiopian who traveled to Jerusalem and was converted to Christianity. Here was additional proof that North Africans of ancient times had been highly civilized.[43]

Williams's politics, then, were reminiscent of the politics of the BCINC: potentially revolutionary because in the end the British Empire could never contain peoples whose nationalist fervor had been fired up; but simultaneously loyalist and moderate in all public pronouncements. "I assure you, you have real and true friends in England who are desirous of ameliorating the condition of your race in Africa; and at the very head of these friends we are proud to be able to say we numbered our late beloved Queen," Williams once assured an audience in Trinidad. Like Naoroji, Williams wanted to pressure British imperialists into living up to their own universalist rhetoric. "If the negroes contributed to the welfare of the Empire, and if they paid their taxes," he argued, "surely they had a right to the name of Britisher, and a title to the protection of the laws of the Empire."[44]

The African Association never condemned British imperialism root and branch as Celestine Edwards had done, possibly because at the close of the nineteenth century the zeitgeist was different from what it had been during the heyday of the New Unionism and the socialist revival. So far removed was Williams from the heady atmosphere of that period that he hedged on his commitment to complete democracy: "Of course he did not for a moment advocate . . . granting the Franchise to the raw, uncultured native."[45] Sounding for all the world like Naoroji yet again, he rebuked the government because its policy requiring South African miners to live in compounds was "un-British." If instead of exploiting colonized peoples, England carried "the light of Christian civilisation into the African lands," he and his colleagues would offer their support. Indeed, then it would be something worth dying for. When the Boer War began, Williams volunteered unsuccessfully to serve in the army.[46]

A contradiction thus lay at the very heart of the African Association's worldview. On the one hand it insisted that Africans within the British Empire share equally in all the rights and privileges accorded to Victoria's white subjects; on the other hand, it adumbrated an independent Pan-African movement. Williams encapsulated the contradiction when he demanded in a lecture that each colonized African be treated as "a Britisher in the true sense of the term," while simultaneously envisioning among Africans an independent and "common mode of thought."[47]

But to dwell upon the contradiction is to miss the main point. It took courage and fortitude in the closing years of Victoria's reign to form an African Association, to publicly demand better treatment for Victoria's subjects of African descent, to petition government officials on their behalf, and to meet with Members of Parliament and heads of radical pressure groups. Williams and his colleagues possessed a toughness which the numerous protestations of loyalty only partially disguised. Occasionally, however, the members of the African Association betrayed the metal in them, especially when they began organizing the famous Pan-African Conference.

The conference itself was a tremendous gesture for the times. For people of African heritage all the currents were flowing the other way. In the United States, Jim Crow laws were at their height. In Africa the imperial "scramble" had left nearly the entire continent in the hands of Europeans. Within the British Empire, repressive laws, many newly strengthened, bore hard on West Indians and Africans alike, and with the outbreak of the Boer War, the mood in Britain itself had turned bumptiously, sometimes ferociously, jingo. Dissidents there were, as we have seen, but root-and-branch opponents of imperialism were rare. In these circumstances the plan to hold a conference at the heart of the empire extolling Pan-Africanism was audacious and visionary.

The conference itself has been carefully studied, although much about it remains obscure. Williams is generally credited as its originator, but he conceived of a meeting confined to the black subjects of the British Empire: "The scheme developed into a Pan-African one."[48] Williams would probably have taken credit for this evolution had it been his idea. The decision to call a Pan-African Conference instead was momentous, endowing the event with a symbolic resonance it would not otherwise have possessed.

On November 19, 1898, Williams persuaded his association to sponsor the meeting, which it scheduled for the spring of 1900, a date later pushed back to the end of July. He circulated invitations, receiving a heartening response. On June 12, 1899, a planning session took place. The African American Booker T. Washington, who happened to be in London then, was among those present. The meeting impressed him: "It is surprising to see the strong intellectual mould which many of these Africans and West Indians possess." Washington agreed to publicize the projected conference in the United States. On July 15 the *Indianapolis Freeman* published his letter describing the preliminary meeting and urging interested readers to contact Williams. During his stay in Britain, Washington visited Street in Somerset and stopped with John Bright's daughter.[49] The links with Catherine Impey and *Anti-Caste* were not completely severed.

Washington deemed the conference very important, but not everybody agreed. The APS thought the event should not take place at all. In a letter of November 4, 1899, Fox Bourne asked Williams to call it off, claiming that the constitution of the African Association did not mandate the convening of international gatherings. Possibly he doubted the association's capacity to pay for the meeting, and there were financial constraints. Williams solicited and received a donation from Naoroji. There was also a substantial subvention from the Anti-Slavery Society.[50] Possibly, however, the secretary of the APS doubted the capacity of West Indians and Africans to organize a conference even if they had enough money. Or possibly he thought that his own society should have been consulted more closely and that the African Association was becoming too independent.

In dealing with Fox Bourne, Williams revealed a little of the steel in his character, and something more. "That the Association has not deviated from its constitution is a certainty beyond contradiction," he asserted robustly in his letter of reply. "A Pan-African Conference will bring the leaders of the people in[to] greater sympathy with the movement and this is a desire to be aimed at." To Booker Washington he wrote, "We are receiving slight opposition from 'The Aborigines Protection Society.'" And then, quoting Washington to himself, the truly revealing remark: "'We must do for ourselves in order to demand and ultimately gain the respect of the other races.'"[51]

This was an attitude to which the leader of the APS was unaccustomed. In Britain the concept of self-help was at least as old as Samuel Smiles, but its advocacy by anti-imperialists suggests a conceptual leap. Catherine Impey, Elizabeth Fyvie Mayo, Dadabhai Naoroji, even Celestine Edwards, all believed that the solution to caste lay in the brotherhood of humankind, in whites lending the colonized peoples a helping hand. The African Association did not despise aid from any quarter, but its race consciousness was something new in Britain. "It is our firm belief that we must employ our own talent and energy," the association declared at one point. And by 1901 Williams was asserting, "No other but a Negro can represent the Negro." Although critics of capitalism had long been saying that workers must represent workers, few British critics of empire would have agreed with Williams's statement.[52]

Race consciousness coexisted in Williams's mind with a more traditional desire to maintain a functioning relation with British Liberals. Now his assiduous networking paid off. The Committee of the New Reform Club entertained delegates to an "At Home" at St. Ermin's Hotel, Westminster, on the evening preceding the opening of the conference. Liberals who spoke at a gathering afterward included P. W. Clayden, treasurer of the New Reform Club and former secretary of the Liberal Forwards, Jane Cobden Unwin, one of Kinloch's early champions, and Dr. Colenso (presumably the son of Bishop Colenso). When the conference began next morning the bishop of London, Mandel Creighton, presided. "No one believed [I] was bold enough, or had brass enough" to invite so important a figure, Williams boasted afterward. But he had written to the bishop, and the bishop had accepted his invitation. At the end of the second day Creighton invited all delegates to tea at Fulham Palace. And at the close of the third and final day, a Liberal M.P. with colonial interests, Gavin Clark, gave the delegates yet another tea on the terrace of the House of Commons followed by a tour of the Palace of Westminster.

At least thirty-two men and women attended the conference, which convened on July 23. Africa sent four delegates, from Abyssinia, Liberia, Sierra Leone, and the Gold Coast; the United States sent eleven, including Du Bois,

34. The Pan-African Conference.
By permission of the British Library.

but not Booker T. Washington, who pleaded a previous engagement; Canada sent one delegate, the West Indies ten, two of whom were doctors training in Edinburgh. Six delegates from London also attended. Then there were a number of attendees who did not list themselves as delegates. "It was not a large audience," commented a journalist, "but it was one eminently representative of the negro and allied races. The Conference embraced nearly every shade and every type of the Ethiopian and those nearly related to him, with a fair sprinkling of pure whites." These would have been journalists plus a few Liberal and Radical sympathizers, representing the Anti-Slavery, Aborigine's Protection, and Quaker societies, all of which received votes of thanks after the conference. Felix Moscheles, the godson of Felix Mendelssohn, friend of Giuseppe Mazzini, and a well-known peace campaigner, also attended as an observer.[53]

No complete record of the conference survives, but the London press covered the meeting in some detail. The *Times* provided the most complete coverage. Mandel Creighton, in his opening address, spoke in the condescending tones of the APS, of which, not coincidentally, he was a member. The conference was worthy, he intoned, because Britons "must look forward in their dealings with other races ultimately to confer on them some of the benefits of self-government that they themselves enjoyed." C. W. French of St. Kitts, on the other hand, spoke in tones still predominating in the BCINC: "The coloured people claimed from the British Government just that recognition which they were entitled to as men—namely that under the Queen's rule men of colour should have equal position and place with the white race." Portions of the conference's proclamation "To the Nations of the World," a document opening with the memorable lines composed by Du Bois, "The problem of the twentieth century is the problem of the colour line," could have been written by Celestine Edwards: "Let not the cloak of Christian missionary enterprise be allowed in the future, as so often in the past, to hide the ruthless economic exploitation and political downfall of less developed nations, whose chief fault has been reliance on the plighted troth of the Christian Church." It was left to the Haitian Benito Sylvain, an aide-de-camp of the Abyssinian emperor Menelik, who had defeated the Italians at Adowa, to speak in language reminiscent of R. C. Sen, the Indian student who had so troubled the India Office spy: "No human power [can] stop the African natives in their social and political development. The question now [is] whether Europe would have the improvement for or against her interests." But Sylvain's was an unrepresentative voice.[54]

Other speakers, including Williams, attempted to focus upon the concrete steps a Pan-African Association must take. It should meet triennially. It should serve as a bureau of information, a resource for people of African descent everywhere. It must establish branches wherever significant numbers of the race had collected. It should sponsor a newspaper, the *Pan-African*. And it should raise public consciousness through meetings, demonstrations, and the like. In short, it should pursue the tried and trusted path of peaceful, constitutional agitation. Appropriately enough at its conclusion the conference offered a petition to Queen Victoria, drawing attention to the disabilities under which Africans labored in Rhodesia and South Africa. Eventually this elicited a response from Chamberlain containing anodyne reassurances.

The conference's most revealing document is the famous proclamation "To the Nations of the World," which begins in nearly defiant tones, "In the metropolis of the modern world, in this the closing year of the nineteenth century, there has been assembled a congress of men and women of African blood, to deliberate solemnly the present situation and outlook of the darker races of mankind." It goes on to predict that the "colour line" will haunt the twentieth century, to contrast the great achievements and powers of past African civilizations with their present weakness, to extol the efforts of Europeans who fought against slavery and racial injustice, to condemn European imperialism, to warn against the further exploitation, ravishment, and degradation of "the black world," and to conclude with an exhortation to all black people to "take heart" and "fight bravely" to demonstrate that they belonged "to the great brotherhood of mankind."[55]

Against the backdrop of caviling qualifications and outright racism which typified most radical and socialist commentary on the empire, the carefully nuanced phrases of the BCINC, and the lonely struggle of Celestine Edwards, the proclamation, the conference as a whole, towers giantlike. It was an extraordinary gesture and achievement for the isolated, struggling few who arranged it.

Some in London understood as much. "The Pan-African Conference which closed its sittings . . . yesterday evening marks the initiation of a remarkable movement in history," predicted the *Westminster Gazette*. "The manifesto which the Pan-African Conference has drawn up and addressed to the Governments of the world is a remarkable document," W. T. Stead acknowledged in the July issue of his *Review of Reviews*. "Is it possible that the much-despised negro race may yet come to the front and lead in the march to a higher stage of human development?" asked a reporter for *Justice*, rather doubtfully, impressed despite himself after attending the conference as an observer. "We should be glad to be able to think so."[56]

But most residents of London remained unaware that a conference had taken place. After all, they inhabited, indeed had helped to construct, a city whose every aspect reflected the glory and power of British imperialism, the inevitability and invincibility of white rule. Against this the anti-imperialists, divided among themselves as we have seen, struggled not absolutely in vain, but without great effect. And what was true of London in this respect was true of the world. The Pan-African Conference was a harbinger, nothing more. The future it foresaw remained far distant in 1900. The symbolism of "a Conference of members of the Negro race gathered together in the world's Metropolis, discussing their wrongs and pleading for justice for the race" was powerful;[57] but the conference's ability to influence events, or even to maintain the spirit evoked for a moment in the imperial metropolis in July 1900, was weak. Delegates returning home discovered that their hands were full coping with racism where they lived and that the international organization broached in London was beyond their power to maintain. The Pan-African Association never met again. Its newspaper lapsed after a short while. Even the London branch broke up.

Williams himself was not a spent force. He struggled unavailingly for some time to keep the new association alive, editing the *Pan-African*, cultivating Liberal politicians,[58] organizing branches in Trinidad and elsewhere in the West Indies. Two of his lectures he published as a long pamphlet or short book, *The British Negro*, in which he argued the usual themes: that the empire was wasting a valuable human resource, that Africans could be proud of their heritage, that they should be treated as all other British subjects were treated. After 1902, however, he seems to have given it up. Perhaps the shifting student population which had supported his early efforts proved decisive; when students finish their studies they go home. In the Pan-African Association Williams appears to have become something of a one-man band.

Also in 1902 Williams crowned his personal ambition. He qualified for the bar and began practicing law, unfortunately with little success. After three years he moved to South Africa, where, briefly and futilely, he sought to establish a practice among the African community. Returned to London he resumed his law practice and appears to have considered a political career. He joined the National Liberal Club and stood as a member of the Progressive and Labour slate for the Marylebone Council. "[My] object would be to serve the working-classes," he told one meeting.[59] Seventeen candidates contested this district, and nine were elected. Williams finished eighth and was therefore successful. Whatever his ambitions may have been, at this stage he abandoned them. In 1908 he returned to Trinidad, where he finally built a successful law practice. He died suddenly and very young, like Celestine Edwards, in 1911, when he was forty-two years old.

❖ ❖ ❖

London's anti-imperialists were the quintessential troublemakers of British politics, as A. J. P. Taylor once called them. Most accepted British imperialist rhetoric at face value and strove mightily to force British imperialists to live up to it. This took courage at a time when politicians, the press, the culture, public opinion trumpeted the empire and the men who had built it as paragons of virtue, bravery, and patriotism.

Although many saw through the hypocrisy and cant expressed in the name of the British Empire and the greed and brutality with which some of its policies were carried out, hardly anyone could imagine a world in which the British Empire had ceased to exist. White critics, Indian nationalists, even Pan-Africans sought, therefore, to make the best of things by stressing the good which the empire might accomplish. It could become a force for progress. It might serve as the basis for a world government, a kind of United Nations. In this dream, if nowhere else, anti-imperialists like Dadabhai Naoroji and Henry Sylvester Williams joined hands with Cecil Rhodes, Alfred Milner, Prime Minister Salisbury. Only an economist like Hobson could pierce this veil of sentiment and wishful thinking.

And Hobson was an anti-Semite. It is hardly surprising that most English troublemakers could not rid themselves of the racist preconceptions of nearly the entire industrialized world. Nor, therefore, is it surprising that Irish and Indian nationalists in London shared them. Only the Pan-Africans placed things in perspective. "To be sure," Du Bois acknowledged in his famous proclamation, "the darker races are today the least advanced in culture according to European standards. This has not, however, always been the case."[60] Williams reiterated the point in his lectures two years later. Even so, most of the men and women who attended the Pan-African Congress believed in the redemptive possibilities of imperialism.

The immediate influence of anti-imperial London was not large. Anglo-Saxon troublemakers, organized in socialist and Aborigine's Protection and Anti-Slavery societies and in ginger groups on the left wing of Liberalism, softened some imperialist policies by drawing public attention to various excesses. No politician likes to defend beastliness once it has been exposed. But Dadabhai Naoroji did not rouse up a public agitation sufficient to abolish the economic drain of India; H. S. Williams did not end the compound system in South Africa. The idea that South Asians and Africans should be treated not as colonized peoples but as British citizens gained little purchase at the turn of the twentieth century.

On the other hand, who would deny that anti-imperial London's most advanced spirits planted the seeds of a movement which would permanently alter British history, or that they were the pioneers of a postimperial metropolis?

Conclusion

CHAPTER 10

THE KHAKI ELECTION OF 1900

L ONDON's imperial reach was prodigous; and the empire's reach into the nooks and crannies of the city and into aspects of its residents' daily lives was equally long. Yet the residents of London were not passive instruments who, for whatever reasons, nourished grand ambitions for their country and its capital. Neither were they mere sponges soaking up imperialist ideas and then spouting them when squeezed. In a myriad of ways London's citizens sought to fashion the imperial metropolis so that it would make sense to them. Workers, women, socialists and Radicals, architects, businessmen, stockholders, dramatists, authors, zoologists, geographers, representatives of the imperialized peoples themselves were among the many we have witnessed taking part in this grand, never-ending shaping and reshaping.

The Khaki Election of 1900 (so called because it took place during the Boer War, when soldiers wore khaki) illuminated the connections between urban life and empire. It cast a searchlight over the megalopolis at the center of the British Empire, highlighting parliamentary candidates who echoed and reechoed themes adduced earlier in this book, offering for public assessment conflicting views of Britain's imperial role and of London's place within the empire. The election foregrounded, too, the men and women who made London what it was by weighing and debating the issues, by voting, if they were men whose names appeared on the electoral rolls, but also by questioning, applauding, jeering the candidates at meetings throughout the metropolis, by discussing in their organizations the issues the politicians had raised, and by commenting on them in print. The Khaki Election allowed Londoners to focus upon the intersection between imperialism and their lives, to participate in a public exchange on the form that that crossroads would take in future, and finally to help shape and define it by supporting candidates who articulated their own ideals and by opposing those who did not.

Enabling Londoners to support or oppose certain politicians, the Khaki Election enabled them, too, to show what kind of empire they believed their city should be the capital of. The Khaki Election, in short, provides a grand finale and fitting concluding chapter to this examination of London in 1900: the Imperial Metropolis.

❖   ❖   ❖

The Conservative government dissolved Parliament on September 24 and called the general election in order to take advantage of public enthusiasm generated earlier in the summer by British victories in the South African war. The ensuing campaign was ill-tempered and characterized by mudslinging. Conservatives emphasized their imperialist accomplishments while warning that to vote for the Liberals was to vote for the Boers. The opposition, much divided, criticized the government either for not being imperialist enough or for being too imperialist, for mismanaging the war, for ignoring important domestic issues, and for allowing crass jingoism to take root among the voters. From this insalubrious contest the Conservatives emerged victorious, renewing their hold on power and slightly increasing their overall majority.[1]

The London campaign generally traced the line followed nationally. "It was a hugger-mugger election, rushed through amid yells of 'Pro-Boer' and 'traitor,'" W. T. Stead observed disgustedly when it was over—and the evidence for London bears him out. "Do you vote for the Queen or Kruger? If for the Queen support Kyd," ran a poster for Whitechapel's Conservative candidate. "Ellis [the Rushcliffe M.P. whose correspondence with the Boers had just been discovered] and Steadman [the Liberal incumbent in Stepney] are pals. Are they not both traitors?" enquired the Conservative candidate, Maj. William Eden Evans-Gordon, in his successful effort to woo East End electors. When voters objected to such name-calling, Conservatives were unapologetic. "Don't you think it's a shame that the Conservative Party should put out bills such as Briton v. Boer?" an elector asked Ernest Gray, the incumbent Conservative for North-West Ham. "No," was the reply. "That's practically my election address and I want to know whether you are going to poll as Briton or Boer."[2]

Like their counterparts throughout the country, London's anti-Conservatives chose diverse, usually ineffective strategies to cope with the onslaught. "You will be told that this election must be fought on the right or wrong of the South African War," George Lansbury, the socialist candidate for Bow and Bromley, argued. "I decline altogether to so regard it and shall do all in my power to keep before you those matters which affect your everyday life and which I feel are of far more importance than any question connected with the war." He lost by 2,145 votes, a relatively large margin in a London constituency. "I am not one of those who fear the responsibilities of Empire if our Empire be free, tolerant and unaggressive," James Stuart, the Radical member for Hoxton recorded defensively in his election address. He went down to defeat at the hands of a member of the Stock Exchange, Claude Hay, who had called him a pro-Boer. William Steadman, trying to deflect the ferocious Major Evans-Gordon, "regretted—deeply regretted—the speeches made by the Irish members in regard to the war, but pointed out that the Liberal party was no more responsible for these than was Lord Salisbury." His regrets too were in vain.[3]

More than seven hundred thousand London men were eligible to vote in the election, choosing sixty-two representatives to the House of Commons, including one from London University.[4] The impression a century later is of a vast battleground, of a city approaching chaos, of a great struggle ebbing to and fro from district to district, of bravery and cowardice among candidates, of violence and near-violence among voters, of huge crowds; above all, of a cacophony of competing voices cheering and jeering, commenting, struggling for purchase and impact. Audiences were not hard to find, although attentive listeners could be scarce. Many whom I have discussed in previous pages took part, repeating, refining, occasionally retooling their understandings not merely of the war and imperialism generally, but of London's role within the empire.

Sir Alfred Newton, Bart., lord mayor of London and chief architect of the CIV, stood for West Southwark. Immediately after announcing his candidacy he discovered a fatherly interest in the district's children, inviting them to the Mansion House for Punch and Judy shows. This displeased the Liberal incumbent, R. K. Causton, who pointed out that the lord mayor had refused previously to contribute to the Southwark public library where poor children went for books.[5]

The contest between Newton and Causton resulted in Liberal victory, rare in London, but otherwise in many respects it typified the metropolitan campaign as a whole. It pitted an aggressive defender of the Conservative government and its imperialist policies against a Liberal whose views on the war and empire were more nuanced. Yet in retrospect the differences between the two candidates seem plain enough.

Certainly Newton's position on London's imperial role differed substantially from Causton's. He viewed the metropolis as a reservoir of volunteer imperialist soldiers. His campaign posters depicted "A City Imperial Volunteer in full uniform bespeaking votes on behalf of Sir Alfred as 'the founder of the CIV and the man who proved the military powers of Great Britain to the world.'" His election address stressed that the CIV, paid for and staffed by City firms and their employees, posed a model for the country, whose regular army must henceforth be "run on business lines." Newton invoked an imperialist militia equipped by free enterprise.[6]

Given his mayoral position, he could not help stressing also the pomp and ceremony which were, in his opinion, essential aspects of an imperial metropolis. He attended functions bedecked in lord mayoral costume, occasionally attended by a sword bearer.[7] He believed not merely that the city's public figures should have an imperial bearing, but also that the metropolis should look like an imperial capital and behave like one, turning out to cheer the heroes returning from South Africa. Already he was planning the grand reception for the CIV, who would return to London at the end of October.

35. Sir Alfred Newton, Bart.
Courtesy of the Guildhall Library.

36. Lady Newton campaigning for her husband in a Southwark pub.
By permission of the British Library.

Causton disagreed. A plainspoken, comfortably-off gentleman reminiscent of Charles Dickens's Mr. Pickwick, he informed the West Southwark Liberal and Radical Association that "the home life of the people . . . was of the first importance." His election address condemned Newton for wrapping himself in the CIV flag. "In my opinion," Causton wrote, "none would more deeply resent the maneouvre which would use them for electioneering purposes than those gallant fellows who belong to the nation." Causton proposed an alternative understanding of how London and the empire should be connected: "I advocate social reforms . . . so that in London . . . the important questions of housing the workers, water, lighting and sanitation may be furthered and the physical and intellectual well-being of our people, so truly essential to the prosperity of our Empire, be advanced." As he put it on another occasion, while "they were all agreed to make the Empire as great as possible, they were not all agreed as to the methods." For Newton the greatness of an empire was measured in square miles claimed, populations subjected by London volunteers, imperial administrators to govern them; for Causton a great empire was one which enacted social reforms at home. This was a crucial divide between the candidates, one replicated in many London constituencies.[8]

Southwark was a poor district. Newton's wife, an assiduous campaigner, confessed that "so much poverty and pathos ... is trying to the feelings." Luckily, however, the mayor "is very much interested in the housing of the poor people and that appeals to them." The tone grated and possibly became a factor in the contest. When Lady Newton entered a Southwark pub to distribute campaign literature "one man asking for and receiving a bill tore it up and threw the pieces on the floor." Nor was this the worst the Newtons endured in their unaccustomed proximity to poverty and democracy. At St. George's Hall, Westminster-Bridge Road, on the evening of October 1, Sir Alfred confronted an unruly audience. He had asked Dadabhai Naoroji's old antagonist at the India Office, Lord George Hamilton, secretary of state for India, to speak on his behalf. Hamilton attempted to do so. "They should support Sir A. J. Newton because he had rendered a great national service in connexion with the equipment and despatch of the City Imperial Volunteers. . . . The most supreme question before the electors was that relating to South Africa." A section of the audience heckled unmercifully. The lord mayor's son, Harry, bolder than he was wise, waded into their midst. "He was hustled by half-a-dozen men" and his head forced through a glass-paneled door. The meeting broke up in disorder, Hamilton failing to complete his speech. Sir Alfred condemned "disreputable Radicals" for the attack. Harry Newton spent the night in hospital and nearly a week convalescing.[9]

In the end Newton lost to Causton by 230 votes, the margin of victory possibly padded by Irishmen who endorsed the Liberal after a meeting with him on September 29. Lord George Hamilton, however, was returned unopposed as Conservative member for Ealing, which he had represented since 1868. The campaign, so hectic elsewhere, provided the secretary of state for India with a period of relative leisure. He composed a magisterial election address in which his main subjects were the inevitable British triumph in South Africa and the need to preserve imperial gains by reelecting the present government. He did not mention the famine in India or an enquiry into its causes. Bitterly *India* pointed out that there was only a single, galling reference in the document to the country of which Hamilton was secretary of state. "In the far East," Hamilton had written, "our Indian troops have once more made known to the world the fighting power and resources which the loyalty and courage of that great dependency can contribute towards Imperial objects."[10]

In fact Hamilton did not believe that Indians should serve as cannon fodder for British imperialists. But as he wrote in his memoirs twenty-two years later, "There is a fixed gulf between European and Asiatic mentalities which will always remain." This was apparent to him even in 1900 and not only with regard to Indians. "The Chinese [too] were a most difficult nation to deal with," he complained to the Primrose League at Weston. It seems strange that Lord Salisbury entrusted to this gentleman rule over large portions of a continent he so little appreciated and understood.[11]

Hamilton, however, recognized his limitations, if not as secretary of state then as orator. "A Cabinet Minister gets out of touch with the tone and trend of the public topics and movements of the day," he conceded in his memoirs. "He soon finds this out when platform-speaking outside his constituency. . . . He has frequently to hunt about to get the tone of his audience and whilst so engaged he not infrequently loses a hold over it which he cannot afterwards regain."[12]

Perhaps he was remembering his own disastrous experiences. Three times during the Khaki Election Hamilton ventured from Ealing to speak on behalf of Conservatives. On one occasion he managed to finish a speech on behalf of Sir Samuel Scott, the sitting Conservative member for West Marylebone, who was serving at the front, but then Conservatives of the district were accustomed to being addressed by Sir Samuel's proxies, including his mother. Twice, however, the secretary of state for India was forced by hecklers to retire from the platform. In addition to the incident at St. George's Hall, there was another, in the Canterbury Music Hall, Westminster-Bridge Road, at which Hamilton, speaking for North Lambeth's Conservative candidate, Fred Horner, could neither find nor hold the tone of his audience. "Lord George Hamilton said the question before the electors was one which mostly affected the industrial interests of London. London was the capital of the largest empire in the world. A great deal of its commerce was dependent upon the city's external connection with the colonies and therefore any question which affected the well-being of the colonies vitally affected the well-being of London." Here was the intersection between urban life and empire most often invoked by Conservatives in 1900. Usually it proved convincing, but not on this occasion. "Lies," shouted the audience, and "for quite five minutes [Lord George] could not get beyond the first words of his sentence." He tried another popular Conservative theme: "The enemies of the country would rub their hands with delight if the present Government was turned out of office." At this his audience made an uproar which "continued unabated until the close of the meeting, the speakers . . . being unable to make themselves heard."[13]

In Ealing, where no campaign meetings took place because his lordship faced no Liberal opponent, a like commotion never occurred. Shortly after the election, however, an outsider ventured into the neighborhood to voice a dissenting view of imperialism and London's role as an imperial capital. Will Crooks, the Lib-Lab from Woolwich, addressed the initial meeting of a newly revived Acton Liberal and Radical Association. Recently, he informed the audience, he had come upon "an old lady residing in a squalid alley" in East London, "and he tried to comfort her by reminding her of her privileges; so he said, 'Don't you know that the Queen reigns over an Empire where the sun never sets?' 'Tell me that agin Bill?' So he told it her again. 'Jes' to think o' that,' replied the old lady, 'where the sun never sets. But the sun never comes down our court.'" What was the empire to such a woman? Crooks demanded of his listeners. What was it even to working-class British soldiers, many of whom would "return from South Africa to find . . . no shelter for themselves and family?" Contrary to what Lord George Hamilton and Sir Alfred Newton believed, there were no positive links between London and imperialism. Crooks concluded, "[My] Imperialism [is] to raise the condition of the people and to help them out of their wretched surroundings."[14]

Crooks, like R. K. Causton, easily pierced the hypocrisy by which many imperial practices were justified. Both were primarily concerned with the London working class, not with the victims of British imperialism abroad. H. Fox Bourne, of the APS, held to yet another version of London's relation to empire. A fitting role for residents of an imperial metropolis, he believed, would be for them to defend aborigines with their ballots. In a letter to the *Times* of September 25, he suggested a series of measures which would result in "much better treatment" for native Africans, Asians, and Australians. "A great deal can be done towards securing the necessary reforms if, in the several constituencies, electors who favour them will press the point on the candidates who ask for their votes." Unfortunately Fox Bourne's well-meant advice was a nonstarter in an imperial metropolis whose anti-imperialists were relatively few and weakened by ambivalencies, especially during so khaki an election as that of 1900. I can find no London constituency in which his appeal played a role.

Other residents of what I have termed anti-imperial London were equally ineffective or entirely invisible. If the Pan-African Association supported or opposed candidates, it left no trace, although H. Sylvester Williams was in London at the time. As for the BCINC, in 1900 not one of its members would stand for Parliament, much to *India's* dismay. Naoroji's name cropped up in several constituencies, but he was too ill to undertake a campaign. One BCINC speaker, Alison Garland, did address provincial constituencies on Indian subjects, but never, apparently, in London.[15]

Within the anti-imperial metropolis only the Irish proved both active and, to an unascertainable degree, effective. Their main political organization, the newly reunited UIL, made its presence known in West Southwark, where it endorsed and presumably assisted Causton's successful campaign for reelection. UIL delegations also waited upon Liberal candidates in Fulham, Hoxton, Clapham, and East Finsbury, receiving assurances on home rule, but these constituencies the Liberals lost. Elsewhere Irish people managed to ask pointed questions at public meetings. "Will [you] or will [you] not vote for a full and comprehensive measure of Home Rule?" one man asked John Bethell, the Radical candidate in North-West Ham. Would he "support the establishment of a Catholic University in Ireland and . . . support voluntary schools in this country?"asked another young Irishman. Bethell satisfied his questioners, but he too lost the election. Still, the *Irish People* thought that London's "Irish voters polled like a well-disciplined army for the friends of Ireland." According to the *Times* the Irish claimed to have the decisive votes in seven London constituencies. In all of London, Liberals won eight seats. Conceivably Irish votes provided the margin of victory in three of them, West Southwark, Camberwell, and Battersea, where at any rate Liberals proved victorious and UIL branches existed.[16]

With Fox Bourne, the Pan-African Association, and the BCINC marginalized during the election and the London Irish concerned primarily to support Liberal home-rulers, candidates who would speak for British imperialism's dark-skinned victims were at a premium. In North-West Ham, where Bethell had satisfied his Irish interlocutors, both he and his opponent, the incumbent Conservative and former head of the teachers' union, Ernest Gray, called for "Justice for the coloured races in South Africa," and one of Gray's Conservative supporters, A. Calver, backed the British effort in South Africa as a precondition to giving "every man, whether white or black, [his] freedom." In Bow and Bromley the Socialist Lansbury drew the attention of electors to "your fellow subjects in India . . . dying by millions of famine and pestilence, and the Imperial Government have refused to grant a single penny to relieve the suffering." In Battersea the Lib-Lab, John Burns, declared his sympathy with the victims of British imperialism in round and vivid tones, as will be shown below. But the primary tone of the campaign was of the opposite persuasion, xenophobic, chauvinistic, jingoist.[17]

Anti-Semitism played an important role in the Khaki Election in London. With tens of thousands of East European Jews flooding the East End, housing shortages had grown acute. There were 315,000 living two in a room, 218,000 three in a room, 99,000 four in a room, and 1,843 cases of eight people living in a single room in the eastern portion of the world's greatest metropolis. In North-West Ham, Gray might demand justice for black South

Africans; simultaneously he was demanding an end to Jewish immigration into London, which "should not be made the dumping ground for the refuse of the world." In South-West Ham, only a stone's throw away, Will Thorne, SDF candidate and ostensible standard bearer of socialist internationalism, condemned the Boer War because it was being "carried out in the interests of a lot of Jews," but surely it was the shortage of housing created in part by Jewish immigration which resonated with his supporters. In Whitechapel, the Conservative candidate, David Kyd, demanded "legislation to restrain the immigration of destitute Aliens." It is obvious whom he had in mind. On September 20, however, the *Pall Mall Gazette* pointed out that fully half the electorate of this district was Jewish. And Kyd's opponent, Stuart Samuel, was himself a Jew as well as being the nephew of the former member Samuel Montagu, likewise Jewish. Stuart was also the brother of Herbert Samuel, who would eventually become high commissioner in Palestine. An anti-Semitic campaign would not work here. Suddenly Kyd discovered that he was a Zionist, a move which enabled him to court Jewish voters while supporting a program that if successful would end the "problem" of Jewish immigration to Whitechapel forever. Even this ingenious maneuver failed to save him, however. He lost the election by seventy-one votes. "All I can say," an uncomprehending Kyd reported afterwards, "is that I am quite unable to give you the reason for my defeat in Whitechapel."[18]

Anti-Semitism, of course, had a long history in London. But many voters snatched at it in 1900 because it connected to the ongoing debate about their city's identity, confirming an exclusive view of it. Could a Jewish population help to define the imperial metropolis too? Not according to the most infamous anti-Semite of the campaign, Major Evans-Gordon, whose nasty tactics against William Steadman have been referred to above. A precursor of the fascist Oswald Mosley, no sooner was the major seated in Parliament than he proposed an anti-alien amendment to the King's Speech from the Throne and launched, in East London, an Anti-Alien League, whose goal was a parliamentary ban on further Jewish immigration.[19]

Yet in the major's case inclusion and exclusion crossed paths in paradoxical fashion. While an army officer in India, Evans-Gordon had behaved like an "Oriental tyrant"; he cannot be described as friendly to critics of British rule there. During the campaign, however, he had taken to calling the subcontinent "the East End of this Empire." A breathtaking enlargement and reinterpretation of the imperial metropolis, the phrase seemed to incorporate an entire nation into the very section of London the major wished to represent in the House of Commons. Yet the Jews must not come in. Either Evans-Gordon conceived of Britain's Indian subjects as white, or at any rate as whiter than the Jews, or he thought that British subjects, whatever their color, were superior to alien Jews.[20]

So the Khaki Election swirled and eddied through the constituencies of London. Against the impregnable walls of high finance, however, it beat in vain. There would be no electoral contest in the Square Mile. Represented by two Conservative members, the City of London could not discover a single Liberal willing to stand against them.

The City's junior Conservative member, Alban Gibbs, a merchant banker, was a colorless figure who made little impact. Among the Gibbs family papers preserved at the Guildhall Library I find only a single letter by him referring to turn-of-the-century politics, a protest to the secretary of the Midland Railway Company: "Since I came back from Scotland I have received many complaints from my constituents . . . who live down your line, of the great inconvenience they are put to owing to a new rule . . . that the trains from Moorgate Street no longer connect with the St. Pancras."[21]

Gibbs's interventions in the House were rare. "[I have] not thought it desirable to speak on many occasions," he confessed to his local Conservative Association. He specialized in introducing votes of thanks to more illustrious figures, however, such as Sir Alfred Newton. "On the Lord Mayor's initiative and under his fostering and watchful care," Gibbs apostrophized the candidate for West Southwark, "had been raised and equipped and sent to the war now happily coming to a glorious and successful end that splendid regiment of citizen soldiers, the City of London Imperial Volunteers, whose brave deeds and excellent qualities have not alone received the repeated high encomiums of Field Marshall Lord Roberts, but compelled the admiration . . ." and so forth and so on, a piling on of subordinate clauses for nearly a column of newsprint.[22]

Few who earned their livings in the Square Mile can have been satisfied with so inconsequential a representative. Gibbs would not step down, but then the City's senior member, Sir Reginald Hanson, Bart., retired. To replace him the local Conservative Association chose Sir Joseph Dimsdale, bank and company director. In the Square Mile an unmediated notion of imperialism and of London's and the imperial government's role held sway. Dimsdale shared these attitudes. "I am myself a member of the great mercantile community of London—a banker," he explained, "and it will be my constant endeavour to promote in every way that I can the commercial and mercantile interests of this City. The action of the present Government during the last five years has shown clearly that they are not unmindful of the great responsibility attendant upon the possession of so vast an Empire as ours." This was a variation on the theme introduced above by Hamilton, that imperialism made Londoners wealthy. "Any question which affected the well-being of the colonies vitally affected the well-being of London," Hamilton had proclaimed. Dimsdale turned it round. He was delighted "to represent the first commercial constituency in this empire, the heart that pumps through the trade and commerce of the civilised world." Not only could imperialism make London rich, but the imperial metropolis could make the empire wealthy too.[23]

Meanwhile the City as a whole was finding the Khaki Election congenial, even bracing. "We do not hesitate to say that the elections have been fixed for a very advantageous period from the City point of view," editorialized the *Financial Times* on September 27. Now that the Boers appeared to be defeated it was expecting a great revival on the Stock Exchange; better to get the general election out of the way first. Halfway through the poll, on October 4, it crowed gleefully that already twenty-three City bankers had been elected to constituencies throughout the country. Of nine members of the Stock Exchange who were also M.P.s, seven Conservatives were returned, of whom three represented London constituencies. One, B. L. Cohen of East Islington, was also president of the Jewish Board of Guardians. He received a letter lauding his contributions in Parliament over the past fifteen years from Lord George Hamilton. "I cannot believe that any sane constituency can do otherwise than retain your valuable services," wrote the man who found Asians nearly impossible to understand and deal with.[24] In this single regard Lord George's vision of the imperial metropolis was more generous than that of many Conservatives, Liberals, and even Socialists.

One London constituency in which imperial issues could not help but play a central role was Bethnal Green North-East, whose sitting member was Sir Mancherjee Merwanjee Bhownaggree, originally of Bombay. The son of a wealthy Parsi merchant, Bhownaggree began his career as a journalist, but in 1872 at age twenty-one assumed his father's position as state agent in Bombay for the territory of Bhavnagar, of which he also became a judicial councillor. He traveled to Britain for the first time the next year, when he performed services for the *thakore* (or governor) of Bhavnagar and the British Liberal Party, demonstrating in the process a precocious understanding of British politics. The thakore wished for a grander salute, more guns to be fired in his honor, than the British accorded him. Bhownaggree arranged for the potentate to send a gift of one hundred thousand rupees to the Liberal Party's Northbrook Club. Shortly thereafter the Liberal government awarded the Order of the Star of India to the thakore, a suitable elevation in status. Now the guns could be fired. A few years later, in 1877, Bhow-naggree translated Queen Victoria's *Leaves from the Journal of our Life in the Highlands* into Gujarati, sycophantically dedicating it to the Prince of Wales. These early efforts cast some doubt upon the work of recent scholars who suggest that Bhownaggree was always something of a critic of British imperial practices.[25]

That the young man was able and ambitious, however, is apparent. In 1881 he became a fellow of Bombay University. The next year found him in London studying law at Lincoln's Inn, (at the thakore's expense). In 1885 he was called to the bar. A year later he helped to organize the Indian and Colonial Exhibition in South Kensington, for which the queen awarded him the Companion of the Indian Empire. Returned to India in 1887 he drew up a constitution for the maharajah of Bhavnagar, receiving as payment an estate which gave him control not merely of land, but of tenants permanently tied to the land. Although he was now a feudal lord in India, however, Bhownaggree's ambitions focused increasingly upon England. "India is solid Conservative," he wrote to George Birdwood. "Why will not the Conservative Party start me as their candidate for some constituency?"[26]

It soon would, even though Bhownaggree was probably mistaken about informed political opinion in his homeland. Conservative Party leaders recognized him as a useful foil to the Liberal and Radical nationalists who dominated the London Indian scene. In 1894 they arranged for Bhownaggree to contest Bethnal Green North-East. It was not a safe seat, having voted Liberal in the past three elections, but now the tides were flowing the other way. During the general election of 1895 Bhownaggree defeated a resentful George Howell by 160 votes. "After ten years hard Labour in Parliament," the old Lib-Lab wrote disbelievingly to a friend, "I was kicked out by a black man, by a stranger from India, one not known in the constituency or in public life."[27]

Thus Bhownaggree entered Parliament. He was the only Indian in the House of Commons, for after his three-year stint for Central Finsbury Naoroji had lost his seat in the general Liberal debacle. Meanwhile Bhownaggree's patrons remained generous. In 1897 Queen Victoria designated him a Knight Commander of the Most Eminent Order of the Indian Empire. He had become Sir Mancherjee Bhownaggree.

Indian nationalists despised Sir Mancherjee Bow and Agree as they called him. *India* was bluntly dismissive. "Strangely enough," it wrote, although it was not strange given Bhownaggree's history, "Sir Mancherjee takes no part in the deliberations of the Indian Parliamentary Committee." Dinshaw Wacha, secretary to the Indian National Congress, thought him "a tool of the

37. Sir Mancherjee Merwanjee Bhownaggree.
Credit: Hulton Getty.

Anglo Indians" who "does harm to India's cause by his abject slavery to them." Even the tolerant and diplomatic Naoroji had misgivings. "About Mr. Bhownaggree," he wrote in a letter to Wacha, "I tried my utmost to keep him straight about India. But, I am afraid, in vain. I cannot help thinking, I may be wrong, that he has sold his soul to his masters."[28]

It cannot be gainsaid, as John Hinnells and Omar Ralph have recently pointed out, that over the course of ten years in the House Bhownaggree loyally defended Indian interests as he understood them, warning the authorities, much the way members of the BCINC did, that there would be a grim reckoning if India's governors continued to ignore the advice of moderates like himself; arguing against excessive taxation and other costs imposed by Britain, and in favor of the construction of technical schools and the promotion of Indian doctors, who currently were being "restricted to inferior posts with trivial salaries."[29] Indian nationalists and a later generation of historians overlooked or minimized these aspects of Bhownaggree's political practice. On the other hand, the essence of Bhownaggree's role was to defend, not criticize, British policies in India, which is what makes his role in Parliament and Bethnal Green so interesting. Certainly this son of imperialized India said nothing critical of British imperial practices in India or anywhere else during the Khaki Election campaign of 1900.

With the general election pending *India* published on September 21 a paragraph which it hoped every well-disposed candidate would include in his election address.

> I undertake to give continuous and sympathetic attention to Indian questions. . . . I promise to support . . . (1) the free grant of at least five millions to the relief of the present famine; (2) the fearless investigation of the economic causes of famine in India with a view to their removal; . . . (3) a fair apportionment of burdens between the United Kingdom and India; (4) the abolition of "Press Committees" in India, the repeal of the repressive sections in the new Law of Sedition, and the repeal of Regulations authorising the imprisonment of British subjects without trial; and (5) the legitimate claims of British Indian subjects in South Africa and throughout the British empire.

Bhownaggree ignored *India*'s advice entirely, an implicit comment not merely upon his opinion of the Indian nationalist movement in London, but also upon the strength of anti-imperialist sentiment in his own constituency. The wrongs done to his country by British imperialists and how they might be righted did not figure in his election address. Indeed there was no mention of India at all, except for a single revealing reference to "our hold on our Indian Empire." Rather Bhownaggree drew attention to his own not inconsiderable efforts on behalf of Bethnal Green's residents (to which I shall return) and launched a starry-eyed celebration of the government's imperialist policies, emphasizing his identification with British imperial interests:

> Our operations in the battlefield of the Soudan, and the Fashoda incident, have not only avenged the unfortunate Gordon massacre, but removed all doubt for the future as to our influence in the region of the Nile; the firm treatment of the belligerent tribes of the Afgan frontier has been of equal effect in fixing our hold on our Indian Empire . . . and to the active part which British arms are taking in quelling the disturbance in China will be due the restoration, at an early date, of peace and the maintenance of our large commercial interests in the far East.

Yet even these accomplishments paled in comparison with "the glorious triumph of our arms in South Africa . . . which . . . finally assures the suzerainty of the British Crown and the safety of British interests in that region."[30] Indian nationalists and other critics of empire could expect little from an M.P., whatever his nationality, who embraced so wholeheartedly the triumphal Conservative imperialism reverberating loudest among all the imperialisms currently echoing throughout London.

Nor, as it transpired, could they look to Bhownaggree's Liberal opponent. Harry Lawson, "an Oxford man, a lawyer, a military officer, a capable steeplechaser," and former Liberal member for West St. Pancras, belonged to the imperialist wing of his party. In his election address he published "striking maps of the Empire and the world to show the iniquity of the Tories in making 'graceful concessions' of territory or trade interests to which apparently . . . we have an exclusive claim against the wide world."[31] Some believed he was a Conservative disguised as a Liberal. The *Daily Graphic* thought the only reason he belonged to the Liberal Party was that somebody had told him he looked like Lord Rosebery. Had the Liberals nominated a pro-Boer or genuine Little Englander to stand in Bethnal Green, the contest would have provided interesting and significant contrasts; instead it pitted two staunch supporters of empire against one another. Their political differences were more apparent than real.

While Britain was engaged in a war to defend its imperial interests, Bhownaggree held an advantage in such a contest, and not simply because, given a choice between two imperialists, a majority of voters in Bethnal Green would probably plump for the one belonging to the party most closely associated with empire. Bhownaggree could not help personifying the empire in a way Lawson never could, first by his name and dark skin, second because of the honors awarded him by Queen Victoria. To make matters worse from Lawson's point of view, shortly before the general election the shah of Persia conferred upon Bhownaggree yet another honor, the Knight Commandership of the Order of the Lion and the Sun in recognition of his efforts on behalf of Persian Parsis. "This honour," a journalist explained, "ranks in importance to our English Knight Commanderships." Despite his privileged background and reputation as an experienced, energetic campaigner, Lawson was at a disadvantage. He appears to have felt himself something of a plain bird in comparison with his much-decorated opponent. Bhownaggree, Lawson acknowledged, possibly in an attempt to appeal to the democratic sensibilities of his audience, "was a prince of the temples of the East," while he was himself "a mere cockney of cockneys."[32]

Paradoxically, then, at a moment when racism ran deep in the imperial metropolis, Bhownaggree's Indian roots were a positive advantage. As J. W. Ward, chairman of the Bethnal Green Conservative Association put it, "they

all felt proud of their Member, Sir M. M. Bhownaggree, who not only represented Bethnal Green but the great Empire of India." Another of his admir-
ers explained at the same meeting that the Conservative incumbent "was constantly being consulted by the Government on Indian matters." The implicit
message was that the government valued Bhownaggree's opinions on India
because he was Indian. Perhaps this line would not have been effective during a different general election. As the *Daily Graphic* pointed out, however, in
1900 Britain was embroiled in a war it could perhaps have avoided if only "one
or two men of South African birth had sat in the House of Commons." (Of
course the *Graphic* did not mean that native Africans should sit in Westminster.) To avert a disaster in India like the one in Africa, "there can be nothing
more desirable than the presence in the House . . . of a man like Sir M. M.
Bhownaggree." Thus was the successor of Dadabhai Naoroji, "Salisbury's
Black Man," awarded the status of an honorary white. That Bhownaggree
was Parsi, monotheistic, associated with a successful trading community
must have helped also.[33]

Englishmen valued Bhownaggree because he personified the image of India they wanted to see, loyal, assimilated, obsequious. They valued him too
because he presented to Indians the image of Great Britain they wished to
publicize on the subcontinent, as the ubiquitous Sir Alfred Newton pointed
out at the unveiling of a bust of Queen Victoria which Bhownaggree had donated, characteristically, to the Victoria Park Chest Hospital. "Their right
hon. friend was widely known in India as well as in Bethnal Green—he was
known in one thing more especially, and that was that in order to make the
people of India more acquainted with the life and ways of their Empress he
had translated the book the 'Life of the Queen in the Highlands' into Hin-
doostani."[34]

Bhownaggree understood his role precisely. "While there were some people who had never travelled out of their own country, so they could not tell
from personal experience what other countries were like," he reminded a local audience, he himself "spoke with knowledge" of India, having not merely
traveled but having been born and raised there. Simultaneously he stressed
his immersion in English life and values. Before the campaign he had condemned the assassination of the king of Italy in shocked and proper tones:
"Extreme teaching had always a very pernicious effect." When he learned
that Lawson was to be his Liberal opponent in Bethnal Green he acknowledged his adversary's qualities in the accents of an English gentleman. They
had met during an ocean voyage and played chess with one another: "Pleasant memories," Bhownaggree murmured.[35]

Above all, as in his election address, he stressed his identification with England's empire. In a long, patriotic speech to the North-East Bethnal Green Conservative Association Bhownaggree acclaimed British imperialism: "With the planting of the flag in Egypt, Africa and India was planted a better kind of government than was ever known before." He defended the government's decision to take up arms in South Africa and berated Liberals of all stripes for lack of national feeling. If voters followed the advice of Little Englanders and "resigned their dependencies . . . they would be reduced to a fourth or fifth rate nation." This would be insupportable—"an inhabitant of a country absolutely annihilated. He might as well give up battling with the world, go up into the mountain-top, say his prayers and live in peace and retirement for the rest of his life."[36] In other words it was precisely because England was an imperial power that Bhownaggree wished to live and work there.

At the close of the meeting a local Conservative, C. B. Blow, rose to speak. Like Bhownaggree, he supported the Boer War. The Dutch in South Africa were an ungrateful lot whom the British were continually having to rescue. "Then came the time when the Zulus wanted to eat them [the Boers], and England went to their assistance and said no, they are whites. They all knew what followed. England fought the Zulus and captured poor old Cetewauo and brought him over here." Would the English have rescued Indians, nonwhites, from Zulu cannibals? (As if the Zulus practiced cannibalism anyway!) Did the Conservatives of Bethnal Green think Bhownaggree was white? If these were questions that occurred to the honorary Englishman who was their parliamentary representative he nevertheless remained silent during Blow's diatribe.

As befitted a constituency M.P., Bhownaggree took demonstrable pride in carrying out the tasks associated with his office and appears to have been good at them, or at any rate conscientious. "An Elector" commented, "One night I find him presiding at one of our several Philanthropic Societies, another at an Angling Society's dinner, as also at a local Flower Show. . . . Then again we discover him helping by his presence . . . the Friendly Societies . . . or attending at some of the Social Gatherings of School Children."[37] But there was more to it than mere attendance and the occasional graceful lecture. In Bhownaggree's approach to local matters may be partially discerned his understanding of the imperial metropolis.

This was not a subject Bethnal Green's Conservative member spoke of directly, but his election address is revealing. In it Bhownaggree mentioned that he had belonged to the parliamentary Select Committee which recommended "the adoption of measures to distinguish between the treatment of the deserving poor and the undeserving." He pointed with pride to his "constant cooperation with philanthropic associations ... which seek to brighten the lives of the inhabitants of this part of the metropolis." There is nothing more here, perhaps, than the typical Conservative notion that local government, which was responsible for paying out relief, must not coddle indolent workers and that charity should play a major role in "brightening" the lives of the poor. But then Bhownaggree mentioned the Bethnal Green Museum, which sponsored "exhibitions, lectures, etc. relating to such staple industries of this locality as silk, furniture, leather and other manufactures." Like any constituency M.P. he wished to advertise local skills and to boost the economy of his district. But he linked these efforts with "the firm Imperial policy of the present Government ... as in such policy alone lies the strength, the safety and the solidity of our ... trade and commerce."[38] In Bhownaggree's mind, then, the fate of Bethnal Green and the fate of the empire were one; only a forward imperialist policy would guarantee the local economy; the South African war was a "knife and fork" question for Londoners. This was the same message Lord George Hamilton had attempted to impart to his audience in North Lambeth and that Dimsdale had offered with slight variation to the City Conservative Association.

It is hard to imagine a colonial figure supporting British imperialism more wholeheartedly or adapting better to the British way of life than Bhownaggree. Against this his opponent was practically helpless. Lawson might charge Bhownaggree with promoting antilabor views (which Bhownaggree vigorously disputed); Bhownaggree charged Lawson, absurdly but woundingly, with holding the views of a Little Englander. The former charge proved a peripheral issue in a campaign which turned upon attitudes toward the empire, the latter was immaterial in a constituency where Bhownaggree held all the cards anyway. His motto during the campaign hung on a large screen outside his central committee room: "Into one Imperial whole! One with Briton heart and soul! One life, one flag, one fleet, one Throne!" The maxim might have served as his epitaph.[39]

Thus during the general election of 1900 the gentleman from Bombay and Bethnal Green had it both ways. He was an Indian and an Englishman, which was just what the district wanted for its representative in Parliament. Bhownaggree defeated Lawson by 379 votes, 2,988 to 2,609, nearly trebling his majority over George Howell in 1895. In one corner of the imperial metropolis voters were content to be represented by "a black man"—partly because the Boer War rendered his skin color invisible or even a positive advantage, more so because Bhownaggree was adept at telling Englishmen what they wanted to hear about empire and the empire what Englishmen wanted it to hear about Britain. Above all he articulated a popular view among many voters, that their own prosperity depended upon the strength and extent of the empire, which Bhownaggree understood better than his opponent and supported more vehemently. The paradox of the Khaki Election in Bethnal Green is that by returning a singular figure to the House of Commons, voters had fortified a common understanding of imperialism and of London's place in the empire.

Across the Thames and only a few miles west of Bethnal Green lay the constituency of Battersea, which also contained a large working-class population. The contrast between incumbent candidates in the two districts, however, could not have been greater. In Battersea the parliamentary member was a Radical Liberal whose political origins lay in the socialist and labor movements. John Burns had passed through the SDF and had played a crucial role in the dockers' great victory of 1889. Elected to Parliament three years later, he gravitated toward the radical wing of the Liberal Party, rather than to the Independent Labour Party. Although in 1900 he declined to join the Labour Representation Committee, forerunner of the Labour Party, he still took every opportunity to condemn jingo imperialism, the Boer War, and the Conservative government he held responsible for both. Where Bhownaggree attempted to blend into the English establishment and to pose as an English gentleman, Burns remained at a stage when he gloried in underlining differences between himself and the "jeunesse dorée" in Parliament who sneered "when anyone less than the son of a marquis asks a question."[40]

"A Collectivist in economics, a Democrat in politics," as he identified himself, Burns was really an old-fashioned Radical patriot who personified the ideals and values, the very look, of the mid-Victorian music hall hero. "Short, broad-shouldered, broad-chested, with powerful hands and legs," he believed in Britain's world mission as a liberatory power. In the Salisbury administration's dealings with foreign governments, however, he discerned only "submission to the strong, truculent intimidation of the weak, or cruel neglect and moral cowardice in helping weaker peoples." This robust figure was not a Little Englander in the conventional sense. His notion was that the British government should remain, as he believed it had been in the main under Gladstone, a force for good in the world. Under Salisbury, however, Burns believed it had become,

> Deferential to the German Emperor ... obtrusively offensive ... to the French; criminally neglectful of our obligation to starving India ... whilst its record in Ashantee, Uganda and Jamaica has been characterised by extravagance and disgraceful interference with native rights and Colonial privileges:

38. John Burns.
Credit: Hulton Getty.

this Government has forfeited the cordial feeling to Britain the smaller nationalities and free peoples hitherto displayed. . . . Britain is ceasing to be the
guardian of the weak, in the interests of human freedom, and has become in
the past five years the champion of a soulless capitalism.

The man capable of so forthright an election address was unlikely to conduct
his ensuing campaign in less stentorian fashion.[41]

His Conservative opponent, Richard Garton, owned shares worth
£54,100 in the Anglo-Bavarian Brewery of Shepton Mallet and William
Cooper and Company, another brewery, of Southampton. He was also chief
partner in a Battersea sugar refinery employing several hundred local men.
His views were conventional. "It was due to the spontaneous way we had
sprung to arms that we had been enabled to keep foreign nations at bay," he
informed a sympathetic audience. "We did not yet know the strength of our

Empire. Increasing danger served only to show up our reserve of power." As for John Burns, "What can we say," Garton queried the Battersea Conservative Association, "of those who apparently cannot do too much to belittle their country, to throw dirt upon it and to aid the enemies of this nation?" Once the campaign began Garton determined not to "allow ourselves to be dragged aside by local or municipal questions." He would make the election a referendum on imperialism, the Boer War, and John Burns's attitudes to both.[42]

Burns was delighted to oblige. "This I can promise Mr. Garton," he told a precampaign meeting, "the issue of the war is now, and will increasingly become, the chief element in the fight at the election. What is more the electors will demand some defense of it other than that which will be offered at smoking concerts and other functions that in Tory quarters take the place of informing the electors." But first he would underline his labor credentials against the employer and capitalist who was his opponent: "Who helped the Gasworkers to get 8 hours with higher pay? Who helped to win the Busmen's Strike for 12 hours? Who helped to get 10 hours for Tramway men? Who helped to include Laundries in the Factory Bill? . . . Who helped to raise the wages of LCC employees, Gardeners, Firemen, Policemen, Laborers and reduced their hours?" The list of workers Burns claimed to have helped continues for more than a page. Against this Garton could only riposte, lamely, that "his men were not called upon to work overtime against their will and . . . when they did work overtime they were paid at nearly time and a half . . . he was a true working man's friend."[43]

Mainly, however, Burns pressed the antiwar and anti-imperial themes, as Garton had hoped he would. In part they reiterated the protest against jingoism noted in an earlier chapter. Britain had become, Burns charged, "khaki clad, khaki mad and khaki bad." In part they incorporated standard Radical criticisms of the Conservative government for poor judgment: "If we had waited patiently until Kruger's death that would have removed the last obstacle to the federation of the whole of South Africa. But Chamberlain was too anxious for the premiership of this country and Rhodes for the presidency of South Africa." But note: a federated South Africa would have been administered by British imperialists. Burns, like so many other anti-imperialists in 1900, did not so much oppose British imperial dominion as British dominion enlarged and maintained at the point of a sword. Contradictorily, however, he also hearkened back to the Gladstonian belief in free trade, in which English dominion played no part: "If you want a big empire of trade, commerce and peaceful industry keep a civil tongue in your mouth. Sell the native[s] goods, have reasonable profits, but respect their freedom as much as you love your own."[44]

Burns's outlook, then, was an amalgam of the typical pro-Boer's, Liberal free-trader's, and Little Englander's, plus something in addition. If he did not condemn imperialism *tout court*, since he believed in a generous and freedom-loving British Empire, he certainly objected to more than the South African War alone. He considered recent expeditions to Ashanti and the Sudan "a re-crudescence on a large scale of our primordial instincts and brutal past-habits of eating each other as we did in ages gone by." He "protested against using soldiers as uniformed commercial travellers, trying to force our ideas on un-willing natives." On the other hand, he did not object to soldiers per se. He was too much the bluff and hearty Englishman not to admire them. But he hated the thought that the cream of Britain's youth should risk their lives in an ill-planned war fought to raise the profits of financiers.[45]

When Britain, already engaged in a war in South Africa which he opposed, prepared to send soldiers to suppress the Boxers in China too, Burns reacted strongly. In this he was not unique among turn-of-the-century critics of em-pire, but he was one of a very few who were capable of carrying a working-class audience on the merits of Chinese as opposed to British civilization. "The Chinese are the oldest people from whom you have learnt many eco-nomical, scientific and cultural notions," he reminded a crowd in Battersea Park, just as the newspapers had begun whipping up fears of the "Yellow Peril." "The Chinese are far more civilised than we." And later in the same speech, "See the Chinaman going to work with his beautiful boots, jacket, pig-tail, fan and umbrella. Contrast that with the 4.30 from Wandsworth-road workmen's [train]. Sixteen of you in a carriage smoking frowsy pipes and wearing the same clothes you had had for months." Burns's belief in the equal-ity of all peoples was hardly complete, as will become apparent below. What-ever his limitations, however, he did not take seriously English claims to su-periority over all other civilizations. He was, in his own way, as much a cultural relativist as Mary Kingsley.[46]

Conceivably Burns's understanding of imperialism owed something to his days in the SDF with Belfort Bax. Well aware of the theories of imperial-ism developed by Hobson, he never accepted British rationales for the Boer War, for example, that it was being fought on behalf of "Outlanders" whom the Boers had denied rights of citizenship, that it would benefit black Africans suffering under the Boer yoke, and so on. "I have persistently opposed this mercenary struggle," he reminded electors. It had been undertaken for sor-did economic reasons and was responsible for "shelving all domestic re-form."[47]

This led him to dispute that the prosperity of the mother country and of his constituents in Battersea depended on the war's success. Contrary to Gar-

ton, Bhownaggree, Hamilton, and Dimsdale, contrary even to a Radical like
R. K. Causton or a Lib-Lab like Will Crooks, both of whom held that the war
was largely irrelevant to the concerns of their constituents, Burns believed
that the imperial war threatened the best interests of Londoners. He preferred to speak, as he thundered to one audience, not of South Africa's Outlanders, but of London's, "who required the £200,000,000 this war will cost
more than the Transvaal Outlanders ever did." What of the 100,000 paupers
in London? he demanded. What of the 400,000 living below the poverty line
as calculated by Charles Booth, and the 160,000 in lodging houses, and "the
50,000 Magdalenes on the streets of London, to be increased because those
upon whom they depended will have laid down their lives in the war?" Instead of Jameson Raids on behalf of immigrants to South Africa "he believed
in a Jameson Raid . . . going to the relief of the beleaguered in poverty."[48]

In short, for all that his anti-imperialism was characteristic of the period,
which is to say that it was limited, Burns posed yet another vision of the intersection between London and empire. War and imperial expansion would
not further his neighbors' interests. He "spoke of peace on earth and good-
will to all men," according to the *Southwestern Star* of July 20, 1900, maintaining that the best way to obtain them was to "take the slums away, get the
anaemic child healthy work and make the women strong." And he spoke from
his heart. Burns could not support imperial adventures which he believed
worked to the detriment of London because he *really* was "a cockney of cockneys," as Harry Lawson had described himself in North-East Bethnal Green.
In the words of one newspaper, "He called the bricks and mortar of the
Shaftesbury Estate 'bone of his bone and flesh of his flesh.' He appealed to the
voters of the district, his old playmates and workfellows to stand by him at
the coming election."[49]

In a contest between such polar opposites as Burns and Garton feelings
were bound to run high. With such a candidate as Burns, many electors, his
former play- and workmates, were destined for a more active role in the campaign than usual. Not for them the relatively passive act of simply casting ballots. They packed the meetings of both nominees, raucous and rowdy, often to
the point of violence. It is possible, sometimes, to hear the authentic voices of
bit players at these gatherings, voices usually unheard or anyway unheeded,
but which went far to defining the imperial metropolis as it really was in 1900.

Garton held his first election meeting on Monday evening, September 24,
at the Primitive Methodist Schoolroom, Plough-road. The building was
packed to overflowing before he or anyone in his retinue appeared. The crowd
grew restless. One section sang the "Dublin Fusiliers . . . heartily in fact, but
being patriotic it was discouraged by some laughter." A gentleman, "appar-

ently of the bricklayer class," called for a song from the other side of the room. Instead the other side called for cheers for John Burns. These were given, upon which three cheers for Garton were also supplied, to much groaning. "The bricklayer shouted 'Arf a mo, I 'ope you'll 'ear bofe sides.'" And later when the cheers for Garton were repeated he called out again, "'I say 'ooray . . . 'E's got a jolly good 'eart to stan' up agin John.'" The bricklayer revealed his own pro-Boer sentiments only a moment afterward, however, when he called for "'free cheers for ole Kroojer.'" There were some groans but the cheers drowned them." Baden-Powell came in for three cheers too, "but the call for cheers for General White only raised a laugh."[50]

Here were the values and opinions of John Burns spread across an entire room. There was support for Britain's gallant soldiers, Irish in this case, who bore the brunt of fighting, support for the man who had directed the miracle of endurance that saved Mafeking from the Boer siege, support above all, it would seem, for the notion of fair play, demonstrated by cheers for both candidates. There was also, however, derisory laughter for run-of-the-mill army officers and for patriotic understandings of the war. Meanwhile the candidate had yet to speak. The meeting was to reveal still more about Battersea voters and the Conservative aspirant who had invited them to hear him.

When Garton finally addressed the restless crowd the essence of his message was, "I shall help to uphold the flag of the British nation all over the world." Here was as complete an endorsement of the imperialist project as could be. The audience bellowed, some with appreciation, the apparent majority with disgust. Garton continued: "I shall never have anything to do with those men who even come to Battersea and throw dirt upon the honour of the country." He was condemning not merely his electoral opponent but half the electorate. Or was he? "You may howl and boo . . . but I tell you this—you'll have to take me for Battersea whether you want it or not." Why was he so confident? Because "I see those here who make a noise but who have no votes." With this supremely impolitic, undemocratic, and revealing statement the meeting broke up. Garton never finished his speech.[51]

Nor did he finish speaking the next time he addressed an election meeting, in Battersea Square on September 26. "From the first it was evident that some of the rougher element of Mr. Burns's supporters were present," the *Daily Mail* recorded with distaste. "Frequent interruptions culminated in the persuasive eloquence of the thick end of a walking stick, with which someone endeavoured to instil sound political principles into a persistent disturber." Garton repeatedly attempted to make himself heard amidst the hubbub, but "the rest of the business consisted of an all-round fight." Finally the police arrived and ended the proceedings.

Many times jingo rowdies broke up meetings of pro-Boers, but there was another side to the story. Hecklers rendered Sir Alfred Newton and Lord George Hamilton speechless on more than one occasion. References to similar disruptions sprinkle the London press for the period of the general election. In Battersea the disruptive element was probably stronger and more numerous than in any other London constituency. "I want to offer myself as a fighting volunteer if you are going to hold a meeting where stout gas-pipe will be of use," one of Burns's supporters wrote to him. "I can also bring a good friend along to help 'hold the fort.'" Burns knew he could count on more than two "good friends." "For every fifty men Garton can send," he boasted at one point, "I'll put up 500—fellows with hands like macadamised roads." He did not encourage his followers to give his opponent a hard time, and surely Burns's correspondent was offering to participate in a defensive action to protect his hero's right to free speech. Despite the received wisdom, however, in Battersea and other parts of London it was the Conservative not the Liberal Party which had to worry about violent disruption of its meetings.[52]

For Garton the climax came on the evening of September 27, at the Battersea Town Hall, when George Wyndham, the undersecretary for war, attempted to speak for him. Several nights previously, in the same room, Burns had "held the undivided attention of a vast audience." This time, however, the hall descended into chaos. Percy Thornton, the Conservative candidate for Clapham, attempted to chair the meeting. "His opening remarks were drowned in shouts of 'Joe's War,' 'Kynochs,' and 'Hoskins,'" the latter two being companies which had profited from the war and of which Chamberlain's relations were major shareholders. When Wyndham took the platform one heckler caught his attention, and "the two engaged in a spirited argument." It turned out that the heckler merely feared Wyndham would turn tail and run. He wanted him to remain for further interaction with the crowd.

Wyndham did remain. He informed the audience that he and Burns had played cricket together in Battersea Park. The response was not what he might have expected. The crowd called for "politics not cricket." It would not be patronized by one who personified the jeunesse dorée Burns so despised. Wyndham then acknowledged that Burns never minced words about the war, "and truth too!" interjected one of his audience, "But he would ask them very seriously, 'did they mean to follow Mr. Burns'—(mingled cries of 'Yes' and 'No,' the former predominating)—who had declared that the war was 'unjust and unnecessary?' (Cheers, during which the right hon. resumed his seat, wearied by the opposition.)" He rose to continue a few moments later, however. "How could we have prevented the war without betraying our brothers in South Africa?" His audience yelled back at him, "What about the Armenians?" whom the British had failed to protect from greater injustices than the Outlanders ever suffered. "I've been there, [to South Africa]" the cabinet minister expostulated, to which the hecklers replied, "Not lately" and, blessedly perhaps, "Sit down." Still he persisted: "'Let me go on'; they answered, 'Why weren't you prepared for it?'" Finally the meeting broke up "amidst a scene of disorder which was repeated when those inside joined the cheering throng in the streets."[53] Again Garton had failed to speak. After this failed attempt he gave up public meetings altogether and concentrated upon canvassing voters instead.

Aroused democracy, at least in Battersea, was no respecter of persons, even cabinet ministers with a share of responsibility for imperial policy. It preferred to defend anti-imperialists (Armenians struggling to free themselves from the Ottomans) than to extend the British Empire by going to war for South African Outlanders whose trials and tribulations it did not much believe in. That Chamberlain's family had purchased shares in companies which then were awarded war contracts only confirmed a more general sense in their minds that the war was being fought for capitalists anyway. And when Wyndham protested his treatment by the crowd, they laughed at him. Burns, the former street-corner agitator who had faced police charges in Trafalgar Square and had stood up to company bullies during the dock strike of 1889, to a snobbish, jeering House of Commons more than once, and to political opponents in Battersea time and again, would have laughed too.

Yet the voice of Battersea was not only the voice of John Burns and his supporters. His opponents also had voices, even if Burns's people often succeeded in drowning them out. On one occasion, however, Garton's backers expressed themselves in surprising fashion. Addressing the Battersea Conservative Association, Garton spoke, as the *Daily Mail* put it, for "villa residents, shop keepers" the residents of "a large number of modern flat-houses" erected since 1892, and, of course, for publicans, who usually voted Tory anyway and who literally carried the Battersea Conservative candidate's beer. He did not speak in the same sense for the workers in his sugar refinery. Nevertheless these men promised to vote for him. They would support Garton's and the government's imperialism as a gesture of defiance against those in the Burns camp who ridiculed them for permitting their boss to exploit them. Convening their own meeting, these South London workers who had promised to uphold the imperialist candidate issued a manifesto in which they insisted that they knew what they were doing when they worked for, and when they voted for, Garton: "We can hold our own with any in Battersea, or in the world, as free men and not slaves." The context suggests that the pro-imperialist votes of such men were the by-product of a perverse class solidarity. Yet Garton's employees too represent the bricks and mortar of which the imperial metropolis was constructed.[54]

By the time October 2, polling day, arrived Battersea had reached a pitch of tension rare in London. "It was clear that the political excitement which has held the district so fiercely . . . is to culminate today in a very remarkable manner," observed the *Westminster Gazette*. Shopkeepers boarded their windows, fearing the consequences if Burns should lose. Conservatives thought he would lose, discerning a backlash among voters against the rough tactics of his supporters. Burns himself was confident, however. "I am in," he told a reporter for the *Daily Mail* the evening before the poll.

The day itself passed in a whirl of activity. Burns wheeled his bicycle out the front gate of his house in Lavender Hill before six in the morning. "Stuck at it all day from district to district," he recorded in his diary, "stimulating workers, plugging leaks, transferring strong men to weak places, hurrying up the laggards and rousing the crowds to the level of their duty in the fight. . . . Worked hard till 8," when the polls closed. Garton dispatched "half a dozen or so motor cars" prominently bedecked with flags to ferry electors to and from voting places. His "healthy-lunged supporters . . . marched through the streets roaring out,

> Oh Battersea is true
> To Red and White and Blue
> We'll have no mad pro-Boer
> So Garton is the man
> We'll have him if we can
> And show John Burns the door.

Meanwhile "sundry voters—principally the better-class villa residents and flat-owners—hurried down the side streets exultantly to the polling booths," avoiding the expected crush of workingmen who would vote after the shops and factories closed for the day.[55]

Ballots were to be counted and the victor proclaimed at the Battersea Town Hall. As afternoon turned to dusk enormous crowds gathered before it. By nightfall "numbers greater than those that make up the sum total of the whole population of the borough" had assembled, "uncountable as the sands, unrestful as the sea." Another observer described "a thick black crowd, fitfully lit up by the flare of gas, naphtha and electricity. And for a mile and more it extended, this human stream, flowing steadily towards the Town Hall which constituted the centre of attraction. Singing, whistling, shouting, tooting, chatting, it crowded round and looked, for three hours, upwards to the white sheet that was to tell the tale." Finally Burns rushed from the building to the balcony overlooking the street. Simultaneously letters and numbers appeared upon the sheet, actually a linen screen, lit from behind by an electric light. They read:

| Burns | 5,860 |
| Garton | 5,606 |

The Battersea Radical had won after all, by a majority of 254, ten votes more than he had received in 1895.

"Such a shout went up as even he had never heard before," wrote the journalist for the *Southwestern Star.* "The solid building seemed to vibrate with the thunderous roar, a roar continuous and ever increasing in volume of sound. Leaning over the balcony, looking down the hill, Mr. Burns thrust out his arms and waved and whirled them with tremendous force. In the delirium of triumph he stamped, he smote with his fist and he frantically beat the air with his hat." The crowd, too, was wild with delight. It "screamed and roared deafeningly. One was compelled to put one's fingers in one's ears." But the crowd was also well behaved, "orderly . . . anxious not to cause any disturbance." Perhaps they were aware of the large contingent of police, horse and foot, waiting in a side street to deal with the expected riots if Burns had lost.

But now the successful candidate was plunging over the balcony and into the crowd. Supporters hoisted him onto their shoulders. "Surging, swaying, tossing, a huge portion of the people with Mr. Burns uplifted as their standard slowly moved towards the foot of the hill." A band led the way "to the 'Square' where 'John' made a speech standing on a drinking fountain." And later, long past midnight, the victor of Battersea sat musing with a few friends in the porch of his house: "What a fight it had been! Ay, and against what odds!"

It would be pleasant to leave it at that, with Burns and his comrades sitting in the porch, savoring his well and hard-earned triumph, to record simply that Battersea had chosen a parliamentary spokesman who would, if he could, reshape the empire and the imperial metropolis into more democratic forms, and to recount his virtues. But John Burns was a type, a representative for good or ill of the old-fashioned, hardfisted, Radical troublemaker who loved his country and wished to see its influence in the world extended so long as it was an influence for good. Like so many critics of empire, Burns was really a critic of specific imperial policies only. Like so many London anti-imperialists he shared many of the prejudices of his age. He could be as chauvinist as any Conservative imperialist. "Vote for John Burns and no Chinese labor!" ran one of his campaign posters, confusingly, given his respectful references to Chinese civilization at Battersea Park. "Equal rights for all white men the world over," he wrote in his election address, a document in which references to equal rights for all, regardless of color, did not appear.

Burns's chauvinism appears most often, however, in another context. He believed that the Conservatives posed only one kind of threat to the idealized version of empire and the imperial metropolis he held in his mind; there was a second, more insidious threat which he was not embarrassed to name: the Jew. His speeches during the campaign often contained anti-Semitic slurs. He wanted, obscurely, "to turn the long-nosed Jew out of the Highland valley" in Scotland; and to obtain the franchise for the "30 per cent of the working classes . . . without votes in Battersea," rather than for "'Ikey Mo' . . . in Pretoria." He believed that the war was being conducted in the interests of German-Jewish financiers in South Africa and the "rich Jews of Park Lane." His diaries are full of distasteful, even shocking, references to Jews. At a cricket match on January 17, 1899, he noted "frowsy, lousy, greasy Jews. No game but grab, no passion but profit, no human playfulness, parasitic; living to work only, and that as a step to exploiting others." Exactly a year later he witnessed the CIV marching through London's streets, "and not a Jew amongst the lot." On November 9, 1900, he shared a railway carriage with "a clever but offensive young cub of a Jew."[56]

Burns's anti-Semitism had an important bearing upon his view of the imperial metropolis. Like Major Evans-Gordon and David Kyd, like the socialist Will Thorne with whom he was well acquainted, he would have relished a letter to the *East London Observer* of September 29 which warned Londoners of "these foreign Jews who will in the near future possess themselves of their homes and expel them from their districts." What was the empire to residents of the imperial metropolis, asked the person who composed this epistle, when they had been "bought out of their houses and their homes without a fight? The Boers did better."

Burns agreed. Five weeks earlier he had written in his diary of a trip to the "East End Jews' Quarter, the condition of Wentworth Street filthy in the extreme. Crowded with Jewesses and children. Chatted with policeman about the Jewish eviction of English from East End." He worried that the city's identity, even his country's identity, was threatened by a wave of immigrants he despised. Standing before the cheering throngs at Battersea Park, the anti-imperialist cried, "I want Russia for the Russians, India for the Indians . . . Britain for the Britons."[57] Ostensibly this was a claim to consistency, every people should run their own affairs; in reality it was a coded reference (which his audience would have understood) to the anti-immigrant campaign already taking shape in Stepney and led by Evans-Gordon. Thus the imperial metropolis envisioned by London's most visible and charismatic critic of empire was not so cosmopolitan, not so all-inclusive, not so generous as one could have wished. Yet the idealized version of what London and the empire might become, which Burns did describe to the voters of Battersea during the Khaki Election of 1900 and which a majority of them endorsed, reflects the complex, ambiguous, ever-shifting construct that London really was.

A nd in the end the elephant had strained to produce a gnat. Of the sixty-one London boroughs, eight returned Liberals in 1895, adding a ninth, William Steadman, at a by-election in Stepney in 1898. In 1900, after all the votes were counted, London had again elected eight Liberals, although there was a slight reshuffling, with Liberal gains in Camberwell and Shoreditch and Conservative gains in Hoxton, Southwest Bethnal Green, and Stepney (where the unfortunate Steadman lost to Evans-Gordon). Conservatives easily defeated the two Socialist candidates, Thorne and Lansbury. Surveying these results, Hyndman observed, more in anger than in sorrow as was his wont, "the poorest districts are generally the most reactionary and chauvinist." He questioned whether universal suffrage was desirable. "If we give the vote to a poverty-stricken, half-educated people we run the risk of strengthening the forces of reaction." Frederic Harrison drew a less pessimistic if still jaundiced conclusion: "The famous Khaki Election of 1900 has proved nothing." But even Harrison was too close to events; he lacked perspective.[58]

Consider the Khaki Election not as part of a political process confirming the status quo, not even as an electoral contest at all, but rather as an opportunity for understanding the imperial metropolis at the apex of its influence and power. For the duration of the campaign London became a great debating chamber in which its relation to empire was a crucial subject. Should the imperial capital govern the nearly defeated and reannexed Boer republics? Should it despatch soldiers to West Africa and to China? Should it continue to rule over Ireland? On the Irish question the UIL mobilized members to vote no "like a disciplined army," but the debate was not stilled. As a typical "loyalist" in North-West Ham put it, "What would it mean if Ireland was granted Home Rule? Its population was ten times as many as that of the Boers in the Transvaal, and if they granted such a measure England would have ten times as bad a case in Ireland as they had in the Transvaal."[59]

Nor was the debate stilled on any of the other questions. Imperial vanity laced with chauvinism ruled the day but not without opposition. Some candidates appealed to Londoners' pride, claiming that citizens of the first city in the empire must prove worthy of their imperial inheritance by shouldering its burdens; others argued, to the contrary, that empire meant little to

most city residents. Many contended that Londoners profited materially
from imperialism, but some claimed the opposite, that imperialism impoverished metropolitan residents by diverting wealth and attention elsewhere.
Still others thought imperialists had their priorities wrong: whatever the
merits of imperial conquests the governors of the imperial capital should focus on uplifting their own constituents before undertaking adventures across
the seas. Sir Alfred Newton thought London should serve as a reservoir of
imperial warriors; H. Fox Bourne might almost have been answering the lord
mayor when he suggested in the *Times* that it should rather provide the victims of British imperialism with a pool of defenders. Members of all parties,
but not all their members, asserted that an imperial metropolis should be exclusive, not a "dumping ground" for Jews, the "refuse" of eastern Europe. Yet
Jews stood victoriously for Parliament in the imperial metropolis too. For
every argument supporting orthodox views of empire and London's place in
it, dissenters posed a contrary argument, though their electoral successes
were few.

While definitions and counterdefinitions swirled and eddied, Londoners
themselves attempted to shape the imperial metropolis. They lobbied politicians through their clubs, trade unions, and religious organizations. The London Irish demanded home rule. Trade unionists endorsed Radicals and Socialists in Battersea, North- and South-West Ham, Whitechapel, Hoxton,
and no doubt elsewhere. They wanted old-age pensions, higher wages, better working and living conditions for the laboring classes. They concentrated
on such issues rather than upon South Africa because they knew, as the socialist and trade unionist Thorne put it, that "the working man had got no
empire" anyway. Unfortunately we hear nothing during the Khaki Election
from Ben Tillett, who would have introduced yet another theme, that an imperial metropolis must treat with due respect the workers who made its functioning possible—that is, treat them as imperial citizens. Tillett, who suffered
from ill health, was out of action for the duration of the campaign. But the
rank and file of his union made their presence felt in Battersea, where they
thought their old friend Burns needed assistance. "Those who broke up Mr.
Garton's meetings were dockers," complained the *Daily Telegraph*. Meanwhile, the third of the original trio who led the dockers to victory in 1889,
Tom Mann, was attempting to provide a meeting ground for "Irish Nationalists, English Liberals, Radicals and Socialists," at the public house Enterprise in Longacre, of which he was current proprietor.[60]

At the opposite end of the political spectrum delegates of the Protestant
Layman's Association quizzed Bhownaggree on "the Romish conspiracy in
the Church" (he responded satisfactorily from their point of view), and a covey

of Wesleyan and Congregationalist ministers condemned Thorne from the pulpit and in the press. They "could not conceive of any respectable—especially Christian—man voting for such a candidate." In Whitechapel Jews mobilized to vote for Stuart Samuel, while Christians extracted from him a promise not to "vote upon Church questions unless he receive[d] a mandate from the electors." Thus the people of London sought to fashion their city into complex, even contradictory, shapes.[61]

Voting booths were repositories for their dreams. In the main Londoners voted for candidates who told them that imperialism would benefit their districts, but sometimes the electors' motives were not straightforward. In Battersea, as we have seen, the workers in a sugar refinery supported the imperialist candidate who happened to be their employer, Richard Garton, in a perverse gesture of defiance: they were not slaves and would cast their ballots as they wished, not as anti-imperialists instructed them to. Likewise an individual in St. George's in the East contributed his mite to London chauvinism by refusing to do what was expected of him. "I ain't a going to vote at all," he was overheard to remark. "There is Mr. Strauss who is a Jew [the Liberal candidate] and there is Mr. DeWar [the ultimately victorious Conservative] who must be a Frenchman. Neither of 'em gets my vote."[62]

Londoners also strove to shape their city when they lobbied and questioned candidates before deciding how they would cast their ballots. Imperialism and their city's relation to it was not always foremost in their minds. "Are you in favour of nationalizing the railways," someone asked Ernest Gray at a North-West Ham meeting. "What about old age pensions?" asked another. "Will Mr. Gray vote for the municipalization of the drink traffic? . . . Will you vote for Sunday closing? . . . Are you in favour of prohibiting the sale of drink to children?"[63]

The overarching theme of the general election, however, was imperialism. So argued almost all the election addresses, and so ran most of the speeches. Who determined it should be this way? Conservative strategists thought their candidates would win votes by appealing to electors' patriotic and imperialist sentiments. Some Liberals, like Harry Lawson in Bethnal Green, thought they could play the imperial card too. But even dissidents like Frederic Harrison recognized that imperialism was "the great issue not only of this election, but of our time."[64] He only wished that Radicals would clearly state their objections to the way the other party practiced it.

Nevertheless, in the dialectical relationship that always obtains between politicians and voters, speakers and audiences, it is not always clear who sets the agenda. In 1900 when candidates strayed from the main topic or voiced opinions with which they disagreed, some audiences quickly reined them in

39. John Burns in action.
London Borough of Wandsworth.

or shouted them down. "Talk politics, not cricket," the crowd had cried to Wyndham. "Lies," they had shouted at Lord George Hamilton, who, when he tried to continue speaking about the benefits imperialism would bring to Londoners, found he was "unable to make [himself] heard."

These were assertions of raw power and of identity in a city whose political arrangements were not yet fully democratic, but whose population was politically energized. I find anti-Conservatives breaking up Conservative meetings throughout the imperial metropolis, as well as better-documented instances of jingoes breaking up pro-Boer meetings. More subtle exercises were also common. As an international force including British troops marched toward Peking to quell the Boxer Rebellion, Will Thorne faced a crowd in West Ham. "How do you propose to settle the Chinese question," asked a man who must have known Thorne already faced difficulties because he opposed sending troops to South Africa. "Are you prepared to give independence back to the Transvaal," an elector queried Alderman Bethell, who had gained Socialist support by opposing the Boer War, but who was trying now to gain electoral support by fudging the matter. Only one candidate appears to have relished taking on questions and comments meant to embarrass him. "What does that man say," John Burns asked at one of his meetings. "'God bless Cecil Rhodes!' Leave me to answer that. I'll make it so hot for him that he will wish he had not spoken."[65]

The Khaki Election, then, serves as a photograph might, capturing the imperial metropolis for a historical moment. It catches Londoners in midstride and midsentence, in all their contradictoriness, all their contrariness. Then the moment passes, the photograph blurs and dissolves, and the great city reawakens. Life rushes onward. London is a process. Already we may discern, in dim outline and in the distant future, an equally complex, fluid, and unfinished postimperial metropolis.

NOTES

CHAPTER 1. LONDON IN 1900

1. London took up seventy-five thousand acres according to a local politician, F. D. Perrott. See his pamphlet "The Lion's Share of London's Profit," n.d., but 1900 or 1901 from internal evidence. Tourist quoted in H. C. Darby, ed., *A New Historical Geography of England* (Cambridge, 1973), Peter Hall, "England *circa* 1900," 741. For the Monument, see *City Press*, February 7, 1900.

2. For the view, see Charles F. G. Masterman, ed., *The Heart of the Empire* (London, 1901), 11. For East London, see esp. Gareth Stedman Jones, *Outcast London* (Oxford, 1971), and William Fishman, *East End 1888* (London, 1988). For the most sophisticated treatment of London during the reign of the Ripper, see Judith Walkowitz, *City of Dreadful Delight* (Chicago, 1992).

3. George Sims, *Living London* (London, 1901–03), Charles Turner, "The City at High Noon," 2:121.

4. Roy Porter, *London, A Social History* (Cambridge, Mass., 1994), 327–29.

5. *Queen*, March 19, 1899, January 27, February 10, March 31, 1900, for the advertisements; see Anne McClintock, *Imperial Leather: Race, Gender and Sexuality in the Colonial Contest* (London, 1995), esp. 207–23, for a discussion of the "commodity racism" embedded in such advertisements.

6. See chapter 2 for an extended discussion of London's docks, which I call the "nexus of imperialism."

7. See chapter 3 for an extended discussion of the City and its links with imperialism.

8. For the Czechs, Italians, and Germans, see Colin Holmes, *John Bull's Island: Immigration and British Society, 1871–1971* (London, 1988), 21–35. In 1911, there were 53,324 Germans resident in England and Wales, 20,389 Italians, and "a Czech colony of a thousand or so in London in the early years of the twentieth century." For the London Irish, see chapter 6. For figures on Irish in London, see J. A. Jackson, "The Irish," in *London, Aspects of Change*, ed. Centre for Urban Studies, University of London (London, 1964), 296; and Alan O'Day, "Irish Influence on Parliamentary Elections in London, 1885–1914, a Simple Test," in *The Irish in the Victorian City*, ed. Roger

Swift and Sheridan Gilley, 99. For the number of Jews resident in London at the turn of the century, see Hall, "England *circa* 1900," 732, and Geoffrey Alderman, *Modern British Jewry* (Oxford, 1992), 104. There is a large literature on Anglo-Jewry and reactions to it. See among others, Bernard Gainer, *The Alien Invasion: The Origins of the Aliens Act* (New York, 1972); Eugene Black, *The Social Politics of Anglo-Jewry* (Oxford, 1988); Lloyd Gartner, *The Jewish Immigrant in England, 1870–1914* (London, 1960); and David Feldman, *Englishmen and Jews: Social Relations and Political Culture, 1840–1914* (Oxford, 1994).

9. Rozina Visram, *Ayahs, Lascars and Princes* (London, 1986), 237, n. 4, quotes C. Kondapi, *Indians Overseas, 1838–1949*, who estimates 7,128 Indians in Britain in 1932. There were 1,319 Chinese in England and Wales in 1911, Holmes, *John Bull's Island*, 32. See also P. J. Waller, "The Chinese," *History Today* (September 1985): 8–15. In the West End there were already Chinese laundries catering to the middle class. See *Westminster Gazette*, September 13, 1900. For those of African descent, see Michael Banton, *The Coloured Quarter* (London, 1955), 27, and James Walvin, *Black and White* (London, 1973), 198. For the Pan-African Conference, see chapter 9.

10. Henry Thompson, "Indian and Colonial London," in Sims, *Living London*, 3:306–08.

11. For explorers and researchers, see esp. Hugh Robert Mill, *The Record of the Royal Geographical Society, 1830–1930* (London, 1930). For missionaries, see the journal *Women in the Mission Field*, sponsored by the Society for the Propagation of the Gospel, as a primary source. Also the *British Emigrant*, first published, however, in May 1907. The demand for women emigrants was high. See Julia Bush, "'The Right Sort of Woman': Female Emigrators and Emigration to the British Empire, 1890–1910," *Women's History Review* 3, no. 3 (1994): 385–400. I am grateful to Chris Clark for information about Waterloo Station.

12. As noted previously this was the title of the volume edited by the Liberal journalist and politician Charles F. G. Masterman, published in 1901.

13. For the location of these offices, see Arthur Beavan, *Imperial London* (London, 1901), 96–101. Victoria Street also contained the Army and Navy Stores, an ex-officers co-op, as it were, with imperial connections; also Artillery Mansions, a grand block of flats inhabited largely by former military men and often decorated in Orientalist fashion. See Richard Dennis, "Imperial Apartments: Apartment Housing in London, 1870–1914," a paper delivered at Royal Holloway College, University of London "Conference on Imperial Cities," May 2, 1997. For the South African offices, see Harold Clunn, *The Face of London* (London, 1932), 142.

14. The Progressives lost their majority to the Moderates in 1907. For more on the history of the LCC, see Susan Pennybacker, *A Vision for London, 1889–1914: Labour, Everyday Life and the L.C.C. Experiment* (London, 1995); and John Davis, *Reforming London: The London Government Problem, 1855–1900* (Oxford, 1988). For Harrison's remarks, see Mark H. Judge, ed., *The Case for Further Strand Improvement* (London, 1906), 6.

15. Asa Briggs, *Victorian Cities* (London, 1963). "London, the World City" was the title of chapter 8.

16. A. J. Hobson's classic work was *Imperialism* (London, 1902). For Lenin's view, see his *Imperialism, the Highest Stage of Capitalism, A Popular Outline* (Moscow, 1975). For the mainstream historians, see Sir John Seeley, *The Expansion of England* (London, 1880); H. A. L. Fisher, *History of Europe* (London, 1936); Ronald Robinson and John Gallagher, *Africa and the Victorians* (London, 1961); C. J. Lowe, *The Reluctant Imperialists: British Foreign Policy, 1878–1902* (London, 1969). Finally, see P. J. Cain and A. G. Hopkins, *British Imperialism: Innovation and Expansion* (London, 1993).

17. For the Manchester University Press series, see among many volumes John MacKenzie, *Propaganda and Empire: The Manipulation of British Public Opinion* (Manchester, 1984); John MacKenzie, ed., *Imperialism and Popular Culture* (Manchester, 1986); J. A. Mangan, ed., *Making Imperial Mentalities* (Manchester, 1990). For some of the feminist approaches, see Nupur Chaudiri and Margaret Strobel, eds., *Western Women and Imperialism: Complicity and Resistance* (Bloomington, 1992); Margaret Strobel, *European Women and the Second British Empire* (Bloomington, 1991); Antoinette Burton, *Burdens of History: British Feminists, Indian Women, and Imperial Culture, 1865–1959* (Chapel Hill, 1995); and Mrinalini Sinha, *Colonial Masculinity: The 'Manly Englishman' and the 'Effeminate Bengali' in the Late Nineteenth Century* (Manchester, 1995).

18. McClintock, *Imperial Leather*; Annie Coombes, *Reinventing Africa: Museums, Material Culture and Popular Imagination in Late Victorian and Edwardian England* (New Haven, 1994). For more on scientific racism, see Nancy Stepan, *The Idea of Race in Science: Great Britain 1800–1960* (London, 1982).

19. The phrase, of course, is Edward P. Thompson's in the preface to his *The Making of the English Working Class* (New York, 1966), 12. See Ron Ramdin, *The Making of the Black Working Class in Britain* (London, 1987); Peter Fryer, *Staying Power: The History of Black People in Britain* (London, 1984); Visram, *Ayahs, Lascars and Princes*; Laura Tabili, *We Ask for British Justice* (Ithaca, 1995).

20. For the gendered language of imperialism, see, for example, Robert H. Macdonald, *The Language of Imperialism* (Manchester, 1994); Graham Dawson, *Soldier Heroes, British Adventure, Empire and the Imagining of Masculinities* (London, 1994); Satya Mohanty "Drawing the Color Line: Kipling and the Culture of Colonial Rule," in Dominick LaCapra, ed., *The Bounds of Race: Perspectives on Hegemony and Resistance* (Ithaca, 1991); Joseph Bristow, *Empire Boys: Adventures in a Man's World* (London 1991). See also Jeffrey Richards, ed., *Imperialism and Juvenile Literature* (Manchester, 1989); Jon Thompson, *Fiction, Crime and Empire* (Urbana, 1993). Then see Antonio Gramsci, *The Prison Notebooks: Selections*, Quinton Hoare and Geoffrey Nowell Smith, eds. and trans. (New York, 1971); and finally Edward Said, *Orientalism* (New York, 1979).

21. It is notable that in a recent, astonishingly well-researched bibliographical essay, John Davis mentions not one work on London and imperialism, although he lists

several on London and racism. John Davis, "Modern London 1850–1930," *London Journal* 20, no. 2 (1995): 56–90. The best works on London government are Davis, *Reforming London,* and Pennybacker, *A Vision for London.* Then see Michael H. Port, *Imperial London: Civil Government Building in London, 1850–1915* (London, 1995); David Feldman and Gareth Stedman Jones, eds., *Metropolis London* (London 1989); and Porter, *London, A Social History.*

CHAPTER 2. THE FACE OF IMPERIAL LONDON

1. The field marshal's statue, a tablet next to it informed the viewer, was cast from guns taken by the Central India field force. The sides of the plinth on which it stood listed Strathnairn's principal military victories. Cleopatra's Needle had been situated originally before the great temple of Heliopolis in Egypt. See Harold P. Clunn, *The Face of London* (London, 1932), 114. For the Colonial Office, see Susan Beattie, *The New Sculpture* (New Haven, 1983), 219, 238.

2. Clunn, *The Face of London,* 141. The statue of Gordon has since been resited on the Victoria Embankment.

3. Rodney Mace, *Trafalgar Square* (London, 1976), 16.

4. Beattie, *The New Sculpture,* 232.

5. For the decline of the Arts and Crafts movement, see Alastair Service, ed., *Edwardian Architecture and Its Origins* (London, 1975), 5. For the Edwardian baroque style, see John Belcher and Mervyn Macartney, eds., *Later Renaissance Architecture in England* (London, 1901), from which the quote is taken (4–5), and, among others, Alastair Service, *The Architects of London* (London, 1979), 155.

6. For English baroque throughout the empire, see Thomas R. Metcalf, *An Imperial Vision: Indian Architecture and Britain's Raj* (Berkeley, 1989), 176–80. For its spread throughout London, see Alastair Service, *London, 1900* (London, 1979), esp. 20, 91–114, 235–37.

7. See David Cannadine, "The Context, Performance and Meaning of Ritual: The British Monarchy and the 'Invention of Tradition,' c. 1820–1977," esp. 112–13, 126–27, in Eric Hobsbawm and Terence Ranger, eds., *The Invention of Tradition* (Cambridge, 1983).

8. Andrew Saint, *Richard Norman Shaw* (New Haven, 1976), 345.

9. For discussion of the many early schemes to cut a north–south route to the Strand, see Dirk Schubert and Anthony Sutcliffe, "The 'Haussmannization' of London?: The Planning and Construction of Kingsway-Aldwych, 1889–1935," *Planning Perspectives* 11 (1996): 115–44; Clunn, *Face of London,* 97; Hermione Hobhouse, quoting the *Architectural Review, Lost London* (London, 1971), 73. The slum contained Holywell and Wych streets.

10. For the Radicals, see the *New Age,* June 22, 1900. For the socialists, see Arthur Page Grubb, *The Life Story of the Right Hon. John Burns* (London, 1908), 121. In the end Burns supported the project. Another Radical, Aneas Smith, "would not vote money for the Strand improvement in its complete form, because he contended that

if they could spend money in London they owed a debt to poor people in the slums rather than in the Strand." Quoted in Davis, *Reforming London*, 123.

11. For Emerson's speech, see the *Journal of the Royal Institute of British Architecture*, May 12, 1900, 348. For Williams, see the *Building News*, April 13, 1900. For the motion, see the *Builder*, February 24, 1900, 187.

12. For the presidential speech, see *Journal of the Royal Institute of British Architecture*, November 11, 1899, 10. For the later speech, see *Journal of the Royal Institute*, June 30, 1900, 409. For the final remark, see *Journal of the Royal Institute*, June 30, 1900, supplement, 8.

13. *Journal of the Royal Institute*, March 1900, 120.

14. For Macartney, see *Architectural Review*, March 1900, 126, and *Architectural Review*, December 1899, 242.

15. Quoted in *Building News*, June 1, 1900, 747.

16. For Emden, see *Building News*, November 23, 1900, 725; for Woodward, see *Building News*, June 1, 1900, 747.

17. For Beachcroft, see the *Builder*, April 14, 1900, 378, but for the views of the editors of the *Builder*, see May 5, 1900, 434.

18. Saint, *Shaw*, 348.

19. James Winter, *London's Teeming Streets 1830–1914* (London, 1993), 213.

20. For Ricardo, see the *Architectural Review*, March 1900, 123. For the views of the editors of the *Architectural Review*, see the issue for October 1899, xxiv. For the scene itself, see Judge, ed., *The Case for Strand Improvement*, photograph facing page 16, in which advertisements for Dewar's Scotch Whiskey, a railway line, and Queen's Hotel and Restaurant are visible among others.

21. For the dithering, see esp. Saint, *Shaw*, 347–49. For Kingsway in the early days, see Hobhouse, *Lost London*, 73, and Grubb, *John Burns*, 126.

22. Judge, *The Case for Strand Improvement*, 8.

23. *Dictionary of National Biography*, 1912–21, E.S.P., 494.

24. For the location of offices, see Clunn, *The Face of London*, 144. For Gaze and Sons advertisement, see *City Press*, January 17, 1900. Shortly thereafter Henry Gaze and Sons went out of business, but not because of their location. They had invested in seats overlooking the route of King Edward's coronation in June 1902. But the coronation had been postponed. See David Kynaston, *The City of London*, vol. 2, *Golden Years, 1890–1914* (London, 1995), 362.

25. For Paddington Station, see Arthur Beavan, *Imperial London* (London, 1901), 287: "Paddington is essentially a terminus where well-dressed and well-to-do people are in the majority. Royalty frequently uses it and there are always personages of more or less importance going to or returning from Windsor." For Victoria's original route, see the *Daily Mail*, June 21, 1897. For "these arrangements," see *Daily Mail*, October 12, 1900. And for the officer, see *Daily Mail*, October 29, 1900.

26. See Winter's *London's Teeming Streets*, photograph on 80.

27. My description of this event is taken entirely from the *Daily Mail*, October 30,

1900. But see also *The C.I.V.: Being the Story of the City Imperial Volunteers and Volunteer Regiments of the City of London, 1300–1900*, 29–30, a work commissioned by the army. It cites no individual author.

28. For Burns's views, see his *The Straight Tip to Workers: Brains Better than Bets or Beer*, Clarion pamphlet no. 36, 1902, 5. For the views of Cox and Harrison, see Judge, ed., *The Case . . . .*

29. Judge, *The Case for Strand Improvement*, 7. A Moderate member of the council, Sir William Richmond, R.A., quit in disgust because its penny-pinching members would not further improve the Strand, for which see 12.

30. Metcalf, *An Imperial Vision*, 176–80.

CHAPTER 3. THE NEXUS OF EMPIRE

1. *Stratford Express*, October 6, 1900.

2. See Col. Henry Yule and Arthur Coke Burnell, *A Glossary of Anglo-Indian Colloquial Words and Phrases and of Kindred Terms* (London, 1886), 319. *Hobson Jobson* was "an Anglo-Saxon version of the wailings of the Mahommedans as they beat their breasts in the processions of the Moharram—'Ya Hasan! Ya Hosain!'" The *Moharram* is (439) "properly the name of the 1st month of the Mahommedan lunar year. But in India the term is applied to the period of fasting and public mourning observed during that month in commemoration of the death of Hasan and of his brother Husain (A.D. 669 and 680), and which terminates in the ceremonies of the 'Ashura-a.'"

3. Britain's second port was Liverpool, which handled a fraction of London's trade. See E. L. Taplin, *Liverpool Dockers and Seamen, 1870–1890* (Liverpool, 1974).

4. For the numbers, see Tom Mann, *The Position of Dockers and Sailors in 1897*, Clarion Pamphlet no. 18, 5. For the actual space occupied, see Public Record Office, MEPO 2/303.

5. John Lovell, *Stevedores and Dockers: A Study of Trade Unionism in the Port of London, 1870–1914* (London, 1969), 19.

6. See London County Council, *Royal Commission on the Port of London* (1900), 18–19.

7. Joseph Conrad, *The Nigger of the Narcissus* (New York, 1979), 137.

8. Charles Booth, *The Life and Labour of the People in London* (London, 1904); Lovell, *Stevedores and Dockers;* Gordon Phillips and Noelle Whiteside, *Casual Labour: The Unemployment Question in the Port Transport Industry, 1880–1970* (Oxford, 1985); Jonathan Schneer, *Ben Tillett, Portrait of a Labour Leader* (London, 1982).

9. For diet, see British Sessional Papers, *Royal Commission on Labour* (1892), vol. 35, Frank Brien, tea porter, responding to question asked by Tom Mann. "The staple food is bread and butter. In fairly good times bread, tea and milk, or tea without milk. Meat at 2d. or 3d. per pound." For crowding, see East London Church Fund, *Quarterly Chronicle*, 1900. Typically the casual docker rented a bed in a doss house or a single room into which he crowded his entire family if he had one. In 1900 there were 4,575 tenements of one room only in the East End, the majority occupied by four or

more people. Of 4,176 two-room tenements, the majority were occupied by six people or more.

10. For fatalities take February as an example: on February 2, Frederick Barnes was trimming coals in the hold of the steamship *Highgate* "when the 'grab came down suddenly crushing him under it," *East End News and London Shipping Chronicle*; on February 9, J. Lawson was crushed by a bag of corn which slipped from a hydraulic crane, and George Nichols was killed by a "deal" of timber at the Surrey Commercial Docks, *East End News*, February 9, 1900; on February 21, Samuel Jeffries died "from injuries sustained from falling into the hold of the steamship *Cornwall* lying in the Albert Dock," *Stratford Express*, February 21, 1900. For other accidents, see British Sessional Papers, *Royal Commission on Labour*, testimony of Tom McCarthy. Ben Tillett testified to the royal commission about the "lusty eight."

11. Ben Tillett in letter to the *Evening Standard*, October 6, 1900.

12. The protesting dock director was Sydney Holland. See Ben Tillett Collection, Modern Records Centre, Warwick University, MSS 74/3/1/32, Holland to Tillett, January 5, 1895. Harry Quelch explained to the royal commission why dockers feared to demand compensation.

13. Beavan, *Imperial London*, 231–37.

14. Hart was musing before the royal commission. He would have thought the literature on the question of the empire's contribution to British prosperity academic to say the least. But see Michael Edelstein, *Overseas Investment in the Age of High Imperialism* (London, 1982); Lance Davis and Robert Huttenback, *Mammon and the Pursuit of Empire* (Cambridge, 1986); and, most provocatively, Avner Offer, "The British Empire, 1870–1914: A Waste of Money?" *Economic History Review* 46, no. 2 (May 1993). For busy Thames police court, see *East London Observer*, February 3, 1900.

15. P.R.O., MEPO 2/303. Mann's report is dated February 17, 1910.

16. Docklands Museum, material found in Box 7 of London and India Joint Committee collection.

17. *East End News*, April 20, 1900; *East London Observer*, April 21, 1900.

18. *Stratford Express*, February 14, 1900; *East End News*, November 23, 1900.

19. *East End News*, January 16, 1900.

20. *East End News*, March 23, 1900; *East End News*, April 17, 1900; *East End News*, May 29, 1900.

21. *East End News*, July 20, 1900.

22. *East London Advertiser*, September 29, 1900; *West Ham Guardian*, January 27, 1900; *East London Advertiser*, March 17, 1900.

23. P.R.O., MEPO 2/303, E. K. Henry to Under Secretary of State, November 23, 1909.

24. V. A. C. Gatrell, "The Decline of Theft and Violence in Victorian and Edwardian England," in *Crime and the Law: The Social History of Crime in Western Europe since 1500*, ed. V. A. C. Gatrell, Bruce Lenman, Geoffrey Parker (London, 1980), 305.

25. *East London Advertiser*, February 3, 1900; *East London Advertiser*, April 17, 1900; Harry Gosling, *Up and Down Stream* (London, 1927), 40.

26. For previous investigations, see, for example, J. H. Grainger, *Patriotisms: Britain 1900–39* (London, 1986), and the essays by Hugh Cunningham, 57–89, and Preben Kaarsholm, 110–26, in Raphael Samuel, ed., *Patriotism: The Making and Unmaking of British National Identity*, vol. 1 (London, 1989).

27. The classic account is Henry Pelling, *The Origins of the Labour Party* (London, 1954).

28. For more on Burns, see, among others, W. G. R. Kent, *Labour's Lost Leader* (London, 1950). For Mann, see Dona Torr, *Tom Mann*, vol. 1 (London, 1956), and, more recently, Joe White, *Tom Mann* (Manchester, 1992), and Chuschichi Tsuzuki, *Tom Mann, 1856–1941* (Oxford, 1991). For Tillett, see Schneer, *Ben Tillett.*

29. For the first few days of the dispute, see *Stratford Express,* June 9, and *West Ham Guardian,* June 13, on which my account is based.

30. For more on the Shipping Federation, see L. H. Powell, *The Shipping Federation* (London, 1950), and Cuthbert Laws, *The Shipping Federation Registry System: Its Advantages and How to Secure Them* (London, n.d.), 5.

31. Powell, *Shipping Federation*, 123. Laws claimed that another, cheaper life belt was just as good.

32. Powell, *Shipping Federation*, 116–17.

33. *East End Advertiser,* June 23, 1900.

34. For strikebreakers from Birmingham, see *West Ham Guardian,* June 23, 1900; from Ipswich and North Shields, see *East End News,* June 19, 1900; for the denial, *Times,* June 16, 1900; for the trip, *Stratford Express,* June 30, 1900.

35. For Morgan's threat, see *West Ham Guardian,* July 7, 1900; for Connolly, *West Ham Guardian,* July 11, 1900; for Carter and Eagle, *Stratford Express,* June 16, 1900.

36. For Dooley, see *West Ham Guardian,* July 7, 1900; for Pearce and Mann, *West Ham Guardian,* July 7, 1900.

37. National Museum of Labour History, Manchester, Amalgamated Stevedores' Labour Protection League, Executive Council Minutes, June 19, 1900.

38. *East End News,* June 26, 1900.

39. *Stratford Express,* April 7, 1900.

40. *Stratford Express,* February 10, 1900.

41. For troop ships being delayed, *East London Advertiser,* June 16, 1900; for "making a virtue . . . ," *East End News,* June 19, 1900.

42. For a description of the docks during the Mafeking celebrations, see *East London Advertiser,* May 26, 1900. For the unfortunate captain, see *Stratford Express,* May 23, 1900.

43. *Stratford Express,* June 9, 1900.

44. *East End News,* July 10, 1900.

45. For counting the money, see *Daily Telegraph,* July 2, 1900. For the socialist attempt to raise money, see *Justice,* July 7, 1900. The three who contributed were "Tattler" a columnist for the newspaper, "H.Q.," who was probably Harry Quelch, an SDF official, and A. P. Hazell, a prominent member of the party. For the final totals, see *Daily Telegraph,* August 18, 1900.

46. *Daily Telegraph*, May 24, 25, 31, 1900; and these are merely a representative sampling.

47. *Daily Telegraph*, June 29, 1900.

48. *Stratford Express*, June 16, 1900.

49. *East London Advertiser*, June 23, 1900.

50. For "refuse heaps," see *East London Advertiser*, June 23, 1900; for Tillett's early anti-Semitism, see British Sessional Papers, *Commission on Sweated Industries* (1888), 21:136, and 136 for Ben Tillett's testimony; for the antiforeign statement, see Ben Tillett, "Our Naval Weakness," *National Review* 27 (March-August 1896): 878; for the antiblack sentiments, see Ben Tillett, *Memories and Reflections* (London, 1931), 228–30; for anti-Semitism in 1910, see Schneer, *Ben Tillett*, 143–45; and for anti-German statements, see Schneer, *Ben Tillett*, 2.

51. For the first factor, see, for example, Douglas Lorimer, *Colour, Class and the Victorians* (Leicester, 1978), and Paul Rich, *Race and Empire in British Politics* (Cambridge, 1986); for "Just plain common sense" and the roots of racism, see *The Empire Strikes Back*, Centre for Contemporary Cultural Studies, University of Birmingham (London, 1982), 47–95; and for Bethnal Green and, particularly, Shoreditch and Stepney as early bastions of antiforeign and racist sentiment, see Christopher Husbands, "East End Racism, 1900–1980," *London Journal* 8, no. 1 (1982): 3–26. For more historicized accounts of British racism, see Fryer, *Staying Power*, and Paul B. Rich, *Race and Empire in British Politics* (Cambridge, 1986).

52. For the lapse in membership, see Lovell, *Stevedores and Dockers*, 146; for the bitter Tillett, see Transport and General Workers' Union Collection, Modern Records Centre, University of Warwick, Dock, Wharf, Riverside and General Labourers' Union, *Eleventh Annual Report*, 1900; for Holland's statement, see Docklands Museum, East and West India Dock Company, *Minutes of Proceedings at the Half-Yearly General Meetings*, February 7, 1901, 4–5.

53. *Stratford Express*, September 8, 15, 22, 1900.

54. For Tillett's statement, see Dockers Union, Eleventh Annual Report, 1900; for Conroy, *East London Advertiser*, July 28, 1900; for Edwards, *Stratford Express*, August 8, 1900.

55. For the contribution of dockland to London's economy, see, for example, Lovell, *Stevedores and Dockers*, and Hall, "England *circa* 1900"; for the contribution to London history, see, for example, Stedman Jones, *Outcast London*, and Paul Thompson, *Socialists, Liberals and Labour: The Struggle for London, 1885–1914* (London, 1967); for the contribution to labor history, Phillips and Whiteside, *Casual Labour*; Schneer, *Ben Tillett*; Lovell, *Stevedores and Dockers*; for labor and popular imperialism see, for example, the essays in MacKenzie, ed., *Imperialism and Popular Culture* and *Propaganda and Empire*; Rich, *Race and Empire*; Grainger, *Patriotisms*; Raphael Samuel, ed., *Patriotism*; Jan Morris, *The Spectacle of Empire* (London, 1982); Nancy Stepan, *The Idea of Race in Science: Great Britain 1800–1960* (Hamden, Conn., 1982); Roger Stearn, "G. W. Steevens and the Message of Empire," *Journal of Imperial and Commonwealth History* 17, no. 2 (January 1989): esp. 219–20; for attitudes toward the Boer War, Richard Price, *An Imperial War and the British Working Class* (London,

1972); and for inwardness, Gareth Stedman Jones, "Working-Class Culture and Working-Class Politics in London, Notes on the Remaking of a Working Class," *Journal of Social History* 7, no. 4 (1974): 717–54, and Standish Meacham, *A Life Apart* (Cambridge, 1977).

CHAPTER 4. THE CITY

1. For the acreage, see Carl Peters, *England and the English* (London, 1904), 64. For more on the architecture of the City, see David Crawford, *The City of London: Its Architectural Heritage* (Cambridge, 1976). For the Mansion House, see *City of London Directory, 1900, 53:* "It is handsomely furnished and supplied with costly plate and jewelled ornaments of the value of about £20,000 or £30,000. State banquets and other civic hospitalities are dispensed here on a scale of sumptuous magnificence, and the traditional splendour of these entertainments has been fully maintained by each successive mayoralty up to the present day. The grand banquet-room is called the Egyptian Hall." For the bank, see Crawford's description in *The City of London*, 24. The top of the monument was reached by means of a large winding staircase of 346 steps. Admission threepence.

2. Crawford, *The City of London*, 54, 131.

3. Beavan, *Imperial London*, 229–30.

4. For Gorgonzola Hall, see Robert Jarvie, *The City of London: A Financial and Commercial History* (Cambridge, 1979), 112; for more description, see Beavan, *Imperial London*, 223.

5. For limiting the number of members, see W. J. Reader, *A House in the City* (London 1979), 66, also the *Financial News*, February 19, 1900; for a description of what members did, see Jarvie, *The City of London*, 100; then see too R. C. Michie, *The London and New York Stock Exchanges, 1850–1914* (London, 1987), 23–24.

6. Peters, *England and the English*, 68.

7. For the theme, see Kynaston, *The City of London*, 153; for the profits, see Beavan, *Imperial London*, 216.

8. Quoted by Antony Brown, in *Cuthbert Heath, Maker of the Modern Lloyd's of London* (London, 1980), 49.

9. Peters, *England and the English*, 80.

10. P. F. William Ryan, "Going to Business in London," in Sims, *Living London*, 1:199.

11. For more on Carl Peters, an extraordinary figure, see his *Lecture . . . on the Future of Africa* (London, 1897), *The Eldorado of the Ancients* (London, 1902), and the *Encyclopaedia Britannica*, 11th ed. (1911), 22:300. For descriptions of the City quoted in this paragraph, see Peters, *England and the English*, preface and 66–67.

12. For the Throgmorton, see the *Financial Times*, October 8, 1900; for description of the more common eateries, see Peters, *England and the English*, 94–95.

13. H. Osborne O'Hagan, *Leaves from my Life* (London, 1929), 1:259–60.

14. For the City's population, Peter Hall, "England *circa* 1900," 743; for its role,

Ronald Michie, *The City of London: Continuity and Change, 1850–1990* (London, 1992), 21. But modern scholars have diverged sharply over the economic, political, and social roles played by the City of London in British history. Michie's is a recent contribution to this growing literature. See also W. P. Kennedy, *Industrial Structure, Capital Markets and the Origins of British Economic Decline* (London, 1987); Martin Weiner, *English Culture and the Decline of the Industrial Spirit, 1850–1914* (Cambridge, 1981); William Rubinstein, *Wealth and Inequality in Britain* (London, 1986); G. Ingham, *Capitalism Divided? The City and Industry in British Social Development* (London, 1984); and S. Newton and D. Porter, *Modernization Frustrated: The Politics of Industrial Decline in Britain since 1900* (London, 1988). For the City overshadowing northern England, Jarvie, *The City of London*, 46–52.

15. For the City's influence on politics, see Peter Cain and Anthony Hopkins, *British Imperialism*, 2 vols. (London, 1993); Youssef Cassis, *City Bankers, 1890–1914* (Cambridge, 1994); Ingham, *Capitalism Divided?*; Kynaston, *The City of London*; Michie, *The City of London*. For the individual histories, see S. D. Chapman, *The Rise of Merchant Banking* (London, 1984); Cassis, *City Bankers*; M. J. Daunton, "Firm and Family in the City of London in the Nineteenth Century: The Case of F. G. Dalgety," *Bulletin of the Institute of Historical Research* 62 (1989): 154–77; R. C. Michie, "Dunn, Fischer and Co. in the City of London, 1906–1914," *Business History* 30 (1988): 195–218; W. J. Reader, *A House in the City: A Study of the City and of the Stock Exchange Based on the Records of Foster and Braithwaite, 1825–1975* (London, 1979). The pointillist is Kynaston in *The City of London*. But then see Cain and Hopkins, *British Imperialism*, and for the discussion of their work, M. J. Daunton, "'Gentlemanly Capitalism' and British Industry, 1820–1914," *Past and Present*, no. 122 (February 1989); W. D. Rubinstein, "Debate: 'Gentlemanly Capitalism' and British Industry 1820–1914, Comment," *Past and Present*, no. 132 (August 1991); and Daunton, "Debate: 'Gentlemanly Capitalism' and British Industry 1820–1914, Reply," *Past and Present*, no. 132 (August 1991). Cain and Hopkins are perfectly aware that there were many important City figures who, while undoubtedly capitalists, were hardly gentlemen.

16. *Financial News*, September 21, 1900.

17. Biographical material on Cade is taken from Thomas J. Rowe, *The Early Pioneers of Ashanti Goldfields 1895–1900* (London, 1991), 11.

18. Guildhall Library, Ashanti Goldfields Corporation Ltd., MS. 24659, Cade to Under Secretary of State, Colonial Office, March 4, 1896.

19. For the report of Chamberlain's views, see Ashanti, MS. 24659, E. Minfield, for Joseph Chamberlain, to Edwin Cade, February 28, 1896. For more on this British expedition, see John Hargreaves, *West Africa Partitioned*, vol. 2, *The Elephants and the Grass* (Basingstoke, 1985), 208–18.

20. For subscriptions for the stamp mill, see Ashanti, MS. 14164 (Minute Book), especially the entries for January 25, March 30, and October 12, 1900. For ounces of gold, see Ashanti, MS. 24,668, G. W. Easton Turner, *A Short History of Ashanti Goldfields Corporation, Ltd., 1897–1947*, issued to employees and stockholders to commemorate the corporation's jubilee, 9.

21. Ashanti, MS. 14170/32–33, Cade to John Daw, January 1, 1900.

22. For Chamberlain's views, see H. Y. Wallach, F.R.G.S., in *Wallach's West African Manual* (London, 1900), viii. Then see Ashanti, MS. 14179/37, January 12, 1900, MS. 14179/46, January 26, 1900, MS. 14179/68, February 23, 1900 and MS. 14164, Minute Book, October 12, 1900.

23. Ashanti, MS. 14170/37, Cade to Daw, January 12, 1900.

24. Ashanti, MS. 24671, "Lecture by John Daw Esq., November 11th, 12th 1902," 7, 53–54."

25. Ibid., 54.

26. *Financial Times*, June 23, 1900.

27. See *Financial Times* for February 1, December 5, and December 19, 1900.

28. For the boast, see *Financial Times*, December 19, 1900. For the continuing rebellion, see the *Daily Mail*, June 30, 1900.

29. For Cade's comment, Ashanti, MS. 14170/91, Cade to Daw, April 11, 1900. And in 1905, as governor-general of British Guyana, Hodgson would provoke yet another native uprising. See Walter Rodney, *A History of the Guyanese Working People, 1881–1905* (Baltimore, 1981), 211–14.

30. Ashanti, MS. 14170/105, Cade to H. L. Webster, June 8, 1900.

31. For Daw's report, *Financial Times*, June 23, 1900; for MacIver and Co., *Daily Mail*, September 7, 1900.

32. *Daily Mail*, October 12, 1900.

33. For enthusiasm, see Joseph Walton quoted in the *Financial Times*, March 14 and April 23, 1900. Walton, a Liberal imperialist, was M.P. for Barnsley. See his *China and the Present Crisis* (London, 1900), 221.

34. *Financial Times*, August 1, 1900.

35. See the *Financial News* for January 13 and 17, 1900.

36. *City Press*, February 17, 1900.

37. For St. James Restaurant, *Financial Times*, March 24, 1900; for Eastman's, *Financial Times*, April 12, 1900; and for the brewery, *Financial Times*, October 1, 1900.

38. See *The C.I.V.*, 9; also the *City of London Directory 1900*, 62–65, and Col. C. G. Boxall, C.B., *Report on the Raising, Organising, Equipping and Despatching the City of London Imperial Volunteers to South Africa* (London, 1900), 3.

39. For more on the volunteers, see *Bankers Magazine*, February 1900, 251; *Financial Times*, January 17, 1900; *City Press*, February 28, 1900; Guildhall Library, City Imperial Volunteers, MS. 17,667 and MS. 19,918.

40. For the unflattering commentary, see C.I.V., MS. 17,666/1, Lt. E. A. Manisty (Inns of Court, Mounted Infantry, C.I.V.) to C. W. Mead, April 19, 1900; and, in print, Maj.-Gen. Mackinnon, "The City Imperial Volunteers on Active Service," *Empire Review* 1, ed. C. Kinloch Cooke (1901): 42–44.

41. *The C.I.V.*, 29.

42. For the lord mayor, *Daily Mail*, January 2, 1900; for the gentlemanly capitalist, see William Sheowring, ed., *British Empire Series*, vol. 2, *British Africa* (London, 1899), 68; and for Lord Gifford, *Financial Times*, March 6, 1900.

43. For reality, *Positivist Review*, January 1900, 10; for "colonising genius," *Financial Times*, January 17, 1900.

44. Sheowring, *British Africa*, 68.

45. *Journal of the Royal Colonial Institute* 31 (May 1900): 433.

46. For Maccatta, *Financial Times*, April 24, 1900; for Shaw, *City Press*, January 24, 1900.

47. For Hichens, *City Press*, May 30, 1900; for Sir Blundell Maple, Bart., *City Press*, February 17, 1900.

48. *City Press*, July 28, 1900.

49. For example, it is a subject entirely ignored in Andrew S. Thompson's otherwise estimable "The Language of Imperialism and the Meanings of Empire: Imperial Discourse in British Politics, 1895–1914," *Journal of British Studies* 36, no. 2 (April 1997): 147–77.

50. For Nichols, see Sheowring, *British Africa*, 308; for the view of Swaziland, see *Journal of the Royal Colonial Institute* 31 (June 1900): 468.

51. See J. A. Hobson on "What are we fighting for?" in the *Speaker*, January 1900, 6.

52. For the Bible class, see City of London Bible Class Union, *Quarterly Review*, no. 2 (January 1900); for the fracas at the Stock Exchange, see *Daily Mail*, January 15, 1900, the *City Press*, February 3, 1900, and Guildhall Library, Stock Exchange collection, MS. 14,600 (vol. 69), "Minutes of Stock Exchange General Purposes Committee," January 15, 22, and 29.

53. *Daily Mail*, May 21, 1900.

CHAPTER 5. POPULAR CULTURE IN THE
IMPERIAL METROPOLIS

1. For museum historians, see especially Coombes, *Reinventing Africa*, 63, which best demonstrates how exhibits invariably extolled the scope, necessity, and benefits of empire to Africans and Britons, as well as a spurious scientific racism on the basis of maps, charts, catalogues, guidebooks, and other explanatory materials which blurred distinctions between the scientific and the popular. See also Tim Barringer, "The Object, the Body and the Imperial Archive: South Kensington, 1857–1886," a paper delivered at Royal Holloway College, University of London, "Conference on Imperial Cities," May 2, 1997. For the Colonial and Indian Exhibit, see John Johnson Collection, Bodleian Library, Oxford, "Exhibitions," Box 5. In all 5,550,745 people attended this exhibit. See Public Record Office, CO 323/436/3769.

2. For the Stanley and African Exhibition, see John Johnson Collection, "Exhibitions," Box 6. For a more detailed discussion of this exhibition, see Felix Driver, "Henry Morton Stanley and His Critics: Geography, Exploration and Empire," *Past and Present*, no. 133 (November 1991): 134–66; and id., "Geography, Empire and Visualisation: Making Representations," Royal Holloway College, University of London, Department of Geography, Research Papers, no. 1, 1994. One portion of the

Stanley and African Exhibition consisted of an "evolutionary" tableaux linking Africans with gorillas and then, ascending the evolutionary ladder, first Egyptians, then Arabs, and then white Europeans. See Coombes, *Reinventing Africa*, 79–80. But Driver has pointed out that British critics of empire offered alternative readings of such exhibitions. See also Nancy Leys Stepan and Sander L. Gilman, "Appropriating the Idioms of Science: The Rejection of Scientific Racism," in LaCapra, ed., *The Bounds of Race*, 72–103, for a discussion of the stigmatized people's attempt to rebut. For more general discussions of colonial exhibitions, see Richard Altick, *The Shows of London* (Cambridge, Mass., 1978); Paul Greenhalgh, *Ephemeral Vistas: The Expositions Universelles, Great Exhibitions and Worlds Fairs, 1851–1939* (London, 1988); and Robert Rydell, *All the World's a Fair: Visions of Empire at American International Expositions, 1876–1916* (Chicago, 1984). For the Greater Britain Exhibition, see Public Record Office, CO 323/436/3769.

3. For Portobello Gardens, John Johnson Collection, "Nigger Minstrels," Box 1; for Royal Agricultural Hall, John Johnson Collection, "Circuses, etc.," Box 1; for Sanger's Hippodrome and Circus, John Johnson Collection, "Circuses, etc.," Box 2; for the Livingstone Exhibition, *Queen*, January 6, 1900; and for Earl's Court, Breandon Gregory, "Staging British India," in J. S. Bratton, ed., *Acts of Supremacy: The British Empire and the Stage, 1790–1930* (Manchester, 1991), 155. Six years earlier, in 1894, this extraordinary park had been the site of a "Stupendous Spectacular Production, 'The Orient,' or 'A Mission to the East,'" in which were traced the interactions of various courageous Britons, wily Arabs, and barbaric Africans.

4. *Dramatic World*, August 1900; and for the sniffy reviewer, *Dramatic World*, September 1899. See also John Johnson Collection, "Exhibitions and Catalogues," Box 20, *Earl's Court, Greater Britain Exhibition 1899, Imre Kiralfy Director General, Daily Programme*.

5. The theater's highest part was 117 feet above ground level; its proscenium and arched stage was 315 feet wide and 100 feet deep. See Gregory, "Staging British India," 152–58; and again see Coombes, *Reinventing Africa*, 99–100, which subtly explores the methods by which exhibitions at the Olympia Theatre were made to fill this didactic purpose. See also B. Shephard, "Showbiz Imperialism: The Case of Peter Lobengula," in MacKenzie, ed., *Imperialism and Popular Culture*, 94–112; and for briefer treatment, Pennybacker, *A Vision for London*, 231–34.

6. For the literature on music hall, see, among many, Peter Bailey, ed., *Music Hall: The Business of Pleasure* (Milton Keynes, 1986), and id., *Leisure and Class in Victorian England* (London, 1978). See also Penny Summerfield, "Patriotism and Empire: Music-Hall Entertainment, 1870–1914," in MacKenzie, ed., *Imperialism and Popular Culture*, 19–34; for the songs and acts listed, see *Dramatic World* for January 1900.

7. *Dramatic World*, January 1900.

8. For Romi Ashton, *Daily News*, January 10, 1900; for biographs, *Dramatic World*, March 1900.

9. *John Bull*, January 10, 1900; *Music Hall and Theatre Review*, March 16, 1900;

Westminster Gazette, August 1, 1900. There is an extensive literature focused on music halls and the messages conveyed by the men and women who performed in them. See above, n. 6. No doubt the message changed over time. In 1900, however, with the Boer War raging, the message in London at least was unabashedly racist and imperialist.

10. *Dramatic World,* January 1900.

11. *Dramatic World,* August–November 1900, and, for "Bootle's Baby," *Westminster Gazette,* February 21, 1900.

12. John Johnson Collection, "Nigger Minstrels," Box 1.

13. See Michael Pickering, "White Skin, Black Masks: 'Nigger Minstrelsy' in Victorian England," in Bratton, ed., *Music Hall: Performance and Syle* (Milton Keynes, 1986), 88.

14. For the zoo's early aims, see Philip Lutley Sclater, *Guide to the Gardens of the Zoological Society* (London, 1900), 3; then see Harriet Ritvo, *The Animal Estate* (London, 1990), 206.

15. Bob Mullan and Gary Marvin, *Zoo Culture* (London, 1987), 110.

16. Information for this paragraph from *Comic Guide to the Zoo,* by W. R. (London, 1907); Richard Kearton, F.Z.S., "The Zoological Gardens," in *Living London,* Sims, ed., 1:346, and P. L. Sclater, *A Record of the Progress of the Zoological Society of London during the Nineteenth Century* (London, 1901).

17. For animals in the zoo, see *Baedeker's London and its Environs* (London, 1898), 288–89, and *Comic Guide to the Zoo.* For visitors to the zoo, see Zoological Society of London, Regent's Park Zoo Archive, "Daily Occurrences Book," for example, September 16, 1900, when sixteen separate schools sent 2,236 children plus teachers.

18. For Clarence Bartlett, see P. Chalmers Mitchell, *Centenary History of the Zoological Society of London* (London, 1929), 71; for deterioration of the zoo and suggested solutions, see Regent's Park Zoo Archives, letter boxes, esp. correspondence of Gambier Bolton.

19. *Saturday Review,* March 16, 1901.

20. The expert was F. G. Aflalo, *A Walk through the Zoological Gardens* (London, 1900), 201; *St. James' Gazette,* August 4, 1901.

21. *Evening News,* April 11, 1901.

22. For Sclater, Regent's Park Zoo Archives, Letter Book, "Humanitarian League," Sclater to Henry Salt, January 22, 1903; for the critics, Regent's Park Zoo Archives, clipping of an article from the *Humane Review* not dated, itself reprinting a letter to the *Morning Leader* also not dated, from a book of newspaper clippings; see also *East London Observer,* February 3, 1903.

23. *Court Journal,* April 20, 1901.

24. Aflalo, *A Walk through the Gardens,* 30, 57.

25. Sclater, *Guide to the Gardens,* 29.

26. For the lion, Aflalo, *A Walk through the Gardens,* 98; for the wildebeest, ibid., 116; for the snakes, *Daily Mail,* August 16, 1900; for the helderm, Aflalo, *A Walk through the Gardens,* 56.

27. For the prince of Wales's elephant, Sclater, *Guide to the Gardens*, 53; for English feminization of Indian men, Sinha, *Colonial Masculinity*.

28. For graceful pacing, *Daily Telegraph*, August 14, 1900; for Kruger's lioness more generally, see *Daily Mail*, August 14, *Daily Telegraph*, August 14, *Daily Graphic*, August 16, and the *Star*, August 14.

29. For guileless lions, L. Beatrice Thompson, *Who's Who at the Zoo* (London, 1902), 11; for devout lions, *Daily Chronicle*, September 3, 1900.

30. For working-man monkey, Kearton, "The Zoological Gardens," in George Sims, ed., *Living London*, 1:347; for "nigger monkey," L. Beatrice Thompson, *Who's Who*, 56; for pearl divers like baboons, Aflalo, *A Walk through the Gardens*, 133–34; for dogs like "their black owners," ibid., 110; and for Paul Kruger like a monkey, L. Beatrice Thompson, *Who's Who*, 46–49.

31. Aflalo, *A Walk through the Gardens*, 63.

32. *My Book of the Zoo* (London, 1905), no author acknowledged.

33. For the emu, Aflalo, *A Walk through the Gardens*, 16; for the ostriches, *Daily Graphic*, May 1, 1899; for the gnu, *Morning Post*, November 16, 1899; for the zebras, *Sphere*, June 14, 1900, and *Daily Mail*, September 21, 1900; for the panthers, *Lady's Field*, June 16, 1900; and for the boars, *Standard*, April 23, 1901.

34. Sir Harry Johnston discovered in the forests of the Congo an animal resembling a horse but actually related to the giraffe, called by local people *o'api*. He reported his find to the society, which promptly renamed the animal *Equus johnstoni*, or Johnston's zebra. See *Proceedings of Zoological Society* (London, 1901), 2:50. Eventually the animal was renamed *Okapia johnstoni*. See Mitchell, *History of the Zoological Society*, 254. For Kingsley's fish, see Katherine Frank, *A Voyager Out: The Life of Mary Kingsley* (London, 1986), 223. For Peel's expedition, see the *Proceedings of the General Meetings for Scientific Business of the Zoological Society of London for the Year 1900*, 6–7.

35. The books were *The Great Boer War* (London, 1901) and *The War in South Africa* (London, 1900); for the invention, see *Westminster Gazette*, February 26, 1900.

36. All quotations taken from *The Annotated Sherlock Holmes*, 2 vols., ed. William S. Baring-Gould (New York, 1992). For Watson, ibid., 1:143; for Holmes, ibid., 1:298.

37. Baring-Gould, *Annotated Holmes*, "A Study in Scarlet," 145.

38. Ibid., "The Adventure of the Empty House," 1:337; ibid., "The Adventure of the Bruce-Partington Plans," 1:432.

39. Ibid., "The Cardboard Box," 2:196; ibid., "The Adventure of the Blue Carbuncle," 1:459.

40. Ibid., "The Sign of the Four," 1:622, 624.

41. Ibid., "The Sign of the Four," 1:625; ibid., "A Study in Scarlet," 1:152.

42. Ibid., "The Man with the Twisted Lip," 1:370–75; ibid., "The Adventure of the Speckled Band," 1:261; ibid., "The Adventure of the Devil's Foot," 2:524; ibid., "The Adventure of the Dying Detective," 1:439, 440–41.

43. Ibid., "The Sign of the Four," 1:667.

44. Ibid., "A Case of Identity," 1:407; ibid., "The Hound of the Baskervilles," 2:13;

ibid., "The Boscombe Valley Mystery," 1:135; ibid., "The Adventure of the Solitary Cyclist," 1:287.

45. Ibid., "The Adventure of the Copper Beeches," 1:132; ibid., "The Adventure of the Three Students," 1:382; ibid., "The Disappearance of Lady Frances Carfax," 2:661.

46. Ibid., 2:250–51 for Downing's thumb. Aside from "The Sign of the Four," the Holmes story in which Conan Doyle indulges his racist sentiments most unabashedly is "The Adventure of the Three Gables." Here Holmes and Watson confront a black boxer: "He would have been a comic figure if he had not been terrific, for he was dressed in a very loud grey check suit with a flowing salmon-coloured tie. His broad face and flattened nose were thrust forward, as his sullen dark eyes, with a smouldering gleam of malice in them, turned from one of us to the other." And so on in nearly the tone of "nigger minstrelsy." See ibid., "The Adventure of the Three Gables," 1:722–23.

47. Ibid., "The Yellow Face," 1:588–89.

48. Ibid., "The Sign of the Four," 1:674–84.

49. Ibid., "The Adventure of Wisteria Lodge," 2:252; ibid., "The Adventure of the Six Napoleons," 2:578, 582–83.

50. Ibid., "A Study in Scarlet," 1:158; ibid., "The Cardboard Box," 2:200; ibid., "The Adventure of Shoscombe Old Place," 2:641.

51. Ibid., 2:194.

52. It attracted 710,000 in 1898. Sclater, *Guide to the Gardens*, 240.

53. For class and music hall, see, among others, Jane Traies, "Jones and the Working Girl: Class Marginality in Music-Hall Song," in Bratton, ed., *Music Hall;* for the "Happy Darkies," see *Queen, the Lady's Newspaper,* January 1, 1898. Amateur "nigger minstrels" performed weekly at the St. Pancras Somers Town Presbyterian Church and in Catford in aid of St. George's Parish Room Fund. See John Johnson Collection, "Nigger Minstrels." Moore, of Moore and Burgess Minstrels, earned a fortune at his trade and wound up living in a mansion in St. John's Wood. *Weekly Dispatch,* April 10, 1904.

54. See above, chap. 3.

55. The so-called new dramatists failed to find a popular audience in London during this period, but they would become more successful during the Edwardian era. See Karl Beckson, *London in the 1890s: A Cultural History* (New York, 1992), 160–85.

CHAPTER 6. LIMNING FEMALE GENDER BOUNDARIES

1. *The Royal Geographical Society's Year-Book and Record* (London, 1899), 2.

2. Women had also organized their own private associations, for example, the Grosvenor Crescent Club near Hyde Park corner, where debates and literary discussions took place every fortnight.

3. For this episode, see the papers of the Royal Geographical Society, especially Box 1, on the admission of female members. See also Dea Birkett, *Spinsters Abroad*

(Oxford, 1989), 211-44, and, less thoroughly, Alison Blunt, *Travel, Gender and Imperialism, Mary Kingsley and West Africa* (London, 1994), 148-59.

4. For the figures, see *Royal Geographical Society's Year-Book* 3. For Stanley, who mentioned Mrs. Bishop, Miss Gordon Cumming, Lady Baker, and Mrs. French Shelden, see RGS, Box 1, verbatim account of meeting held on December 28, 1892.

5. A piquant example: at the department store of Messrs. Debenham and Freebody on Wigmore Street, E. P. Veeraswamy gave classes in Indian cookery, teaching London's women to appreciate simultaneously an appropriately gendered activity and one of the benefits of Britain's imperial dominion. As *Queen, the Lady's Newspaper* (March 5, 1898), put it, "Considering India is part of Her Majesty's dominions, we ought to be as keenly interested in, and as ready to adapt Indian as Continental" cuisine, advertising Veeraswamy's demonstrations and lessons in that subject on both a private basis and at the Wigmore Street store.

6. Of course, male gender roles are also constructed, but that is not my subject here. See especially Graham Dawson, *Soldier Heroes: British Adventure, Empire and the Imagining of Masculinities* (London, 1994); Joseph Bristow, *Empire Boys: Adventures in a Man's World* (London, 1991); J. A. Mangan and James Walvin, eds., *Manliness and Morality: Middle-Class Masculinity in Britain and America, 1800–1949* (Manchester, 1987). For the intersection of feminist and imperialist scholarship, see Antoinette Burton, who argues that interaction between colonized and colonizer was reciprocal: "A 'Pilgrim Reformer' at the Heart of the Empire: Behramji Malabari in Late-Victorian London," *Gender and History* 8, no. 2 (August 1996): 175-96. Others have argued that British women played a larger imperial role than has been acknowledged, that the *practice* of British imperialism was gendered, and that imperialism affected attitudes toward gender in Britain. They have also argued that native women in the colonies experienced imperialism differently from men. See Ronald Hyam, *Sexuality and Empire* (Manchester, 1991); Ann Laura Stoler, "Carnal Knowledge and Imperial Power: Gender, Race, and Morality in Colonial Asia," in Micaela di Leonardo, ed., *Gender and the Crossroads of Knowledge: Feminist Anthropology in the Postmodern Era* (Berkeley, 1991), 51-100. For "maternal imperialism," see Julia Bush "'The Right Sort of Woman': Female Emigrators and Emigration to the British Empire, 1890–1910," *Women's History Review* 3, no. 3 (1994): 385-400. For the gendering of imperialism, see Nupur Chauduri and Margaret Strobel, eds., *Western Women and Imperialism, Complicity and Resistance* (Bloomington, 1992), and Margaret Strobel, *European Women and the Second British Empire* (Bloomington, 1991). Finally see McClintock, *Imperial Leather*, esp. 207-23, who has argued that empire and domesticity were linked late in the nineteenth century through advertising campaigns which established the "civilizing" nature of commodities commonly found in the British home—e.g., Pears and Monkey Brand soaps, the beef extract Bovril, and Eno's Fruit Salts.

7. Edmund Gosse, *Lady Dorothy Nevill, An Open Letter* (London 1913), 10. This is a memoir of Lady Dorothy Nevill, privately printed and circulated.

8. Frances, Countess of Warwick, *Afterthoughts* (London, 1931), 49; Ralph Nevill, *The Life and Letters of Lady Dorothy Nevill* (London, 1919), 107; British Li-

brary, Carnarvon Papers, Add. Ms. 61060/124, Lord Charles Beresford to Lady Jeune, n.d.

9. Gosse, *Nevill*, 5–6.

10. For names of Nevill's guests, see Nevill, *Life of Lady Nevill*, 108; Lady St. Helier, *Memories of Fifty Years* (London, 1909), 210.

11. For the guinea pig, see Gosse, *Nevill*, 8; for fear of Hardie, see University of Birmingham, Joseph Chamberlain Collection, JC5/56/89, Nevill to Chamberlain, n.d.; for coaxing Chamberlain, see Chamberlain Papers, JC5/56/76, Nevill to Chamberlain, November 1, year uncertain; for coaxing Burns, see British Library, John Burns Collection, Add. Ms. 46299/136, Nevill to Burns, November ?, 1906; for flattering Chamberlain, see Chamberlain Collection, JC5/56/89, Nevill to Chamberlain, n.d.; and for flattering Burns, see Burns Collection, Add. Ms. 46301/184, Nevill to Burns, October ?, 1910.

12. For her antidemocratic and feminist views, see Lady Dorothy Nevill, *My Own Times* (London, 1912), 134–35.

13. For the prediction that Chamberlain was about to marry Beatrice Potter, see British Library, Thomas Hay Sweet Escott Collection, Add. Ms. 58788, NE25, n.d. but "Bef. 8 June 1885." Beatrice Potter went on, of course, to marry Sidney Webb. For Lady Tweedale's marriage, see Chamberlain Collection, JC5/56/92, Nevill to Chamberlain, n.d.; for the helpless female, see Chamberlain Collection, JC5/56/86, Nevill to Chamberlain, n.d.; for "You are a saviour," see Chamberlain Collection, JC5/56/89, Nevill to Chamberlain, n.d.; for Nevill's discretion, see Escott Collection, NE29, Nevill to Escott, n.d., and Chamberlain Collection, JC5/56/88, Nevill to Chamberlain, n.d. except "12th August."

14. For Gorst and Fawcett, Escott Collection, NE31, Nevill to Escott, "Bef. 6 Nov. 1884"; for Russell and Baring, Chamberlain Collection, JC5/56/92, Nevill to Chamberlain, n.d.

15. Frances, Countess of Warwick, *Afterthoughts*, 48, 103–04.

16. Quoted in H. Montgomery Hyde, *The Londonderrys, A Family Portrait* (London, 1979), 63; Lady Londonderry's papers at the Public Record Office of Northern Ireland in Belfast hold hundreds of letters from leading Conservatives concerning the "Die-hard" resistance.

17. Brian Masters, *Great Hostesses* (London, 1992), 45.

18. For the first description, Masters, *Great Hostesses*, 103; for the second, Colonel Repington, military correspondent of the *Times*, quoted in Anne de Courcy, *Circe, the Life of Edith Marchioness of Londonderry* (London, 1992), 36; for the last, Masters again, 40.

19. For the description, see de Courcy, *Circe*, 34. Lady Londonderry also owned Wyngard, a great estate in Northern Ireland where, again, she entertained on a lavish scale but without the same political effect.

20. E. F. Benson, quoted in Masters, *Great Hostesses*, 40.

21. Nevill, *Life of Lady Neville*, 109.

22. Northern Ireland Public Record Office, Belfast, Papers of Theresa Susey

Helen Vane-Tempest-Stewart, wife of 6th marquess of Londonderry, D.2846/2/14/68, Milner to Lady Londonderry, December 20, 1898; D.2846/2/13/70, Buller to Lady Londonderry, October 4, 1899; D.2846/2/19/27, Chamberlain to Lady Londonderry, March ?, 26, 1900; D.2846/2/20/14, Balfour to Lady Londonderry, n.d.

23. For the Aga Khan, Lady Londonderry Collection, D.2846/2/6/1, in August 1902; for Rhodes, D.2846/2/7/84–95; for the king, D.2846/2/18/8, Knollys to Lady Londonderry, March 6, 1901.

24. Countess of Warwick, *Afterthoughts*, 49; Morley quoted in de Courcy, *Circe*, 34; Lady Londonderry Collection, D.2846/2/32/82, Sir A. D. Wolff to Lady Londonderry, January 22, 1896; D.2846/2/22/20, Harcourt to Lady Londonderry, [month illegible] 29, 1900; D.2846/2/22/19, Harcourt to Lady Londonderry, April 13, 1900; D.2846/2/14/71, Milner to Lady Londonderry, February 2, 1900; D.2846/2/19/114, Wyndham to Lady Londonderry, February 14, 1896.

25. Lady Londonderry Collection, D.2846/2/18/1, Dawson to Lady Londonderry, May 6, 1905.

26. Lady Londonderry Collection, D.2846/2/22/24, Harcourt to Lady Londonderry, November 1, 1900; D.2846/2/22/23, Harcourt to Lady Londonderry, October 31, 1900; D.2846/2/32/74, Matthew Ridley to Lady Londonderry, n.d., but obviously 1900.

27. Lady Londonderry Collection, D.2486/2/21/54, Lord Lansdowne to Lady Londonderry, July 5, 1899; D.2846/2/18/5&6, Knollys to Lady Londonderry, May 10 and May 17, 1897; de Courcy, *Circe*, 36; Masters, *Great Hostesses*, 36.

28. Lady Londonderry collection, D.2846/2/19/67, Rosebery to Lady Londonderry, July 2, 1894.

29. Lady Londonderry Collection, D.2846/2/13/98, Maude Buller to Lady Londonderry, November 24, 1899.

30. Lady Londonderry Collection, D.2846/2/13/62, Buller to Lady Londonderry, June 23, 1899; D.2846/2/13/63, Buller to Lady Londonderry, July 8, 1899.

31. Lady Londonderry Collection, D.2846/2/13/70, Buller to Lady Londonderry, October 4, 1899; D.2846/2/13/72, Buller to Lady Londonderry, November 17, 1899; D.2846/2/13/75, Buller to Lady Londonderry, March 4, 1900.

32. Lady Londonderry Collection, D.2846/2/13/89, Buller to Lady Londonderry, October 11, 1901; D.2846/2/6/88, Buller to Lady Londonderry, March 18, 1901.

33. de Courcy, *Circe*, 36.

34. Lady Londonderry Collection, D.2846/2/6/67, Buller to Lady Londonderry, September 4, 1899.

35. For biographical details, see E. Moberly Bell's hagiographical *Flora Shaw* (London, 1947).

36. Ibid., 70.

37. Oxford University, Rhodes House, Perham Collection, MS Perham, Box 308, file 1, "Extract from Miss Shaw's Private Diary . . . ," November 29, 1889.

38. Rhodes House, Anti-Slavery Society Papers, MS. BritEmp. S.18, Shaw to Allen, December 13, 1889.

39. Bell was the son of a leading English merchant in Alexandria who had become the *Times*'s correspondent in Egypt. According to T. P. O'Connor, the Irish journalist and politician, Bell's "telegrams, letters and arguments before during and after the Arabi Rebellion of 1882, secured the attention of Gladstone and Granville, Dufferin and Northbrook, and they, looking about for a policy and a guide, had the good sense to go for advice to the master-critic of the moment." *M.A.P.*, October 13, 1900, 342.

40. Perham Collection, Box 308, file 7, Lady Lugard to Chamberlain, n.d., but written between July and November 1902; Lady Lugard, "West African Negroland," *Journal of the Royal Colonial Institute* (June 1904): 438; Perham Collection, Box 309, file 1, Lady Lugard to Frederick Lugard, March 31, 1905.

41. *Times*, January 8, 1897.

42. A. H. Keane, "The Struggle of the Races, An Ethnico-Political Forecast," *The Imperial and Colonial Magazine*, January 1901, 323; Flora Shaw, *Letters from South Africa* (London, 1893) (reprinted from the *Times* of July, August, September, and October 1892), 80, 83, 92; Lady Lugard, "Nigeria," *Journal of the Society of Arts*, March 18, 1904, 372, 375.

43. Shaw, *Letters*, 1.

44. Lady Lugard, "West African Negroland," 486.

45. For Shaw's consultations with Goldie, see John E. Flint, *Sir George Goldie and the Making of Nigeria* (Oxford, 1960), 258; for an example of a worshipful article on Rhodes, *Times*, January 30, 1899; then see Rhodes House, MS Brit. Emp. S54, Shaw to Lugard, November 7, 1895, and Oliver Woods and James Bishop, *The Story of The Times* (London, 1983), 160.

46. For the telegrams, see Woods and Bishop, *Story of The Times*, 169–70. The originals are to be found in the *Times* Archive, file on Jameson Raid. For the entire episode see especially the *Times* Archive, Jameson Raid file, "The Connection of *The Times* with the Jameson Raid," a carefully researched and most illuminating sixty-four-page typescript written by Shirley Dolne (1975).

47. For Shaw's worries, see the *Times* Archive, E. F. Moberly Bell file of letters from Flora Shaw, January 17, 1897; *Saturday Review*, July 10, 1897.

48. Woods and Bishop, *Story of The Times*, 170.

49. For Labouchere, see clipping in the *Times* Archive of *Truth*, but n.d.; Rhodes House, Cecil Rhodes Collection, Grey of Howick to Rhodes, July 1897.

50. Quoted in Woods and Bishop, *Story of The Times*, 179.

51. Public Record Office, C.O. 323/458/4040.

52. The *Times* Archive, E. F. Moberly Bell file, Shaw to Bell, February 20, 1899.

53. For Shaw's view of Buller, see the *Times* Archive, "Miscellaneous file" relating to Flora Shaw, Shaw to Bell, from "Somewhere in South Africa," January 1902; *Times*, February 22, 1900.

54. Rhodes House, Micr. AFR.4B, Rhodes-Stead Correspondence with one letter from Flora Shaw to Stead, n.d., but from internal evidence written in 1891. This let-

ter is interesting for another reason. What can the dynamics of the relationship between Rhodes and Shaw have been in 1895, as plans for the Jameson Raid took shape, if four years earlier Rhodes had acknowledged Shaw as his teacher?

55. The *Times* Archive, Foreign Editor's Letter-books, #2: August 29, 1893—May 29, 1895: Wallace to Shaw, February 7, 1894, 362; Wallace to Shaw, March 19, 1894, 436.

56. Perham Collection, Box 308, file 9, "A rough 'appreciation' by E. J. Lugard [Lord Lugard's brother], in a vain endeavour to string together various letters from which the Biographers could deal with the matter delicately"; Box 309, file 1, Lady Lugard to Frederick Lugard, November 13, 1904; Lady Lugard to Lord Lugard, n.d., but filed with other letters written during 1904-05.

57. Perham Collection, Box 308, file 4, Shaw to Lugard, March 4, 1899.

58. Perham Collection, Box 309, file 1, Lady Lugard to Lord Lugard, n.d.; Lady Lugard to Lord Lugard, November 13, 1904.

59. Bell, *Shaw*, 229.

60. For letters from Nigeria, see, for example, Perham Collection, Box 308, file 7, Lady Lugard to Joseph Chamberlain, n.d., except July-September 1902; for the interview with Churchill, Box 309, file 1, Lady Lugard to Frederick Lugard, November 6, 1905.

61. For the projected partnership, see Perham Collection, file 5, Flora Shaw to Frederick Lugard, December 13, 1901; on Sir Reginald Antrobus, who was assistant undersecretary at the Colonial Office from 1898 to 1909, Box 309, file 1, Lady Lugard to Frederick Lugard, April 12, 1905; for the domestic sphere, Box 309, file 1, Lady Lugard to Frederick Lugard, April 11, 1905.

62. Of perhaps a dozen biographies, the best are Frank, *A Voyager Out*, and Dea Birkett, *Mary Kingsley, Imperial Adventuress* (Worcester, 1992). See also Blunt, *Travel, Gender, and Imperialism*, and, for a revisionist view, E. Flint, "Mary Kingsley—A Reassessment," *Journal of African History* 4, no. 1 (1963).

63. For Kingsley's pro-English views, see Rhodes House, John Holt and Company Ltd. Collection, MSS Afr.s.1525, Box 16, file 3, Kingsley to Holt, December 26, 1898. But see also Box 16, file 8: While aboard the ship taking her to South Africa and her death, Kingsley wrote a much-quoted letter to the editor of the *New Africa*, published in Monrovia by Dr. A. P. Camphor and Bishop Hartzell, both belonging to the Episcopal Missionary Society. In it she reiterated her belief in the existence and worth of African laws, culture, and religion, "which I confess is a form of my own religion," and argued against African assimilation of European values. "The African is *different* from the European," Kingsley wrote, "yet . . . he is a very fine fellow and we can be friends." Perhaps this was nothing more than a reassertion of her by now familiar cultural relativism (for which see below), yet the letter suggests something more. It blames imperialists for interfering with Africa and for hypocritically claiming to be doing so on behalf of the Africans themselves; and it reproaches European-educated Africans for attempting to defend themselves by appealing to Europe's Christian conscience, a strategy that was and always would be hopeless in Kings-

ley's opinion. She urged her correspondents instead to straightforwardly explain to Europe the worth of their own institutions. She warned that unless they did so Africans would be dispossessed of their homeland and made to suffer the fate of the Jews and the Irish Catholics.

But if Africans were in the same boat as other exploited and oppressed peoples, then the remedy for their sufferings lay, as Kingsley suggested in her letter, in nationalism, in the African equivalent of a Zionist or even a home rule movement. Such a movement was already in embryo, although Kingsley did not realize it. The first Pan-African Conference met in London in July 1900, little more than a month after she died. Had she lived, Pan-Africanism would have possessed a powerful, resourceful, and imaginative ally.

64. For Maxwell, see Holt Collection, Box 16, file 4, Kingsley to Holt, April 26, 1898; for handy knowledge, Box 16, file 4, Kingsley to Holt, May 7, 1898; for "quantities of blacks," see Box 16, file 4, Kingsley to Holt, September 15, 1898. Edward Wilmot Blyden, 1832–1912, was a West Indian active in Liberian and Sierra Leonean politics and precursor of Marcus Garvey as an advocate of the "back-to-Africa" movement; Arthur Barclay, 1854–1938, was a West Indian who rose to become president of Liberia from 1904 to 1912.

65. *Spectator*, December 28, 1895, quoted in Birkett, *Mary Kingsley*, 64.

66. Mary Kingsley, "The Development of Dodos," *National Review*, March 1896, quoted in Frank, *A Voyager Out*, 69.

67. For "Vauxhall Road," see Frank, *A Voyager Out*, 157; for Kingsley on native law, see Holt Collection, Box 16, file 4, Kingsley to Holt, April 26, 1898.

68. Holt Collection, Box 16, file 4, Kingsley to Holt, undated fragment of a letter probably written late in 1899; Box 16, file 4, Kingsley to Holt, August 28, 1899.

69. For "androgens," Royal Geographical Society Archive, file of Mary Kingsley letters to Dr. Scott Keltie, January 12, 1899; for "lecturing," see Holt Collection, Box 16, file 3, Kingsley to Holt, November 14, 1898.

70. Holt Collection, Box 16, file 3, Kingsley to Holt, February 20, 1899.

71. Holt Collection, Box 16, file 3, Kingsley to Holt, November 9, 1898.

72. For the "Salisbury-Balfour set," Holt Collection, Box 16, file 4, Kingsley to Holt, July 16, 1898; for the discussion with Chamberlain, Box 16, file 1, Kingsley to Holt, March 19, 1898.

73. Holt Collection, Box 16, file 4, Kingsley to Holt, May 5, 1898.

74. For "thinskinned," Holt Collection, Box 16, file 1, Kingsley to Holt, March 21, 1898; for "cocktailed ass," Box 16, file 3, Kingsley to Holt, November 2, 1898; for Cromer, Box 16, file 4, Kingsley to Holt, n.d. but September 1899.

75. For Maclean and young Winston Churchill, Holt Collection, Box 16, file 4, Kingsley to Holt, May 10, 1899; for plot, Box 16, file 4, Kingsley to Holt, July 28, 1899.

76. For including "the native," Holt Collection, Box 16, file 4, Kingsley to Holt, April 29, 1898; for "powerful enough," Box 16, file 4, Kingsley to Holt, September 30, 1899; for "gall and wormwood," Box 16, file 4, Kingsley to Holt, May 29, 1899.

77. For more on Kingsley's scheme, see Birkett, *Mary Kingsley*, 132–33, Frank, *A Voyager Out*, 240–42, and Flint, "Mary Kingsley," 103–05.

78. *Saturday Review*, February 11, 1899.

79. Holt Collection, Box 16, file 4, Kingsley to Holt, June 21, 1899.

80. For De Manville, Holt Collection, Box 16, file 3, Kingsley to Holt, December 13, 1898 (the name of the French ambassador to Britain in 1898 was actually A. de Courcel); for Mrs. Antrobus, Box 16, file 3, Kingsley to Holt, March 4, 1899.

81. For drawbacks to crowded dinner parties, Holt Collection, Box 16, file 1, Kingsley to Holt, December 13, 1897; for Toby, M.P., Box 16, file 4, Kingsley to Holt, June 27, 1899.

82. For Shaw to Bird, see Birkett, *Mary Kingsley*, 138; then see Perham Collection, Box 308, file 4, Lugard to Shaw, February 23, 1899.

83. For Kingsley on Shaw on Kingsley, Holt Collection, Box 16, file 1, Kingsley to Holt, n.d.; for Kingsley on the *Times*, Box 16, file 4, Kingsley to Holt, July 2, 1898; for "sarcasm . . . my natural weapon," Box 16, file 4, Kingsley to Holt, May 7, 1898; for detesting the *Times*, Box 16, file 1, Kingsley to Holt, February 16, 1898.

84. Holt Collection, Box 16, file 3, Kingsley to Holt, April 25, 1899.

85. First impression of Lugard, Holt Collection, Box 16, file 1, Kingsley to Holt, December 13, 1897; but then see Box 16, file 3, Kingsley to Holt, January 23, 1898, "Lugard . . . now depends on personal influence, conversation, not *letters*. I would show you his long screed [?] but I cannot because of its abuse of Liverpool. . . . It is unfair and unfounded . . . as I frequently tell him"; for not rising up against, Box 16, file 3, Kingsley to Holt, December 7, 1898; and finally, Box 16, file 3, Kingsley to Holt, January 19, 1899.

86. For Kingsley's designs on Goldie, Holt Collection, Box 16, file 4, Kingsley to Holt, May 5, 1898; for the tug-of-war, Box 16, file 3, Kingsley to Holt, February 11, 1898.

87. Holt Collection, Box 16, file 4, Kingsley to Holt, July 11, 1899.

88. There is a curious endnote to what can only be viewed as the rivalry between Kingsley and Shaw. Shaw seems never to have mentioned Kingsley in her private correspondence or published journalism, but on August 7, two months after Kingsley's death, she published a letter in the *Times* defending British medical practices in South Africa, which had recently come under attack. She quoted in their support an unfinished letter to her by Mary Kingsley which she had only just received. We cannot know why Kingsley wished to contact Shaw, nor whether she really believed, as Shaw maintained she did, that British hospitals in South Africa were well run. In any event the more interesting part of Shaw's letter is the part which snidely questions Kingsley's patriotism. Would a woman possessing "Imperialistic sympathies" have "found herself employed in the work of nursing Boer prisoners in Simonstown"? Shaw implies that this is an incongruence which requires "an explanation."

89. Bell, *Shaw*, 77.

90. Actually to John Holt, but the argument is still correct. See Holt Collection, Box 16, file 2, Kingsley to Holt, October 29, 1898.

91. For Shaw on female emigrators, *Times*, April 11, 1899; for Kingsley on the need for female nurses in Africa, *British Empire Review*, October 1899; for "maternal imperialism," Bush, "The Right Sort of Woman," 396.

CHAPTER 7. LONDON'S RADICAL AND CELTIC FRINGE

1. See Bernard Porter, *Critics of Empire* (London, 1968), A. P. Thornton, *The Imperial Idea and its Enemies* (London, 1985), Stephen Howe, *Anticolonialism in British Politics: The Left and the End of Empire* (Oxford, 1993).

2. For Russell, see the *Speaker*, February 17. See also A. E. Fletcher in *New Age*, September 30, 1897, "The main purpose for which the Liberal Forwards exist is to insist that Great Britain should continue to play her historic part as the refuge of the enslaved and the oppressed and the defender of freedom and national independence all round the world." For empire wreckers, see *Westminster Review*, February 1900; for the pamphlet, see John Johnson Collection, "Creeds, Parties, Policies," Box 5, "The Treatment of the Natives in South Africa."

3. When Stead read William Digby's *Prosperous British India* (1901), which claimed to prove a steady growth of poverty among the Indian masses under British rule, he shrank from the obvious conclusion. "I should be delighted if you could give me some solid assurance that in your judgement Mr. Digby is all wrong," he wrote to the Indian historian and nationalist G. K. Gokhale. "If he is right, then—but I recoil with horror from such a conclusion." British Library, India Office, Gokhale Papers, IOR POS 11706, Stead to Gokhale, January 27, 1902. For Courtney, see the *Aborigine's Friend*, May 1897.

4. *Review of Reviews*, May 1900, 442.

5. *Fortnightly Review*, April 1898, "Liquor Traffic with West Africa," by Mary Kingsley; for the second critic, see *Justice*, June 30, 1900; for Stead, see *Review of Reviews*, July 1900.

6. *New Age*, September 9, 1897; Alfred Haggard, brother of the novelist, in the *Positivist Review*, November 1900.

7. For Hodgkin, see the *Aborigine's Friend*, July 1896; for Creighton, *Aborigine's Friend*, April 1900; for Fox Bourne, *Humane Review*, April 1900 to January 1901, 172.

8. H. Fox Bourne, *The Aborigines Protection Society: Chapters in its History* (London, 1899).

9. The inspection took place before Savage South Africa appeared at Earl's Court. See Rhodes House, MSS Brit. Emp. S18, C150/174, Correspondence of H. Fox Bourne, Secretary, Aborigines Protection Society, Cleary to H. R. Fox Bourne, July 24, 1899; then see Henry Fox Bourne, *Aborigines Protection Society*, and the *Aborigine's Friend* for April 1900, 526.

10. For Butler, see Vron Ware, *Beyond the Pale* (London, 1992), 156; for overlapping memberships, see, for example, *Humane Review*, which led the crusade on behalf

of the zoo animals, vol. 1, April 1900—January 1901, article by H. Fox Bourne, secretary of the APS, entitled "The Claims of Uncivilised Races," 162–72. Also, the Christian socialist journal *New Age* reported Humane Society Meetings, e.g., May 11, 1899; for "Zoophilist," see *Humane Review*, April 1903—January 1904, 173. But see Coombes, *Reinventing Africa*, 33, for a less jaundiced view of Fox Bourne. She also points out that it was common for Britons to compare Africans with wild animals, e.g., 102, in quoting a review of the Savage South Africa show: "Frank Fillis has achieved some wonderful results in the training of the troupes of savages and, incidentally, of the horses also."

11. For fastidious shrinking, see John Trist, "Our National Imbroglio," *Westminster Review*, April 1900, 405; the elitist pro-Boer was E. B. Husband in "Reflections: Wage Earners and the South African War," *Westminster Review*, September 1900, 358. The staunch democrats belonged to the Land and Labour League. *Land and Labour*, January 1900.

12. For Harrison, see Martha S. Volger, *Frederic Harrison* (Oxford, 1984). The Positivists took their doctrine from Auguste Comte, who, rejecting traditional religions, argued for rationalism, science, and service to humanity. Harrison led the most important London branch of the Positivist movement. Strongest during the 1880s, by 1900 its 150-seat auditorium had become too large. Typical Sunday meetings now attracted approximately 50 people. Ibid., 245. For the annual address, see the *Positivist Review*, February (supplement), 1900.

13. For Harrison's jeremiad, see BLPES, London Positivist Society Collection, LPC 4/1, handwritten transcript of speech by Frederic Harrison to a Positivist audience, n.d. but from internal evidence delivered in 1900. For the Positivist meetings, see Minute Book of Monthly Meetings, LPS1/2, 1899–1901. They discussed such subjects as "The Proposed Peace Conference," "British Rule in India," "The War," "South African Fallacies," "China," "The South African and Chinese Wars," "Farm Burnings in South Africa," "Pro-Boers and Imperialists." On September 27, 1901, Harrison decreed that these meetings be opened to women as well as men. For satisfied Harrison, see the *Positivist Review*, October 1900.

14. For the condemnation of racism, see the *Positivist Review*, supplement for October 1900, 180. For the National Liberal Club speech, see London Positivist Society Collection, LPS2/8, "A Toast of Empire," by Frederic Harrison, n.d.

15. For more on Hobson, see his *Confessions of an Economic Heretic* (London, 1938), and, for more recent appraisals, John Allett, *New Liberalism: The Political Economy of J. A. Hobson* (Toronto, 1981), Jules Townshend, *J. A. Hobson* (Manchester, 1990), and Michael Schneider, *J. A. Hobson* (Basingstoke, 1996).

16. For Hobson on the real purpose of the Boer War, see the *Speaker*, January 1900; for the "real Imperialism," see *Contemporary Review*, January 1900. See too Porter, *Critics of Empire*, esp. chaps. 4, 6. Hobson set out his arguments in a series of authoritative articles for Liberal and Radical journals and newspapers, and in three books, *The War in South Africa* (London, 1900), *The Psychology of Jingoism* (London, 1901), and *Imperialism* (London, 1902).

17. G. Spillar, *The Ethical Movement in Great Britain: A Documentary History* (London, 1934), 13.

18. For the Independent Labour Party, see, for example, the anti-imperialist motion successfully proposed by J. Frederick Green, a Londoner, at the party's annual conference in 1900, which says in part, "regarding the less civilised or weaker people, we should pursue a policy of protection without interference with their own self-development as races and nations . . . and . . . immediately [begin] to withdraw the iron and unnatural dominance of our forms of rule." For the *New Age* see, for example, "The effective answer to the Jingo Imperialism and militarism from which we now suffer is to declare that it is not England's duty to master other nations or peoples, but to serve them." *New Age*, November 2, 1899. On the other hand in 1900 the *New Age*, under the editorship of A. E. Fletcher, was unique in London for its numerous and forthright denunciations of "colour lunacy" and the frequency with which it printed letters from black readers and articles by black writers. For Beatrice Webb's attitudes, see Edmund Silberner, *Historica Judaica* 14 (April 1952): 27–38, and more recently Deborah Epstein Nord, *The Apprenticeship of Beatrice Webb* (Amherst, 1985), 170–74. For the Fabians, see A. M. McBriar, *Fabian Socialism and English Politics, 1884–1918* (Cambridge, 1962), 126. And finally see George Bernard Shaw, *Fabianism and the Empire* (London, 1900), 23.

19. *Justice*, August 25, 1900. See also the issue for May 1, 1900.

20. For Hyndman's anti-Semitism, see *Justice*, March 10, 1900; for Bax, see *Justice*, September 29, 1900.

21. *Justice*, August 11, 1900.

22. *Justice*, October 6, 1900.

23. John Johnson Collection, "Empire and Colonies," Box 2, H. M. Hyndman, *The Approaching Catastrophe in India* (London, 1897).

24. For instrumental anti-imperialism, see Bax in *Justice*, May 1, 1900, "It has become essential for capitalists to . . . employ the political power of the State directly for the purpose of obtaining for their capital fresh outlets in which they . . . shall have a monopoly. . . . This means the bringing of all the barbarous and savage countries of the earth . . . under th[eir] political control . . . conduc[ing] to one end solely, the prolongation of the capitalist system." For moral anti-imperialism, see *Justice*, May 5, 1900, "Imperialism, imperial federation, the dominance of one nation, of one people, of one race, it is our duty, for the cause of humanity, to oppose to the utmost."

25. For some of the numbers, see David Fitzpatrick, "A Curious Middle Place: The Irish in Britain, 1871–1921," in *The Irish in Britain, 1815–1939*, Roger Swift and Sheridan Gilley, eds. (London, 1989), 11–13; then see also, Alan O'Day, "Irish Influence on Parliamentary Elections in London, 1885–1914: A Simple Test," in *The Irish in the Victorian City*, Roger Swift and Sheridan Gilley, eds. (London, 1985), 99. On the other hand Paul Thompson puts the figure at 350,000 in 1900. See his *Socialists, Liberals and Labour: The Struggle for London, 1885–1914* (London, 1967), 25. See John Lovell, "The Irish and the London Dockers," for a more detailed account of their presence among the dock labor force, *Bulletin of the Society for the Study of Labour History*,

no. 35 (Autumn 1977); for where they lived, see Thompson, *Socialists, Liberals and Labour,* 25. Finally see Lynn Hollen Lees, *Exiles of Erin: Irish Migrants in Victorian London* (Manchester, 1979), 242. See also Roger Swift, "The Outcast Irish in the British Victorian City: Problems and Perspectives," *Irish Historical Studies* 25, no. 99 (May 1987): 264–76.

26. See O'Day, "Irish Influence on Parliamentary Elections in London."

27. These were the Irish Literary Society, the Gaelic League of London, the Irish Social Club, the Irish Medical Graduates Union, the London Irish Rugby Football Club, the London Irish Rifles (16th Middlesex), the Ulster Association, the London Young Ireland Society, the Gaelic Athletic Association, the Shandon Athletic Club, the Irish National Club, the Irish National League of Great Britain, the Irish Texts Society, the Catholic Five Hundred, the Catholic League of South London, and the Tower Hamlets Catholic League.

28. For O'Brien, see *Irish People,* October 27, 1900; for "Mr. P. T. MacG," see *Half-Yearly Magazine of the Gaelic League of London,* 1904, 21–22.

29. Mark F. Ryan, *Fenian Memories* (Dublin, 1945), 157–69. See also R. F. Foster, *W. B. Yeats: A Life* (Oxford, 1996), 1:59–257, for a wonderful evocation of the Irish literary scene in London during these years.

30. For the enthusiast, see *Irish Weekly Independent,* July 21, 1900; for Redmond's promise, *Irish Weekly Independent,* March 10, 1900.

31. For the debates, *Irish Weekly Independent,* January 6, 20, 1900; for the crowds, *Irish Weekly Independent,* November 17, 1900; for the Gaelic League meetings, *Irish Weekly Independent,* February 3, 1900.

32. *Irish Weekly Independent,* May 12, 1900.

33. See Ryan, *Fenian Memories,* 184–85; for Lough's lecture, see *New Ireland,* March 31, 1900.

34. He took an "ardent interest" in the Gaelic Athletic Association, for example, "with the object of securing recruits for the physical force movement." Ryan, *Fenian Memories,* 169.

35. For the Irish National Club, see ibid., 171–201, and *New Ireland,* September 22, 1900.

36. For Fenian principles, Ryan, *Fenian Memories,* 192; for the speech-making, O'Brien Collection, MS 13,456, O'Brien to William O'Brien, November 11, 1899; for Mulcahy, *New Ireland,* March 17, 1900; for Mulcahy's speech, *New Ireland,* March 17, 1900.

37. Ryan, *Fenian Memories,* 169, 192, for example.

38. Public Record Office, H.O.144/1537/3.

39. For example, Robert Kee in *The Bold Fenian Men* (London 1976), who refers to "self-indulgent pseudo heroics," 129.

40. For the number of branches, Lees, *Exiles of Erin,* 236; Thompson, *Socialists, Liberals and Labour,* 26. In changing its name the INLGB was accepting the lead of the newly reunited Irish Parliamentary Party, which on January 18 had elected the Parnellite John Redmond as leader. The branches making reports in the spring of the

year were Tower Hamlets, South Islington, Bermondsey, Battersea, Clapham, Deptford, Southwark, Woolwich, Greenwich, Holborn, Marylebone, Walworth, Walthamstow, and Wapping. For the Hoxton branch, *Irish People*, May 19, 1900, for dues, November 3, 1900, for membership; for Bermondsey, *Irish Weekly Independent*, May 26, 1900.

41. For O'Brien, see his unpublished autobiography, National Library of Ireland, J. F. X. O'Brien Collection, MSS 16,696. For more on Denvir, see his autobiography, *The Life Story of an old Rebel* (Dublin, 1910). For "enemy's country," see J. F. X. O'Brien Collection, MSS 13,429, O'Brien to Thomas Sexton, M.P., June 3, 1901.

42. National Library of Ireland, MS 9576/ACC 2036, Minute Book of Father Purcell Branch of INLGB, London, 1892-95.

43. For Denvir to the Peckham branch, see *Irish People*, April 21, 1900; for the Father Purcell branch, see National Library of Ireland, MS 9576/ACC 2036, both resolutions carried on January 1, 1893.

44. For sorrow at surrender of Cronje, *Irish People*, March 10, 1900; for Davitt upon leaving London for South Africa, see F. Michael Sheehy-Skeffington, *Michael Davitt, Revolutionary Agitator and Labour Leader* (London, 1908), 205.

45. For East Finsbury, *Irish People*, May 26, 1900; for J. F. X. O'Brien in Bermondsey, *Irish People*, November 25, 1899; for Mr. Brogan in Deptford, *Irish Weekly Independent*, March 3, 1900.

46. For the Irish-Indian connection, see Mary Cumpston, "Some Early Indian Nationalists and Their Allies in the British Parliament, 1851-1906," *English Historical Review* 76 (April 1961): 279-97. See also Frank H. O'Donnell, *A History of the Irish Parliamentary Party* (London, 1970), 2:426-40. See also below, chap. 8. For O'Brien, see *Irish People*, June 30, 1900.

47. See John Scurr, *Labour in India* (London, 1920); for Scurr at Bermondsey, *Irish Weekly Independent*, March 3, 1900; for Scurr at Bow and Bromley, *Irish People*, April 28, 1900; for Scurr's talents as a speaker, *Irish People*, February 24, April 28, 1900.

48. For "purer and higher air," *Irish Free Press*, October 6, 1893; for Webb's natural allies in Parliament, see Friends Library, Swanbrook House, Donnybrook, Dublin, Alfred Webb unpublished autobiography, 478-82; for Webb on "oppressed people," Webb, unpublished autobiography, 394.

49. For Webb on people of African decent, *Freeman's Journal*, n.d. Taken from one of three volumes of newspaper clippings devoted to Webb's life and given by his wife to J. F. X. O'Brien after Webb's death, O'Brien Collection, MS 1745; for Webb and Ida B. Wells, unpublished autobiography, 474; for Webb and Henry Sylvester Williams see below, chap. 9.

50. For example, "at the magnificent demonstration of London Irishmen at the Bermondsey Town Hall," *Irish People*, November 25, 1899.

51. For "stupid yokels," *Irish People*, September 30, 1899; for O'Brien, *Irish People*, May 19, 1900; for minimizing the Irish contribution to empire, *New Ireland*, May 12, 1900.

52. *Irish People*, May 19, 1900.

53. For Hoxton, *Irish People*, June 23, 1900; for anti-Dreyfusard sentiments in the *Irish Weekly Independent*, see, for example, December 29, 1900. "The impudent complacency with which Zola assumes the innocence of the ex-Captain of the Artillery shows that the man is not to be reasoned with. . . . And this at a time when the Devil's island prisoner and his treachery were fast sinking into the oblivion of forgetfulness."

54. For anti-Chinese sentiments, *Irish People*, July 21, 1900; for racist sentiments regarding Africans, *Irish People*, July 7, 1900; for pro-Finnish sentiments, *Irish Weekly Independent*, April 14, 1900. Not that the Finns did not deserve their sympathy; the point, however, is that these Irish nationalists did not sympathize with nonwhite victims of imperialism.

55. *Irish People*, May 19, 1900.

56. *New Ireland*, December 15, 1900.

CHAPTER 8. DADABHAI NAOROJI AND THE SEARCH FOR RESPECT

1. But I am guessing about the Indian population in London. C. Kondapi estimated that in 1932 there were 7,128 Indians in Britain in *Indians Overseas, 1838–1949* (New Delhi, 1951), 528. See also Rozina Visram, who endorses this estimate, *Ayahs, Lascars and Princes*, 237. As for those who were politically active: in 1882, according to Mary Cumpston, 250 Indians inaugurated the Indian Constitutional Reform Association at a meeting in Kensington, "Some Early Indian Nationalists," 284. A spy for the India Office reported 150 Indians at a meeting of the London Indian Society on December 28, 1898, British Library, India Office, L/P&J/6/66; but at another meeting of the same organization on May 24, 1901, an India Office spy estimated the audience at between 250 and 300, "including about 50 natives." See India Office, L/P&J/6/570/970. In 1903 an unidentified correspondent of G. K. Gokhale states positively that there were "nearly 90" Indians studying law at Gray's Inn. India Office, Gokhale Collection, IOR POS 11710.

2. R. P. Masani, *Dadabhai Naoroji: The Grand Old Man of India* (London, 1939), introduction by Gandhi, 7. For a useful brief resume of Naoroji's career, see John Hinnells, *Zoroastrians in London* (Oxford, 1996), 156–74.

3. Harish P. Kaushik, *The Indian National Congress in England (1885–1920)* (New Delhi, 1974), 5. For more on the very early Indian nationalist movement in England see Fryer, *Staying Power*, 262–67, and Visram, *Ayahs, Lascars and Princes*, 76–102.

4. See India Office, L/P&J/6/66, for example, for the report of a meeting held by the London Indian Society on December 28, 1898; and also L/P&J/6/570/970 for the report of a meeting held on May 24, 1901, at Westminster Town Hall.

5. For the Irish connection, see Cumpston, "Some Early Indian Nationalists," 279–97. See also O'Donnell, *History of the Irish Parliamentary Party*, 413–45.

6. For Hume, see Sir William Wedderburn, Bart., *Allen Octavian Hume, C.B.* (London, 1913). For Bonnerjee's speech, see Kaushik, *Indian National Congress*, 11.

7. Quoted in B. R. Nanda, *The Moderate Era in Indian Politics* (Delhi, 1983), 11.

8. Quoted in Wedderburn, *Hume*, 86.

9. India Office, William Digby Collection, MSS EUR, D767, Motilal Ghose to William Digby, August 1, 1901.

10. British Library, Lord Ripon Collection, British Museum, Add. Ms. 43618, Wedderburn to Lord Ripon, March 4, 1889.

11. For the BCINC as moderate model, see Nanda, *The Moderate Era;* for the need to connect with British workers, see Visram, *Ayahs, Lascars and Princes*, 81.

12. For the description of Wedderburn, see S. K. Ratcliffe, *Sir William Wedderburn and the Indian Reform Movement* (London, 1923), 96; for Wedderburn in the Humanitarian League, see *New Age*, May 11, 1899. See Hyndman's references to Digby in *The Unrest in India*, verbatim report of a speech delivered at Chandos Hall, Maiden Lane, London, on May 12, 1907. For more on Digby, see the *Dictionary of National Biography*, supplement, 1901–11, 502.

13. India Office, Digby Collection, Ghose to Digby, June 9, 1900; for some of Digby's activities, see Kaushik, *Indian National Congress*, 25.

14. For Caine on "the Bradlaugh-Digby combination," see Digby Collection, Ghose quoting Caine to Digby in a letter of December 6, 1900; for more on Caine, see *Dictionary of National Biography*, supplement, 1901–11, 291.

15. Ratcliffe, *Wedderburn*, 109. For example, in July 1900, Wedderburn organized a breakfast meeting at the Westminster Palace Hotel "to meet Mr. Vaughan Nash, Special Correspondent of the *Manchester Guardian*, on his return from the famine districts of India." Nash's articles had created a sensation in Britain for their vivid depiction of Indian suffering at a time when the government was still reluctant to admit that anything out of the ordinary was going on, and the BCINC was delighted to provide him with an additional forum. Perhaps the "large and distinguished company" Wedderburn managed to bring together on this occasion illustrates a change in emphasis since the Radical Digby's day. Included in the party were three lords, a bishop, twenty-two MPs from the two major parties, including Lloyd George and Leonard Courtney, the entire executive committee of the BCINC, a number of leading Positivists, the publisher T. Fisher Unwin, prominent journalists, and others. See *India*, July 20, 1900.

16. For the number of meetings, see Kaushik, *Indian National Congress*, 35; for Garland, see *India*, September 14, 1900.

17. For meetings with Radical and socialist organizations a few examples just for the year 1900: M. B. Moulavie, a Muslim belonging to the BCINC, spoke on the future of India to the South Place Institute on February 23, Professor Murison, a lawyer and well-known advocate of Indian reforms, delivered an address to the Fabian Society on the same subject precisely a month later, G. P. Pillai, member of the BCINC and editor of the *Madras Standard*, delivered an address on the Indian famine at the Mayall Progressive Club, Brixton, on August 26, Naoroji addressed the Metropolitan Radical Federation on July 21 and the Mildmay Radical Club at Stoke Newington on December 7, and Garland spoke before the National Union of Women Workers on November 6. See *India* for those dates. For meetings in more "respectable" venues, see

India for the same period: Wedderburn addressing the political committee of the National Liberal Club on one occasion and the New Reform Club at St. Ermin's Hotel, Westminster on another, Garland speaking to the Women's Liberal Federation, the Paddington Women's Liberal Association, the distinctly tony Grosvenor Crescent Club, and any number of drawing room meetings, and Naoroji delivering remarks to the London Patriotic Club, the St. John's Literary and Debating Society, and numerous "Garden Meetings" at fashionable addresses. For Stead's query, see India Office, Gokhale Collection, IOR POS 11706, W. T. Stead to Gokhale, January 27, 1902.

18. For a more typical example of English reformers' attitudes, see the discussion of the government's plan to raise from ten to twelve the age at which Indian girls might marry, in Sinha, *Colonial Masculinity*; for Bonnerjee's visit to the House, see Kaushik, *Indian National Congress*, 110.

19. India Office, Digby Collection, Ghose to Digby, December 24, 1902.

20. For Caine on Wedderburn, India Office, Gokhale Collection, IOR POS 11697, Caine to Gokhale, September 30, 1897; for Goodridge on Hume, Wedderburn, and Naoroji, Gokhale Collection, IOR POS 11710, Goodridge to Gokhale, May 18, 1899; for Wood on himself, Gokhale Collection, IOR POS 11709, Wood to Gokhale, September 29, 1905; and for Hume on Digby, India Office, Digby Collection, Ghose to Digby, August 1, 1901.

21. Gokhale Collection, IOR POS 11701, Wedderburn to Wacha, May 6, 1901; for Naoroji's donations, Gokhale Collection, Naoroji to Wedderburn, October 12, 1902; for Wedderburn's, Gokhale Collection, Naoroji to Gokhale, September 27, 1901.

22. *Dadabhai Naoroji Correspondence*, vol. 2, part 1, *Correspondence with D. E. Wacha, 4.11.1884 to 23.3.1895*, R. P. Patwardhan, ed. (New Delhi, 1977), xxxiv; *Dadabhai Naoroji's Speeches and Writings* (Madras, n.d.), speech to Toynbee Hall, "The Condition of India," January 31, 1901; Naoroji speaking before the Metropolitan Radical Federation, *India*, July 21, 1900.

23. Gokhale Collection, IOR POS 11701, Naoroji to Gokhale, July 19, 1894; Gokhale Collection, IOR POS 11701, Romesh Dutt to Gokhale, August 30, 1901.

24. (Naoroji to Undersecretary of State, June 29):—I am thankful to read that for the appointments to be made by the Secretary of State for India "there is nothing to prevent the selection of the Natives of India." Now the . . . [Indian] applicant . . . has . . . to apply through the chief educational officer of the Province. This officer has to forward the application to the Provincial Government who have to send it on to the Government of India, and the Government of India have to send it to the Secretary of State. I wish to know whether the Indian applicant will be allowed time enough to have his application received by the Secretary of State and fully and carefully considered by him.

(Naoroji to Undersecretary of State, July 15):—I am glad to know that Indians desiring to be considered candidates for appointment in the higher Indian Education Service should forward their applications with testimonials and references direct to the Secretary of State for India at the India Office. . . . But I trust that the Secretary of State will be good enough to give some guidance as to the standard or particulars of qualification for which testimonials and references should be furnished by the candidate.

(Naoroji to Undersecretary of State, August 7):—I trust that the Secretary of State will act fairly and impartially in deciding according to merit. [But] the second paragraph of your letter amounts to this. In the Higher Educational Service the Europeans are afforded every advantage of distinction in their own universities in this country, while Indians are altogether denied similar advantages of distinction in their own universities in India, thus indirectly giving almost a monopoly to the Europeans on the basis of race-distinction, and thereby doing a serious injustice to Indians. According to this arrangement any highly distinguished M.A. of an Indian University can have no chance at all for admission, while an inferior graduate of an English University is given the right to be preferred. Can anything be more unjust, and in violation of the most solemn pledges, in the face of acts of Parliament and Proclamations of the Queen?

The entire correspondence is located at the India Office, L/P&J/6/555/2168.

25. For Naoroji at Stoke Newington, *India*, December 7, 1900; *Dadabhai Naoroji's Speeches*, "Speech to Toynbee Hall."

26. For Pillai, *India*, July 20, 1900; for the letter to Gokhale, Gokhale Collection, IOR POS 11710, Ollivant to Gokhale, October 14, 1897.

27. Gokhale Collection, IOR POS 11697, Hume to Gokhale, August 24, 1897; Naoroji to Hyndman, n.d., quoted in Masani, *Dadabhai Naoroji*, 400.

28. For Naoroji, *India*, July 27, 1900; for Gokhale, see *Progress in Women's Education in the British Empire*, being the Report of the Education Section, Victorian Era Exhibition, 1897, ed. the Countess of Warwick (London, 1898), 254; for Caine, see India Office, L/P&J/6/66. This is a nearly verbatim report of a London Indian Society meeting, December 28, 1898, compiled by an India Office official for the secretary of state for India, Lord George Hamilton; and for Gandhi, Maureen Swan, *Gandhi: The South African Experience* (Johannesburg, 1985), 89.

29. *India*, January 5, 1900.

30. For "ignorant Kaffirs," *India*, May 11, 1900; for Mullick, India Office, L/P&J/6/570/970; see also, *India*, June 8, 1900.

31. Dadabhai Naoroji, *The Poverty of India* (London, 1878); Romesh Dutt, *Open Letters to Lord Curzon on Famine in India* (London, 1900).

32. For "capitalists ever stronger," *India*, September 21, 1900; for the subcontinent as a vast market, *India*, July 6, 1900.

33. For Carpenter, *India*, October 26, 1900; for Hyndman, *Justice*, September 15, 1900; for Indian loyalty, *India*, June 1, 1900; and for "true British friends," *India*, May 11, 1900.

34. The *Indian Sociologist, an organ of freedom and of political, social and religious reform*, ed. Shyamaji Krishnavarma, January 1905. This is the first issue of the journal.

35. For "haughty language," Hyndman to Naoroji, March 29, 1900, quoted in Masani, *Dadabhai Naoroji*, 411; for "thick end of wedge," ibid., Hyndman to Naoroji, July 24, 1900, 412.

36. Quoted in ibid., 400–01, but no date given for these letters.

37. Gokhale Collection, IOR POS 11704, Naoroji to Gokhale, July 19, 1894; Gokhale Collection, IOR POS 11704, Naoroji to Gokhale, September 23, 1896.

38. For "discontented group," India Office, L/P&J/6/66, Mahtab Singh speaking at London Indian Society meeting, December 28, 1898; for Dutt, India Office, L/P&J/6/570/970, another nearly verbatim account of a second conference "of all the Indians resident in the United Kingdom [*sic*]" held May 24, 1901, and quoted by the India Office official sent to keep tabs on the meeting, H. J. Tozier; for Dal, India Office, L/P&J/6/570/970; for Naoroji, India Office, L/P&J/6/555/2168, Naoroji to Lord George Hamilton, October 12, 1900.

39. India Office, L/P&J/6/66.

40. For Webb, see above, chap. 7; for Webb and Williams, see Louis Harlan and Raymond Smock, eds., *The Booker T. Washington Papers*, vol. 5, 1899–1900, Henry Sylvester Williams to Booker T. Washington, July 17, 1899, "I heard of you through our friend Mr. Alfred Webb." Also in that year Alison Garland began supplementing her duties for the BCINC by lecturing for the Aborigine's Protection Society, which was then largely, although not exclusively, concerned with African questions. See the *Aborigine's Friend*, August 1900. At the Women's Liberal Federation annual meeting she moved an antislavery resolution. See the *Anti-Slavery Reporter*, March-May, 1899. Finally see Fryer, *Staying Power*, 286.

41. India Office, L/P&J/6/570/970.

CHAPTER 9. ROOTS OF THE PAN-AFRICAN CONFERENCE

1. James Walvin, *Black and White* (London, 1973), 199.

2. Quoted in Herbert Aptheker, ed., *Writings of W. E. B. Du Bois in Non-Periodical Literature* (New York, 1982), 11.

3. See, for example, J. R. Hooker, *Henry Sylvester Williams, Imperial Pan-Africanist* (London 1975), 34–42; Owen Charles Mathurin, *Henry Sylvester Williams and the Origins of the Pan-African Movement, 1869–1911* (Westport, 1976), 55–77; Clarence G. Contee, *Henry Sylvester Williams and the Origins of Organizational Pan-Africanism: 1897–1902* (Washington D.C., 1973); David Levering Lewis, *W. E. B. Du Bois, Biography of a Race, 1868–1919* (New York, 1993), 248–50; Elliot Rudwick, *W. E. B. Du Bois, A Study in Minority Leadership* (Philadelphia, 1960), 208–09; Imanuel Geiss, *The Pan-African Movement*, trans. Ann Keep (London, 1974), 174–98; Ron Ramdin, *The Making of the Black Working Class in Britain* (London, 1987), 50–55; Fryer, *Staying Power*, 280–87; J. Ayodale Langley, *Pan-Africanism and Nationalism in West Africa, 1900–1945: A Study in Ideology and Social Classes* (Oxford, 1973), 29.

4. Stephen Yeo, "A New Life: The Religion of Socialism in Britain, 1883–1896," *History Workshop Journal* 4 (1977): 5–56.

5. *Anti-Caste,* March 1895. All future quotations from this journal are taken from the issues of March and June-July 1895.

6. Ware, *Beyond the Pale,* 173–78.

7. They included Hallie Q. Brown, fundraising for Wilberforce University, G. F. Richings lecturing on "present day negro life in America," D. E. Tobias, a student of the British penal system, the Fisk Jubilee Singers led by Frederick Loudin.

8. For more on the antilynching campaign and the relationship between Impey and Mayo see Ware, *Beyond the Pale,* 170–220. The two women did not remain friends for long, and Impey quit the society, though remaining on good terms with Ida Wells. When Edwards died prematurely on July 25, 1894, Impey briefly resumed publication of *Anti-Caste.*

9. *Lux,* November 3, 1894.

10. *Lux,* September 29, 1894. These and other biographical details come from a series of articles written by R. V. Allen, September 15, 1894, January 4, 1895.

11. For Tillett, see Schneer, *Ben Tillett.* I have noticed that Moses Da Rocha, a frequent letter writer to the *New Age,* was a student at the Edinburgh University medical school; also John Alcindor, who later practiced as a physician in London, see Jeffrey P. Green, "West Indian Doctors in London: John Alcindor (1873–1924) and James Jackson Brown (1882–1953)," *Journal of Caribbean History* 20 (1985–86): 49–77; also "a young West African now studying medicine in Scotland," almost certainly not Da Rocha, who always identified himself, *New Age,* January 20, 1898.

12. The friend was R. Allen, *Lux,* November 10, 1894; for Edwards's conversation, *Lux,* August 25, 1894; for the lecture, Edwards, *Political Atheism: A Lecture by S. J. Celestine Edwards, delivered on February 12th, 1889, to 1,200 people;* for additional sterling qualities, *Lux,* December 8, 1894 and April 27, 1895.

13. *Lux,* October 27, 1894.

14. *Lux,* November 24, 1894.

15. *Lux,* December 29, 1894.

16. *Lux,* November 17, 1894.

17. For Edwards and Mr. Atheist, *Lux,* December 8, 1894; *Lux,* December 15, 1894.

18. For Edwards in Bishop's Waltham, *Lux,* August 25, 1894; for packed halls, *Lux,* May 13, 1893.

19. For Edwards on *Anti-Caste,* see *Fraternity,* July 1893; for Edwards on "scientific racism," *Lux,* December 10, 1892; for Edwards on Knox and Baker, *Lux,* February 18, 1893; and finally, *Lux,* August 27, 1892.

20. *Lux,* January 6, 1894.

21. For Edwards on the need for faith, see his pamphlet *Political Atheism;* for his impatience with the church, *Lux,* December 10, 1892. Socialists who left the church, at least temporarily, include Tillett, who at one point had been a lay preacher, George Lansbury, though he later returned to Anglicanism with a vengeance, and Tom Mann, who at one point hoped to train as an Anglican minister, although he eventually joined

the Communist Party. For his tolerance, see his lecture *Does God Answer Prayer?* praising "the Mohammedan, as you call him," and so-called primitive peoples who "in the absence of priests, in the absence of rites, in the absence of sacrifice, in the absence of holy shrines . . . perform acts that cannot be called by any other name than Prayer."

22. *Lux*, August 20, 1892.

23. *Lux*, January 12, 1895.

24. *Lux*, August 25, 1894.

25. *Lux*, May 19, 1894, March 10, 1894.

26. *Lux*, January 12, 1895.

27. This small circle included but was not limited to the composer Samuel Coleridge-Taylor, the physician John Alcindor, the African-American law student D. E. Tobias, the medical student John Archer, Celestine's mentor in Antigua, the Rev. Henry Mason Joseph, and of course Henry Sylvester Williams. For Coleridge-Taylor, see Avril G. Coleridge-Taylor, *The Heritage of Samuel Coleridge-Taylor* (London, 1979); for Alcindor, see Jeffrey Green, "West Indian Doctors in London"; for Williams, see Hooker, *Henry Sylvester Williams*, and Mathurin, *Henry Sylvester Williams*. There are no biographies of John Archer, although as a local Labour Party activist he later represented Battersea on the London County Council, or of Rev. Henry Mason Joseph.

28. For some details of Williams's early life, including the possible cloud, note the dinner in his honor in Port of Spain, Trinidad, in 1901, when one of his former teachers said, "We observed many years ago that he was a young man full of vigour, full of life, and determined by some means or other to make a way for himself. Circumstances perhaps over which he had no control took him away from his native home." *Port of Spain Mirror*, July 8, 1901; for his arrival in England, Rhodes House, Anti-Slavery Papers, MSS. BritEmp.S18, C91/11, Dr. Greville Walpole, MA, LLD, Chairman, National Thrift Society, to Travers Buxton, Secretary, British and Foreign Anti-Slavery Society, May 13, 1902: "Mr. H. Sylvester Williams . . . came to England in 1896"; for Williams's law studies, see Contee, *Henry Sylvester Williams*, 7.

29. Anti-Slavery Papers, C91/11.

30. But Contee refers to R. J. Colenso as Francis Ernest Colenso.

31. *Port of Spain Gazette*, June 2, 1901.

32. Ibid.

33. For Williams's determination, ibid.; for the first gathering, see Geiss, *Pan-African Movement*, 174; Geiss cites the Record of Proceedings of the Pan-African Conference as his source; for the group's aims, *Aborigine's Friend*, November 1897; for the ratification, Geiss, *Pan-African Movement*, 147. Mrs. Kinloch returned to South Africa, however, in February 1898, see *Aborigine's Friend*, March 1898.

34. For mention of the sixteen meetings, *Aborigine's Friend*, March 1898; for the forty-seven members, *Lagos Standard*, February 8, 1899.

35. In contrast to the argument of Fryer, *Staying Power*, who sees Edwards as their main progenitor, 278.

36. *New Age*, January 20, 1898.

37. The historian can trace these changes of address through Williams's corre-

spondence with the British and Foreign Anti-Slavery Society, Rhodes House, MSS. BritEmp. S18; see, too, Geiss, *Pan-African Movement*, 194.

38. For Williams's lectures, see Contee, *Henry Sylvester Williams*, 9, and the *Lagos Standard*, February 8, 1899.

39. *The Memorial of the African Association on the Distress in the West Indies*, March 30, 1898.

40. *Lagos Standard*, December 28, 1898.

41. *Port of Spain Gazette*, April 6, 1899.

42. For the speech in Ipswich, *Port of Spain Mirror*, January 8, 1902; for speech at the South Place Institute, Henry Sylvester Williams, *The British Negro: A Factor in the Empire* (London, 1902), 13.

43. For education and culture, Williams, *The British Negro*, 14; for "the enlightenment of the so-called Negro and Negroid races," see again Williams, *The British Negro*, 10 (evidently Williams delivered this speech to more than one audience); *The Ethiopian Eunich* is printed in the volume entitled *The British Negro*. The quotation is from page 28.

44. For Williams in Trinidad, *Port of Spain Gazette*, June 2, 1901; then see *Port of Spain Mirror*, January 8, 1902.

45. *Port of Spain Gazette*, June 2, 1901.

46. For "un-British," *Port of Spain Gazette*, June 2, 1901; for volunteering, *Port of Spain Mirror*, January 8, 1902.

47. Williams, *The British Negro*, 15, 26.

48. *Westminster Gazette*, July 26, 1900.

49. Harlan and Smock, *Booker T. Washington Papers*, 155.

50. Rhodes House, British and Foreign Anti-Slavery Society Papers, MSS. BritEmp. S18, C91/7 and C91/8, Williams to Buxton, May 31, 1900, and August 30, 1900.

51. For the letter of reply, Rhodes House, British and Foreign Anti-Slavery Society Papers, MSS. BritEmp. S18, C153/40 Williams to Fox Bourne, November 11, 1899; Harlan and Smock, *Booker T. Washington Papers*, 570, Williams to Washington, June 29, 1900.

52. For "our own talent," see Contee, *Henry Sylvester Williams*, 13; for "no other but a Negro," *Pan-African*, October 1901.

53. For the attendees, Geiss, *Pan-African Movement*, 182–83; for the journalist, *Westminster Gazette*, July 24, 1900.

54. For Creighton, French, and Sylvain, *Times*, July 24, 1900.

55. Aptheker, *Writings of W. E. B. Du Bois*, 11.

56. *Justice*, July 28, 1900.

57. *Lagos Standard*, October 17, 1900.

58. "Far from the [Pan-African Association] being defunct as our detractors would like our friends to believe, we are getting on quietly and have enlisted the sympathy of the leaders of the Liberal Party in the great cause. E. Lazare, Vice Pres., P.A.A." *Port of Spain Mirror*, September 4, 1902.

59. *Marylebone and West London Gazette*, October 6, 1906. See also the *Marylebone Times*, November 2, 1906.

60. Quoted in Aptheker, *Writings of W. E. B. Du Bois*, 11.

CHAPTER 10. THE KHAKI ELECTION OF 1900

1. The *Conservative Election Manifesto* called for a mandate to "rebuil[d] upon durable foundations ... the Imperial Power over the territories of the two South African Republics," and for endorsement of its imperialist activities generally. See the *Conservative Manifesto*, written by the prime minister, the marquess of Salisbury, *British General Election Manifestos 1900–1974*, F. W. S. Craig, ed. (London, 1975), 2–3. Conservative election leaflets listed the government's imperialist accomplishments in China, Burma, India, Egypt, Khartoum, Ashanti, Benin, Rhodesia, and South Africa. See also Bodleian Library, John Johnson Collection, "Creeds, Parties, Policies," Box 6, which contains Conservative election leaflets for 1900, "Foreign Series," "Lord Salisbury's Foreign Policy," a selection of titles includes the following: "South Africa: How the Gentle Boers Treat the Unarmed British Refugee," "The Evils of Boer Government, How the Gentle Boers Treat the Natives Under It," "The Gentle Boer and His Brutal [expanding Mauser] Bullet," "Why this War?" "The South African Question, Opinions of Ministers of Religion." See, too, John Johnson Collection, "South African War," Box 5, "Transvaal Series" of Conservative Party leaflets, 1900. For attacks on Liberals, the following is typical: "Electors!! Will you be represented in Parliament by Radicals who take the Enemy's side? If not, vote for the Unionist candidate and be true to your country." Bodleian Library, John Johnson Collection, Box 5, "South African War," "Transvaal Series." According to Liberal imperialists, on the other hand, British interests had been "gratuitously sacrificed" in India, Siam, Tunis, and Madagascar. Craig, *General Election Manifestos*, 4–6. For the following election results, see Elizabeth York Enstam, "The 'Khaki' Election of 1900 in the United Kingdom" (Ph.D. diss., Duke University, 1967), iii:

	1895	1900
Liberals	189	182
Irish	83	83
ILP	3	—
Conservatives & Liberal Unionists	402	399

2. For Stead, *Review of Reviews* 22 (October): 329; for Kyd, *Westminster Gazette*, October 4, 1900; for Evans-Gordon, *East London Observer*, October 9, 1900; for Gray, *West Ham Guardian*, September 26, 1900.

3. For Lansbury, *Justice*, September 29, 1900, and Jonathan Schneer, *George Lansbury* (Manchester, 1990), 204; for Hay, *Hackney Express and Shoreditch Observer*, September 29, 1900; for Steadman, *East London Advertiser*, September 29, 1900.

4. The number of registered voters was 702,114. According to Renwick Seager, head of staff at the offices of the London Liberal and Radical Union, however, up to

20 per cent of the London electorate had been disenfranchised by the failure to compile an up-to-date register. *East London Observer,* September 25, 1900. See also New Bodleian Library, Archives of the British Conservative Party, Harvester Microfilm, Series One, Pamphlets and Leaflets, Part I, Card 86, "National Union Gleanings"; also Enstam, *The 'Khaki Election,'* 149.

5. *Southwark and Bermondsey Recorder,* September 29, 1900.

6. For the poster, *City Press,* September 26, 1900; for the election address, *Southwark and Bermondsey Recorder,* September 22, 1900.

7. See, for example, the *City Press* for September 26 and September 29, 1900.

8. For "home life of the people," *Southwark and Bermondsey Recorder,* July 14, 1900; for social reforms, *Southwark and Bermondsey Recorder,* September 29, 1900; for "methods," *Times,* September 25, 1900.

9. Mrs. Newton quoted in the *Labour Leader,* October 13, 1900; for the episode in the pub, *City Press,* September 26, 1900; for the fight, *Southwark and Bermondsey Recorder,* October 6, 1900.

10. For the meeting with Irishmen, *Irish People,* September 29, 1900; *India,* September 28, 1900, both for commentary and for Hamilton's election address.

11. Lord George Hamilton, *Parliamentary Reminiscences and Reflections, 1886–1906* (London, 1922), 2:279; *Acton and Chiswick Gazette,* September 14, 1900.

12. Lord George Hamilton, *Parliamentary Reminiscences,* 260.

13. For the speech on behalf of Sir Samuel Scott, see *Daily Telegraph,* September 30, 1900; for the disrupted meeting, see *Middlesex and Surrey Express,* October 6, 1900.

14. *Acton and Chiswick Gazette,* November 2, 1900.

15. Williams was in correspondence with Travers Buxton of the Anti-Slavery Society during the period of the campaign, conveying thanks for the financial assistance the society had rendered the Pan-African Conference. See, for example, Rhodes House, Anti-Slavery Papers, MSS. BritEmp.S18, C91/9, Williams to Buxton, October 10, 1900; for Garland's speeches, see *India,* October 12, 1900.

16. For questions put to Bethell, see *West Ham Guardian,* September 26, 1900; for the UIL during the election, see the *Irish People,* September 29, October 6, 1900, and *Times,* September 26, 1900.

17. For Bethell and Gray, *West Ham Guardian,* September 22, 1900; for Calver, *West Ham Guardian,* September 26, 1900; for Lansbury, *Justice,* September 29, 1900.

18. For overcrowding, *East London Advertiser,* September 29, 1900; for Gray, *East London Advertiser,* September 29, 1900; for Thorne, *East London Advertiser,* September 22, 1900; for Kyd, *Daily Telegraph,* September 22, 1900, and for his campaign more generally, British Library of Political and Economic Science (BLPES), Clapham Conservative Party Collection, volume of news clippings.

19. See Bernard Gainer, *The Alien Invasion* (London, 1972), 67–68.

20. For "Oriental tyrant," *Morning Leader,* October 2, 1900, quoted in *India,* October 5, 1900, and for "East End of Empire," *Morning Chronicle,* October 2, 1900, also quoted in *India,* October 5, 1900.

21. Guildhall Library, Antony Gibbs and Sons Collection, Ms.11039, Gibbs to "the Secretary, Midland Railway Co.," August 31, 1900.

22. For Gibbs's confession, *City Press*, September 1, 1900; for his encomium to the lord mayor, *Daily Telegraph*, September 30, 1900.

23. For choosing Dimsdale, see *Financial Times*, October 1, 1900; for Dimsdale's self-description, *City Press*, September 26, 1900; finally see *City Press*, October 3, 1900.

24. *City Press*, September 29, 1900.

25. John Hinnells and Omar Ralph, *Bhownaggree* (London, 1995), and Hinnells, *Zoroastrians in Britain*, 174-93, from which all biographical details are taken.

26. Quoted in Hinnells and Ralph, *Bhownaggree*, 13.

27. For anti-Conservative, or anyway anti-Bhownaggree, sentiment in India, see *The Indian Political Estimate of Mr. Bhavnagri, M.P., or the Bhavnagri Boom Exposed* (Bombay, 1897). The author chose anonymity but was probably Dinshaw Wacha of the INC; for Howell, see F. M. Leventhal, *Respectable Radical: George Howell and Victorian Working Class Politics* (Cambridge, Mass., 1971), 212.

28. *India*, October 12, 1900; in a letter of January 16, 1897, to Dadabhai Naoroji, quoted in Hinnells, *Zoroastrians in Britain*, 175; India Office, Gokhale Collection, IOR POS 11707, Naoroji to Wacha, October 8, 1896.

29. Hinnells, *Zoroastrians in Britain*, 183.

30. *East London Observer*, September 29, 1900.

31. *Daily Graphic*, October 3, 1900.

32. For the knight commandership, *Eastern Argus and Hackney Times*, September 1, 1900; for Lawson's modesty, *Eastern Argus and Hackney Times*, May 5, 1900.

33. For Bhownaggree's importance, *Eastern Argus and Hackney Times*, June 12, 1900; *Daily Graphic*, October 3, 1900.

34. *Eastern Argus and Hackney Times*, August 21, 1900.

35. *Eastern Argus and Hackney Times*, July 7, 1900; *East London Observer*, August 4, 1900; *Eastern Argus and Hackney Times*, May 5, 1900.

36. *Eastern Argus and Hackney Times*, July 7, 1900.

37. *Eastern Argus and Hackney Times*, September 22, 1900.

38. *East London Observer*, September 29, 1900.

39. Did Bhownaggree mean "One with Briton" or "One with Britain"? Either way the sense of identification is revealing.

40. House of Lords Records Office, St. Loe Strachey Papers, S/3/3/3, Burns to Strachey, July 12, 1900. For biographies, see Kenneth Brown, *John Burns* (London, 1977), William Kent, *John Burns: Labour's Lost Leader* (London, 1950), and Grubb, *Life Story of John Burns*. Burns eventually became a tame Liberal cabinet minister, to the despair of his former comrades. He resigned from Asquith's government when it declared war on Germany in 1914.

41. For the physical description, Grubb, *Life Story of John Burns*, 167; for the indictment of Salisbury's administration, John Burns's election address, *Westminster Gazette*, September 25, 1900.

42. For Garton's background, BLPES, Coll. Misc. 246, Electioneering Matter,

1892–1924, John Burns, election leaflet produced on Burns's behalf by four local churchmen and three local teetotalers, also *Times*, September 26, 1900; for "strength of Empire," *Southwestern Star*, March 2, 1900; for Garton on Burns, *Southwestern Star*, February 23, 1900; for "municipal questions," *Southwestern Star*, August 24, 1900.

43. For Burns's promise and list of achievements, BLPES, Coll Misc. 246, Electioneering Matter, 1892–1924, John Burns, *Battersea Labour Gazette*, September 29, 1900. This "Organ of the Trades and Labour Progressive Movement" appears to have been published only during the general election campaign of 1900; for Garton's riposte, *Daily Telegraph*, September 26, 1900.

44. For "khaki Britain," see Kent, *John Burns*, 102; for Burns on Chamberlain and Rhodes, *Southwestern Star*, September 14, 1900; for "respect their freedom," *Southwestern Star*, July 13, 1900.

45. For "forcing our ideas," *Southwestern Star*, September 28, 1900; for admiring soldiers, see British Library, John Burns Collection, Add. MSS. 46317, diary entry for February 2, 1900, and January 17, 1900: "Regent's Park . . . saw Scots Guards, a fine lot of men."

46. *Southwestern Star*, July 13, 1900.

47. We know Burns was acquainted with Hobson because on January 25, 1900, he recorded in his diary, "Had a long chat with Hobson on general position and the imperialism of the day;" for more on his views of the war, see *Westminster Gazette*, September 22, September 25, 1900.

48. *Southwestern Star*, June 15, 1900.

49. *Southwestern Star*, September 14, 1900.

50. *Southwestern Star*, September 28, 1900.

51. See also the *Daily Mail*, September 25, 1900.

52. For the "fighting volunteer," Burns Collection, Add MSS. 46297, f. 284, Arthur Fields to John Burns, February 14, 1900; for "macadamised roads," *Daily Mail*, October 1, 1900.

53. *Westminster Gazette*, September 28, 1900.

54. For Garton the spokesman, *Daily Mail*, September 24, 1900; for Garton's employees, *Times*, September 28, 1900.

55. See *Daily Mail*, *Westminster Gazette*, and *Southwestern Star*, October 2, 3, 1900, from which all quotations describing polling day in Battersea are taken.

56. For "the long-nosed Jew," *Southwestern Star*, July 20, 1900; for "Ikey Mo," *Southwestern Star*, June 15, 1900; for "rich Jews," *Westminster Gazette*, September 25, 1900.

57. *Southwestern Star*, July 20, 1900.

58. *Justice*, November 3, 1900; *Positivist Review*, November 1900.

59. *West Ham Guardian*, October 1, 1900.

60. For trade unionists endorsing candidates, in South-West Ham, Gasworkers for Thorne, Railwaymen for Bethell; in Whitechapel, Costermongers' and Street Sellers' Union for Samuel, *Daily News*, October 1, 1900; in Hoxton, according to the *Hackney Express and Shoreditch Observer* of September 29, 1900, the Printers' Machine

Minders' Society, the Ivory and Wood Turners' Society, the Bookbinders' Society, and the Engineers among others supported the Radical, Professor James Stuart; for Thorne, *West Ham Guardian*, September 29, 1900; for Tillett, see Schneer, *Ben Tillett*, 113–14 (throughout his career Tillett would summon reserves of nervous energy to face a crisis like the dock strike earlier in the summer and, once the crisis had passed, suffer a nervous collapse); *Daily Telegraph*, September 30, 1900; for Tom Mann, *Irish Weekly Independent*, May 12, 1900.

61. For Protestant Layman's Association, *Eastern Argus and Hackney Times*, September 28, 1900; for ministers opposed to Thorne, *West Ham Guardian*, October 3, 1900, and *Stratford Express*, September 26, 1900; for Samuel, *Daily Telegraph*, September 22, 1900.

62. *East London Observer*, October 13, 1900.

63. *West Ham Guardian*, September 26, October 1, 1900.

64. *Positivist Review*, November 1900, 195.

65. For anti-Conservative rowdies in Bethnal Green, *East London Observer*, October 2, 1900, in Bermondsey, *Times*, October 3, 1900, in addition to Battersea, Southwark, and Marylebone; the most infamous of the jingo disruptions in London occurred not during the general election but in February, when a meeting in Mile End descended into a free fight, *Justice*, February 17, 1900; for Thorne's questioner, *West Ham Guardian*, September 29, 1900; for Bethell's, *West Ham Guardian*, September 29, 1900; for Burns, Grubb, *Life Story of John Burns*, 169.

BIBLIOGRAPHY

COLLECTIONS

UNIVERSITY OF BIRMINGHAM

Joseph Chamberlain Collection

BODLEIAN LIBRARY, OXFORD UNIVERSITY

Archives of the British Conservative
  Party (microfilm)
John Johnson Collection
Gilbert Murray Collection

BRITISH LIBRARY

Balfour Papers
John Burns Papers
Campbell-Bannerman Papers
Carnarvon Papers
Thomas Hay Sweet Escott Papers
Montagu Guest Papers
Lord Ripon Collection

BRITISH LIBRARY OF POLITICAL AND ECONOMIC SCIENCE

Electioneering Matter, 1892–1924
Clapham Conservative Party Collection
London Positivist Society Collection

CITY OF WESTMINSTER ARCHIVES CENTRE

City of London Conservative Associa-
  tion
St. George's Conservative Association
Strand Conservative Association

DOCKLANDS MUSEUM

East and West India Dock Company
  Papers
London and India Docks Joint Commit-
  tee Papers

FRIENDS LIBRARY, SWANBROOK HOUSE, DONNYBROOK, DUBLIN

Unpublished autobiography of Alfred
  Webb

GUILDHALL LIBRARY

Ashanti Goldfields Corporation Ltd.
  Collection
Reginald Archer Bennett Papers
Henry Ross Boot Papers
Dodwell Company Limited Papers

City Imperial Volunteers Collection
Empire of India & Ceylon Tea Company Limited Papers
Antony Gibbs and Sons Collection
Charles Hammond & Sons, Stockbrokers, Collection
Stock Exchange Collection

HOUSE OF LORDS RECORDS OFFICE

St. Loe Strachey Papers

INDIA OFFICE (BRITISH LIBRARY)

William Digby Collection
Gokhale Collection
Files on London Indian Society
Files on Dadabhai Naoroji

MODERN RECORDS CENTRE (UNIVERSITY OF WARWICK)

Ben Tillett Collection
Transport and General Workers Union Collection

NATIONAL LABOUR HISTORY MUSEUM (MANCHESTER)

Amalgamated Stevedores Labour Protection League Collection

NATIONAL LIBRARY OF IRELAND

Alfred Webb Collection
J. F. X. O'Brien Collection
Irish National League Collection

Father Purcell Branch
Misc. Pamphlets

NEWS INTERNATIONAL ASSOCIATED SERVICES LTD (ARCHIVE OF THE *Times*)

Flora Shaw Collection

NORTHERN IRELAND PUBLIC RECORD OFFICE, BELFAST

Papers of Theresa Susey Helen Vane-Tempest-Stewart (1858–1919), wife of 6th Marquess of Londonderry

PUBLIC RECORD OFFICE

Colonial Office files
Home Office files
Metropolitan Police Office files

REGENT'S PARK ZOO LIBRARY AND ARCHIVE

Volumes of Newspaper Clippings
Daily Occurrences Book
Council Minutes

RHODES HOUSE LIBRARY, OXFORD UNIVERSITY

Aborigine's Protection Society Papers
Anti-Slavery Society Papers
Cecil Rhodes Collection
John Holt and Company Ltd. Collection
Lugard Papers
Overseas Nursing Association Papers
Pamphlets on the History of the Transvaal
Margery Perham Collection (of Lugard Papers)
W. T. Stead Correspondence (microfilm)

ROYAL GEOGRAPHICAL SOCIETY

Mary Kingsley Letters
Minute Book of General Council

ZOROASTRIAN HOUSE (WEST
HAMPSTEAD, LONDON)

Papers relating to Sir Mancherjee
Bhownaggree

DAILY AND WEEKLY NEWSPAPERS

Acton and Chiswick Gazette
Acton Express
Architect and Contract Reporter
Battersea Beacon
Builder
Building News
City Press
Clapham District Gazette
Contemporary Review
Daily Graphic
Daily Mail
Daily News
Daily Telegraph
Dramatic World
*East End News and London Shipping
  Chronicle*
East London Advertiser
East London Observer
Eastern Argus and Hackney Times
Financial News
Financial Times
Hackney Express and Shoreditch Observer
India
Irish People
Irish Weekly Independent
John Bull

Justice
Labour Leader
Lagos Standard
Lambeth Times
Lux
Marylebone Times
Marylebone and West London Gazette
Middlesex and Surrey Express
Mirror (Port of Spain, Trinidad)
Music Hall and Theatre Review
New Age
New Ireland
Pall Mall Gazette
Port of Spain Gazette
Queen, the Lady's Newspaper
Review of Reviews
Southwark Recorder
Southwestern Star
Star
Stratford Express
The Times
West Ham Citizen
West Ham Guardian
Westminster Gazette
Westminster Review

JOURNALS

Aborigine's Friend
Anti-Caste
Anti-Slavery Reporter
Architectural Review
Banker's Journal
Banker's Magazine
British Empire Review

Economist
Empire Review
Fraternity
Fortnightly Review
Geographical Journal
*Half-Yearly Magazine of the Gaelic
  League of London*

Humane Review
Imperial and Colonial Magazine
Imperial Institute Journal
Indian Sociologist
Journal of the Royal Colonial Institute
Journal of the Royal Institute of British
    Architecture
Land and Labour
Pan-African
Positivist

Positivist Review
Quarterly Review (City of London Bible
    Class Union)
Royal Geographical Society's Yearbook
    and Record
Saturday Review
Social Democrat
Spectator
Women in the Mission Field

Aborigine's Protection Society. *Annual Reports* 1895–1905.
———. *Native Labour in South Africa.* London, 1903.
Adler, Rev. Dr., Chief Rabbi. *The Queen and the War.* London, 1900.
Aflalo, F. G. *A Walk through the Zoological Gardens.* London, 1900.
African Association. *The Memorial of the African Association on the Distress in the West Indies.* London, 1898.
Alderman, Geoffrey. *Modern British Jewry.* Oxford, 1992.
Altick, Richard. *The Shows of London.* Cambridge, Mass., 1978.
Anonymous. *A Day at the Zoo.* London, n.d.
———. *Comic Guide to the Zoo.* London, 1907.
———. *Dadabhai's Speeches and Writings.* Madras, n.d.
———. *My Book of the Zoo.* London, 1905.
Aptheker, Herbert, ed. *Writings by W. E. B. DuBois in Non-Periodical Literature Edited by Others.* New York, 1982.
Bailey, Peter, ed. *Music Hall: The Business of Pleasure.* Milton Keynes, 1986.
———. *Leisure and Class in Victorian England.* London, 1978.
Banton, Michael. *The Coloured Quarter.* London, 1955.
Baring-Gould, William S., ed. *The Annotated Sherlock Holmes.* New York, 1992.
Bartlett, A. D., and Edward Bartlett, eds. *Wild Animals in Captivity.* London, 1899.
Bartlett, M.P., Sir E. Ashmead. *British Natives and Boers in the Transvaal.* London, 1894.
Barty-King, Hugh. *The Baltic Exchange: The History of a Unique Market.* London, 1977.
Beattie, Susan. *The New Sculpture.* New Haven, 1983.
Beavan, Arthur. *Imperial London.* London, 1900.
Beckson, Karl. *London in the 1890s, A Cultural History.* New York, 1992.
Belcher, John, and Mervyn Macartney. *Later Renaissance Architecture in England.* London, 1901.
Bell, E. Moberly. *Flora Shaw.* London, 1947.
Benjamin, H. W. "The London Irish: A Study in Political Activism, 1870–1910." Princeton University, 1976.

Berwick Sayer, W. C. *Samuel Coleridge-Taylor, Musician, His Life and Letters.* London, 1927.

Birkett, Deborah. *Spinsters Abroad.* Oxford, 1989.

———. *Mary Kingsley (1862–1900), A Biographical Bibliography.* Bristol, 1993.

———. *Mary Kingsley, Imperial Adventuress.* Worcester, 1992.

Bishop, James, and Oliver Woods. *The Story of The Times.* London, 1983.

Black, Eugene. *The Social Politics of Anglo-Jewry.* Oxford, 1988.

Blackham, H. J. *Stanton Coit, 1857–1944.* London, 1949.

Blomfield, Sir Reginald. *Richard Norman Shaw, R.A.* London, 1940.

Blunt, Alison. *Travel, Gender and Imperialism: Mary Kingsley and West Africa.* London, 1994.

Blunt, Wilfrid. *The Ark in the Park.* London, 1976.

Blyden, Edward W. *The African Society and Miss Mary H. Kinsgley.* London, 1901.

Bolt, Christine. *Victorian Attitudes to Race.* London, 1971.

Boulenger, E. G. *Zoo Cavalcade.* London, 1933.

Boxall, Col. C. G. *Report on the Raising, Organising, Equipping and Despatching of the City of London Imperial Volunteers to South Africa.* London, 1900.

Bratton, J. S., ed. *Music Hall: Performance and Style.* Milton Keynes, 1986.

———. *Acts of Supremacy: The British Empire and the Stage, 1790–1930.* Manchester, 1991.

Briggs, Asa. *Victorian Cities.* London, 1963.

Brightwell, L.R. *The Zoo Story.* London, 1952.

Bristow, Joseph. *Empire Boys: Adventures in a Man's World.* London, 1991.

British Sessional Papers. 1888, vol. 21, *Minutes of Evidence taken before the Royal Commission on Sweated Industries;* 1892, vol. 35, *Minutes of Evidence taken before the Royal Commission on Labour.*

Brown, Antony. *Hazard Unlimited: The Story of Lloyd's of London.* London, 1973.

———. *Cuthbert Heath, Maker of the Modern Lloyd's of London.* London, 1980.

Brown, John. *The Colonial Missions of Congregationalism.* London, 1908.

Brown, Kenneth. *John Burns.* London, 1977.

Burke, Thomas. *London in My Time.* London, 1934.

Burnell, Arthur Coke, and Col. Henry Yule. *A Glossary of Anglo-Indian Colloquial Words and Phrases and of Kindred Terms.* London, 1886.

Burns, John. *Labour's Death Roll, the Tragedy of Toil.* Clarion Pamphlet No. 29, 1899.

———. *The Straight Tip to Workers: Brains Better than Bets or Beer.* Clarion Pamphlet No. 36, 1902.

Burton, Antoinette. *Burdens of History: British Feminists, Indian Women, and Imperial Culture, 1865–1959.* Chapel Hill, 1995.

———. "A Pilgrim Reformer at the Heart of the Empire, Behramji Malabari in Late-Victorian London." *Gender and History* 8, no. 2 (August 1996).

Bush, Julia. "'The Right Sort of Woman': Female Emigrators and Emigration to the British Empire, 1890–1910." *Women's History Review* 3, no. 3 (1994).

Caine, Peter, and Anthony Hopkins. *British Imperialism: Innovation and Expansion.* Volume 1. London, 1993.

Cannadine, David, and David Reeder, eds. *Exploring the Urban Past: Essays in Urban History.* Cambridge, 1982.

Cassis, Youssef. "The Banking Community of London, 1890–1914: A Survey." *Journal of Imperial and Commonwealth History* 12, no. 3 (May 1985).

———. *City Bankers, 1890–1914.* Cambridge, 1994.

Centre of African Studies, University of Edinburgh. *The Theory of Imperialism and the European Partition of Africa.* Edinburgh, 1967.

Centre for Contemporary Cultural Studies, University of Birmingham. *The Empire Strikes Back.* London, 1982.

Centre for Urban Studies, University of London. *London, Aspects of Change.* London, 1964.

Chapman, S. D. *The Rise of Merchant Banking.* London, 1984.

Chauduri, Nupu, and Margaret Strobel, eds., *Western Women and Imperialism: Complicity and Resistance.* Bloomington, 1992.

Choo, Ng Kwee. *The Chinese in London.* London, 1968.

City Liberal Club Rules and Regulations and List of Members. London, 1900.

City of London Directory. 1900.

The C.I.V., Being the Story of the City Imperial Volunteers and Volunteer Regiments of the City of London, 1300–1900. London, 1900.

Clunn, Harold. *The Face of London.* London, 1932.

Cockerill, Hugh. *Lloyd's of London, A Portrait.* Cambridge, 1984.

Coleridge-Taylor, Avril. *The Heritage of Samuel Coleridge-Taylor.* London, 1979.

Collison, William. *The Apostle of Free Labour.* London, 1913.

Colls, Robert, and Philip Dodd. *Englishness, Politics and Culture.* London, 1986.

Contee, Clarence. *Henry Sylvester Williams and the Origins of Organizational Pan-Africanism: 1897–1902.* Washington, D.C., 1973.

Coombes, Annie. *Reinventing Africa: Museums, Material Culture, and Popular Imagination in Late Victorian and Edwardian England.* New Haven, 1994.

De Courcy, Anne. *Circe, the Life of Edith Marchioness of Londonderry.* London, 1992.

Craig, F. W. S., ed. *British General Election Manifestos 1900–1974.* London, 1975.

Crawford, David. *The City of London, Its Architectural Heritage.* Cambridge, 1976.

Cronin, Sean. *Irish Nationalism, A History of its Roots and Ideology.* Dublin, 1980.

Cumpston, Mary. "Some Early Indian Nationalists and their Allies in the British Parliament, 1851–1906" *English Historical Review* 76 (1961).

Darby, H. C., ed. *A New Historical Geography of England.* Cambridge, 1973.

Daunton, M. J. "'Gentlemanly Capitalism' and British Industry 1820–1914." *Past and Present,* no. 122 (February 1989).

———. "Debate: 'Gentlemanly Capitalism' and British Industry 1820–1914, Reply [to William D. Rubinstein]." *Past and Present,* no. 132 (August 1991).

———. "Firm and Family in the City of London in the Nineteenth Century, the Case of F. G. Dalgety." *Bulletin of the Institute of Historical Research* 62 (1989).

Davis, John. *Reforming London: The London Government Problem, 1885–1900*. Oxford, 1988.

———. "Modern London, 1850–1930." *London Journal* 20, no. 2 (1995).

Davis, Lance, and Robert Huttenback. *Mammon and the Pursuit of Empire: The Political Economy of British Imperialism*. Cambridge, 1986.

Davitt, Michael. *The Boer Fight for Freedom*. London, 1902.

Dawson, Graham. *Soldier Heroes, British Adventure, Empire and the Imagining of Masculinities*. London, 1994.

Denvir, John. *The Life Story of an Old Rebel*. Dublin, 1910.

Dictionary of South African Biography, 1977.

Digby, William. *Prosperous British India*. London, 1901.

Dilke, Sir Charles. *The British Empire*. London, 1899.

Dorn, Robert. *Irish Nationalism and British Imperialism*. Dublin, n.d.

Driver, Felix. "Stanley and His Critics: Geography, Exploration and Empire." *Past and Present*, no. 133 (November 1991).

———. "Geography, Empire and Visualisation: Making Representations." Royal Holloway College, University of London, Department of Geography, Research Papers No. 1, 1994.

Duffield, Ian. "Pan-Africanism, Rational and Irrational." *Journal of African History* 18 (1977).

Dutt, Romesh. *Economic History of India under Early British Rule*. London, 1902.

———. *Open Letters to Lord Curzon on Famine and Land Assessments in India*. London, 1900.

Edelstein, Michael. *Overseas Investment in the Age of High Imperialism*. London, 1982.

Edwards, Celestine. *Political Atheism*. London, 1889.

———. *Does God Answer Prayer?* London, n.d.

Enstam, Elizabeth York. "The 'Khaki' Election of 1900 in the United Kingdom." Duke University, 1967.

Etherington, Norman. "Hyndman, the Social-Democratic Federation and Imperialism." *Historical Studies* 16 (1974).

Eyges, Thomas. *Beyond the Horizon*. Boston, 1944.

Feldman, David. *Englishmen and Jews: Social Relations and Political Culture, 1840–1914*. Oxford, 1994.

Feldman, David, and Gareth Stedman Jones. *Metropolis London*. London, 1989.

Fisher, H. A. L. *History of Europe*. London, 1936.

Fishman, William. *East-End Jewish Radicals, 1875–1914*. London, 1975.

Fleming, Rev. Canon. *Weeping for the Slain*. A sermon preached at St. Michael's Church, Chester Square (London SW), on Sunday morning, February 11, 1900. London, 1900.

Flint, John E. *Sir George Goldie and the Making of Nigeria*. Oxford, 1960.

———. "Mary Kingsley—A Reassessment." *Journal of African History* 4, no. 1 (1963).

Foster, Roy. *Paddy and Mr. Punch*. London, 1993.

————. *W. B. Yeats: A Life*. Volume 1. Oxford, 1996.

Fox Bourne, H. *The Aborigines' Protection Society, Chapters in its History*. London, 1899.

————. *Blacks and Whites in South Africa*. London, 1900.

Frank, Katherine. *A Voyager Out: The Life of Mary Kingsley*. London, 1986.

Fryer, Peter. *Staying Power: The History of Black People in Britain*. London, 1984.

Fyfe, Hamilton. *T. P. O'Connor*. London, 1934.

Gainer, Bernard. *The Alien Invasion*. London, 1972.

Gallagher, John, and Ronald Robinson. *Africa and the Victorians*. London, 1961.

Gartner, Lloyd. *The Jewish Immigrant in England, 1870–1914*. London, 1973.

Garvin, Tom. *The Evolution of Irish Nationalist Politics*. Dublin, 1981.

————. *Nationalist Revolutionaries in Ireland, 1858–1928*. Oxford, 1987.

Gatrell, V. A. C., Bruce Lenman, and Geoffrey Parker, eds. *Crime and the Law: The Social History of Crime in Western Europe Since 1500*. London, 1980.

Geiss, Imanuel. *The Pan-African Movement*. Translated by Ann Keep. London, 1974.

Gibb, D. E. W. *Lloyd's of London, A Study in Individualism*. London, 1957.

Gilley, Sheridan, and Roger Swift, eds. *The Irish in Britain, 1815–1939*. London, 1989.

————. *The Irish in the Victorian City*. London, 1985.

Gooch, G. P. *The War and its Causes*. London, 1899.

Gore, John. *Sydney Holland: Lord Knutsford, A Memoir*. London, 1936.

Gosling, Harry. *Up and Down Stream*. London, 1927.

Gosse, Edmund. *Lady Dorothy Nevill, an Open Letter*. London, 1913.

Grainger, J. H. *Patriotisms: Britain 1900–39*. London, 1986.

Green, Jeffrey. "West Indian Doctors in London: John Alcindor (1873–1924) and James Jackson Brown (1882–1953)." *Journal of Caribbean History* 20 (1985–86).

Greenhalgh, Paul. *Ephemeral Vistas: Expositions Universelles, Great Exhibitions and Worlds Fairs, 1851–1939*. London, 1988.

The Grosvenor Crescent Club. London, 1900.

Grubb, Arthur. *The Life Story of the Right Hon. John Burns*. London, 1908.

Gupta, J. N. *Life and Work of Romesh Chunder Dutt, C.I.E.* London, 1911.

Haldane, Richard. *Education and Empire*. London, 1902.

Hamilton, Lord George. *Parliamentary Reminiscences and Reflections 1886–1906*. Volume 2. London, 1922.

Handy Notes on Current Politics, A Monthly Vade-Mecum for Conservatives and Unionists.

Hargreaves, John. *West Africa Partitioned*. Volume 2. *The Elephants and the Grass*. Basingstoke, 1985.

Harlan, Louis, and Raymond Smock, eds. *The Booker T. Washington Papers*. Volumes 4, 5. Urbana, 1975.

Hinnells, John. *Zoroastrians in Britain*. Oxford, 1996.

Hinnells, John, and Omar Ralph. *Bhownaggree*. London, 1995.

Hobhouse, Hermione. *Lost London*. London, 1971.

Hobsbawm, Eric, and Terrance Ranger. *The Invention of Tradition*. Cambridge, 1983.

Hobson, J. A. *The War in South Africa: Its Causes and Effects*. London, 1900.

————. *Imperialism*. London, 1902.

Holland, Sydney. *In Black and White.* London, 1926.

Holmes, Colin. *John Bull's Island: Immigration and British Society, 1871–1971.* London, 1988.

———, ed. *Immigrants and Minorities in British Society.* London, 1978.

Hooker, J. R. *Henry Sylvester Williams, Imperial Pan-Africanist.* London, 1975.

Howe, Stephen. *Anticolonialism in British Politics: The Left and the End of Empire, 1918–1964.* Oxford, 1993.

Husbands, Christopher. "East End Racism, 1900–1980." *London Journal* 8, no. 1 (1986).

Huttenback, Robert. *Racism and Empire.* Ithaca, 1976.

———. *Gandhi in South Africa.* Ithaca, 1971.

Hyam, Ronald. *Sexuality and Empire.* Manchester, 1991.

Hyde, H. Montgomery. *The Londonderrys, A Family Portrait.* London, 1979.

Hyndman, H. M. *Incipient Irish Revolution, An Expose of Fenianism Today.* London, 1889.

———. *The Indian Political Estimate of Mr. Bhavnagri, M.P., or the Bhavnagri Boom Exposed.* Bombay, 1897.

———. *The Approaching Catastrophe in India.* London, 1897.

———. *The Ruin of India by British Rule.* London, 1907.

———. *The Unrest in India.* London, 1907.

———. *The Record of an Adventurous Life.* London, 1911.

Ingham, G. *Capitalism Divided? The City and Industry in British Social Development.* London, 1984.

Irving, Robert Grant. *Indian Summer.* New Haven, 1981.

Jackson, John. "The Irish in East London." *East London Papers* 6, no. 2 (December 1963).

Jarvie, Robert. *The City of London: A Financial and Commercial History.* Cambridge, 1979.

Judge, Mark, ed. *The Case for Further Strand Improvement.* London, 1906.

Kaushik, Harish. *The Indian National Congress in England (1885–1920).* New Delhi, 1974.

Kee, Robert. *The Bold Fenian Men.* London, 1976.

Kennedy, W. P. *Industrial Structure, Capital Markets and the Origins of British Economic Decline.* London, 1987.

Kent, William. *John Burns: Labour's Lost Leader.* London, 1950.

Kondapi, C. *Indians Overseas, 1839–1949.* New Delhi, 1951.

Kosmin, B. A. *A Journal of History; London's Asian M.P.s.* London, 1991.

Koss, Stephen, ed. *The Pro-Boers: The Anatomy of an Antiwar Movement.* Chicago, 1973.

Kushner, Tony, and Kenneth Lunn, eds. *Traditions of Intolerance: Historical Perspectives on Fascism and Race Discourse in Britain.* Manchester, 1989.

Kynaston, David. *The City of London.* Volume 2. *Golden Years, 1890–1914.* London, 1995.

LaCapra, Dominick. *The Bounds of Race: Perspectives on Hegemony and Resistance.* Ithaca, 1991.

Lady Dorothy Nevill. *Reminiscences.* London, 1906.

————. *Under Five Reigns.* London, 1910.

————. *My Own Times.* London, 1912.

Lady St. Helier (Mary Jeune). *Memories of Fifty Years.* London, 1909.

Langley, J. Ayodele. *Pan-Africanism and Nationalism in West Africa, 1900–45: A Study in Ideology and Social Classes.* Oxford, 1973.

Laws, Cuthbert. *The Shipping Federation Registry System: Its Advantages and How to Secure Them.* London, n.d.

Lees, Lynn. *Exiles of Erin: Irish Migrants in Victorian London.* Manchester, 1979.

Lenin, V. I. *Imperialism, the Highest Stage of Capitalism, A Popular Outline.* Moscow, 1975.

di Leonardo, Micaela. *Gender and the Crossroads of Knowledge: Feminist Anthropology in the Postmodern Era.* Berkeley, 1991.

Lest We Forget. Dublin, 1908.

Leventhal, F. M. *Respectable Radical, George Howell and Victorian Working-Class Politics.* Cambridge, Mass., 1971.

Lewis, David Levering. *W. E. B. DuBois, Biography of a Race, 1868–1919.* New York, 1993.

Little, Kenneth. *Negroes in Britain.* London, 1972.

The London Chamber of Commerce Official Report of the Fourth Congress of Chambers of Commerce of the Empire. London, 1900.

London County Council. *Royal Commission on the Port of London.* 1900.

Lorimer, Douglas. *Colour, Class and the Victorians.* Leicester, 1978.

Lovell, John. *Stevedores and Dockers: A Study of Trade Unionism in the Port of London, 1870–1914.* London, 1969.

————. "The Irish and the London Dockers." *Bulletin of the Society for the Study of Labour History,* no. 35 (Autumn 1977).

Low, D. A., ed. *The Indian National Congress, Centenary Hindsights.* Oxford, 1988.

Lowe, C. J. *The Reluctant Imperialists: British Foreign Policy, 1872–1902.* London, 1969.

Lynch, Hollis. *Edward Wilmot Blyden: Pan-Negro Patriot, 1832–1912.* Oxford, 1967.

Lyons, F. S. L. *The Irish Parliamentary Party, 1890–1910.* London, 1951.

MacDonagh, Oliver, W. F. Mandle, and Pauric Travers. *Irish Culture and Nationalism, 1750–1950.* Dublin, 1983.

MacDonald, Robert. *The Language of Imperialism.* Manchester, 1994.

Mace, Rodney. *Trafalgar Square, Emblem of Empire.* London, 1976.

MacKenzie, John, ed. *Imperialism and Popular Culture.* Manchester, 1986.

————. *Propaganda and Empire.* Manchester, 1984.

Makers of Modern Africa: Profiles in History. London 1991.

Mangan, J. A. *The Games Ethic and Imperialism.* Middlesex, 1986.

————, ed. *"Benefits Bestowed"? Education and British Imperialism.* Manchester, 1988.

————. *Making Imperial Mentalities: Socialisation and British Imperialism,* Manchester, 1990.

————. *The Imperial Curriculum: Racial Images and Education in the British Colonial Experience.* Manchester, 1993.

Mangan, J. A., and James Walvin, eds. *Manliness and Morality: Middle-class Morality in Britain and America, 1800–1949.* Manchester, 1987.

Mann, Tom. *The Position of Dockers and Sailors in 1897.* Clarion Pamphlet No. 18, 1898.

Marvin, Gary, and Bob Mullin. *Zoo Culture.* London, 1987.

Masani, R. P. *Dadabhai Naoroji: The Grand Old Man of India.* London, 1939.

Masterman, Charles. *The Heart of the Empire.* London, 1901.

Masters, Brian. *Great Hostesses.* London, 1982.

Mathurin, Owen. *Henry Sylvester Williams and the Origins of the Pan-African Movement, 1869–1911.* Westport, 1976.

Maude, Aylmer. *War and Patriotism.* London, 1900.

McBriar, A. M. *Fabian Socialism and English Politics, 1884–1918.* Cambridge, 1962.

McClintock, Anne. *Imperial Leather: Race, Gender and Sexuality in the Colonial Contest.* London, 1995.

Meacham, Standish. *A Life Apart.* Cambridge, 1977.

Metcalf, Thomas. *An Imperial Vision: Indian Architecture and Britain's Raj.* Berkeley, 1989.

Michie, Ranald. *The London and New York Stock Exchanges, 1850–1914.* London, 1987.

————. "Dunn, Fischer and Co., in the City of London, 1906–1914." *Business History* 30 (1988).

————. *The City of London, Continuity and Change.* London, 1992.

Mill, Robert. *The Record of the Royal Geographical Society, 1830–1930.* London, 1930.

Miller, M. G. "The Continued Agitation for Imperial Union, 1895–1910." Corpus Christi College, Oxford, 1980.

Mitchell, P. Chalmers. *Centenary History of the Zoological Society of London.* London, 1929.

Moody, T. W. *Davitt and Irish Revolution.* Oxford, 1981.

————. "Michael Davitt and the British Labour Movement, 1882–1906." *Transactions of the Royal Historical Society,* 5th ser., 3 (1953).

Morris, Jan. *The Spectacle of Empire.* London, 1982.

Morrison, Arthur. *Zig-Zags at the Zoo.* London, 1894.

Nanda, B. R. *The Moderate Era in Indian Politics.* Delhi, 1983.

Naoroji, Dadabhai. *The Poverty of India.* London, 1878.

————. *Poverty and UnBritish Rule in India.* London, 1901.

Nevill, Guy. *Exotic Groves, A Portrait of Lady Dorothy Nevill.* London, 1984.

Nevill, Ralph. *The Life and Letters of Lady Dorothy Nevill.* London, 1919.

Newton, Scott, and Dilwyn Porter. *Modernization Frustrated: The Politics of Industrial Decline in Britain since 1900.* London, 1988.

Nord, Deborah Epstein. *The Apprenticeship of Beatrice Webb.* Amherst, 1985.

O'Day, Alan. *The English Face of Irish Nationalism: Parnellite Involvement in British Politics, 1880–86.* London, 1977.

O'Donnell, Frank. *A History of the Irish Parliamentary Party.* Volume 2. London, 1970.

Offer, Avner. "The British Empire, 1870–1914: A Waste of Money?" *Economic History Review* 46, no. 2 (May 1993).

O'Hagan, H. Osborne. *Leaves from My Life.* Volume 1. London, 1929.

Padmore, George, ed. *Colonial and Coloured Unity, A Programme of Action: History of the Pan-African Congress.* Manchester, 1947.

Parssinen, Terry. *Secret Passions, Secret Remedies.* Manchester, 1983.

Patriotic Association. *The Truth about the Conduct of the War: Concentration Camps.* London, 1901.

Patwardhan, R. P. *Dadabhai Naoroji Correspondence.* Volume 2, Part 1, Correspondence with D. E. Wacha, 4.11.1884 to 23.3.1895. New Delhi, 1977.

Pennybacker, Susan. *A Vision for London, 1889–1914: Labour, Everyday Life and the L.C.C. Experiment.* London, 1995.

Perham, Margery. *Lugard, The Years of Adventure, 1858–98.* London, 1956.

———. *Lugard, The Years of Authority, 1898–1945.* London, 1960.

Perrot, F. D. *The Lion's Share of London's Profit.* London, n.d.

———. *The Unrest in India,* London, 1907.

Peters, Carl. *The Future of Africa.* London, 1897.

———. *Lecture Delivered by Carl Peters on the Future of Africa at the Society of Arts.* London, 1897.

———. *The Eldorado of the Ancients.* London, 1902.

———. *England and the English.* London, 1904.

Phillips, Gordon, and Noel Whiteside. *Casual Labour: The Unemployment Question in the Port Transport Industry, 1880–1970.* Oxford, 1985.

Port, Michael. *Imperial London: Civil Government Building in London, 1850–1915.* London, 1995.

Porter, Bernard. *Critics of Empire.* London, 1968.

———. *The Lion's Share.* London, 1975.

Porter, Roy. *London, A Social History.* Cambridge, Mass., 1994.

Powell, L. H. *The Shipping Federation.* London, 1950.

Price, Richard. *An Imperial War and the British Working Class.* London, 1972.

Ramdin, Ron. *The Making of the Black Working Class.* London, 1987.

Rappaport, Erika. "The West End and Women's Pleasure: Gender and Commercial Culture in London, 1860–1914." Rutgers University, 1995.

Ratcliffe, S. K. *Sir William Wedderburn and the Indian Reform Movement.* London, 1923.

Reader. W. J. *A House in the City: A Study of the City and of the Stock Exchange Based on the Records of Foster and Braithwaite, 1825–1975.* London, 1979.

A Record of the Progress of the Zoological Society of London during the 19th Century. London, n.d.

Rich, Paul. *Race and Empire in British Politics.* Cambridge, 1986.

Richards, Jeffrey, ed. *Imperialism and Juvenile Literature.* Manchester, 1989.

Ritvo, Harriet. *The Animal Estate.* London, 1990.

Robinson, J. Armitage. *Holy Ground: Three Sermons on the War in South Africa,* preached in Westminster Abbey. London, 1900.

Rocker, Rudolf. *The London Years.* London, 1956.

Rowe, Thomas. *The Early Pioneers of Ashanti Goldfields 1895–1900.* London, 1991.

Rowntree, Joshua. *The Imperial Drug Trade.* London, 1905.

The Royal Geographical Society's Year-Book and Record. London, 1899.

Rubinstein, William. *Wealth and Inequality in Britain.* London, 1986.

———. "Debate: 'Gentlemanly Capitalism' and British Industry 1820–1914, Comment." *Past and Present,* no. 132 (August 1991).

Rudwick, Elliot. *W. E. B. Du Bois, A Study in Minority Leadership.* Philadelphia, 1960.

Ryan, Mark. *Fenian Memories.* Dublin, 1945.

Rydell, Robert. *All the World's a Fair: Visions of Empire at American International Expositions, 1876–1916.* Chicago, 1984.

Said, Edward. *Orientalism.* New York, 1979.

Saint, Andrew. *Richard Norman Shaw.* New Haven, 1976.

Samuel, Raphael, ed. *Patriotism: The Making and Unmaking of British National Identity.* Volume 1. London, 1989.

Sayers, R. S. *The Bank of England, 1891–1944.* Volume 1. Cambridge, 1976.

Scherren, Henry. *The Zoological Society of London.* London, 1905.

Schneer, Jonathan. *Ben Tillett: Portrait of a Labour Leader.* London, 1982.

———. *George Lansbury.* Manchester, 1990.

Schubert, Dirk, and Anthony Sutcliffe. "The 'Haussmannization' of London?: The Planning and Construction of Kingsway-Aldwych, 1889–1935." *Planning Perspectives* 11 (1996).

Sclater, Philip. *Guide to the Gardens of the Zoological Society of London.* London, 1900.

Seeley, Sir John. *The Expansion of England.* London, 1880.

Service, Alastair. *London 1900.* London, 1979.

———. *The Architects of London.* London, 1979.

———, ed. *Edwardian Architecture and its Origins.* London, 1975.

Shaw, George Bernard. *Fabianism and Empire.* London, 1900.

Shaw, Flora. *Letters from South Africa.* London 1893.

———. *A Tropical Dependency: An Outline of the Ancient History of the Western Soudan with an Account of the Modern Settlement of Northern Nigeria.* London, 1905.

Sheey-Skeffington, F. *Michael Davitt, Revolutionary Agitator and Labour Leader.* London, 1908.

Sheowring, William, ed. *British Africa.* London, 1899.

Silberner, Edmund. "British Socialism and the Jews." *Historica Judaica* 14 (April 1952).

Sims, George, ed. *Living London.* London, 1901–03.

Sinha, Mrinalini. *Colonial Masculinity: The 'Manly Englishman' and the 'Effeminate Bengali' in the Late Nineteenth Century.* Manchester, 1995.

Spiller, G. *The Ethical Movement in Great Britain, A Documentary History.* London, 1934.

Stearn, Roger. "G. W. Steevens and the Message of Empire." *Journal of Imperial and Commonwealth History* 17, no. 2 (January 1989).

Stedman Jones, Gareth. *Outcast London.* Oxford, 1971.

———. "Working-Class Culture and Working-Class Politics in London: Notes on the Remaking of a Working Class." *Journal of Social History* 7, no. 4 (1974).

Stepan, Nancy. *The Idea of Race in Science: Great Britain 1800–1960.* London, 1982.

Strauss, E. *Irish Nationalism and British Democracy.* London, 1951.

Strobel, Margaret. *European Women and the Second British Empire.* Bloomington, 1991.

Stuart, James. *Reminiscences.* London, 1912.

Swan, Maureen. *Gandhi: The South African Experience.* Johannesburg, 1985.

Swift, Roger. "The Outcast Irish in the British Victorian City: Problems and Perspectives." *Irish Historical Studies* 25, no. 99 (May 1987).

Tabili, Laura. *We Ask for British Justice.* Ithaca, 1995.

Taplin, E. L. *Liverpool Dockers and Seamen, 1870–1890.* Liverpool, 1974.

Taylor, Miles. "John Bull and the Iconography of Public Opinion in England, 1712–1929." *Past and Present,* no. 134 (February 1992).

Temperley, Howard. *British Anti-Slavery, 1833–1870.* London, 1972.

Thompson, Andrew S. "The Language of Imperialism and the Meanings of Empire: Imperial Discourse in British Politics, 1895–1914." *Journal of British Studies* 26, no. 2 (April 1977).

Thompson, Jon. *Fiction, Crime and Empire: Clues to Modernity and Postmodernism.* Urbana, 1993.

Thompson, L. Beatrice. *Who's Who at the Zoo.* London, 1902.

Thompson, Paul. *Socialists, Liberals and Labour: The Struggle for London, 1885–1914.* London, 1967.

Thornton, A. P. *The Imperial Idea and its Enemies.* London, 1985.

Tidrick, Kathryn. *Empire and the English Character.* London, 1990.

Tillett, Ben. *Memories and Reflections.* London, 1931.

Turner, Easton G. W. *A Short History of Ashanti Goldfields Corporation Ltd., 1897–1947.* London, 1947.

Vadgama, K. *India in Britain.* London, 1984.

Van Reenen, Rykie. *Emily Hobhouse: Boer War Letters.* Cape Town, 1984.

Vevers, Gwynne. *London's Zoo.* London, 1976,

Visram, Rozina. *Ayahs, Lascars and Princes.* London, 1986.

Volger, Martha. *Frederic Harrison.* Oxford, 1984.

Walker, Mabel. *The Fenian Movement.* Colorado Springs, 1969.

Walkowitz, Judith. *City of Dreadful Delight.* Chicago, 1992.

Wallach, H. Y. *Wallach's West African Manual.* London, 1900.

Waller, P. J. "Immigration into Britain: The Chinese." *History Today* (September 1985).

Walton, Joseph. *China and the Present Crisis.* London, 1900.

Walvin, James. *Black and White*. London, 1973.

Ware, Vron. *Beyond the Pale: White Women, Racism and History*. London, 1992.

Warwick, Countess of. *Afterthoughts*. London, 1931.

———. *Life's Ebb and Flow*. London, 1929.

———. *Progress in Women's Education in the British Empire*. London, 1898.

Wedderburn, Sir William. *Allan Octavian Hume*. London, 1913.

Weiner, Martin. *English Culture and the Decline of the Industrial Spirit, 1850–1914*. Cambridge, 1981.

Weinthal, Leo, ed. *Memories, Mines and Millions: Being the Life of Sir Joseph B. Robinson, Bart*. London, 1929.

Whyte, Frederic. *The Life of W. T. Stead*. Volume 2. London, 1925.

Wilkins, Mira. "The Free-standing Company, 1870–1914: An Important Type of British Foreign Direct Investment." *Economic History Review*, 2d ser., 41, no. 2 (1988).

Williams, H. S. *The British Negro: A Factor in the Empire*.

———. *The Ethiopian Eunuch*. London, 1902.

Winter, James. *London's Teeming Streets*. London, 1993.

Woman's Exhibition. Earl's Court, 1900, Daily Programme.

The Womens' Institute. London, 1900.

Yajnik, Indulal. *Shyamaji Krishnavarma, Life and Times of an Indian Revolutionary*. Bombay, 1950.

Yeo, Stephen. "A New Life: The Religion of Socialism in Britain, 1883–1896." *History Workshop Journal*, no. 4 (1977).

Ziegler, Philip. *The Sixth Great Power, Barings 1762–1929*. London, 1988.

Zoological Society. *Proceedings of the General Meetings for Scientific Business*. London, 1900.

Prof. Lord Zuckerman, ed. *The Zoological Society of London, 1826–1976*. London, 1976.

ACKNOWLEDGMENTS

I T has taken me eight years to research and write this book, by far the most difficult and complex of my career, and many people have helped along the way. I wish to thank first of all Tania Alexander, who provided me with a home away from home in London. Over the course of seven successive summers her unstinting hospitality and generosity transformed my experience of London. And I want to thank John Grigg for introducing me to Tania.

Numerous friends have discussed aspects of the project with me and have read portions of the manuscript, steering me to relevant literature, saving me from countless errors of fact, misinterpretations, and infelicities of style. I wish to thank my colleagues at Georgia Tech, Greg Nobles, Andrea Tone, John Tone, and Joan Sokolovsky. Others who have read critically individual chapters are Stephen Brooke, Peter Caine, Dina Copelman, Margo Finn, Ewen Green, Geoffrey Tyack, and Judy Walkowitz. Chris Clark proved a trenchant reader and, as always, a steadfast friend; likewise Jim Cronin, with whom I discussed the project many times, always to my advantage. Finally Jonathan Prude read nearly the entire manusucript with a critic's eye and a friend's heart. I hope I may prove as helpful to him, and to all those mentioned above, as they have been to me.

Over the years I have read draft sections of the manuscript to many conferences and seminars both in the United States and in Great Britain, always with profit to myself at least. I would particularly like to thank members of seminars at Oberlin College, the University of Arizona, Harry Ransom Humanities Center at the University of Texas at Austin, Center for European Studies at Harvard, Sidney Sussex College, Cambridge, the Center for Social History at University of Warwick, and the Institute of Historical Research in London.

I wish to thank the Georgia Institute of Technology for generously supporting my research and granting me leave from teaching. Here the key figures have been Robert Hawkins and Kenneth Knoespel, dean and associate dean, respectively, of the Ivan Allen College at Georgia Tech; also the successive chairs of my department, Gus Geibelhaus, Robert McMath, and Greg Nobles. I wish also to thank Clare Hall, Cambridge University, St. Catherine's College, Oxford University, and Worcester College, Oxford University, for awarding me Visiting Fellowships which enabled me to pursue my research.

I wish to express my gratitude, too, to archivists and librarians throughout the United Kingdom and Ireland, especially those at the Public Record Office in Belfast, the National Library of Ireland and the Friend's House in Dublin, the Guildhall Library, the British Library including the India Office and the Newspaper Library at Colindale, and the British Library of Political and Economic Science in London, and the old and new Bodleian Libraries and Rhodes House Library in Oxford.

Finally, and as always, thanks to my family for putting up with the inevitable disruptions and distractions which accompany these long-term scholarly projects and for sustaining me in every way throughout.

INDEX

H

I

Impey, Catherine, 204–05, 220, 221, 299n8
Independent Labour Party (ILP), 162,
   169, 198, 211, 291n18
India, 93–94, 164–65, 234–35. *See also*
   Indian nationalists
India, 37–38, 191, 197, 199; and Khaki
   Election of 1900, 234, 236, 241, 243
India for the Indians—and for England, 190
Indian and Colonial Exhibition, 241
Indianapolis Freeman, 220
Indian Constitutional Reform Associa-
   tion, 294n1
Indian National Congress Agency, 189
Indian National Congress (INC), 181; and
   the BCINC, 187–89, 194. *See also*
   British Committee of the Indian Na-
   tional Congress
Indian nationalists: and Khaki Election of
   1900, 241–42, 243, 244; leadership,
   190–92, 193–94; organizations of,
   185–89; Radicals/Irish nationalists
   and, 170–71, 179, 181; strategies of,
   192–93, 194–202
Indian Political Agency, 188
Indians, in London, 184, 266n9, 294n1
India Office, 9, 195
India Reform Society, 185–86
Indigenous populations, 80–82, 94–95,
   110–12, 236; and Flora Shaw, 137–38;
   and Mary Kingsley, 147, 148–49,
   286n63. *See also* Racism
Insurance companies, 67
Irish, 7, 291n25; anti-imperialism and the,
   171–83; influence on Indian national-
   ists, 187, 189–90; and Khaki Election
   of 1900, 234, 237, 259
Irish Literary Society of London, 173, 174
Irish National Club, 174, 175–76
Irish National League of Great Britain
   (INLGB), 174, 177, 187, 292n40. *See
   also* United Irish League
Irish Parliamentary Party, 172, 181,
   292n40
Irish People, 172, 182, 237
Irish Republican Brotherhood (IRB), 172,
   175
Irish Texts Society, 172, 174

Irish Weekly Independent, 177, 182, 294n53
Italians, in London, 7, 265n8

J

Jackson, T. G., 24
Jameson Raid, 139–42
Japanese, 8
Jeune, Mary. *See* St. Helier, Lady
Jews, 7–8, 172–73; and Khaki Election of
   1900, 237, 260, 261. *See also* Anti-Semi-
   tism
Johnston, Sir Harry, 280n34
Jones, Gareth Stedman, 12
Joseph, Rev. Henry Mason, 206, 214, 215,
   217, 300n27
Journalism: and Flora Shaw, 134–35,
   142–45; and Mary Kingsley, 150
Justice, 58, 169, 170, 199, 224, 291n24

K

Kahn and Herzfelder, 91
Kay, Harry, 170
Keane, A. H., 138
Kelly, William, 48
Keltie, Scott, 150
Khaki Election of 1900, 302n1, 302n4; and
   Bhownaggree election, 240–48; debate
   over imperialism, 229–31, 234–40,
   244–48, 259–63; and John Burns,
   248–59; Newton/Causton contest,
   231–34
Kingsley, Charles, 147
Kingsley, George, 147–48
Kingsley, Mary Henrietta, 146–58, 149
   (photo), 159, 160–61, 164, 286n63,
   288n88
Kingsway, 24, 26 (photo), 27
Kinloch, A. V., 213–14, 215, 300n33
Kiralfy, Imre, 10, 95
Klein, Melanie, 12
Knollys, Lord, 131
Kruger, Paul, 132, 137, 142
Kyd, David, 238